ALSO BY CHRISTOPHER BENFEY

DEGAS IN NEW ORLEANS

THE DOUBLE LIFE OF STEPHEN CRANE

EMILY DICKINSON AND THE PROBLEM OF OTHERS

THE
GREAT WAVE

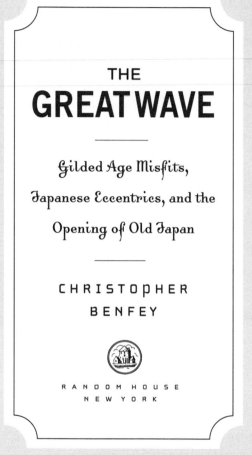

THE
GREAT WAVE

Gilded Age Misfits,

Japanese Eccentrics, and the

Opening of Old Japan

CHRISTOPHER
BENFEY

RANDOM HOUSE
NEW YORK

All rights reserved under International and
Pan-American Copyright Conventions. Published
in the United States by Random House, an imprint of
the Random House Ballantine Publishing Group,
a division of Random House, Inc.,
New York, and simultaneously in Canada by Random
House of Canada Limited, Toronto.

RANDOM HOUSE and colophon are registered
trademarks of Random House, Inc.

Owing to limitations of space, acknowledgments of
permission to use illustrative material will be found
on page 332.

LIBRARY OF CONGRESS CATALOGING-IN-PUBLICATION DATA

Benfey, Christopher E. G.
The great wave / Christopher Benfey.
p.   cm.
ISBN 0-375-50327-7
1. Japan—Civilization—1868–1912.   2. Japan—
Civilization—1600–1868.   3. United
States—Civilization—1865–1918.   4. United
States—Civilization—1783–1865.   5. United States—
Civilization—Japanese influences.   I. Title.
DS822.3 .B46   2003
303.48'27305'09034—dc21   2002031750

Random House website address: www.atrandom.com

Printed in the United States of America
on acid-free paper

24689753

FIRST EDITION

Book design by Barbara M. Bachman

To my brother Stephen and to Mickey, Tommy, and Nicholas

CONTENTS

INTRODUCTION

THE MAP

>< >< ><

Toward the end of the nineteenth century, and especially during the quarter
century that followed the Centennial of 1876, there was a tremendous
vogue in the United States for all things Japanese—Japanese prints and
porcelain, judo and Buddhism, geisha and samurai. In retrospect, this
great wave of interest seems both unlikely and inevitable. Unlikely, because for most of the nineteenth century Japan was a tiny and backward
country, a spray of inconsequential dots on the map of the Pacific. Inevitable, because once the westward expansion of the United States, all
but complete by the end of the century, arrived at the Pacific Ocean, the
idea of a new frontier even farther west was in the air—or water. "The
same waves wash . . . the new-built Californian towns, but yesterday
planted by the recentest race of men, and lave the faded but still gorgeous
skirts of Asiatic lands, older than Abraham," wrote Herman Melville,
"while all between float milky-ways of coral isles, and low-lying, endless,
unknown Archipelagoes, and impenetrable Japans."

   No region of the United States was more enamored of Japan than New
England. This affinity, too, was perhaps to be expected. Through its great
ports of Salem and Boston, Nantucket and New Bedford, New England had
sent merchant ships and whaling ships into Asian waters—past Java and
Japan, and on to Shanghai and Calcutta—since the late eighteenth century.

Occasionally a ship from New England foundered off the xenophobic shores of Japan, which had been closed to foreigners since the Shogun's declaration in 1639 that Christians and other "outside barbarians" were a menace to Japan. And sometimes an American ship rescued a Japanese fisherman adrift in the wide expanses of the Pacific. After voyages that could last for years, sea captains returned with exotic curiosities—fans and furnishings, swords and screens, seashells and bamboo—to adorn their mantelpieces and, later, to fill the museums of New England. It was no accident that the tax revolt known as the Boston Tea Party—when casks of Asian tea were tossed unceremoniously into the harbor—took place in Boston, the heart of the Asia trade.

Even as its power as a financial and trading center was eclipsed by New York after the Civil War, Boston insisted on its role—reaching back to the Puritan divines, and renewed during the age of Emerson—as spiritual guide to the nation. Emerson and his disciple Henry Thoreau had looked to the Asian religions of Hinduism and Buddhism for sustenance as early as the 1840s. That interest in Asian spiritual practices increased as Protestant fervor waned. The Reverend Phillips Brooks, imposing rector of Boston's Trinity Church, visited in 1883 the great Indian temple of Buddha-gaya—where the Buddha is said to have reached enlightenment after six years of sitting under a bo-tree. "In these days, when a large part of Boston prefers to consider itself Buddhist rather than Christian," Brooks wrote, "I consider this pilgrimage to be the duty of a minister who preaches to Bostonians, and so this morning before sunrise we started for Gaya and the red Barabar Hills."

The large part of Boston that considered itself Buddhist was not, of course, the Irish workers. Brooks meant the Protestant elite—those old Boston families who might be counted on to attend Trinity on any Sunday. It was among the artists and intellectuals of this congregation—the Lodges and the Adamses, the Bigelows and Brookses—that Buddhism had its hold, and Phillips Brooks was hardly the only Boston "Brahmin" who made the pilgrimage to the East. Deeply disaffected by the vulgarity and superficiality of American culture during the decades immediately following the Civil War, these self-styled young aristocrats looked elsewhere for a social order more attuned to their temperament. The historian Richard Hofstadter has succinctly described their disillusionment:

The coarse, materialistic civilization that emerged in the United States during the years after the Civil War produced among cultivated middle-class young men a generation of alienated and homeless intellectuals. Generally well-to-do, often of eminent family backgrounds, clubmen, gentlemen, writers, the first cluster of a native intellectual aristocracy to appear since the great days of Boston and Concord, the men of this class found themselves unable to participate with any heart in the greedy turmoil of business or to accept without protest boss-ridden politics. Money-making was sordid; politics was dirty; and the most sensitive among them made their careers in other ways.

Edith Wharton called this uneasy era the Age of Innocence; her friend Henry James called it the Awkward Age. But it was Mark Twain who named it, indelibly, the Gilded Age. Americans in love with prosperity alone, Twain implied, would never achieve a Golden Age, that idea of a harmonious utopia in the remote, sun-spangled past. The best they could hope for was a gold veneer, with dross hidden beneath.

Why was "Old Japan"—Japan as they imagined it before it was "opened" to Western visitors and trade in 1854—such a magnet for these alienated young New Englanders? Why did Boston become the repository of much of the knowledge about Japan, and of many of her most highly prized works of art? There is no simple answer, and it is difficult to generalize about radically varied characters and temperaments. But two major events hung over New England during the Gilded Age: one was the devastation of the Civil War, which threw so many prewar certainties into doubt; the other was the rapid industrialization of the region, and the consequent loss of the predictable rhythms of farm and village life. A longing for a more rooted connection to the soil, and for the aesthetic and spiritual satisfactions of a simpler life—these inchoate yearnings found a response in what Bostonians could glean of Old Japan.

Many of Hofstadter's aristocratic New Englanders discerned in the traditions of Old Japan an alternative social order of hereditary aristocracy, austere religion, and aesthetic cultivation. In the self-sacrifice of the samurai, they detected the stern ethos of their own Puritan forebears. (Were they not themselves, amid the corrupt governance of the Gilded

Age, leaderless *ronin* in search of a cause worth fighting for?) In the martial arts of judo and archery, they discovered something like that soldierly virtue lost in an age of soft prosperity—the "Gelded Age" of American millionaires. And in Zen austerity and reserve, they found confirmation of their own recoil from Victorian excess and ostentation. In Old Japan, in short, they thought they glimpsed a Golden Age, a world they were eager to visit before it disappeared.

The irony was that just as Bostonians were falling in love with Old Japan, Japan was reinventing herself as a modern state, evolving in the space of twenty-five years from a feudal backwater to an international power. This is the period known as the Meiji Era (1868–1912), which corresponds almost year for year to America's Gilded Age. The parallel rise of the two young nations, the United States and the "New" Japan, initiated some of the major power struggles—both military and economic—of the twentieth century. But underneath Japan's confident modernization, other feelings festered—feelings remarkably similar to those of disaffected Bostonians. In Natsume Soseki's novel *Sorekara* (*And Then,* 1909), the protagonist— an aesthetically minded young man of excellent family—looks back at his father's generation, the generation that transformed Japan: "There was a time when his father had looked like gold to him. Many of his seniors had looked like gold. Anyone who had attained a certain high level of education had looked like gold. Therefore, his own gold plating had been all the more painful, and he had been impatient to become solid gold himself. But once his keen eyes penetrated directly to the inner layers of those other people, his efforts suddenly came to seem foolish." The Meiji Era itself, in Soseki's view, was more gilded than golden. The transformation prompted by an armada commanded by a naval officer from Newport, Rhode Island, had brought ambiguous gains to "impenetrable Japan."

The fabled opening of Japan is often told as though Japan were an oyster, tightly closed for 250 years until Commodore Matthew Calbraith Perry sailed with his Black Ships into Yokohama Bay in 1854 to apply the knife. But Perry's historic venture did not in truth open up very much. While his heavily armed ships forced Japan to open her major ports to Western ships and Western trade, a more significant opening of Japan happened much more slowly, and asked more of those doing it. It was one thing to fire a few cannonballs across Edo Bay and run a miniature railroad along the beach. It was quite another to grasp the subtle moves of judo, the tenets of Esoteric Buddhism, or why the most highly prized vessel in the tea ceremony was a dun-colored water jar that had buckled in the kiln. This second opening was the work of men and women who realized that Japan had things to offer besides safe harbor for whalers and supplies for Salem traders bound for Calcutta and Canton. This cultural opening of Japan is the subject of this book.

Even after the restoration of the Emperor Meiji in 1868, and the subsequent efforts to modernize along Western lines, Japan carefully controlled her image in the West. Visitors who wished to venture beyond the "treaty ports" of Yokohama, Kobe, and Nagasaki had to follow carefully laid-out routes, and stay in the same few Western-style hotels. The journey by rail and jinricksha from the burial shrines of Nikko, past the views of Mount Fuji in Hakone, and on to the hillside temples of Kyoto became as familiarly exotic as the journey up the Nile. A few foreigners, hired to teach their expertise to the Japanese, acquired a more sophisticated sense of the country than a couple of weeks and a guidebook allowed. But for most Westerners, Japan remained a secretive island with strange customs and impeccable taste. World's fairs and art museums gave Japan further opportunities to stage her reputation abroad. Such achievements as the high rate of literacy in Meiji Japan could be publicized in exhibits, but the Japanese quickly learned that it was their excellence in art that most impressed foreign audiences—and foreign buyers. Millions of Americans first became aware of Japanese arts and crafts at the Philadelphia Centennial Exhibition of 1876. Subsequent fairs in New Orleans, Chicago, and St. Louis confirmed Japanese ingenuity, and for some American viewers supremacy, in the arts.

This book tells the story of a tightly knit group of travelers—connoisseurs, collectors, scientists—who dedicated themselves to exploring and preserving what they referred to as Old Japan. A sense of urgency impelled them, for they were convinced—Darwinians that they were—that their quarry was on the verge of extinction. Most were New Englanders and several were hired by the Japanese to impart instruction on moderniza- tion in the Western mode. But they left Japan persuaded that preserva- tion of the old was far more important than aping of the new. They were joined in this view by several prominent Japanese officials. Precisely what constituted Old Japan remained something of a moving target. But the image of an island realm of aristocratic customs and stately ritual, of high art and high ceremony, appealed to them all. They left behind some of the masterworks of American literature, painting, and sculp- ture, and helped to found some of the greatest museums in the world, in America and Japan. Along the way, in the hidden mountains and valleys of Japan, they had extraordinary adventures, of the body, the mind, and the spirit.

In one sense, Old Japan vanished at the moment of its discovery. "For Old Japan was like an oyster:—to open it was to kill it," as the longtime res- ident Basil Chamberlain lamented. But it turned out that something of Old Japan—like the shrines carried in the great Shinto festivals—was portable, and recoverable. It could be relocated in Boston, or Chicago, or Washing- ton, D.C.—even in the White House itself—and assume a second life. This recovery was the work of men and women who realized that to open Japan culturally meant to open themselves in turn, and to risk transformation in the process. For the opening of Japan occurred as much in the hearts and minds of individuals as in some particular location in Japan or Mas- sachusetts. A lyrical passage from Joseph Conrad's novel *Lord Jim* captures their necessary readiness: "To us, their less tried successors, they appear magnified, not as agents of trade but as instruments of a recorded destiny, pushing out into the unknown in obedience to an inward voice, to an im- pulse beating in the blood, to a dream of the future. They were wonderful; and it must be owned they were ready for the wonderful."

The eight chapters of this book play out in chronological order, keyed to the moment of encounter with Japan. A first chapter sketches the strange and porous world of the Pacific islands—both the stationary archipelagoes and the floating ones with sails—before Perry. Two drifters—the Japanese fishing boy Manjiro and the American whaler-writer Herman Melville— are taken to be representative of this "floating world." The chapters that follow chart the cultural opening of Japan after Perry among an intersecting circle of American friends and their Japanese associates—the shell collector turned Japanese preservationist Edward Morse; the historian Henry Adams and the artist John La Farge; the connoisseur-collectors William Sturgis Bigelow, Kakuzo Okakura, and Isabella Stewart Gardner; the astronomer Percival Lowell and the astronomer's wife, Mabel Loomis Todd; the exoticist writers Lafcadio Hearn and Mary Fenollosa; and President Theodore Roosevelt.

Some of these people are of course extremely well known—though not for their involvement with Japan, an involvement that casts them in a different and revealing light. Fringe characters in one chapter emerge as central in succeeding chapters. This structural device is itself meant to be an opening, or unfolding. A closing coda identifies the year 1913 as the end of an era in the American encounter with Japan. And that is part of the argument, too: that the American fascination with Japan did not begin during the 1950s with the Beat poets, or during the 1920s with the Imagists. It began much, much earlier, and shows no signs of abating.

The march of chapters is not merely chronological, however; they proceed from local detail—a drab snail in a Maine garbage heap, a cup of green tea, a waterfall in a garden—to increasingly larger cultural perspectives. Spatially, and spiritually, the experience of reading this book should play out—to borrow the Reverend Phillips Brooks's term—as a pilgrimage, from modest beginnings to unexpected arrivals. The result, I hope, is as much a map of intersecting journeys as a history. The burden of the narrative will be to get the meaning and shading of those journeys right. As the poet Elizabeth Bishop put it in her poem "The Map": "More delicate than the historians' are the map-makers' colors."

The great wave of my title is meant to be suggestive rather than strictly descriptive. It alludes, of course, to Hokusai's most famous image, *Under the Wave off Kanagawa*, popularly known as "The Great Wave." The first installment in Hokusai's series of woodblock prints *Thirty-six Views of Mount Fuji* (early 1830s), the print depicts three small fishing boats caught in turbulent seas. An enormous wave with clawlike froth breaks above them while, in the background, the snowy cone of Mount Fuji looms like another, distant wave. Hokusai's image became the best-known Japanese print in Europe and America, and inspired Debussy's *La Mer* among other works of art. In Japan, it helped—along with the other views in Hokusai's series—to make Mount Fuji the symbol of the whole country, and the one sight all travelers to Japan must see.

Such cultural exchange between Japan and the West is the overarching meaning I hope to capture with my title: both the great wave of American visitors to Japan after Perry's opening and the counterwave of Japanese influence in America. But it also alludes to the great wave, or tsunami, that tore the roof from the monumental bronze Buddha at Kamakura. It picks up the meaning of the leaderless samurai called *ronin*, or "wave-men," as well as the storms at sea endured by the sailor-*ronin* Melville and Manjiro on their Pacific crossings. And it alludes to the Taoist sense of flux and falling water that John La Farge and Henry Adams discerned in Japanese thought and religion. Finally, it seeks to capture a shared mood in both the Gilded Age and the Meiji Era, amid superficial promise and prosperity, of an overmastering sense of precariousness and impending peril.

A Note on Japanese Names

In encounters between East and West, Japanese names often suffer indignities. In this book, Japanese names are generally ordered according to the Western system, family names last. This practice may jar Japanese-speaking readers but will seem less confusing to readers without Japanese. Exceptions to the Western order are when the person is best known by his or her "artist's name" (e.g., Natsume Soseki or Yokoyama Taikan), or when pre–Meiji Era names are so well known (Sen no Rikyu, for example) that reordering them seems a needless deformation. Diacritical marks are not employed.

THE
GREAT WAVE

THE FLOATING WORLD

>< >< ><

If that double-bolted land, Japan, is ever
to become hospitable, it is the whale-ship alone
to whom the credit will be due;
for already she is on the threshold.

—HERMAN MELVILLE, *MOBY-DICK* (1851)

Imagine the following scenario. Two fatherless boys on opposite sides of the earth take to the sea within days of each other, in search of adventure and a livelihood. Their paths cross on an archipelago in the middle of the Pacific Ocean, where they encounter some of the same helpers, and hinderers. One arrives after years of wandering at the other's port of departure. The other falls just short but writes an extraordinary book that completes the journey. One deserts a whaling ship while the other is rescued by one. One discovers the joys of savage life while the other discovers the ambiguous joys of civilization. Each dreams of "opening" the other's country, and each is changed utterly in the process; their reward is gloom and isolation. Now, let us give these lost boys and Pacific drifters names and dates.

I. The May Basket

During the waning hours of a warm spring evening in 1843, in the coastal village of Fairhaven, Massachusetts, sixteen-year-old John Mung hung a May basket on the knocker of his classmate Catherine Terry's door. A note was hidden among the buttercups:

Tis in the chilly night
A basket you've got hung.
Get up, strike a light!
And see me run
But no take chase me.

Mung, according to age-old New England custom, ran off into the enveloping night—anonymous except for that telltale fifth line. Catherine Terry had reason to believe that the basket was "hung" by none other than John Mung, whom on occasion she had smiled at demurely during recess.

One Sunday morning, during that same spring of 1843, John Mung sat in Captain Whitfield's pew in the Fairhaven Congregational Church. After the service one of the elders of the church approached Captain Whitfield and quietly suggested that Mung should sit in the section reserved for escaped slaves. Mung was distracting the other worshipers, the elder explained, and would be more at home among the Negroes in the balcony.

Two years earlier John Mung had no idea that the town of Fairhaven, Massachusetts, existed. He had never heard of the United States or of the English language. Rituals such as May baskets and the Christian Mass would have seemed to him impossibly foreign, and remote. In fact, no one by the name of John Mung existed in 1841. Call him Manjiro instead.

On January 5, 1841, in the Year of the Ox, the boy Manjiro, fourteen years old, boarded a boat with four other fishermen on the coast of Shikoku, the smallest of the four main islands of Japan. Manjiro, who lived with his mother in the tiny village of Nakanohama, had wandered up the coast in search of work. Captain Fudenjo of the village of Usa, near Tosa, had found Manjiro asleep on the sand and asked him to join his crew: his two brothers, Jusuke and Goemon, and another fisherman called Toraemon. In the fixed feudal order of Old Japan, peasants like Manjiro had only one name, and one life to look forward to. Like his father, who died when Manjiro was nine, and his grandfather and great-grandfather back into the mists of time, Manjiro would be a fisherman. What knocked him loose from this order established across millennia was a storm—the "great wind" called the typhoon.

Fudenjo's twenty-four-foot boat with a square sail, like all boats made in Japan, was equipped to hug the shore—to go farther out was strictly against the national laws and punishable by death. The nets came up empty for two days. On the third the crew suddenly found themselves in a school of mackerel. In their excitement they barely noticed that the wind-whipped waves had risen. They tugged hurriedly at the heavily laden nets, but by the time they had retrieved them the storm was in full force. Their efforts to gain control of the boat led to disaster; the sails were torn and the rudder split in two. Tempest-tossed, they watched helplessly as they drifted farther and farther out to sea. The next morning the color of the sea, dark indigo, confirmed their worst fears. They were

Manjiro, View of Torishima (Bird Island), *1852*.

caught in the Kuroshio, or Black Current, a Pacific counterpart of the Gulf Stream. The best they could hope for was an island in their path. For these five superstitious and illiterate men, the sea was boundless—until somewhere, without warning, one dropped off the edge. Through eight days of terror, they drifted in the ice-cold water, living on raw fish and on icicles plucked from the ruined rigging.

Suddenly birds wheeled on the horizon—first just a few, like children's kites entangled in the sky, and then a gathering din, swooping and feeding. Below the swarm of birds was a tiny speck of bleak land, Torishima, or Bird Island, its steep volcanic cliffs jutting above the waves. The battered fishing boat capsized in the crashing surf and was smashed to pieces on the rocks. The five men dragged themselves to shore and collapsed—Jusuke's leg was badly mauled in the landing. Barely two miles in circumference and all but barren of vegetation or animal life, as the men discovered, Torishima was little more of a refuge than the drifting fishing boat. Birds, nothing but birds kept the men company. Six months of a hand-to-mouth existence out of *Robinson Crusoe* ensued: eating great-winged albatross that came so close that Manjiro, the most agile of the men, could kill them with a stone; scavenging for birds' eggs in the lava crevices; drinking brackish water scooped from rocks with a scallop shell. Then, as spring edged into burning summer, the birds too began to depart.

One clear morning three wavering sticks rose above the horizon. On the lookout, Manjiro tied a ragged kimono to a fragment of driftwood and waved it wildly from the shore. The apparition of a ship—huge and ungainly and indescribably odd, as it seemed to the Japanese fishermen—came steadily closer, like something dreamed in their abject desperation. Then bizarre sailors, some with light skin and some very dark, rowed in a small boat toward the island. In sign language, friendly invitations were issued, and the starved castaways were conveyed to the mother ship.

Captain William H. Whitfield, a stern New Englander with a clipped beard and piercing eyes, had brought the *John Howland* from her home port of Fairhaven, Massachusetts, in 1839, in search of whales in the waters east of Japan. Whaling captains had first discovered the fabled "Japan whaling grounds" twenty years earlier, as the overfished North Atlantic yielded fewer and fewer whales. Whitfield's crew had approached Torishima in hopes of finding giant sea turtles to relieve the monotony of their pota-toes-and-hardtack diet. Instead they found five gaunt islanders—the Americans had no idea from whence they came and could make no sense of their language. They fed and clothed the shivering castaways, who looked at their rescuers with puzzled eyes.

Captain Whitfield then steered the *John Howland* on an eastward course toward the Sandwich Islands, hunting whales as he found them. Manjiro, quick-eyed and curious, was a favorite with the crew; they shortened his name to Mung, and added John in honor of their ship. Manjiro was astonished at the efficient violence practiced by these strangers. Four light whaling boats manned by six men each were lowered from the ship. With a sail or muffled oars, they approached the unwitting sperm whale and threw barbed harpoons into the domed head, holding on for dear life—the so-called Nantucket sleigh ride—as the whale tried desperately to free himself from the weapons lodged in his flesh. A boat could be dragged for miles, and at any moment the whale could dive downward or attack the boat, hurling the men into the sea. If all went well, the captured whale was butchered in the sea, and the flesh and blub-ber hacked into pieces and boiled down in vats on deck. These whalers, unlike the Japanese, did not eat the whale meat. The oil was what they were after, to light the houses of New England.

On November 20, 1841, the *John Howland,* with fourteen hundred barrels of sperm whale oil in its hold, dropped anchor in the port of Ho-nolulu, on the southern coast of Oahu. The Sandwich Islands (later re-named Hawaii) were nominally an independent monarchy, with a king closely in league with American missionaries. With its dusty checker-board streets lined with adobe walls, and a sprinkling of New England cottages incongruously mixed in among dingy native huts, Honolulu was part missionary town and part pleasure ground for sailors. Grogshops, brothels, and gambling dens had followed the onward march of civiliza-tion. With its strategic position along trade and whaling routes, Honolulu was the mid-ocean switching point for communications and travel in the

Pacific, an obligatory stopping point for whalers, merchant ships, and naval vessels. Mail exchanged hands; newspapers were swapped; crew members could be hired and the sick or mutinous discharged.

Perched on the roof of his coral-pink church, Dr. Gerrit Parmele Judd was surprised to see his old friend Captain Whitfield, somber-clothed as always, leading five exotic strangers dressed in sailors' white duck along the main road. Dr. Judd, a Presbyterian missionary trained in medicine, was attaching the final shingles to his enormous new church, the Kaiwa-iaho or "stone church." Hacked block by block by Hawaiian converts from coral reefs offshore, and built to house two thousand worshipers, the structure was the visual embodiment of Dr. Judd's far-reaching power and influence. From humble origins on the New England frontier, Dr. Judd had risen to high places. A tough-minded man with a jaw firmly clenched, he had won the confidence of King Kamehameha III and persuaded hundreds of native islanders, including the hard-drinking king, to sign a temperance pledge. Dr. Judd had also prevented Catholic priests from entering on British ships, keeping the islands pure of religious and national contamination.

Dr. Judd had seen many exotic islanders pass through the Sandwich Islands; he was particularly eager to identify the origins of Captain Whitfield's sea drifters. He spread a map of the Pacific on the ground before the fishermen, but they had never seen a map and had no idea what it signified. Then, from his house near the church, Dr. Judd brought some Japanese coins and pipes left by an earlier group of shipwrecked sailors. Manjiro and his friends smiled in happy recognition. Dr. Judd bowed low with his palms together. The men cried "Dai Nippon," and all five prostrated themselves on the ground. Satisfied that he had cracked the code, Dr. Judd quickly offered to hire Fudenjo, along with his brothers, Goemon and Jusuke, as house servants in his own household, with menial tasks such as drawing water and chopping firewood. Toraemon, more independent, found work as a carpenter and boat builder.

These arrangements left in doubt the fate of "John Mung." Captain Whitfield had been struck aboard ship by Manjiro's quick intellect and cheerful outlook. Manjiro picked up English words much faster than the other castaways. Nothing was lost on him, and for everything he sought an explanation and a name. Manjiro was particularly intrigued by the secrets of navigation and—in his broken English—asked question after question about how the ship could find its way with no visible landmarks by which to chart its course. The captain had a plan. A childless widower, he wished to take Manjiro back to Massachusetts with him, give him an education, and eventually adopt him as his son. Manjiro eagerly accepted the offer, and Captain Fudenjo gave his assent. As the *John Howland* made the long journey around Cape Horn in April 1843, and up the coasts of South and North America, Captain Whitfield had ample time to prepare Manjiro for what he might expect in the whaling town of Fairhaven, Massachusetts.

Spires jutting into the sky like the straight masts of ships and a bridge that broke in two so that tall ships could pass through: these were the sights that Manjiro, now sixteen years old, saw as the *John Howland* approached Fairhaven on May 7, 1843. The town, at the top of the jagged notch below Cape Cod known as Buzzards Bay, is true to its name: a protected harbor of deep and quiet water. A drawbridge spans the Acushnet River where it enters the harbor, connecting Fairhaven to the neighboring town of New Bedford. As Captain Whitfield explained the mechanism of the drawbridge, Manjiro, mesmerized by its operation, sketched it carefully. Then Whitfield pointed to a stone breakwater on the Fairhaven side and looming above it the proud battlements of Fort Phoenix, where the first naval engagement of the American Revolution took place.

Fairhaven, once called Poverty Point, has benefited from cycles of wealth and penury. The wealth accounts for the handsome Greek Revival houses of stone and clapboard that still line the narrow streets. The poverty accounts for the time-capsule preservation of so much of the town—money tends to mar. What wealth came to Fairhaven came from whales. Quaker shipowners in Fairhaven and New Bedford sent agents into the New England countryside to round up younger sons in search of more adventure than family farms could provide. Seasoned seamen were not fooled by the pitch; they signed instead with merchant ships bound for China or India. Only the gullible and the desperate fell for the whaler's promise of a minuscule share of the profits—minus whatever the owner claimed to have spent on the upkeep of the crew. Whaling ships were notorious for cruelty and hardship; they almost never returned with their crews intact. Even the *John Howland*, with an unusually civil captain, had lost eleven men, eight of whom deserted, during its three-and-a-half-year trip.

Manjiro, circa 1880.

Captain Whitfield had found a son; he now went in search of a wife. He placed Manjiro temporarily in the household of a sailor friend and asked a teacher in the local school, Jane Allen, to tutor the boy after hours. After a week of tutoring sessions, Allen was so impressed with Manjiro's progress and aptitude that she enrolled him in the one-room stone school of Fairhaven. When Captain Whitfield returned with his bride, Albertina Keith, the Whitfields bought a farm on Sconticut Neck, and Manjiro joined them there as a member of the family, helping with daily chores and learning to ride a horse. Less enjoyable were the months he spent apprenticed to an impoverished cooper in New Bedford, learning the trade of barrel making. Neither the life of the farmer nor that of the tradesman appealed to Manjiro. The sea was his vocation, and somewhere in the back of his mind he retained the hope of returning to Japan to see his mother.

Those skills he had begun to learn onboard the *John Howland*—celestial navigation and the English language—Manjiro was able to perfect in Fairhaven, on the banks of the Acushnet River. The Christian Bible, an exotic tale of wizards and fishermen, meant little to Manjiro; his humiliation in the Fairhaven Congregational Church killed whatever enthusiasm he might have felt for the alien religion. Far more compelling was *The New American Practical Navigator*, by the Salem mathematician Nathaniel Bowditch, the guide to celestial navigation often called the sailor's bible. For this castaway who knew the perils of the open sea, Bowditch seemed the true savior. If Bowditch was a navigational tool on the perilous sea, *Webster's Dictionary* was for orientation in the world of men. These lessons—in language and navigation—proved to be the keys that opened the world for Manjiro.

II. Acushnet

What caught Herman Melville's eye as he roamed the narrow, frigid streets of lower Manhattan during the Christmas season of 1840 was a notice for a whaling voyage, aboard a new ship called the *Acushnet*, scheduled to depart within the week from Fairhaven, Massachusetts. Longhaired, bearded, and barely twenty-one, Melville had nothing whatsoever to look forward to during the new year. He had tried on several ill-fitting professions. He had taught school, served as cabin boy on a merchant ship bound for Liverpool, and wandered westward on the Erie Canal in a vague search for a purpose in life. He had seen the Mississippi and the distant city of Chicago. Now, back in his native city of New York, he was looking for work at the worst possible time—after the market crash of 1837—and finding nothing. Whaling—three or four years at sea—seemed a solution, and Melville seized it.

And so it was that two fatherless boys in search of adventure took to the sea within two days of each other, and following opposite itineraries. On January 3, 1841, Melville boarded the *Acushnet* in Fairhaven, bound for the coastal waters of Japan. On January 5, 1841, the boy Manjiro boarded Fudenjo's fishing boat in Shikoku, bound—though he did not know it—for Fairhaven.

The disreputable profession of whaling, which attracted the roughest sort of men, was hardly the future promised by Herman Melville's aristocratic ancestry. Heroes of the Revolutionary War graced both sides of the family. Melville's maternal grandfather, General Peter Gansevoort, defended Fort Schuyler, protecting Albany and New York City from British attack in 1777. Melville's Boston-born grandfather, Major Thomas Melvill (Herman added the final *e*), was a close friend of Samuel Adams and other Sons of Liberty. Melvill had joined in the rowdy protest in December 1773 against the East India Company, preventing three ships from unloading their cargo of heavily taxed tea. The protesters disguised themselves as American Indians, in feathers and war paint, boarded the ships, and pitched the crates of "the East India Company's Souchong" into Boston Harbor. The Melvill family retained a vial of confiscated tea leaves, brought home in the major's shoes, to commemorate his participation in the Boston Tea Party, the first salvo of the American Revolution.

The next generation could not maintain this heroic tradition. Melville's father, Alan, was a feckless dealer in luxury hats and furs; his special skill in life was to stay a step ahead of his creditors. His death in 1832 opened the books. Herman was cast adrift, fatherless and penniless, into the world. He made his way to Fairhaven by New Year's of 1841 and signed up as a "green hand" on the *Acushnet* with a 1/175th share of the profits. He was sailing southward, out of the merciless winter, five days later. His brother Gansevoort, in Fairhaven to see Melville off in his red flannel shirt and duck trousers, told their mother that he had never seen Herman "so completely happy."

Valentine Pease, captain of the Acushnet, *was probably no worse than the av-*erage whaling captain. He ran a tight ship in a single-minded quest for whales—already off Bermuda the *Acushnet* made its first kills and sent the oil home from Rio de Janeiro. After rounding Cape Horn in rough weather, however, they sighted no whales for weeks at a time. Ill-tempered and in poor health, Captain Pease sought to placate his restless crew and prevent their defection. Failing to flush sperm whales off the coast of Chile, he shuttled for distraction among the Galápagos Islands. The ten islands were called the Encantadas because they seemed, as if by enchantment, to wander on the charts. For Melville—as for Charles Darwin, who had explored the islands six years earlier aboard the *Beagle*—the Galápagos opened a vision of creation devoid of divine intervention. The islands seemed to Melville a desolate, bird-infested world from which God had withdrawn his presence. He noted the "demoniac din" of birds on the towering Rock Rodondo, which he called "the aviary of Ocean. Birds light here which never touched mast or tree: hermit-birds, which ever fly alone; cloud-birds, familiar with unpierced zones of air." Giant sea turtles were the quarry of the *Acushnet*, a delicacy for men ravenous for fresh meat. In one of his sketches about the Encantadas, Melville noted that "most mariners . . . believe that all wicked sea-officers, more especially commodores and captains, are at death (and, in some cases, before death) transformed into tortoises." If so, the crew of the *Acushnet* feasted for days on dead captains boiled in soup.

As the *Acushnet* veered westward past Robinson Crusoe's isle of Juan Fernandez, and on toward the Marquesas in the South Pacific, boredom was Melville's dominant mood, as bad food, equatorial heat, and monotony took their toll. If the *Acushnet* seemed an experiment in deprivation—"the sky above, the sea around, and nothing else"—the Marquesas were rumored to be a mariner's paradise. When the *Acushnet* anchored off the main island of Nuku Hiva, and young girls dressed in nothing but a strip of tapa cloth swam out to greet the crew, Melville was ready to answer the siren call. On July 9, 1842, Herman Melville and a fellow sailor named Richard Tobias Greene slipped into the tropical underbrush near the beach of Nuku Hiva and made a run for the purple-tinged mountains they had admired from the harbor. Desertion was a serious offense, punishable by flogging, imprisonment, or worse, yet it seemed an easy choice. Nor were they alone in their decision to escape Captain Pease's iron routine. Before the *Acushnet* returned home four years later, half of her crew had deserted and one man had killed himself.

Melville lived among a native tribe in Nuku Hiva for four weeks. Then he boarded an Australian whaling ship, on which conditions were even worse than aboard the *Acushnet*. After a night of drunken merriment in the harbor of Tahiti, the whole crew was arrested by French authorities and imprisoned. Having escaped once again, Melville boarded the Nantucket whaler *Charles and Henry*, and sailed to Lahaina in the Sandwich Islands, where he was discharged on May 2, 1842. Lahaina, on Maui, was a favorite port for New England ships, but it offered little amusement for restless sailors. Melville quickly made his way to more freewheeling Honolulu, got a job setting up pins in a bowling alley, and prepared to spend a quiet summer.

Then Melville encountered Dr. Gerrit P. Judd and his coral-pink church. No pages in *Typee*, Melville's autobiographical novel about his adventures in the South Seas, are more scathing than those that treat the hypocrisy and cruelty of the Christian missionaries in Honolulu. Manjiro had left Honolulu six months earlier, but his companions—Captain Denzo (as Fudenjo now called himself) and his two brothers—were still in Dr. Judd's employ. Although Jusuke and Goemon were house servants in Dr. Judd's strict religious household, and Denzo worked for a time as a waiter in a missionary school, none of the Japanese fishermen converted to Christianity—an indication, perhaps, that Dr. Judd was not as benevolent as he seemed.

Melville was indignant to find the missionaries "dwelling in picturesque and prettily-furnished coral-rock villas," while the natives lived in misery around them. Servants seemed little more than slaves. "Not until I visited Honolulu," he wrote, "was I aware of the fact that the small remnant of the natives had been civilized into draught horses, and evangelized into beasts of burden. But so it is. They have been literally broken into the traces, and are harnessed to the vehicles of their spiritual instructors like so many dumb brutes." He tells of watching "a robust, red-faced, and very lady-like personage, a missionary's spouse," out for a pleasure drive in "a little go-cart drawn by two of the islanders." One of this naked pair of "*draught* bipeds" is an old man, the other a youngster. As they begin to climb a hill, the small wheels are caught in the sand. "Will the tender-hearted lady, who has left friends and home for the good of the souls of the poor heathen, will she think a little about their bodies and get out, and ease the wretched old man until the ascent is mounted? Not she; she could not dream of it. To be sure, she used to think nothing of driving the cows to pasture on the old farm in New England." The description, right down to the old farm in New England, suggests that Mrs. Judd is the robust lady.

Melville had other reasons to despise the Judds. Soon after his arrival in Honolulu, he witnessed a tense face-off between American and British authorities over the governance of the islands. British residents had complained of ill treatment by the native population and the American missionaries who controlled them. Dr. Judd's policy of excluding British Catholic priests from the islands was not well received. The Sandwich Islands, it was felt, were becoming an American protectorate, hostile to British interests. An English naval officer, Lord George Paulet, was sent to investigate, and he occupied the islands from February 11, 1843, onward. Paulet sought a personal interview with King Kamehameha III; he was told that he would have to communicate instead through the king's chief minister, Dr. Gerrit Judd.

Melville, employed at the time by an English merchant in league with Paulet, had no difficulty choosing sides between the American missionaries and the British navy. He discounted whatever imperialist designs Great Britain might have on the Sandwich Islands. Once again the missionaries inspired his greatest wrath.

> High in the favor of the imbecile king at this time was one Dr. Judd, a sanctimonious apothecary-adventurer, who, with other kindred and influential spirits, were animated by an inveterate dislike to England. The ascendancy of a junto of ignorant and designing Methodist elders in the councils of a half-civilized king, ruling with absolute sway over a nation just poised between barbarism and civilization, and exposed by the peculiarities of its relations with foreign states to unusual difficulties, was not precisely calculated to impart a healthy tone to the policy of the government.

To Melville, Dr. Judd seemed a sort of evil wizard, a Prospero who had bewitched the natives, supplanted the drunken king, and ruled the island from his pink-coral cell.

The arrival of an American naval frigate on July 11 brought the conflict to a head. Lord Paulet withdrew, the Hawaiian flag was restored, and ten days of what Melville called "universal broad-day debauchery by royal decree" ensued. This "Polynesian saturnalia" was one more indication, in Melville's view, that Dr. Judd had managed to destroy one order of society—the healthy native one—without establishing another to replace it. "The history of these ten days . . . furnishes an eloquent commentary on the results which have flowed from the labors of the missionaries. Freed from the restraints of severe penal laws, the natives almost to a man had plunged voluntarily into every species of wickedness and excess, and by their utter disregard of all decency plainly showed, that although they had been schooled into a seeming submission to the new order of things, they were in reality as depraved and vicious as ever."

Four years later, in the summer of 1847, Melville was still railing at Judd. Evert Duyckinck, godfather of American writers at mid-century, noted in his diary: "A visit from Herman Melville with a picturesque account of Dr Judd at Lahaina, making up his diplomacy from fat natives lolling in the shade."

During his sojourn in Honolulu, Melville found a quiet refuge in the reading room of another missionary, the Reverend Samuel Chenery Damon, chaplain of the Seamen's Bethel. The Bethel, an architectural reminder of New England, was a plain white building of two stories with a cupola on top. A plainspoken Massachusetts man and a graduate of Amherst College, the Reverend Mr. Damon was vigorous and open-minded, except with regard to alcohol. He took a lively interest in visitors from the West and from Asia, and almost single-handedly ran the communications operation in Honolulu. Damon published a weekly paper called *The Temperance Advocate and Seamen's Friend,* mixing extracts from religious and literary texts with advertisements and news of Pacific ports and whaling ships. The *Friend* was the newspaper of the Pacific, treasured by whaling men far from home and passed from ship to ship. Damon was also happy to hold and redirect mail left in his hands for safekeeping. In the chapel's reading room, Melville wrote letters, read American newspapers, and browsed among Damon's books.

The surprise arrival a few weeks later of the *Acushnet* cut short Melville's sojourn in Honolulu. Fearing that Dr. Judd would inform Captain Pease of his presence, Melville sought a means of escape. As the *Acushnet* prepared for one more venture to the coast of Japan in search of the sperm whale, Melville enlisted in the American navy and shipped aboard the frigate *United States*. By the time the ship arrived in Boston, on October 3, 1844, Melville was ready to try his hand at a new profession.

Melville's first book, Typee, *was published in 1846, less than two years after* his return, and sold well enough to make him famous as a sort of modern Robinson Crusoe. A sequel, titled *Omoo*—the Marquesan word for "rover," or rather, Melville specified, "a person wandering from one island to another"—appeared the following year. *Typee* is really two books: an idyll about native life in the Marquesas and a bitter diatribe against missionaries in Hawaii. The suspense Melville kindles around the identity of the tribe that welcomes him—cannibal Typees or peace-loving Happars—is quickly dissipated. In a scene reminiscent of Dr. Judd's identification of the Japanese sea drifters, Melville learns, to his horror, that he has stumbled into a camp of cannibals.

The discovery that he is indeed among the Typees sets in motion a deeper investigation into native psychology and customs, contrasted with those of Melville's own tribe of civilized Europeans and Americans. Melville finds among the Marquesans no crime, no poverty, no sickness, but rather "universally diffused perceptions of what is *just* and *noble*." He suggests that the missionary traffic ought to be reversed: "Four or five Marquesan Islanders sent to the United States as Missionaries might be quite as useful as an equal number of Americans dispatched to the Islands in a similar capacity."

The Typees are beautiful, in body and soul, and if their warriors occasionally eat an enemy's flesh in a solemn ceremony, what of that? Among the Typees, Melville finds his Friday: the "beauteous nymph" Fayaway. Crusoe—as his crusading name implied—converted Friday to Christianity. Melville, by contrast, wants to be deconverted by Fayaway and her tribe. Part fairy or fay, and "faraway," Fayaway is the embodiment of all Melville's longings. No pages are more idyllic, or made a greater

Herman Melville, 1861.

impression on Melville's readers, than those that describe Melville and
Fayaway adrift in a canoe on a lake in the valley. Ever the rover, Melville
reclines in the stern while Fayaway, the lookout, stands in the bow and
unfurls her tapa robe to the wind. "We American sailors pride ourselves
upon our straight clean spars, but a prettier little mast than Fayaway
made was never shipped a-board of any craft."

How much of this actually happened? It hardly matters. The green
world of the islands was always a dream—for Melville, Gauguin, and later
"Omoos." The point was to keep the spoilers out, to prevent Dr. Judd and
his sanctimonious crew from chipping away at the coral reefs and confin-
ing the native women in cotton smocks. If the missionary plague spread
from Hawaii to the Marquesas, there was always Japan, which had wisely

expelled her Christian missionaries during the early seventeenth century and locked the doors. "So, hurrah for the coast of Japan! Thither the ship was bound," Melville wrote wishfully at the end of *Omoo*. Japan was the ultimate "other," a world arrested in the sleep of centuries, promising not the unfettered freedom of Fayaway and the Marquesas but something more courtly and stern, an island fortress impregnable and unbreached.

III. The Adventurer

By 1846, when Typee *appeared, Manjiro was determined to go to sea again.* Tired of the dusty and confined cooper's trade and bored with helping around Captain Whitfield's farm, he eagerly accepted the invitation of Captain Ira Davis of Fairhaven, who had served as Whitfield's harpooner, to join the crew of the whale ship *Franklin*. The ship made a first stop in Boston—Manjiro carefully sketched the harbor—and then crossed the Atlantic and sailed around the Cape of Good Hope, reaching the Pacific from the west. Manjiro began the voyage as cook's assistant, a lowly job (one senses prejudice at work), but soon showed his acuity at navigation and other skills. Once, when some of the sailors failed to harpoon a huge turtle from the ship, Manjiro put a knife between his teeth and dived into the ocean in hot pursuit. He disappeared below the surface for a long time and emerged triumphantly with the turtle, its throat slit.

While hunting whales near the island of Guam, in February 1848, Captain Davis began to behave strangely, flying into rages and threatening the crew with a musket. The men met in secret and determined to restrain the captain for his own safety. It was a daring decision; the crew knew that the charge of mutiny was a serious one. When the captain was put in chains in his cabin, and dropped off in Manila to be hospitalized, the crew held an election to replace him. The navigator took charge of the ship, and Manjiro was chosen as first mate—a signal honor under the circumstances. Manjiro, now a seasoned seaman and navigator, returned to Fairhaven at the end of August 1849, after a voyage of three and a half years.

Within days of Manjiro's return to Fairhaven, news reached New England that gold had been discovered in huge quantities in California. Manjiro joined other young men of the region in the race across the continent in search of wealth and adventure. By now he had another goal as well. He hoped to find enough gold in the Sacramento Valley to pay a sea captain willing to drop him on the forbidden coast of Japan. Manjiro, the castaway, the orphan, the picaresque hero, the loyal Confucian—Manjiro wished to see his mother before she died. With mules and provisions purchased at the shantytown of San Francisco, Manjiro made his way into the mountains. Working on his own, he was sufficiently successful panning gold to buy his way aboard a steamship to Honolulu. The friends he had left behind were delighted to see him, and apprised him of their lives in the intervening eight years. Denzo and Goemon said they were ready to join him, despite the considerable risks, in a return voyage to Japan. Toraemon, happy with his new life in Hawaii, begged off. Jusuke, whose leg wound suffered in the surf of Torishima had never properly healed, had died a few years before.

It was the Reverend Samuel Damon, chaplain of the Seamen's Bethel in Honolulu, who took Manjiro's case to heart. Damon raised money for Manjiro's return to Japan through an announcement on December 14, 1850, in the *Friend*. Someone contributed a copy of Nathaniel Bowditch's *Practical Navigator* for the venture. Damon helped find the captain of a ship, the *Sarah Boyd*, willing to take the three Japanese within reach of their home islands. Meanwhile, Manjiro had located a used whaleboat that he could afford to purchase as a landing craft. People who met Manjiro often used words such as *fearless* and *adventurous* to describe him. Calling his whaleboat *Adventurer* shows that he endorsed this view of himself. These whaleboats—shaped like canoes with oars, and carried on board whaling ships instead of lifeboats—were used to pursue whales; they were beautiful craft, as Melville wrote—"like noiseless nautilus shells their light prows sped through the sea." Damon knew the dangers Manjiro was risking. He knew that by Japanese law Manjiro was a criminal subject to execution for leaving Japan and returning. But he also saw Manjiro, schooled in the methods of the United States and the modern world, as someone who might "open" Japan to the benevolent West.

IV. Melville's Japan

Mid-December 1850. As the Reverend Mr. Damon in Honolulu scrambled to outfit Manjiro with Bowditch and a whaleboat, Damon's other rover,

Herman Melville, was completing his own imaginary journey to the coastal waters of Japan. Holed up in his snow-girt farm in the Berkshire town of Pittsfield, Massachusetts, Melville was writing the final chapters of *Moby-Dick.* "I have a sort of sea-feeling here in the country, now that the ground is covered with snow," he wrote to his friend Evert Duyckinck on December 13, 1850. "I look out of my window in the morning when I rise as I would out of a port-hole of a ship in the Atlantic. My room seems a ship's cabin; & at nights when I wake up & hear the wind shrieking, I almost fancy there is too much sail on the house, & I had better go on the roof & rig in the chimney."

Melville at thirty-one was respectably married—to Elizabeth Shaw, daughter of Chief Justice Lemuel Shaw of the Massachusetts Supreme Court—and the author of four books of maritime adventure, none of which had examined the disreputable trade that had taken him to the Pacific in the first place. *Moby-Dick* had begun to take shape during the spring of 1850. That summer, while vacationing in the Berkshires in western Massachusetts, Melville first met Nathaniel Hawthorne, fifteen years his senior and already regarded as a major American writer. Melville hoped to give his White Whale some of the same symbolic force that Hawthorne had accorded his own just-published *Scarlet Letter.* In September, determined to live near his new mentor, Melville bought the Pittsfield farm he called Arrowhead, and by Christmas, in less than a year of writing, he had finished drafting *Moby-Dick,* which he dedicated to Hawthorne.

Moby-Dick is both an unsurpassed novel of adventure and a book of extraordinary cultural reach. Everyone knows the bare outlines of the plot. A bookish schoolteacher named Ishmael, who confides he has "nothing particular to interest me on shore," takes to the sea aboard a whaling ship. "With a philosophical flourish Cato throws himself upon his sword," Ishmael says; "I quietly take to the ship." The grim suicidal joke turns out to be a premonition. The captain of the *Pequod,* one Ahab of Nantucket, is a monomaniacal madman obsessed with tracking down the Pacific-roving whale that chewed off one of his legs. While the novel is as damning as *Typee* concerning the soul-killing constrictions of "snivelization," there are no idyllic islands inhabited by half-naked nymphs in *Moby-Dick.* The only means of escape is the floating island of the *Pequod*, the only destination the White Whale's shifting haunts. And no country figures more prominently in the plot and symbolism of Melville's dark masterpiece than Moby Dick's favorite refuge, the waters of Japan.

From the outset, the journey of the Pequod *is shadowed by hostile and mysterious Japan.* Ishmael travels from his home island of Manhattan to New Bedford, where he visits Father Mapple's Seamen's Bethel—the New Bedford counterpart to the Reverend Mr. Damon's Bethel in Honolulu. Ishmael contemplates the memorial tablets on the chapel wall, including one that foreshadows the fate of the *Pequod* and its mad captain:

THE LATE

CAPTAIN EZEKIEL HARDY,

WHO IN THE BOWS OF HIS BOAT WAS KILLED BY A

SPERM WHALE ON THE COAST OF JAPAN

The *Pequod*, Ishmael soon learns, has already met with near disaster in the typhoon-tossed waters off Japan. Her three straight masts of pine were "cut somewhere on the coast of Japan, where her original ones were lost overboard in a gale." If the *Pequod* was literally "dismasted" off the coast of Japan, so metaphorically was its captain, Ahab, in a previous encounter with Moby Dick. "Aye, he was dismasted off Japan," says one of the *Pequod*'s harpooners, "but like his dismasted craft, he shipped another mast [i.e., a wooden leg] without coming home for it." As if he has not made it sufficiently clear that the *Pequod*'s fate is intimately linked to Japan, Ishmael adds: "You may have seen many a quaint craft in your day, for aught I know: square-toed luggers; mountainous Japanese junks . . . but take my word for it, you never saw such a rare old craft as this same rare old Pequod."

Straight toward the islands of Japan—east from Nantucket around the Cape of Good Hope, past Australia and into the Pacific Ocean—Ahab is determined to go to wreak his revenge on the White Whale. As the *Pequod* approaches its destination, Melville's descriptions evoke a Japan of lacquerware and rising suns, and of burning spiritual clarity: "Now, some-

times, in that Japanese sea, the days in summer are as freshets of efful-
gences. That unblinkingly vivid Japanese sun seems the blazing focus of
the glassy ocean's immeasurable burning-glass. The sky looks lacquered;
clouds there are none; the horizon floats; and this nakedness of unre-
lieved radiance is as the unsufferable splendors of God's throne. Well
that Ahab's quadrant was furnished with colored glasses, through which
to take sight of that solar fire."

"Eyeing the same sun with him," but with no need of colored glasses,
is Ahab's closest associate among the exotic crew of the *Pequod*, the inef-
fable harpooner Fedallah; "only the lids of his eyes half hooded their
orbs, and his wild face was subdued to an earthly passionlessness." If
Fedallah's origins "remained a muffled mystery to the last," Melville asks
us to picture him as one of those who "glide among the unchanging Asiatic communities, especially the Oriental isles to the east of the continent—those insulated, immemorial, unalterable countries, which even
in these modern days still preserve much of the ghostly aboriginalness of
earth's primal generations." Fedallah, writes Melville, "was such a creature as civilized, domestic people . . . only see in their dreams"—a
dream, we can now be specific, of "insulated, immemorial, unalterable"
Japan.

The crisis in *Moby-Dick*, when it is made clear that Ahab's quarry is
not whale oil but a particular white whale, takes place—and Melville insists upon it—off the coast of Japan. The first mate, Starbuck, enters Captain Ahab's cabin to inform him that oil is leaking from some of the
barrels (called Burtons) in the hold. "And so Starbuck found Ahab with a
general chart of the oriental archipelagoes spread before him; and another separate one representing the long eastern coasts of the Japanese
islands—Niphon, Matsmai, and Sikoke." (Melville was mistaken about
the nonexistent island of "Matsmai," an emblem of American ignorance
of Japan in 1850, but "Sikoke" is Manjiro's island of Shikoku.) Always attentive to the contracted goal of the *Pequod*'s voyage, namely to hunt
whales, Starbuck is for pausing in order to bring up the barrels to repair
the damage. Ahab, convinced that Moby Dick may well be summering in
the cool waters of Japan, will have none of it. "Up Burtons and break out?
Now that we are nearing Japan; heave-to here for a week to tinker a parcel of old hoops?" When Starbuck insists, Ahab seizes a loaded musket

from its rack and points it at his first mate. Nothing will stand in the way of the *Pequod*'s fatal encounter with its quarry.

As though the murderous whale is insufficient menace, a storm suddenly swoops down on the *Pequod*, ripping the canvas from her masts. "Warmest climes but nurse the cruellest fangs," Ishmael muses in a phrase worthy of Shakespeare; "in these resplendent Japanese seas the mariner encounters the direst of all storms, the Typhoon." Spliced from a Chinese word meaning "big wind" and the name of the Greek god of the winds, Typhon, the word *typhoon* is itself a wondrous meeting of East and West. "It will sometimes burst from out that cloudless sky, like an exploding bomb upon a dazed and sleepy town," says Ishmael. As the crew cowers on the deck of the "bare-poled" *Pequod*, and Fedallah kneels reverently with head bowed, Ahab is defiant. He has not traveled halfway around the world to escape the dangers that haunt the Japanese seas; he has come to confront them. He has studied his maps of Niphon and Sikoke. He has survived one typhoon and will survive another. The lightning that spangles the sky, Ahab proclaims, "but lights the way to the White Whale!"

Moby-Dick *is a work of the imagination, a prodigious dream of journeying* into the unknown. The hostile archipelago into whose waters the *Acushnet* had ventured twice, though only after Melville had jumped ship, was an ideal destination for Ahab's doomed quest. In plotting the *Pequod*'s course, Melville could complete in his imagination the journey from Fairhaven to Japan that he had aborted in 1843. And he could invite his American readers to imagine the menacing allure of this country that faced California across the seemingly "serene Pacific" traversed by whaling ships: "The same waves wash the moles of the new-built Californian towns, but yesterday planted by the recentest race of men, and lave the faded but still gorgeous skirts of Asiatic lands, older than Abraham; while all between float milky-ways of coral isles, and low-flying, endless, unknown Archipelagoes, and impenetrable Japans."

But *Moby-Dick* is also a work of deep research, and Melville drew on actual events for many of the Japanese details of the voyage of the *Pequod*. No writer has given a richer sense of the multinational Pacific world of lost boys and drifters than Herman Melville. When he refers to how whaling crews include "queer castaway creatures" found on "blown-off Japanese junks," he is alluding to stories like Manjiro's, as chronicled in the Reverend Mr. Damon's *Friend*. The masts of the *Pequod* "cut somewhere on the coast of Japan, where her original ones were lost overboard in a gale," also have a historical analogue. In 1845 the whaling ship *Manhattan* rescued two groups of shipwrecked Japanese sailors, eleven on Manjiro's Torishima and another eleven from a "blown-off Japanese junk." When the Americans tried to return the men to Edo (the city later renamed Tokyo), they were initially rebuffed, but the Shogun's leading minister, Masahiro Abe, overruled the decision. Americans were not allowed to leave the ship, but the Japanese, in gratitude, gave them a number of gifts and supplies, including "4 large cedar poles to replace storm-battered masts." An account of the adventures of the *Manhattan* appeared in the Reverend Mr. Damon's *Friend* in 1846; we know Melville was familiar with it.

Perhaps the most tantalizing of the historical analogues is the possibility that the critical scene off the coast of Japan in which Ahab threatens Starbuck with a musket is drawn from an episode aboard the *Franklin*, Manjiro's ship, when the insane Captain Davis "for no apparent reason . . . would fly into a rage, even going so far on occasion as to brandish a sword or gun." Starbuck's nervous fantasy of what it would take to confine Ahab belowdecks is precisely what the crew of the *Franklin* did to Captain Davis. "News of this incident," as the scholar Sister M. Blish concludes, "may have reached Melville and helped him shape Chapter 123, 'The Musket,' which contains the reference to 'locked Japan.' " Melville would have learned of Manjiro's adventure through the Reverend Mr. Damon and his *Friend*, the man and the magazine that kept careful track of those drifters Melville and Manjiro.

Among the great digressions that interrupt the narrative of Moby-Dick, *as* the *Pequod* makes its way toward the Pacific haunts of the sperm whale, is the key twenty-fourth chapter, entitled "The Advocate," in which Melville posits the case for the importance of whaling in the history of the modern world. He makes two major claims for the hunters of whales. First (in the decades before petroleum was discovered underground, bringing an abrupt end to the whaling industry), whale oil was the light of the world, "for almost all the tapers, lamps, and candles that burn round the globe, burn, as before so many shrines, to our glory!" Melville's second claim is even more encompassing. Whale ships not only bring light "round the globe" but themselves have discovered its remotest corners. "For many years past the whale-ship has been the pioneer in ferreting out the remotest and least known parts of the earth. She has explored seas and archipelagoes which had no chart, where no Cook or Vancouver had ever sailed. If American and European men-of-war now peacefully ride in once savage harbors, let them fire salutes to the honor and the glory of the whale-ship, which originally showed them the way, and first interpreted between them and the savages." "The uncounted isles of all Polynesia confess the same truth," Melville writes, "and do commercial homage to the whale-ship, that cleared the way for the missionary and the merchant, and in many cases carried the primitive missionaries to their first destinations."

And in the midst of this history, Melville ventures a bold prophecy. If parts of the world are still closed off, it is the whaling ship that will "open" them. Two years before Commodore Perry's mission, Melville proclaims that whaleboats, not gunboats, will open Japan. "If that double-bolted land, Japan, is ever to become hospitable, it is the whale-ship alone to whom the credit will be due; for already she is on the threshold."

Just as the whaling ship will unlock the as yet undiscovered country of Japan, it will be the key to opening an unmapped region (a sort of interior Japan) inside Ishmael—and by extension Herman Melville—as well. Having boasted of the whaling ship's wide-ranging explorations, Ishmael adds a final note: "And, as for me, if, by any possibility, there be any as yet undiscovered prime thing in me; if I shall ever deserve any real repute in that small but hushed world which I might not be unreasonably ambitious of . . . if, at my death, my executors, or more properly my creditors, find any precious MSS. in my desk, then here I prospectively ascribe all the honor and the glory to whaling; for a whale-ship was my Yale College and my Harvard." In 1851, just before the publication of *Moby-Dick*, Melville learned that the *Acushnet* of Fairhaven, his model for the *Pequod*, had run aground on St. Lawrence Island, off the coast of Alaska. The ship was a total loss, smashed to bits in heavy seas, but the crew was saved, and safely conveyed to Honolulu.

V. The Threshold

In January 1851, as though to fulfill Melville's prophecy of that very year, Manjiro and his whaleboat *Adventurer* were on the "threshold" of Japan. Manjiro visited the Reverend Mr. Damon's chapel reading room for the final time and wrote a letter to Captain Whitfield expressing his gratitude. "I never forget your benevolence to bring me up from a small boy to manhood. I have done nothing for your kindness till now. Now I am going to return with Denzo and Goemon to native country. My wrong doing is not to be excused but I believe good will come out of this changing world, and that we will meet again." Exactly ten years had passed since Manjiro and his shipmates had lost their way in the Kuroshio current. The *Adventurer* was lowered from the whaling ship under cover of night, and the three men rowed through a rough sea to a beach on the island of Okinawa. After being questioned by some native villagers, who spoke a dialect difficult to understand, Manjiro, his companions, and the *Adventurer* were taken to the nearby port city of Kagoshima, the castle town at the southern tip of the island of Kyushu.

The first European visitors to Japan had landed in Kagoshima in 1549, when the Jesuit Francis Xavier had begun his mission to make Japan a Christian country, only to have the Shogun turn violently against the Christian missionaries fifty years later. In Kagoshima, the castle town of the great clan of Satsuma province, Manjiro and his shipmates met with unexpected luck. The Satsuma leader, Lord Shimazu, was one of the few Japanese to favor a more open policy toward Europe and the United States. With a snap of his fan, Lord Shimazu dismissed his attendants; alone in the castle, he eagerly questioned Manjiro about Western miracles such as steam-powered ships. How, he wondered, did they move without sails? Then, like some unreasonable king in a fairy tale, Lord Shimazu ordered Manjiro to build a whaling ship in Kagoshima harbor. For forty-eight days Manjiro and his companions labored on the ship, with local help, and launched it successfully, much to their relief.

Then came an order for the shipwrecked fishermen to be brought to Nagasaki, ninety miles up the Kyushu coast, to be subjected to a far less sympathetic interrogation. In a "trial" devised two centuries earlier to root out secret Christians, Manjiro and his companions were ordered to trample barefoot on icons called *fumi-e*, representations of the Crucifixion or the Virgin Mary. The fear of eternal damnation had led many converts to refuse and suffer the consequences: immediate execution. Untroubled, Manjiro walked over the images. Asked how he felt doing so, he replied that his feet were cold since he had become accustomed to wearing shoes.

During his ensuing nine months of imprisonment and interrogation in Nagasaki, the surreal gulf between questions and answers widened—to the distance of the Pacific. Did the Milky Way, the interrogators wondered, really reach all the way to the land called Massachusetts? Could Americans standing outside at night really see the multitrunked katsura tree that grows on the moon? And what was the climate like in that faraway land? "The climate of New England is like that of Japan," Manjiro replied. He was questioned about American churches. He was questioned about American toilets. The latter are "placed over holes in the ground," Manjiro said. "It is customary to read books in them."

Manjiro was again asked about steamships, and he explained how a fire in the hold of the ship gave off steam that turned wheels on each side of the ship. Then he described a "land ship":

> They have an iron box about thirteen feet square containing fire which creates steam. This fills the box and then issues out through an iron pipe. The construction is like that of a steamship. [The engine] is followed by twenty-three or four iron boxes chained together, on top of which the cargo is placed, and within which the passengers sit. These boxes have two or three windows with glass panes. When one looks through them when the train is in motion its swiftness is so great that all objects appear obliquely and are seen only for an instant. When possible the route chosen is along flat ground, avoiding the mountains. This land ship runs on iron rails.

Manjiro showed his questioners his watch and remarked that even American children wore watches. When he tried to explain the telegraph, invented eight years earlier by Samuel Morse, he seems to have betrayed even his own skepticism: "It uses a wire stretched high above the road and the letter hung on it goes from one station to another without the aid of a messenger. To prevent the letter from colliding with another they use a device which I do not understand. I think the letter is drawn by a magnet iron."

Having awed his interlocutors with these references to American technological prowess, Manjiro turned to the superiority of the American government. He displayed his American passport (the first to be issued to a Japanese) and explained the workings of the United States government, insisting on its peaceful intentions toward Japan. He contrasted Japanese pomp with American simplicity, and the fixed feudal order of Japan with America, where "there is no distinction between classes." The American president, he said, "is chosen from the people for his talent and learning. . . . He lives very simply and goes about on horseback, followed by a single retainer. Officials are hard to distinguish as they never display the authority of their office. They do not demand courtesies from citizens along the road."

Manjiro concluded with a passionate plea for the opening of Japan:

> American ships entering ports of Japan have been ordered to leave immediately, and compelled to do so without accomplishing any results. When a whale ship or a trading ship is delayed by a storm there is a shortage of water and fuel. The Americans seek permission to get these things and if necessary would be willing to leave a hostage. In spite of their humble proposals, the Japanese made a great commotion, to the astonishment of the Americans. . . . The Americans are better tempered than the Japanese. Their country *being opened*, they have no desire to annex any other country. In sailing from California to China a ship is carrying so many passengers and such a quantity of goods that it is impossible to load enough provisions . . . [and] it is impossible to make the long voyage back to California to get coal when it has run short. So I understand that they want to get a storage place for coal in Satsuma, Nippon. I read this report when I was in Oahu last year in a newspaper called *Friend*.

After a nervous night spent in the tiny cells of the Nagasaki prison, Manjiro and his companions were officially released and allowed to re-

turn to their homes in Shikoku. The lost child Manjiro had a joyful reunion with his aged mother. She took him to the village graveyard of
Daikakuji Temple to see the boulder she had placed in his honor. She was
too poor to afford a proper memorial stone.

VI. The May Basket

In the 114th chapter of Moby-Dick, *as the* Pequod *is "penetrating further*
and further into the heart of the Japanese cruising ground," Melville
pauses for a bucolic moment, imagining the rolling waves as so many
"mild blue hill-sides . . . you almost swear that play-wearied children lie
sleeping in these solitudes, in some glad May-time, when the flowers of
the woods are plucked." Even Ahab enters into the mystic mood, as the
sun—the "Gilder" of the chapter's title—"did seem to open in him his own
secret treasuries." Ahab, in an extraordinary vision suggesting the Buddhist concept of reincarnation, meditates on the course of a man's life:

> There is no steady unretracing progress in this life; we do not ad-
> vance through fixed gradations, and at the last one pause:—
> through infancy's unconscious spell, boyhood's thoughtless faith,
> adolescence' doubt (the common doom), then scepticism, then
> disbelief, resting at last in manhood's pondering repose of If. But
> once gone through, we trace the round again; and are infants,
> boys, and men, and Ifs eternally. Where lies the final harbor,
> whence we unmoor no more? In what rapt ether sails the world, of
> which the weariest will never weary? Where is the foundling's fa-
> ther hidden? Our souls are like those orphans whose unwedded
> mothers die in bearing them: the secret of our paternity lies in
> their grave, and we must there to learn it.

VII. The Language-Bearer

In a sense, the boy Manjiro, the illiterate fisherman lost at sea, had died, and
his mother was right to erect a stone in his memory. The man Manjiro,
trying to put together his twin worlds of Fairhaven and Shikoku, had exactly three days and nights to enjoy his reunion with his mother. The

"changing world" he had mentioned to Captain Whitfield caught up with him again. The daimyo of the Tosa clan required his assistance. He accorded Manjiro samurai status—he was now required to wear a sword—and asked him to teach his retainers about the West. Manjiro began with language: there could be no knowledge of foreign lands without foreign words. He taught his students the English alphabet. He taught them to sing the letters to the tune he had learned in Fairhaven and thus bequeathed it to Japanese children forever after. He wrote the first Japanese guide to the English language, "Shortcut to Anglo-American Conversation," with phrases like "How do you do, sir?" in English with Japanese translation.

For the Shikoku-born writer Kenzaburo Oe, winner of the Nobel Prize in literature in 1994, Manjiro's greatest gift to Japan was as a carrier of language. Manjiro, with brush and ink, painted the English alphabet on innumerable Japanese fans, such as the one invoked in Oe's novel *The Silent Cry*, most of which is set in Shikoku near Manjiro's home village: "The fan painting that hung in the alcove in the room beyond bore a Roman alphabet, crudely written in Chinese ink and barely distinguishable by now against paper browned with age . . . the signature 'John Manj' in the bottom right-hand corner." Oe invokes Manjiro at several points in his novel as a traveler between worlds, and a precursor of Oe's twentieth-century rovers.

VIII. **The Black Ships**

In the spring of 1854, Manjiro was abruptly summoned to Edo, the seat of the ruling Tokugawa clan. American ships under the command of Commodore Matthew Calbraith Perry had returned to Japan, fulfilling the threat that Perry had made the previous year, when he brought an armada of "Black Ships" into Edo Bay. Manjiro was selected to serve the Tokugawa Shogun in negotiations with the invaders. In recognition, he was promoted again. Now he was accorded two swords and a family name. He chose Nakahama in honor of his home village of Nakanohama.

Japan's more progressive thinkers knew that its "closed country" policy was doomed. The Industrial Revolution, so vividly described in Manjiro's recitation in Nagasaki, had shifted the balance of power decisively toward the West. Japan must either find a strategy for catching up or risk the humiliating dismemberment of neighboring China after the so-called Opium War. When the imposing flotilla of Commodore Perry's *kurofune* (or "black ships") entered Edo Bay on the evening of July 2, 1853, it confirmed their worst nightmares. The steam-powered warships were called black not only for their sooty color but also for the uncertain fate they foretold for Japan. Commodore Perry assured the Japanese that his intentions were friendly, and that what he requested, as spelled out in a letter from President Millard Fillmore, was entirely reasonable. He asked for safe haven for shipwrecked sailors and whalers who washed up on Japanese shores, a refueling station for steamships in need of coal, and the opening of a few Japanese ports to American trade. At the same time, Perry made sure that his superior weaponry was abundantly on view. With a few playful cannon blasts across the bay, he demonstrated what might be in store if his "pacific overtures" were rebuffed. He promised to return the following year for an answer.

Amid the panic that ensued among Japanese officials, nothing was more evident than the need for an interpreter they could trust, someone who knew both languages and both countries. The Shogun's foreign minister, Lord Egawa of Ise, recommended Manjiro for the position. An interesting correspondence ensued, testifying to the deep distrust still harbored against the "half-American" Manjiro. "When you came here today, you told me about Manjiro," Prime Minister Masahiro Abe wrote Egawa. "I do not think that Manjiro has any thoughts of treason, but upon getting on board [Perry's] ship, there is no telling what might happen. Considering the fact that Manjiro was taken to America by a foreigner, we do not know what method he might use in talking to the men on the ships." Another samurai suggested that Manjiro might be a spy, brainwashed by his crafty rescuers. "I wonder . . . if that American barbarian educated Manjiro as part of a scheme. After all, he must have realized that Manjiro was young and impressionable."

Despite such objections, Manjiro accompanied the Japanese delegation to meet with Perry at Yokohama and sign the Treaty of Amity, accepting the Americans' demands. By that time Prime Minister Abe had outlined a strategy. The Japanese would risk a temporary opening to the West in order to learn everything they had to learn, about weaponry and other technological innovations, to catch up with the Western powers. Once they had achieved these goals, they could reevaluate their relations with the West. To celebrate the agreement, the Japanese delegation staged a sumo match, and the Americans countered with a minstrel show. A ceremonial exchange of gifts starkly revealed the technological gap between the parties. The Americans received a teapot, a ceramic vase, a bronze temple bell, and a lacquer writing case with enamel overlay. The Japanese were given American machinery, including a telegraph machine, a daguerreotype camera, and, most impressive of all, a quarter-scale steam-powered railroad train on a circular track, large enough for the delighted samurai to ride atop the cars. These technological wonders, which confirmed the magical powers Manjiro had described to his skeptical inquisitors in Nagasaki, were entrusted to Manjiro himself, as official curator of Commodore Perry's gifts, since only he among the Japanese knew what they were for.

IX. The Commodore

On the morning of December 28, 1854, while serving as United States consul in Liverpool, England, Nathaniel Hawthorne received an unexpected visit. "Commodore Perry called to see me this morning," Hawthorne wrote in his journal. The grave and grim-faced commodore had not been accorded the hero's welcome he had expected in Washington. The capital had other things than Japan to worry about in those years leading up to the Civil War. Hawthorne described the visit: "He soon introduced his particular business with me—it being to inquire whether I could recommend some suitable person to prepare his notes and materials for the publication of an account of his voyage [to open Japan]. He was good enough to say that he had fixed upon me, in his own mind, for this office, but that my public duties would of course prevent me from engaging in it. I spoke of Herman Melville." Having served as midwife for *Moby-Dick*, Hawthorne came close to delivering a second Pacific epic by Melville to American literature. But Commodore Perry, who seemed "to have some acquaintance with the literature of the day," was not enthusiastic. "It would be a very desirable labor for a young literary man, or, for that matter, an old one," Hawthorne concluded wistfully; "for the world can scarcely have in reserve a less hackneyed theme than Japan."

X. Found at Sea

The terror of being lost at sea was the defining experience of John Manjiro's life; his greatest gift to the Japanese was his translation of the "sailor's Bible," Nathaniel Bowditch's *The New American Practical Navigator*, which he had first studied in Fairhaven. Finding one's bearings by the position of the moon and the stars must have seemed miraculous to Manjiro, who assured Japanese officials that Bowditch's volume contained the secrets for sailing in the open ocean. He undertook the translation around 1855, and completed it in two years. John Manjiro had, in a profound sense, no native language; his main challenge turned out to be not the English language but the Japanese, which he had been assiduously studying since his return. New words were needed for scientific concepts new to Japan. Scribes were hired to help Manjiro with the calligraphy, and with the diagrams and logarithmic tables. Manjiro joked that the labor of translation had turned his hair white.

Around the time the translation was begun, a marriage was arranged for Manjiro. His sixteen-year-old bride was the daughter of a famous master swordsman of the samurai class. She was skilled in the tea ceremony and in ikebana, the art of arranging flowers. It was a marriage of Old Japan, just as Japan was on the verge of entering a new era.

XI. Pacific Man

"From my twenty-fifth year I date my life," Melville told Hawthorne, referring to the year he returned from his Pacific journey. Melville the Omoo, the rover among islands, never quite "settled" after his return to domestic life. He wrote unceasingly, and descended into black moods that alarmed his wife and family; at one point they consulted with a minister about arranging a legal separation. Melville's true home was somewhere in the Pacific Ocean—"my dear Pacific," as he had called it in *Moby-Dick*, his first view of which had answered "the long supplication of my youth." During the last decades of his long life, Melville sought to return to the Pacific— both in his imagination and aboard ship.

Melville was a man who had seen an unsettling vision, but not the

Christian version. His antipathy toward the coercive moralizing and tepid spiritual life of Dr. Judd and his missionary company, living high in Honolulu on the backs of native islanders, convinced him that there was nothing in that direction worth preserving. What Melville was after was something deeper and darker, primordial and prehuman. Call it a Pacific vision, and Melville a "Pacific man"—the phrase is the poet Charles Olson's, in his remarkable study of Melville. It is something like the vision vouchsafed to Pip, the little African American boy dear to Ahab. In a chapter called "The Castaway," Pip falls unnoticed out of a whaleboat and sinks deep, deep, into the darkest depths of the Pacific, "where strange shapes of the unwarped primal world glided to and fro before his passive eyes . . . :

> and among the joyous, heartless, ever-juvenile eternities, Pip saw the multitudinous, God-omnipresent, coral insects, that out of the firmament of waters heaved the colossal orbs. He saw God's foot upon the treadle of the loom, and spoke it; and therefore his shipmates called him mad. So man's insanity is heaven's sense; and wandering from all mortal reason, man comes at last to that celestial thought, which, to reason, is absurd and frantic; and weal or woe, feels then uncompromised, indifferent as his God.

During the fall of 1856, two years after Perry's visit, Melville himself called on Hawthorne in England. Melville's father-in-law, Judge Lemuel Shaw of Boston, alarmed by his son-in-law's financial concerns and habitual gloom, paid for the trip, a voyage of recuperation to the Continent and the Holy Land. Judge Shaw had looked into the possibility of a consulship for Melville—the post in Honolulu was vacant, and so was Florence—but behind-the-scenes maneuvering by Shaw and Hawthorne (a friend of President Franklin Pierce) had come to nothing. So Melville was wandering again, still groping for the spiritual certainties that eluded him. He arrived in Liverpool on November 10, and the two men spent a few days together, walking and talking on the beach at Southport, Lancashire.

Melville's account was laconic: "Took a long walk by the sea. Sands &

grass. Wild & desolate. A strong wind. Good talk." Hawthorne, in his journal for November 12, was more expansive, and provides the best analysis of Melville's ongoing spiritual quest:

> We took a pretty long walk together, and sat down in a hollow among the sand hills (sheltering ourselves from the high, cool wind) and smoked a cigar. Melville, as he always does, began to reason of Providence and futurity, and of everything that lies beyond human ken, and informed me that he had "pretty much made up his mind to be annihilated"; but still he does not seem to rest in that anticipation; and, I think, will never rest until he gets hold of a definite belief. It is strange how he persists—and has persisted ever since I knew him, and probably long before—in wandering to and fro over these deserts, as dismal and monotonous as the sand hills amid which we were sitting. He can neither believe, nor be comfortable in his unbelief; and he is too honest and courageous not to try to do one or the other. If he were a religious man, he would be one of the most truly religious and reverential; he has a very high and noble nature, and better worth immortality than most of us.

The pilgrimage to the Holy Land already seemed foolhardy. Melville confided, Hawthorne said, that he "did not anticipate much pleasure in his rambles, for that the spirit of adventure is gone out of him. He certainly is much overshadowed since I saw him last." When Melville boarded a steamer on November 18, Hawthorne was struck by how little he carried in a single carpetbag: "This is the next best thing to going naked; and as he wears his beard and moustache, and so needs no dressing-case—nothing but a tooth-brush—I do not know a more independent personage. He learned his travelling habits by drifting about, all over the South Sea, with no other clothes or equipage than a red flannel shirt and a pair of duck trousers."

Melville found nothing particularly holy in the Holy Land. His holy land was elsewhere, in those Pacific regions in which he had drifted about in a red flannel shirt. So in 1860, at the age of forty, he tried again to cross the Pacific in quest of Asia. His plan was to accompany his brother Thomas, captain of the clipper ship *Meteor*, around South America and westward, eventually circling the world. On the rough passage around Cape Horn, Melville read wayfaring books that reminded him of his primal vision of the Pacific. In Chapman's translation of Homer he underscored a line from the fifth book of the *Odyssey*, "The sea had soak'd his heart through." He boarded a whale ship encountered near the equator, spending a nostalgic hour there, and reported that there were "eight or ten of the 'wild people' aboard," picked up from the island of Roratonga "to help pull in the whaleboat when they hunt the whale." He was back in his element.

On October 12, 1860, the *Meteor* anchored in San Francisco. The *Daily Evening Bulletin* reported that "Mr. Melville is traveling in pursuit of health, and new experiences to turn to account in a literary way." And then, without explanation, Melville's journey to the East was abruptly aborted. On October 18, the *Daily Alta* reported a change of plans. "This well known author . . . intends to return by the next steamer to New York." The voyage of the *Meteor* was Melville's final attempt to regain his past self. "I feel so much disappointed," his mother, Maria, wrote on November 5. "I had fondly hoped that a Voyage to India under kind Tom's care would have quite brought Herman back to health."

XII. The Errand-Bearers

Just a few months before Melville's abrupt departure from San Francisco in the fall of 1860, the Daily Alta *reported the presence there of another famous rover,* John Manjiro. With his familiarity with the United States and the English language, Manjiro had been named chief interpreter for the Japanese mission to Washington and New York to ratify the Treaty of Amity that the American consul, Townsend Harris, had drawn up after Commodore Perry's mission. Two ships, one American and one Japanese, carried the delegation across the Pacific. The Japanese ship, with Manjiro aboard, was the legendary clipper *Kanrin Maru*. Soon after departure, the ship ran into one of the worst typhoons ever documented in the Pacific. When the Japanese captain fell ill, an American naval officer called John Brooke, with Manjiro as navigator, took charge of the ship. It was the first time that a Japanese ship navigated by a Japanese had crossed the Pacific.

"Manjiro is certainly one of the most remarkable men I ever saw," Brooke wrote in his journal. "He has translated Bowditch into the Japanese language. Manjiro is an adventurous character. . . . He is very communicative and I am satisfied that he has had more to do with the opening of Japan than any other man living."

The 1860 mission, so critical to Japanese-American relations—the historian Marius Jansen calls it "the first fully authorized voyage abroad by a Japan about to reorient itself toward the wealth and strength it sensed in the Western world"—received considerable press attention in the United States. *The New York Times* on June 26 called the parade of the samurai down Broadway "decidedly the most magnificent display our city has ever seen." The next day the *Times* published a poem by Walt Whitman called "The Errand-Bearers." For Whitman, standing among the Broadway crowds, the "errand" of the Japanese delegation represented a decisive reversal in the westward march of civilization.

> *Over the Western sea hither from Niphon come,*
> *Courteous, the swart-cheek'd two-sworded envoys,*
> *Leaning back in their open barouches, bare-headed, impassive,*
> *Ride to-day through Manhattan.*

Whitman saw rich symbolism in the "guests from the islands" advancing between the imposing buildings of lower Broadway:

> *Where our tall-topt marble and iron beauties range on opposite sides,*
> *   to walk in the space between,*
> *To-day our Antipodes comes.*

The United States, in Whitman's view, was now "the space between," where "venerable Asia" and European civilization encountered each other.

> *The sign is reversing, the orb is enclosed,*
> *The ring is circled, the journey is done,*
> *The box-lid is but perceptibly open'd, nevertheless the perfume pours*
> *   copiously out of the whole box.*

Whitman invoked the American ships that had opened Japan: "My sail-ships and steam-ships threading the archipelagoes . . . Commerce opening." At the same time, he praised "Asia, the all-mother," and asked the United States to "bend your proud neck to the long-off mother now sending messages over the archipelagoes to you."

Meanwhile John Manjiro, back in San Francisco, oversaw repairs to the Kanrin Maru. A newspaper reporter noted that Manjiro "astonished a sta-tioner not a little by asking, in excellent English, for a copy of *Webster's Dictionary.*" He also purchased a daguerreotype camera to photograph his mother ("when that is done," he said, the camera "will be useless!") and an early sewing machine. On the return trip via Hawaii, Manjiro sought out his old friend and sponsor the Reverend Samuel Damon, who pub-lished an extended account of their visit in the *Friend* for June 1, 1860. Manjiro gave Damon a copy of his translation of Bowditch, calling it "a long and laborious work." "I have had charge of some of the presents which were brought by Commodore Perry," Manjiro said. "I am thirty-six years old. I am married, and have three children. I am captain in the navy, and at home, have charge of a vessel." "He is the first native of the Japanese Empire," Damon noted, "who navigated a vessel, out of sight of land, according to scientific principles."

This upbeat assessment of Manjiro's career concealed darker cur-rents. The year 1860 was a critical one for Japan; its prime minister was assassinated by samurai resistant to continuing Tokugawa leadership. Upon his return to Japan in the summer of 1860, Manjiro was placed under house arrest, under suspicion of passing secrets to the Americans. A letter had been circulating among high-ranking samurai claiming that Manjiro was an American spy.

Nonetheless, Manjiro had many contacts among the Western popu-lation of Yokohama—one of the treaty ports opened to Westerners under the document just signed. The missionaries and merchants that Melville had predicted would follow the whaling ships over the "threshold" had indeed arrived. Francis Hall, a bookseller from Elmira, New York, who had opened an import-export firm in Yokohama, reported in his diary of

July 16, 1860, that Manjiro, confined to his house in Tokyo, had given his mother the sewing machine only to meet with her disappointment that the tight seams could not be ripped out, according to Japanese practice, for cleaning. Hall, an amateur photographer, also learned from associates of the missionary Dr. James Hepburn that Manjiro, with the other modern invention he had acquired in San Francisco, was "taking daguerreotypes at Yedo [Edo] with considerable success."

XIII. **The No Play**

While Manjiro took photographs, Melville wrote poems. These two "Pacific men," so admirably suited by wide travel, intellectual acumen, and linguistic brilliance to participate in the continuing evolution of their respective countries, found it increasingly difficult to secure a place suited to them. Both sought to participate in the conflicts that rent Japan and the United States during the early 1860s, as the two countries struggled with the inheritance of feudal ways of life. Melville sought in vain an officer's position in the U.S. Navy; he wrote poems about the great battles of the Civil War instead.

Manjiro's expertise in navigation and his familiarity with the West contributed to his continuing rise in Japan. In 1862 he was appointed a naval instructor and captained the first Japanese whaling ship, teaching the skills he had learned aboard American ships. After the Meiji Restoration of 1868, Japan began an industrious process of modernization. Manjiro was named an instructor at the Kaiseijo School, or Institute for Western Books, the precursor of Tokyo Imperial University. But an edict of 1876 also revoked the special privileges of samurai; the two swords Manjiro had been entitled to wear were now meaningless. In the meantime, Manjiro's personal life was in disarray. After the death of his first wife, he married a second time, to a young woman who gave him two children. They separated soon after, and Manjiro took a third wife. Rumors spread through Tokyo concerning his visits to brothels in the pleasure quarters, and his intimacy with geisha.

Suspicion continued to surround Manjiro's political views. In 1870 he was invited to accompany a Japanese mission to Europe to look into the Prussian military strategy in the Franco-Prussian War. During a five-day stopover in New York, Manjiro received permission to travel by train to Boston and on to Fairhaven to visit Captain Whitfield. The reunion was a happy one: "If it is not John Mung!" Whitfield exclaimed. "I have been looking forward to this for twenty years." On his return to Japan, Manjiro and the head of the delegation were disciplined for the visit to Fairhaven—the suspicion that he was a spy lingered on.

Manjiro's final decades were marred by illness and depression, as he lived, according to one of his biographers, "in near seclusion in his Tokyo home." In 1884 the Reverend Mr. Damon sought out Manjiro in Tokyo and wrote a report for the *Friend:* "Long shall we cherish the memory of our visit to Japan, but among the most pleasing incidents of that visit were the repeated interviews with Nakahama Manjiro, the wrecked sailor-boy, the successful adventurer in returning to his native land and the translator of Bowditch's Navigator." Damon glossed over the sadness, noting only that Manjiro was "not possessed of a large amount of this world's goods, being dependent upon his sons for support. We most sincerely wish the Japanese government might honor itself by honoring its old and faithful servant with a liberal pension."

A truer picture comes from the English explorer and travel writer Isabella Bird, who had met Damon in Honolulu while she was writing a book about the Sandwich Islands. As she was preparing to undertake her influential book *Unbeaten Tracks in Japan,* based on travels through the Japanese countryside in 1878, Damon urged her to seek out Manjiro in Tokyo if she possibly could arrange it. She wrote to Damon on November 16, 1879, describing a lunch she had had with "Mangero":

> Mangero is quite an old-looking and sad-looking man. His party is out of power and himself out of employment, and he lives on a plot of land some distance from Tokyo. He brightened very much when he heard of you, and especially when I gave him your photo and message. I urged him to write to you, but he has nearly forgotten English. Your thought of him seemed to be quite a gleam of brightness in his depressed condition, and I am glad you gave me the message to find him.

By 1888 Manjiro was sufficiently well known for a Nō play in the classical style to be written about him and performed. The famous actor Sadanji played the part of Manjiro, the drifter from Tosa. The play opens with a scene of Manjiro's mother praying in a village temple on the thirteenth anniversary of his death. The central plot concerns the suspicions harbored by a group of *ronin*, or leaderless samurai. The *ronin* believe that Manjiro had served as an advance scout for Commodore Perry and was responsible for the invasion of the Black Ships. They conspire to assassinate him. In the course of the play, Manjiro persuades them of his innocence. The play closes with a ceremonial wrestling match—a version of the sumo matches held for Commodore Perry—in which a Japanese overcomes an African American.

Manjiro, at age sixty-one, attended the play, accompanied by a young woman who served as his companion. Despite the fact that Sadanji portrayed Manjiro as a frequenter of the pleasure quarters and a connoisseur of courtesans, Manjiro was satisfied that the play contained no charges of treason. He lived for another ten years, sickly and poor, and died in Tokyo, in 1898, at the age of seventy-one.

XIV. Typee Dreams

Melville's last years are darker than Manjiro's. After Moby-Dick *failed to* cause the stir he had anticipated, he turned away from the sea in his writing, which, except for a few masterly short tales, became hermetic and obsessive: the incestuous romance *Pierre*, the intellectual long poem *Clarel*. Lobbying by friends for a government sinecure had failed. Melville for twenty years, beginning in 1866, was reduced to filling out forms in the Customs House in lower Manhattan, writing poetry at night, and returning one last time to the sea in *Billy Budd*, the late masterpiece he never published. One of his sons put a bullet through his own head in 1867; the other, Stanwix, sailed aboard the *Yokohama* to Shanghai before dying of tuberculosis in San Francisco in 1886. The following year Melville received his last royalty statement from his publisher, which hadn't printed any of his books for a decade. By the time of his death, in September 1891, he was almost forgotten. "Probably, if the truth were known," ran the obituary in the *New York Press*, "even his own generation has long thought him dead, so quiet have been the later years of his life." The *Times*, more forgetful still, gave his name as Henry Melville.

Only boyhood readers of *Typee*, still smitten with the vision of Fayaway in her skiff, kept Melville's memory alive. Lafcadio Hearn, longing to leave New Orleans and venture into the Pacific himself, wrote in 1886 of being "bewitched" by *Typee*. In the year Melville died, the painter John La Farge, roving the South Pacific with his traveling companion Henry Adams, had *Typee* on his mind: "The name recalls so many associations of ideas, so much romance of reading." As Adams and La Farge explored Tahiti, looking for Melville's haunts and traces, "Nothing but dreams of Typee sustain[ed] us," Adams wrote. It was the vision of *Typee*, and more precisely of Fayaway, that inspired these South Sea rovers, and for a new edition of *Typee*, published in 1892, La Farge supplied a frontispiece: naked Fayaway, her tapa spread above her like a spinnaker. La Farge did more versions of the picture, finally achieving something closer to Melville's intensity in a watercolor of 1895. Best though is a little pencil sketch, in which the windblown garment looks like a thought unfurling from Fayaway's head. La Farge wrote of "how Melville passed from those records of exterior life and scenery to a dwelling within his mind—a following out of metaphysical ideas, and a scheming of possible evolution in the future of man."

And what evolution was that? The afterimage of the twinned stories of Melville and Manjiro is one of ships in full sail. First, the Acushnet *on her maiden voyage, carrying Melville out of Fairhaven in January 1841, and the* John Howland *returning to Fairhaven with the first Japanese boy to seek an American education. In 1851: the* Pequod *in tempest-tossed Japanese waters in search of the White Whale, and Manjiro's* Adventurer *beached on Okinawa. Then the two clippers of 1860, the* Meteor *with Melville onboard and the* Kanrin Maru *navigated by Manjiro, crossing paths in San Francisco. New visions crossing old ones, Bibles and dictionaries, mariners mixing with missionaries. And these roving pioneers of the Pacific, Melville and Manjiro, pointing the way for others in their restless wake.*

A COLLECTOR OF SEASHELLS

>< >< ><

Nothing we know of our own actions enables us to
imagine what it may be that so gracefully modulates
these surfaces, element by element, row by row,
without other tools than those contained in the thing
that is being fashioned; what it may be that so
miraculously harmonizes and adjusts the curves, and
finishes the work with a boldness, an ease, a
precision which the most graceful creations of the
potter or bronze founder are far from equaling. . . .
Perhaps what we call <u>perfection</u> in art (which all do
not strive for and some disdain) is only a sense of
desiring or finding in a human work the sureness of
execution, the inner necessity, the indissoluble bond
between form and material that are revealed to us by
the humblest of shells.

—PAUL VALÉRY, "MAN AND THE SEA SHELL"

A typhoon was blowing across the island of Kyushu, turning roads into rivers and cliffs into waterfalls. Sheltered from the wind and the driving rain, the American professor and the former samurai sipped bitter green tea in a fisherman's hut. For the humble fisherman and his wife, it was like the arrival of a pair of mythical gods—they had never entertained an "outside barbarian" beneath their ramshackle roof, nor had a high-ranking samurai like the governor of the prefecture ever sought their company. A group of villagers had circled the hut to gawk at the exotic visitors. One of the villagers, hearing that the professor was a collector of old things, shouted above the pelting rain that there was a burial cave nearby. With "curious embarrassment," as the professor noted in his journal, they explained that they had never seen the burial urns, nor had their fathers. Their grandfathers, however, "had handed down the story that when a narrow road had been built on the side of the hill the workmen had broken through the roof of the cave and had seen the vessels." The professor, who had seen similar caves farther north, called for brush and paper and quickly made a sketch of the sort of pottery he expected to find there.

Conditions for collecting were hardly ideal. A few miles of climbing through mud and standing water, wind and torrential rain, brought them to the cave. Even after a temporary dam and sluice were put in place to divert a rushing stream, it was still going to be a challenge to descend into the underground cemetery. "Only a muskrat or a beaver could stem a current like that," remarked the professor—he was from New England. The villagers warned the professor about disturbing the dead. None was willing, even when offered generous payment, to allow himself to be lowered into the cave. Brushing aside such superstitious nonsense—he was from Salem, Massachusetts—the professor insisted that he would make the descent alone. If there were pots down there, he was determined to find them. Ancient beliefs must yield to modern science. The villagers knew better. Their fathers had warned them. Their grandfathers had warned them. But the professor *would* go down.

Two of the muscular jinricksha runners grabbed the professor by the hands and lowered him into the cave. "It was as dark as a pocket," he noted, "and the little light from a rainy sky was cut off by the curious and awe-stricken crowd that shaded the hole. I stretched out my legs in vain to find something to touch, and finally jerked my hands from the grasp of the men and dropped into the water nearly up to my middle. There was a momentary silence and then shouts of horror came echoing down from the opening."

The professor reassured everyone that there was no cause for concern. He was bearing up fine in the subterranean—and increasingly submarine—cemetery. "I called to my assistant that I was all right, when in agitated tones he told me that great poisonous centipedes were crawling out of the opening! I had on my wide-brimmed hat and a slippery rubber coat, and what I had supposed to be crumbs of earth and pebbles tumbling from the sides of the ragged hole were huge centipedes dropping on me! I stood literally in a cascade of the venomous creatures."

As his eyes grew accustomed to the dim light, the professor noted that there were centipedes "by the hundreds" floating in the water in which he was half-submerged. A lesser man would have panicked at this revenge-of-the-dead scenario. But the professor, clearheaded, waited for the current to carry the centipedes away and groped in the sand for pots. "Had I not been so excited over the pottery," he recounted, "my loathsome position in this dark and noisome cave, crouching in a cascade of centipedes, would have horrified me."

Then the professor did something unexpected. He took an interest in the centipedes. In addition to four specimens of pottery, he made sure to get "three specimens of the creatures"—the centipedes, that is. In no hurry, he carefully made a sketch of the wall of the cave toward the opening, and only then had the rope lowered so that he could be yanked aboveground. That the pots he retrieved exactly matched the drawings he had made in the fisherman's hut confirmed the villagers' sense that there was something a little scary, and a little wonderful, about Professor Edward Sylvester Morse of Salem, Massachusetts.

All this happened in 1879, eleventh year of the Meiji Era, on Kyushu, the southernmost island of Japan. Edward Sylvester Morse, professor of zoology at the Imperial University in Tokyo, was touring the region, by jinricksha and on foot, in search of specimens—seashells, ancient pottery, bones—for the museum of natural history he planned to build in Tokyo. Kyushu was, in more ways than one, a landscape of ruins. Two years earlier, civil war had devastated the major cities in the area in the Satsuma Rebellion. The proud warlords of Satsuma had led the battle against the Tokugawa family, whose shoguns had ruled an isolated Japan for 250 years. In place of the shoguns, they had restored the emperor Meiji to power. But the intentions of the Meiji regime to modernize Japan along Western models, abolishing along the way the feudal distinctions of the Tokugawa Era, did not appeal to the profoundly conservative Satsuma clans. Satsuma led a rebellion against the curtailment of the hereditary rights of the samurai class, and it was the resulting devastation that Morse observed all around him. During his travels in Kyushu, Morse had visited the ancient port of Kagoshima, burned to ashes during the rebellion, and also Kumamoto, where the governor showed him how cannonballs had damaged the great castle. From Kumamoto, Morse had traveled south to Yatsushiro.

Morse and his traveling companion, a former samurai who held the post of governor of Yatsushiro prefecture, had made a ten-mile journey on foot and in jinricksha up the mountainous western coast of the island. Their destination—it was the reason the professor had come to Kyushu in the first place—was the shell heaps of Onomura. Morse had seen similar shell heaps, garbage dumps of Stone Age peoples, along the coast of the American South. In Onomura, he and the governor spent a few hours in the driving rain digging among the discarded seashells of this prehistoric waste dump, finding bits of broken pottery and other artifacts. "We got many bones," the professor noted in his journal, "among them fragments of human bones . . . showing evidences of cannibalism." It was then that, soaked and covered with mud, they sought refuge in the fisherman's dilapidated hut and humbly requested lunch.

The centipedes and burial urns are typical of the strange poetry of Edward Sylvester Morse's life. The poetry was not lost on his contemporaries. With his spreading brown beard and his twinkling eyes, Morse became a sort of pied piper who drew important people to Japan: the museum founder Isabella Stewart Gardner, the art collector and Buddhist convert Dr. William Sturgis Bigelow, the astronomer Percival Lowell, the connoisseur Ernest Fenollosa. All these intellectually and emotionally restless Bostonians went to hear Professor Morse's lectures at the Lowell Institute in Boston in 1881, and they all came away with a desire to travel to Japan, as Morse had done, and to see the marvelous things that he had seen. At various times during his long life—he lived from 1838 to 1925—Morse was an archaeologist and a zoologist, a student of the tea ceremony and the No drama, an expert on Japanese architecture and archery, a researcher in folklore, criminology, and the mysteries of Mars. He was a tireless collector—of everything, one is tempted to say—and a founder and director of museums. In three fields in particular he excelled—was indeed the world's authority: marine brachiopods, Japanese ceramics, and Japanese houses.

"To renew the old world"—that, according to the German polymath Walter Benjamin, is "the collector's deepest desire." Morse looked at everything as though he were seeing it for the first time. For Morse, one thing led to another, and his curiosity recognized no limits. He learned to eat, raw, the marine worms he had come to Japan to study. Then he drew the arrangement of the worms on the serving plate and carefully noted the clay, the glaze, and the provenance of the plate itself, comparing it with other plates he had seen. Then he examined the joints of the table on

Edward Sylvester Morse.

which the plate was set, the walls and construction of the room, the house itself and its surroundings. He was one of those people, as his friend Henry James would say, on whom nothing was lost. Morse had another skill that proved invaluable. He had an uncanny way of turning private crises in his life into occasions for personal "opening" and intellectual growth. Stalled in one direction, he embarked with renewed energy in another. If poisonous centipedes blocked his way to burial urns, he would collect the centipedes.

Edward Morse's special genius as a collector was to cherish the drab, the nondescript, and the overlooked. As a boy growing up in Portland, Maine, Ned Morse (as he was known) was an avid shell collector, drawing and classifying the monochromatic whelks, conches, and hard-shell clams of the North Atlantic. Collecting shells had several attractions for restless New England boys like Morse. There was adventure and risk in retrieving live specimens from tidal pools and surf. One could barter and banter with sailors, themselves inveterate shell collectors. And since seashells were an aesthetic craze in nineteenth-century New England, with abalones and helmet shells rubbing knobby shoulders with fine porcelain on many a mantelpiece, there was money to be made.

But seashells were more than a boyhood passion for Morse. The thread of his life, like a pilgrim's quest, was strung with shells.

During the Middle Ages, pilgrims made their way across the Pyrenees on foot to the great shrine of Santiago de Compostela, in Spain, where the apostle James was reputed to be buried. There the pilgrims were rewarded with a pilgrim's badge that displayed the scallop shell of Galicia. The scallop shell soon became a symbol throughout Europe for pilgrimages. Seashells brought Morse to Japan, and they brought him home again. Three shells in particular determined the course of Edward Morse's life.

I. The Land Snail

Edward Sylvester Morse was born into a pious family in coastal Maine. His father made a meager living in furs and beaver hats, and turned to Christianity with a vengeance when Ned's older brother died unbaptized at the age of nineteen. His mother, horrified at the fire-and-brimstone funeral sermon, vowed never to enter a church again. She turned instead to spiritualism, the erratic faith that the dead were reachable with teacups and séances. Edward Morse, who was twelve when his brother died, grew up hostile to authority of all kinds, especially religious authority. A troublemaker who was kicked out of three schools in succession, with a taste for liquor and other forbidden things, Morse had found, by the age of twelve, two things he loved: collecting shells and drawing.

For a boy like Morse, restless and with a vivid imagination, collecting shells could seem like virtual travel, a way to escape the intellectual confines of Portland. When an English ship called the *Sarah Sands* ran aground in Portland harbor, Morse hurried to the scene: "I got acquainted with the boatswain and a sailor on board . . . and they promised to get me a lot of shells. Especially the sailor, for he had been a fisherman. He said that he would go a-dredging. . . . And get them alive and perfect and sell them in the shell stores in Liverpool. . . . He also stated that he got a dozen shells in Egypt . . . and had looked in all the Shell stores in Liverpool and had only seen two like them." Something else was driving Morse's collecting, pushing it beyond the aesthetic, the mercenary, and ("a dozen shells in Egypt") the exotic. Even after he ambitiously determined to make a comprehensive collection of *all* the shells in the state of Maine, he could have scoured the coastline and left it at that, ticking off each find against the listings in the already plentiful handbooks for shell collectors.

But Morse developed a sudden interest in *land* shells, which offered no reward either in beauty or in monetary value. Land snails tended to be tiny, drab, and nondescript, making their humdrum homes in garbage heaps and piles of manure. Here is a typical passage from one of Morse's letters to a boyhood friend and fellow collector:

October 29, 1854: I have found the *Helix minuta* at the Portland Company's works. I suppose you know where the stable is. On the bank running down to the water near the Stable is the *Helix minuta* by the 100,000,000. Yes, sir. The specimens are very nice and I have got a great many of them. I have bought a microscope for $3.00, a very nice one.

Here we can already detect the collector of genius, willing to look where no one else has looked, and willing to value the apparently valueless, plucking his treasures from an oozing stream of horse manure.

A hundred million snails would not pay for a microscope, so Morse was forced to turn to his second passion to support himself. He worked as a draftsman off and on at the Portland locomotive works, spending his spare time adding to his collection. One September day in 1856 he came upon a tiny snail—drab like the rest, dirt-colored, one thirty-second of an inch long—that was new to him. A month later, encouraged in his passions by a teacher at the local Bethel Academy, he took the train to Boston and read a description of the snail at the Boston Society of Natural History. He was profoundly gratified when a member of the society reported "the communication read at the last meeting from Mr. E. S. Morse of Portland, Maine, on a species of *Helix*, the most minute any yet observed . . . [and] believed to be a distinct species."

Morse's early reports in natural science journals attracted the attention of influential men. In 1858, he received an invitation from the world-renowned naturalist Louis Agassiz to come to Harvard and work with him. It was like a summons from a god. Agassiz, the Swiss-born genius who had stunned the world by announcing that Europe and America were once covered by glaciers, was among the most famous scientists alive. In Agassiz, Morse met a man as consumed by collecting as he himself was. Agassiz was active on many fronts—as professor at Harvard, popular lecturer, researcher and writer, and houseparent for the elite school for girls that his wife, Elizabeth, ran on the second floor of his Cambridge house.

But Agassiz' dream was to establish a museum of comparative zoology at Harvard to house his extraordinary collections of natural objects. By 1858 he had managed to raise the necessary funding from private donors and from the state of Massachusetts to build the museum. What he needed, urgently, were talented and energetic young men to catalog and arrange its holdings. Morse, enthralled by the brilliant and fatherly Agassiz, went to work at once identifying marine animals under the microscope and drawing their constituent parts.

The devout Agassiz was at that time carrying on his doomed intellectual battle with Charles Darwin, arguing passionately that species were fixed and unchanging in their God-created forms and not, as Darwin

claimed, incessantly evolving. Early on he assigned his gifted young lieu-
tenant Morse a role in the battle. In late December 1859, Morse wrote a
long letter to his mother that included these lines:

> Today I have been at work in the Museum. I could never begin to
> write you what a truly good man Prof Agassiz is. He shows it in a
> thousand ways. He has such a jolly "Good Morning" and his
> "goodnight" breathes of kind wishes. He always says it; I can hear
> him now "Good night, Mr. Morse, good night." His voice is ten-
> der. Ah, he is one of the best men that ever lived. . . . Prof told me
> the other night he wished me to read Shakespeare thoroughly in
> order, he said, to be able to write classically. Tonight he gave me
> earnest work to do. It is this: there are thousands of species of
> shells found fossil in England and France which authors have con-
> sidered the same as recent living species. Prof don't believe they
> are the same and he wishes me to examine closely and make com-
> parisons of those species in order to prove their difference.

The letter leaves the unsettling impression that the affection "Prof"
felt for his gifted student just might be contingent on Morse finding
"proof" of significant differences between fossil and living specimens.
The specimens that Agassiz assigned Morse to examine were the shelled
organisms known as brachiopods. Common in the fossil record but rare
in Atlantic waters, the brachiopods, with their fluted twin shells, resemble the common scallop shell. If Morse could discover, contrary to Darwin's claims of the adaptation and modification of species over time, that
fossil and living animals had nothing to do with each other, he was doing
Agassiz' (and God's) work.

Morse found just the opposite: fossil and living organism were
clearly related, the one—dare one say it?—having presumably descended
from the other. The steady erosion in his own mind of Agassiz' authority
had begun. And Morse found something else as well. He was able to show,
by careful dissection and observation under the microscope, that brachiopods, despite their superficial resemblance to seashells, weren't
mollusks at all, as Agassiz had claimed. They were in fact a variety of marine worm.

Morse's gradual adoption of Darwin's system, complete by the year 1873, had the force of a conversion. "My chief care," Morse noted in a letter, "must be to avoid that 'rigidity of mind' that prevents one from remodeling his opinions; there is nothing [more] glorious . . . than the graceful abandoning of one's position if it be false." There was, for Morse, an accompanying deconversion. Having grown up in a pious household, he now felt a sense of liberation. So, along with Agassiz' rigid dogmas went the Christian religion as well. To Morse's gratification, his systematic research on marine brachiopods from the Maine coast southward, and his announcement that brachiopods were distinct from mollusks, attracted the enthusiastic notice of Charles Darwin, himself a passionate admirer of earthworms. "What a wonderful change it is to an old naturalist," wrote Darwin, "to have to look on these 'shells' as 'worms.' " Agassiz, by contrast, replied that he would hold on to Morse's pamphlet until, as Morse angrily wrote, "he ascertains whether my position is tenable or not!"

Something else contributed to Morse's break with Agassiz after two years of discipleship: the Swiss-born Agassiz' lukewarm response to the outbreak of the Civil War in 1861. Morse's father had died the previous year, and he returned to Portland with a mixed bag of resolutions: he wanted to support his mother and siblings; he wanted to marry his sweetheart; and he wanted to join the Union Army. When the last option proved impossible—he failed the army physical because of bad teeth and chronic tonsilitis—he settled in Portland and supported himself for seven years by lecturing and teaching.

Then seashells brought him to Salem, Massachusetts.

Few American towns can match Salem for sheer oddity. None can match its importance during the first half century of fraught encounters between Asia and the United States. Salem's notorious history combines an appealing cosmopolitanism with the most appalling insularity. It is known for the intrepid captains of its China trade and for putting its witches to death. Perhaps these extremes were related in some occult way. In opening itself to strange influences, Salem found itself subject to periodic convulsive collapse.

Nathaniel Hawthorne, Salem's resident scribe and conscience, was born during the seaport's prime and returned to work as an official in the Salem Custom House during its autumnal eclipse, when the upstart ports of Boston and New York stole her clipper trade. During the pivotal year of 1845, when, according to Samuel Eliot Morison in *The Maritime History of Massachusetts*, "Salem ceased to be an important seaport," Hawthorne holed up on the top floor of the Custom House and began writing *The Scarlet Letter*. The grand dimensions of the port remained: the great wharf with its endless promenade jutting far into the harbor, the huge gold dome of the Custom House itself, a beacon to nothing much. Salem shrank in stature, and you can almost feel the shrinkage in Hawthorne's haunted House of the Seven Gables, down among the narrow streets by the waterfront. "Salem clung desperately to her minor specialties," Morison notes, "such as the trade with Fiji, Zanzibar, and the West Coast of Africa. But these were poor substitutes for the Calcutta, the China, and the Sumatra voyages." Salem went the way of other Massachusetts towns, shifting, as Morison puts it, "from wharf to waterfall." It became a factory town.

Even as trade subsided, however, in one crucial respect Salem managed to expand her global reach. She became a world-class repository of collections, a monument to her glorious sea-roving past. The big houses of the sea captains, topped by their viewing cupolas and widows' walks, had long housed exotic collections—cabinets filled with curiosities culled from islands where men ate human flesh or whales washed up on the sand. A few captains had pooled their collections—"of natural and artificial curiosities, particularly such as are to be found beyond Cape of Good Hope or Cape Horn"—in 1799 to form the East India Marine Society in a large hall in Salem.

This odd institution, along with the natural science collections of the Essex Institute, caught the generous eye of the fabulously rich George Peabody, a native of Essex County and banking partner in London of Junius Spencer Morgan, father of J.P. In 1854 Peabody made one final tour of New England, dispensing Peabody museums of one kind or another at Yale and Harvard; wishing to sow something similar in his sister's town of Salem, he showered gold on the sea captains' collecting club. The result was the founding of the Peabody Academy of Science (renamed, in 1914, the Peabody Museum).

Edward Morse and three other Agassiz alums, all of whom had helped to build Agassiz' museum, were invited to Salem to put the collections in order according to the tenets of modern science rather than the whims of the traveler. The Peabody, like its cousins at Harvard and Yale, was to be a pioneering institution in the emerging fields of anthropology and ethnology, as well as the natural sciences. For Morse, initially hired as curator of seashells in 1868, it was to be a lifelong commitment. He built a house on Linden Street—the only house he ever owned. A delightful drawing he made during his first happy months in Salem shows a land snail looking through a microscope—a self-portrait of sorts. But Morse's horizons were about to expand in a hurry.

II. **The Cockle Shell**

The collector of seashells is, in a modest way, a kind of explorer. He wanders desert sands in search of the extraordinary. What better backdrop could there be than a monotonous expanse of sand to set off the vivid polychrome effects of the seashell? It is as though a traveler in the desert were to come upon a marvel of early creation, a sphinx or a phalanx of pyramids, and not once but repeatedly, all along the break line of the surf. For the collector who knows the North Atlantic coast, with its hard-shell clams with purple thumbprints—the wampum shells—and its occasional moon shells and conches and whelks, a visit to the Pacific can be overwhelming. It is as though one had grown up on black-and-white movies and suddenly fell into a world of Technicolor. Along the Pacific shore, especially its southern latitudes, all is Oz—abalones, cones, indigo murexes, helmet shells. And the rarest shell of all, the alphabet cone— with its hieroglyph patterns that no one can read. "No one who is not a collector," wrote Edward Morse, "can realize the delight of picking up rare tropical shells of a species entirely new to him."

During a lecture tour in California in the spring of 1874, Morse happened to hear of the extraordinary wealth of brachiopods in Japan. This confirmed what he had read in Commodore Perry's account of the abundance of seashells along the Japanese coastline. Morse immediately determined to go and see for himself. "I first visited Japan solely for the purpose of studying various species of Brachiopods in the Japanese seas," he wrote in the preface of his journal *Japan Day by Day*. When he visited the World's Fair in Philadelphia in 1876, which introduced so many Americans to the art and culture of Japan, a trip to Japan was on his mind. "The Japanese exhibit at the Centennial exposition in Philadelphia came to us as a new revelation," he later observed; "and the charming onslaught of that unrivalled display completed the victory. It was then that the Japanese craze took firm hold of us." At the fair, presumably by prior arrangement, Morse was approached by Japanese officials, including David Murray, formerly a mathematics professor at Rutgers. Murray had been appointed by the Japanese government to develop a public school system, from grade school to university, on American models. Morse's expertise in the natural sciences made him particularly attractive to these officials. He was eager to travel to Japan on account of the wealth of brachiopods in Japanese waters. They were eager for him to teach Darwin and modern scientific methods to Japanese students. No specific terms were discussed, but it was made clear that Morse would be more than welcome.

The Japanese were in a hurry. They were determined to establish an educational system comparable to the best schools in Europe and the United States. What these countries had perfected over many generations the Japanese hoped to acquire in a couple of years. They wanted it immediately, and they were willing to pay. During the early years of the Meiji Era, one-third of the Imperial budget went to the Ministry of Education, or Mombusho. The Mombusho developed a sophisticated strategy whereby foreign advisers would be imported to Japan for a limited period of time to help set up institutions and train Japanese experts. David Murray was one of the most influential of these advisers. At the same time, many of the most gifted Japanese young men were sent abroad, also for a limited period of time, to learn the ways of the West.

Edward Morse arrived in Yokohama on June 18, 1877, his thirty-ninth birthday. As a reminder to keep his eyes open, he had copied a journal entry from Hawthorne, his fellow Salem writer, on exact observation: "Begin to write always before the impression of novelty has worn off from your mind, else you will be apt to think that the peculiarities which

at first attracted you are not worth recording; yet these slight peculiarities are the very things that make the most vivid impression upon the
reader. Think nothing too trifling to set down, so it be in the smallest
degree characteristic. You will be surprised to find, on re-perusing your
journal, what an importance and graphic power these little peculiarities
assume." Morse took Hawthorne's injunction to heart. The opening
pages of Morse's Japan diary show how perfectly attuned he was to sheer
looking and observing, how alert to "slight peculiarities." This quality
runs counter to almost all the other writers on Japan of Morse's time,
who arrived with minds stocked with images from Hokusai and Hiroshige, and could not stop saying that Japan was just like the prints.

Morse took exploratory walks and jinricksha rides from his rooms at
the Yokohama Grand Hotel. Good student of Darwin that he was, he noticed "varieties" of each species of object. The workers' clogs, for example, were of "two types, one consisting of an oblong piece of wood with
two thin pieces fastened crosswise, the other carved out of a solid block of
wood." There were "two types of buildings . . . going up." "Their head-
coverings were of two kinds." Later he wrote a virtuoso passage on the
many uses of the Japanese fan:

> While in most parts of the world the fan is used for cooling the face
> or for shading the eyes, in Japan one notices not only a great vari-
> ety of fans, but that they are utilized for many purposes: an oil-
> paper fan is dipped in water and thus, in fanning, the air is cooled;
> a fan takes the place of the bellows in kindling the fire; a Japanese
> fans his soup if it is too hot and the dancing girls make great use of
> the fan in their graceful posturing. Fans are educational as well,
> information of various kinds being printed on one side, such as
> the best inns and tea-houses to stop at, or the productions of the
> province, while a map of the region is printed on the other
> side. . . . In feudal times high officers directed the maneuvers of
> an army by waving a large fan, either white with red disk, red with
> gold disk, or gold with red disk.

How much like the zoological classifier this sounds. Not at all the way an
art connoisseur would describe an array of fans.

Edward Morse did not just look, he listened. He was, in fact, a collector of sounds—the odder and more varied, the better. Particularly sensitive to sound, even obsessively so, he gained his first impression of the Japanese through his ears. A launch from the Grand Hotel in Yokohama arrived alongside Morse's steamer to scull the foreigners across two miles of water to the quay, or Bund, of the city. Morse recorded the chants of the scullers. "And such a peculiar series of grunts they made, keeping time with each other with sounds like *hei hei cha, hei hei cha,* and then varying the chanty, if it were one, putting quite as much energy into the grunts as they did into the sculling. The noise they made sounded like the exhaust of some compound and wheezy engine." It was in search of a variety of sounds that Morse later took lessons in No singing—he was the first foreigner to do so.

The morning after his arrival in Yokohama, Morse took the newly constructed train to Tokyo. Six miles shy of the city, near the village of Omori, he happened to glance out the window at the railroad embankment. There, luminous in the morning sun, lay a weathered cockleshell, *Arca granosa,* five thousand years old. "I had studied too many shell heaps on the coast of Maine not to recognize its character at once," he wrote. What Morse had noticed in the railway cut was a prehistoric kitchen midden, a scrap heap of ancient pottery shards, bones, shells, and the like.

Morse was traveling to Tokyo to call on David Murray, the Ministry of Education official he had met in Philadelphia. Murray had an office at the Imperial University, which had officially opened just three weeks earlier near Ueno Park. The university—so central to Japanese intellectual life during the following quarter century—was more an idea than an institution when Morse first saw it. But Morse was accustomed to turning ideas into institutions. He had done so in Cambridge with Agassiz and with Agassiz' students in Salem, where great museums had emerged from cases of specimens. He talked with Murray, and they began to develop a plan.

Morse had traveled to Japan alone. Leaving his family behind in Salem, he had planned a summer's stay, long enough to gauge the richness and variety of brachiopods, long enough to give Murray and his

Japanese associates advice on how to teach the natural sciences at the new university. But the more Murray saw of Morse, the more he saw the man's potential value. Murray was particularly taken with Morse's excitement about the seashell at Omori. With Murray's assistance, and official government permission to stray from the usual routes traveled by foreigners, Morse returned to Omori a few days later with a team of students to excavate the site. "I was quite frantic with delight, and the students shared in my enthusiasm. We dug with our hands and examined the detritus that had rolled down and got a large collection of unique forms of pottery, three worked bones, and a curious baked-clay tablet." Morse's discovery of the Omori shell heap was the beginning of Japanese archaeology.

David Murray, on the basis of the Omori find, could tell that Morse was the kind of person who noticed things. He invited Morse to accompany him on a journey to Nikko, the forested mountain refuge ninety miles north of Tokyo where the Tokugawa shoguns had erected spectacular mausoleums. To be invited to Nikko in 1877 was a signal honor. For a foreigner, it was unheard of. Nikko was among the most sacred sites in all Japan. The Tokugawa family had been overthrown a decade earlier, but the tombs retained their awful power. Morse hurried back to Yokohama to retrieve his luggage, then joined Murray for the two-day trek by horseback and jinricksha to Nikko. Morse admired the shrines with their rococo layering of detail, but he was more attentive to the natural habitats above Nikko. At Lake Chuzenji, a serene expanse of water surrounded by mountains, he was delighted to find snails uncataloged by naturalists.

Meanwhile, Murray's Japanese associates, Hattori and Toyama, had been crafting a proposal for Morse. Deeply impressed by Morse's knowledge and efficiency, they were convinced that this was the man who could introduce Darwinian ideas to the Japanese. Murray asked what it would take to keep him in Japan. Morse named an exorbitant sum. Murray accepted on the spot. The plan was that Morse would remain in Japan through the summer and early fall, dredging for brachiopods on the coast, collecting specimens for the museum, and lecturing on Darwin at the Imperial University. Then in November he would travel to the United States, fulfilling his lecture engagements there, and return to Japan in the spring with his family for a stay of two years.

With the support of the university, Morse established a makeshift marine laboratory on the scenic island of Enoshima, just off the coast from the ancient capital of Kamakura, and an easy ride from Yokohama. The blue waters and twelfth-century lacquered shrines of Enoshima, and the unobstructed view of Mount Fuji, are known throughout Japan. Thousands of pilgrims come to Enoshima each year to worship at the shrines, which are built into the rock cliffs. A single narrow street leads up to the Shinto shrines, and pilgrims can linger at shops along the sacred way to purchase curious objects made from shells. Morse, in his typically down-to-earth way, outfitted a fisherman's hut on the shore as his temporary laboratory, and let it be known to the local fishermen that he would pay for peculiar specimens of marine life. "Conceive my astonishment and delight," he reported on July 30, when the first haul "brought up twenty small *Lingula,*" the brachiopods "that first induced me to come to Japan." For the most part Morse ignored the pilgrims and pilgrimage sites, though one day he did row around the island to the cave dedicated to the goddess Benten, protector of seafarers. The rock carvings interested him less than other inhabitants of the cave. "I scanned the walls closely for evidence of twilight insects," he wrote. "To my delight I found two little spiders, two very small sow-bugs, and, better than all, two cave crickets with exceedingly long antennae, much smaller than ours, mouse-colored, and having a good set of compound eyes."

III. **The Scallop Shell**

In April 1878, Edward Morse was back in Japan, this time with his wife and eleven-year-old son, John, in tow. They settled in the Imperial University's walled compound for foreigners, a former samurai villa called the Kaga Yashiki. With his habitual vigor, Morse threw himself into his activities at the university. Soon work was under way on the museum for the natural sciences that he had promised to oversee. And he embarked on an ambitious series of public lectures on Darwinian ideas of evolution. He was impressed by how receptive the Japanese were to these ideas and

speculated that Buddhism, with its cycles of extinction and reincarnation, was more compatible with Darwin than was Christianity.

Then came one of those mercurial and perspective-enlarging shifts
of direction in the face of crisis that made for the poetry of Morse's life.
By the fall he had developed some sort of psychological distress, presumably depression, affecting his nerves and digestion. Nervous disorders
among American men of his generation were common enough—among
Morse's own circle of friends, the Harvard philosopher William James
and the astronomer Percival Lowell both succumbed for a time to mysterious "nervous" complaints. To calm and distract his patient, Morse's
Japanese physician prescribed a daily walk of five miles. Morse complained of the monotony. "Find some hobby," countered the doctor,
"some interest to pursue during your walks."

Walking one day along a shopping street in Tokyo, where the open-
fronted stalls lined the road, Morse noticed a small ceramic dish, the
kind on which the slivers of raw fish called *sashimi* are served. The dish,
with its fluted sides, was a perfect replica of a pecten shell, or scallop, the
traditional badge of the European pilgrim. No one was home when Morse
burst in to announce his discovery—which loomed as large in his mind as
the land snail in Portland or the fossil shell in the railroad cut at Omori.
No one was home, that is, except the twelve-year-old playmate, Tsunejiro
Miyaoka, of his son. Miyaoka, later a world traveler himself, witnessed
the beginning of Morse's pilgrimage.

Morse began to look for more pots resembling seashells, as though
the back streets of Tokyo—and Tokyo, according to Morse, had nothing
but back streets—were a beach and he a beachcomber. In a way, he was re-
capitulating an ancient development in the history of pottery. Potters had
long seen a resemblance between pots and shells; porcelain, for example,
resulted from the efforts of potters to imitate the exquisite cowrie shell.
Excitedly, Morse showed his treasures to his Japanese friends, who were
unimpressed. They showed him their own collections of pottery—which
often included (shades of those land snails!) drab little bowls used for
serving tea. Morse learned that there was a hierarchy of Japanese pottery,
and that his scallop-shell saucer occupied one of the lowest rungs. He was
invited to attend special pottery-identifying parties, where the guests
took ceremonial green tea together and competed in guessing the origins

of a succession of valuable ceramic objects. The game appealed to the tax-onomist in Morse.

Then, in one of those leaps of imaginative and acquisitive ambition that mark his whole career, Morse determined to make a comprehensive collection of Japanese pottery. For this he needed an expert guide, and he found one in Noritone Ninagawa. Ninagawa was a scholarly collector and connoisseur who had written a major work on Japanese pottery. Each Sunday afternoon, Ninagawa would come to Morse's library to examine Morse's purchases. They would discuss the different kinds of clay, the varieties of glazes, and the identifying marks of the various potters, fa-mous and lesser-known. Within a year Ninagawa was dead, but he had passed on much of his expertise to Edward Morse.

Through Ninagawa, Morse discovered that many of the most trea-sured works of Japanese pottery were associated with the tea ceremony. Morse took lessons in this ancient ritual of serving and partaking of pow-dered green tea; he was assured by his teacher that he was the first for-eigner to do so. Through the tea ceremony, Morse discovered in turn the whole aesthetic world of "tea taste," with its emphasis on rustic simplic-ity, irregularity, muted colors, and contrasts of rough and smooth. This is the *wabi* aesthetic associated with the sixteenth-century tea master Sen no Rikyu, who recast the tea ceremony as we know and practice it today. Morse learned why certain apparently nondescript ceramic water jars and tea bowls are among the most prized treasures in all of Japanese art.

In the domain of tea, as in his other interests, Morse was by no means simply a classifier of objects. He took note not only of external traits of structure and decoration. He was just as interested in context and habi-tat. Consequently, Morse went far deeper than most foreign visitors in penetrating Japanese aesthetic principles. During the time Morse was learning all about tea, his friend and associate Ernest Fenollosa (whom Morse hired to teach at Tokyo Imperial University) was considered the world's foremost expert on Japanese art. But Fenollosa had no interest in tea. "Fenollosa never took up chanoyu," the art historian Christine Guth notes. "Why Fenollosa, unlike Morse, remained so aloof from tea and ap-parently ignorant of its influence in the development of Japanese taste is puzzling." Guth is right to suggest that Fenollosa may have been "less in-terested in appreciating Japanese art according to native aesthetic and decorative guidelines than he was in promoting his own approach to Japanese art history." But Darwin was also a guide for Morse in this realm of tea. Morse was looking for the deep organic processes that shaped a tea bowl from Kyushu in one way and a dish from Tokyo in another. The elaborate ideas and procedures associated with the tea ceremony were among these processes. Varieties of pottery led Morse directly to tea—he could see that the evolutionary principles of the production of pottery involved tea ideas and ideals.

Indeed, through the tea ceremony Morse discovered a whole, sophisticated aesthetic that matched, in an uncanny way, his already highly developed temperamental preference for the drab, the irregular, and the apparently nondescript. The Japanese pleasure in nature's "caprices" was in harmony with Morse's Darwinian bent. "In one balcony rail I saw a rough plank with irregular holes in it: one would say, a rude and ungainly object fit only for fire wood, and yet the Japanese enjoy the natural results of nature's caprices: the fungus-stained wood, a plank cut from the outside of an irregular tree-trunk." Tea and Darwin were oddly in tune.

During the final weeks of Morse's sojourn, in late 1879, the former president Ulysses S. Grant arrived on his tour around the world. During his presidency Grant had done much to help Japan in her quest for modernization. He had sent his commissioner of agriculture, Horace Capron—who had served as a general in the Civil War—to help the Japanese develop an agricultural policy on the fertile island of Hokkaido in the north. Capron had also arranged arms deals for the Japanese in their own civil war, the Satsuma Rebellion of 1877. In their efforts to make Grant feel at home, the Japanese welcomed him to Nikko, where the "American Mikado" was invited to cross the sacred bridge of red lacquer—Grant declined—formerly reserved exclusively for the Tokugawa shoguns. A huge reception, which Morse attended, was held back in Tokyo at Ueno Park, the central park of the city. There Morse noted approvingly that Grant, known for his drinking, was moderate and well behaved.

At the end of his two-year stay, in 1880, Morse packed up his pots, crate after crate, to return to Salem. On the ship bound for San Francisco, the Morses were surprised to find among the passengers President Grant and his party. Grant spent much of the journey teaching Morse's son to play chess. Morse returned to Salem and to the Peabody Academy of Science as its director, a position he held until 1914.

Morse's third and final trip to Japan, in 1882, had an entirely different character from the others. This time he went as a collector, pure and simple. By now Morse had an acute sense that Old Japan, as he had known it, was on the verge of extinction. In the mania for Western things, ancient practices and objects were rapidly being replaced with their Western counterparts—Morse himself had witnessed the disappearance of the cosmetic practice of blackening women's teeth, for example, and Western clothes were everywhere in evidence. Good Darwinian that he was, Morse wished to preserve the fossil record of a vanishing civilization. The idea that took root in his imagination, and which he conveyed to other like-minded and well-endowed Bostonians, was that if the Japanese did not intend to preserve Old Japan, then someone else would have to do it. Why not the museums of Boston and environs—specifically the Museum of Fine Arts in Boston and the Peabody Academy of Salem?

In 1881, a year into his directorship, Morse delivered a series of lectures on Japanese folkways at the Lowell Institute in Boston. It is difficult to imagine a lecture series having a greater impact on a more influential group of people. So fascinating were these lectures to prominent Bostonians that some of the excitement seems to have rubbed off on Morse himself. Young Percival Lowell, chafing at the boredom of piling up money when he already had enough, was in the audience. Within a year Lowell was in Japan, writing his influential books about the country and its culture before turning his restless attention to the mysteries of Mars. Isabella Stewart Gardner came to hear Morse, whom she promptly invited to repeat his lectures in the more intimate environs of her house on the Fenway. When, a few months later, Mrs. Gardner's only child, an infant son, died, it was to Japan that the Gardners traveled to mourn their loss. Mrs. Gardner's lifelong interest in Japanese things dates from this time.

Dr. William Sturgis Bigelow was in the audience, and he promptly invited Morse to visit his male-only retreat on Tuckernuck Island, just off the coast of Nantucket. Bigelow, son of the most distinguished physician in Boston, had reached a crisis in his own medical career. He had trained for two years under Louis Pasteur in Paris and knew as much about bacteriology as anyone in the United States. But his work in emergency surgery (at his father's insistence) depressed him; a sense of lassitude and drift had set in. In January 1881 he took a break to visit his favorite cousin (their mothers were sisters), Clover Adams, wife of the historian Henry Adams, in Washington, D.C. "Sturgis Bigelow appeared at midnight on Thursday," Clover reported to her father on January 30; "we found him on coming back from a mild carouse. He seems happy and not eager to go back to his work and his native town." In Morse's lectures at the Lowell Institute, Bigelow glimpsed an alternative to the drudgeries and respectable behavior of Boston.

All these gifted people—Lowell, Gardner, Bigelow—heard something in Morse's lectures that spoke to their own most intimate needs. It wasn't simply the possibility of escape, though certainly escape was part of the appeal. But Morse sketched out a country of simplicity and taste, of good manners and aesthetic contemplation. Whatever one was suffering from in the modern metropolis of Boston—the loss of a child, professional or sexual alienation—Morse made Japan seem the right destination for a pilgrimage. It was a place where one could open oneself to powerful new (and age-old) influences and make oneself whole.

Relaxing on the veranda of Bigelow's Tuckernuck estate, with the Atlantic surf pounding in the distance, Morse and Bigelow hit on a plan. They would travel to Japan together. Bigelow, rich and restless, his personal fortune derived from Salem ship captains in the Asia trade, wanted to collect objects for the Museum of Fine Arts in Boston, to which he had close ties. (While in Paris with Pasteur, Bigelow had already purchased a great many Japanese prints for the museum.) For his part, Morse would augment his pottery collection, also destined for the MFA, and collect all manner of Japanese household things for the Peabody. It was a sort of cultural raiding party that the two men embarked on, though they convinced themselves that their aim was preservation.

"After an absence from Japan of two years and eight months I arrived for the third time in Yokohama on June 5, 1882," Morse wrote in his journal. "Doctor William Sturgis Bigelow, an ardent admirer and collector of Japanese art, was my companion." Bigelow and Morse were lodged in a little house in the neighborhood of the university: "Back of the house is the insane hospital, and we are lulled to sleep by the songs of the maniacs, enlivened now and then by the shrieks of some cases of acute mania." By now Bigelow was as passionate a preservationist as Morse. Soon after their arrival, at a gathering of university friends, Bigelow made an after-dinner speech. "He urged the importance and necessity of the Japanese adhering to their own methods of drawing and painting," Morse noted.

Their plan was to travel from Tokyo west toward the cultural treasure house of Kyoto, then south to Hiroshima and down into Kyushu to visit Nagasaki. For the Kyoto portion of the trip, they were joined by another Salem man passionate about Japan, Ernest Fenollosa. Morse had met Fenollosa in Salem, when Fenollosa had just graduated from Harvard with a degree in philosophy. At Morse's invitation the younger man had accepted a position at the Imperial University in Tokyo. Fenollosa, who had trained as a painter before attending Harvard, developed a passion for traditional Japanese and Chinese painting. Like Morse, he had contracted the collecting bug. With his favorite student and interpreter, Kakuzo Okakura, he was happy to join the collecting triumvirate. "We shall see a little of the life of old Japan," Morse wrote in his diary, as they headed for Kyoto. "I shall add a great many specimens to my collection of pottery; Dr. Bigelow will secure many forms of swords, guards, and lacquer; and Mr. Fenollosa will increase his remarkable collection of pictures, so that we shall have in the vicinity of Boston by far the greatest collection of Japanese art in the world."

Morse and Bigelow were drawn to a rougher, rawer version of Old Japan than was the fastidious Fenollosa. Together they admired the strenuous samurai sports—archery, falconry, sword fighting, sumo wrestling. "We were greatly entertained by this ancient sport [of falconry], seen for the first time," Morse wrote, "and the Doctor vowed that when he got home he would establish it." They were intrigued when "a peculiar kind of wrestling called *jujitsu* was demonstrated. . . . In this method of wrestling, a weaker man is taught how to take advantage of the efforts of a stronger man." On another occasion, Bigelow "went wild" over a collection of ancient swords, and Morse noted approvingly that the swords allowed "a genuine glimpse of one of the many interesting features of old Japan." Morse and Bigelow enjoyed Japanese food—especially raw fish, "of which the Doctor has become very fond." A jar of cooked grasshoppers? "The Doctor and I ate a number of them and found them very good."

Fenollosa preferred his Japan well cooked, and these contrasting tastes in food eventually led him to abort his trip, as Morse reported disdainfully. "Fenollosa, being disgusted with the so-called foreign food of the night before, lost all interest in Hiroshima and our intended visit to Miyajima and Iwakuni, and . . . started back to Osaka and Kyoto." Rid of their annoying companion, Morse and Bigelow sailed on a small boat across the inland sea, "through one of the most picturesque and beautiful waterways in the world," and resumed the easy camaraderie they had enjoyed on Tuckernuck. Morse recounted, "I fairly enjoyed the rapturous comfort the Doctor seemed to take as he sat on the roof of the cabin. Leaning back against a pile of matting with a box of Manila cigars by his side, he held his post the entire day, either dozing or admiring the varied scenery, which was indeed beautiful."

During his pleasurable wanderings with Bigelow, Morse noticed—he was always noticing things—that there was great variety in the houses of Japan. His interest in houses was a natural extension of his interest in seashells and Darwinian adaptation. The Japanese house, he argued, "is as thoroughly adapted to [Japanese] habits and wants as ours is to our habits and wants." And just as he had collected the outer shells of mollusks and brachiopods, he determined to make a comprehensive study of these outer shells of human beings. Morse's book of 1885 titled *Japanese Homes and Their Surroundings* was dedicated to Bigelow, "in memory of the delightful experiences in the 'heart of Japan.' " Probably Morse's single most influential book, *Japanese Homes* is both an analytic taxonomy of the variety of Japanese domestic architecture and a sophisticated essay on Japanese aesthetics, in particular the *wabi* aesthetic of sixteenth-century Japan, associated with rustic simplicity and voluntary poverty.

Morse was one of the first observers to see in Japanese houses an architecture of absence. To American eyes, he noted, a Japanese house may seem like hardly a house at all, "so many features are absent that go to make up a dwelling at home,—no doors or windows . . . no attic or cellar; no chimneys, and within no fire-place, and of course no customary mantel; no permanently enclosed rooms; and as for furniture, no beds or tables, chairs or similar articles,—at least, so it appears at first sight." But examined with care, the Japanese house, so flexible, light, and inexpensive, turns out to be perfectly adapted to Japanese inhabitants and Japanese needs. Challenging an English critic who had recognized "little merit in the apparently frail and perishable nature" of Japanese houses, Morse found virtue in impermanence and transience. If the Japanese could not afford fireproof houses, they did the next best thing and "built a house whose very structure enables it to be rapidly demolished in the path of a conflagration. Mats, screen-partitions, and even the board ceilings can be quickly packed up and carried away."

Morse went farther, finding in Japanese austerity a welcome corrective to the plush excesses of American Victorian taste—what his friend Percival Lowell called America's "abject enslavement to tawdry upholstery":

> After studying the Japanese home for a while . . . one comes to realize that display as such is out of the question with them, and to recognize that a severe Quaker-like simplicity is really one of the great charms of a Japanese room. Absolute cleanliness and refinement, with very few objects in sight upon which the eye may rest contentedly, are the main features in household adornment which the Japanese strive after, and which they attain with a simplicity and effectiveness that we can never hope to reach. Our rooms seem to them like a curiosity shop, and "stuffy" to the last degree. Such a maze of vases, pictures, plaques, bronzes, with shelves, brackets, cabinets, and tables loaded down with bric-à-brac, is quite enough to drive a Japanese frantic.

At a time when no one in America or Europe was giving much attention to such things, Morse made a bold effort to define some of the key components of Japanese taste: the pleasure in the irregular and the quaint, the resistance to mirrors and other modes of repetition, the preference for neutral tints and subdued tonalities, the contrasting textures of rough and smooth.

Morse's book on Japanese homes was a landmark in the history of American architecture. Its decisive influence on Japan-inspired architects such as H. H. Richardson and Frank Lloyd Wright is only now becoming clear. (Like Morse, Wright was a collector of seashells. "Here in these shells," he told his students, "we see the housing of the life of the sea. It is the housing of a lower order of life, but it is a housing with exactly what we lack—inspired form.") Morse's *Japanese Homes* became a pattern book for American builders of Victorian houses during the late 1880s and the 1890s. All across New England, thanks to him, one finds vestiges of Japanese practices in rooflines and sheds, balconies and alcoves, and in a willingness to leave empty spaces for the imagination to dwell in. Morse had set out with Bigelow to collect traditional Japanese pottery, saving it, in his view, from the ravages of modernization. He returned to Salem in 1883 with plenty of pottery, most of which made its way to the Museum of Fine Arts in Boston. But he also returned with the materials and drawings for his study of Japanese houses, as well as cases full of ordinary household objects to reconstitute Old Japan in his Salem museum.

Edward Sylvester Morse lived for another forty years, but he never returned to Japan after 1883. This reluctance was not for lack of invitations or opportunities. He remained an intrepid traveler, visiting the great collections of Asian art and natural history in Europe and making a pilgrimage to the country estate of his idol, Charles Darwin. Morse's easy explanation was that Japan had changed so rapidly that the country he loved no longer existed. New Japan had supplanted Old Japan, which survived only in Morse's extensive collections in Salem and Boston. Morse's friends were left with the impression that he lamented the changes. But this view is too simple and misses Morse's deeper motivations as a collector.

It was his old traveling companion Sturgis Bigelow who insisted, many years later, that Morse should publish his journal. Morse had informed Bigelow that he had a leave of absence from the Peabody Museum to finish some articles on mollusks and brachiopods. Bigelow replied:

The only thing I don't like in your letter is the confession that you are still frittering away your valuable time on the lower forms of animal life, which anybody can attend to, instead of devoting it to the highest, about the manners and customs of which no one is so well qualified to speak as you. Honestly, now, isn't a Japanese a higher organism than a worm? Drop your damned Brachiopods. They'll always be there and will inevitably be taken care of by somebody or other as the years go by, and remember that the Japanese organisms which you and I knew familiarly forty years ago are vanishing types, many of which have already disappeared completely from the face of the earth, and that men of our age are literally the last people who have seen these organisms alive. For the next generation the Japanese we knew will be as extinct as Belemnites.

Bigelow's letter meant a great deal to Morse, and it reveals a key aspect of his life as a collector. For Edward Morse was not interested in preservation per se, out of some nostalgic commitment to a simpler or more aesthetic past. Darwin had schooled him too well in the unavoidable fact of extinction. Through years of intellectual struggle, Morse had graduated from Agassiz' commitment to fixity and embraced instead Darwin's universe of flux. The collector's task was not to arrest evolution—as though that were possible—but to preserve the fossil record, the fact, over time, of *variety*. What Morse liked in Japanese houses and acknowledged in evolution was transience, impermanence, the bird's nest rather than the brick mansion.

In 1885, the year in which he published his survey of Japanese houses, Morse also produced a brief comparative study of what he called arrow release. The ancient Japanese art of archery, with which Morse had an abiding fascination, is an apt symbol for his mercurial temperament. From a close observation of Japanese archers, which he had witnessed in Bigelow's company, Morse proceeded to compare the ways in which other groups—American Indians, Hawaiian islanders, Europeans, Chinese—held and released arrows from their bows. He distinguished what he called the primary release, as practiced by children the world over and by so-called primitive peoples like the Ainu of Hokkaido, from other modes of release: holding the arrow with a ring, for example, or with a crooked finger. The evolutionary danger, again, was extinction without a record, and the consequent importance of "preserving the methods of handling a weapon which is rapidly being displaced in all parts of the world by the musket and rifle." Morse discovered—or invented—a whole new field for ethnographic research, catching the winged arrow as it flies.

Morse's varied career can seem like a virtuoso performance of random and scattershot interests. But there was a beautiful and internal progression to his passions. What Morse possessed was a mind set free, and an extraordinary eye that he had trained to be as innocent as possible. In the introduction to *Japanese Homes,* he includes a devastating account of the typical foreign book on Japan:

> . . . the record of an itinerary of a few weeks at some treaty port, or a brief sojourn in the country, where, to illustrate the bravery of the author, imaginary dangers were conjured up; a wild guess at the ethnical enigma, erroneous conceptions of Japanese character and customs,—the whole illustrated by sketches derived from previous works on the same subject, or from Japanese sources, often without due credit being given . . . [and] an account of the progress its public were making in adopting outside customs, with no warning of the act of *harakiri* their arts would be compelled to perform in the presence of so many influences alien to their nature.

The rippling effect of Darwin's ideas went far beyond the challenge to biblical accounts of the creation, and was hardly limited to the vulgarities about social class and racial destiny popularized by Herbert Spencer, inventor of the phrase "the survival of the fittest." What Darwin gave Morse was a fresh and dynamic way to think about *all* existence. So a Japanese seashell (the protective outer covering of a mollusk) isn't that different from a Japanese house (the protective outer covering of a person). Both can be studied in their astonishing variety as responses to given sets of conditions. Morse examined seashells and houses with the same painstaking attention to detail and difference. Similarly, the extraordinary variety of Japanese pottery, scattered over the islands of Japan like the finches of the Galápagos, could be seen in evolutionary terms.

The collector thrives by turning chaos into order. His patron saint is Noah—two of each. Once his taxonomy is secure, the rest can perish in the flood for all he cares. And is there, in turn, a taxonomy of collectors? Do they, too, come in distinctive kinds? There is the collector as connoisseur—Fenollosa is a perfect example—who has in mind a set of supreme values derived from somewhere else. So the painter Okyo is the Japanese Giotto. Then there is the collector as seeker—for which Bigelow may serve as a model. Bigelow collected tokens of an alternative life: exotica, erotica, Buddhist icons, samurai swords. And then there is the collector as preserver. Edward Morse is a supreme example. Only God (or Nature) can truly create. Humans, as Morse kept reminding his friends and his students, have a choice. They can destroy or preserve.

THE BOSTON TEA PARTY

> < > < > <

Under certain circumstances there are few hours in
life more agreeable than the hour dedicated to the
ceremony known as afternoon tea.

—HENRY JAMES, *THE PORTRAIT OF A LADY*

During the spring of 1906, a little book with a green cover was published in
Boston. Ostensibly about the intricacies and meaning of the Japanese tea
ceremony, it was called *The Book of Tea*, and its author was Kakuzo
Okakura. Bostonians, at least the sorts of Bostonians who attended the
symphony and the opera, were familiar with Okakura. They had seen him
dressed in darkly formal kimono sitting in the private box of Isabella
Stewart Gardner, the stylish and flamboyant collector of art and interesting people. They had seen him, imperious and surprisingly tall for a
Japanese, at her private museum on the Fenway, "bowing among the
Titians," as T. S. Eliot (substituting Hakagawa for Okakura) remembered
him in "Gerontion." To Bostonians in search of something more spiritually intense than their own diluted Christianity, Okakura's sad eyes and
proud demeanor radiated the wisdom of the East. It was known that he
was intimate with Mrs. Gardner. It was known that she hung on his every
word. But where he had come from and what sort of life he lived, as he
shuttled between Japan and Boston, remained a mystery.

A cosmopolitan and compulsive traveler, equally at home in China,
India, and Europe, and blessed with an extraordinary gift for languages,
Okakura was a perfect cultural ambassador for an insecure Japan. After a

romantic scandal interrupted his remarkable career in Japan, during which he founded museums and schools, and helped shape the cultural policy of the young nation, Okakura pursued an impressive career in the United States. From 1904 to 1913 he headed the Japanese collection of the Museum of Fine Arts in Boston, then and now the greatest and most comprehensive repository of Japanese art outside Japan. It was during this period that Okakura emerged as a charismatic celebrity—the very embodiment of Japan in dress, deportment, and the ritual serving of tea—in the Boston of his most enthusiastic patron, "Belle" Gardner. Okakura's accomplishments—as connoisseur, art historian, arts administrator, spiritual guru, and writer—were conspicuous and varied. His influence on a diverse array of artists and thinkers, including Frank Lloyd Wright and Wallace Stevens, Rabindranath Tagore and Martin Heidegger, adds to the fascination and enduring mystery of this remarkable man, whose thought, as his close friend John La Farge put it, ran "as a stream runs through grass—hidden, perhaps, but always there."

Kakuzo Okakura was born on December 23, 1862, in Yokohama, the port city for Tokyo. It was near Yokohama, with its sweeping bay and excellent harbor, that Commodore Perry's Black Ships had first announced, just nine years before Okakura's birth, that Japan would henceforth be a destination for American ships. Yokohama was among the first of the treaty ports, planned as a narrow conduit for goods to enter and exit Japan. Unlike the chaotic tangle of Tokyo, Yokohama was laid out in an orderly European grid, broad avenues enclosing the green expanse of a central cricket field. On the outskirts, however, the city had grown in the makeshift, opportunistic way of expanding ports. Its mood—profane, opportunistic, mongrel, with periodic eruptions of violence and disease—reminded some visitors of the boomtowns of the American West; others compared it with the vice-ridden ports of New Orleans or Vera Cruz. Missionaries of various faiths looked askance at the brothels and beer dives. Edward Sylvester Morse wrote in a letter in 1878 that Yokohama, "the city which contains the greatest number of representatives of Christian nations, is notoriously the most licentious, profane, indecent and corrupt city in Japan."

Yokohama's long, straight waterfront was lined with foreign businesses, hotels, and concessions. Small launches and junks sailed out into the harbor to meet foreign ships and bring passengers to shore. A busy canal marked off one corner of the wharf, or Bund, as it was called. The Yokohama Grand Hotel stood at the confluence of canal and harbor. Across the canal, the ground rose abruptly to the wooded and walled neighborhood known as the Bluff, where European and American merchants had their well-staffed clubs and residences. "The Bluff is very pretty with a New England prettiness," wrote Isabella Bird on her visit in 1878, "and everything is neat and trim." Inland from the Bund were teeming neighborhoods of Chinese immigrants, and a large Japanese population concerned mainly with the two great exporting industries of silk and tea. On windless days, the smell of roasting tea filled the air.

With its extraordinary mix of cultures, Yokohama offered an attentive child a microcosm of the wider world, and especially of the late nineteenth-century clash of the values of East and West. From an early age, Okakura was educated in two worlds, one cosmopolitan and forward-looking, the other rooted in the traditions of Old Japan. Okakura's father, Kan'emon, was born a samurai of the proud Echizen domain. Sent to Yokohama to purvey the silk produced in Echizen, he left a wife and four children behind as he smoothly made the transition from the swordsman's life to that of a successful merchant. When his wife died, he took up with a tall and capable woman he had glimpsed on a business trip to Tokyo. Their matter-of-fact relations can be gleaned from the only name for her on record, Kono. Lacking the evocative Chinese characters of Japanese names, Kono is short for *kono onna*, "this woman."

This woman was Okakura's mother. But beyond the biological bond, mother and elder son had little to do with each other. Even the naming of the child was offhand, provisional, for Kakuzo means simply "corner warehouse"—Okakura later changed the Chinese characters to conceal the prosaic meaning. The father was determined that Kakuzo and his younger brother, Yoshisaburo, would be equipped for the economy of the New Japan. Both boys were enrolled at the missionary school of James Hepburn, situated by the canal right around the corner from the Yokohama Grand Hotel.

The Hepburns had lived in Japan since 1869, braving the periodic waves of antiforeign sentiment. Travelers from the West made a point of visiting their house in Yokohama; the Hepburns had known John Manjiro and other Pacific wanderers. A gifted linguist, Hepburn compiled the first Japanese-English dictionary, translated the New Testament into Japanese, and invented the system for romanization of Japanese words, a version of which is still in use. It was from Hepburn's wife, a sharp-eyed woman of considerable energy, that Kakuzo received his first taste of maternal affection, even as he began learning the perfect English that was to be his most important acquisition in life. The affection the Hepburns conveyed toward their Japanese charges was tinged with scorn. As Isabella Bird reported, Dr. Hepburn "is by no means enthusiastic about the Japanese, or sanguine regarding their future in any respect, and evidently thinks them deficient in solidity."

At age eight, in 1870, came another blow for Kakuzo: the death of his mother, Kono. The boy was placed in a foster household, quickly expelled for requesting a second serving of food, and then placed in another. Even as he acquired skills in English and the other disciplines of the West, this child of the Black Ships was increasingly estranged from anything resembling family, and from Japan itself. The depth of that estrangement was made clear during that same year, when Kakuzo's father took him along on a business trip to Tokyo. On the train, the father made a stunning discovery concerning his precocious elder son. Kakuzo, so gifted in both speaking and writing English, could not read a single Japanese character on the signs outside the train. In the Japanese language he was completely illiterate. This unexpected development, so iconic of Kakuzo's cultural estrangement, led to another rupture in his zigzagging life. He would now acquire, at his father's offended insistence, the traditional Japanese culture—Chinese classics, Japanese music, religious instruction in Shinto and Buddhism—that the Hepburns had set out to eradicate.

So Kakuzo found himself living in a Buddhist temple, amid the whole pre-Perry world of gongs and shuffling slippers, meditation by candlelight, and green tea. Now, instead of St. Paul and the Gospels, Kakuzo studied the sayings of Confucius and Mencius. Instead of scales at the piano and Methodist hymns in the choir with his fellow pupils, Kakuzo became adept at the koto. And starting far too late to acquire the facility with the brush of his contemporaries (he later hid his shortcomings be-

hind an aggressively eccentric style), Kakuzo learned enough of the rudi-
ments of calligraphy to know just how rich were the traditions of the Chinese written character.

In 1873, when a worldwide depression temporarily ruined the market for silk, Okakura's father moved the family to Tokyo and started an
inn. At the age of fifteen, Kakuzo, with his gift for English, enrolled in the
Faculty of Letters at the newly founded Tokyo Imperial University. This
was the fledgling, unabashedly Western institution of Hattori, Toyama,
and Edward Sylvester Morse, the shell-collecting professor from Salem.
With its majestic Red Gate at the far corner of Ueno Park, its cluster of
Western-style buildings with high ecclesiastical windows, and its hopeful
young oaks and elms, Tokyo Imperial University circa 1878 was an institution more hypothetical than real. But Professor Morse had had a year to
fan Darwinian fires, as well as to lure some congenial New England
minds to help him in his tasks. During his brief visit to New England in
the fall of 1877, Morse had identified a young physicist named Thomas
Mendenhall and a Harvard student of political philosophy called Ernest
Fenollosa as promising candidates for Tokyo professorships. Fenollosa—
as mentor, colleague, and finally rival—was to be the decisive influence
on Okakura.

Salem born and bred, Ernest Fenollosa had come by his exotic name through
his father, Manuel, a professional musician from Spain who had married
into the old Salem family of Silsbee. Since his graduation from Harvard
with first-class honors in 1874, Ernest Fenollosa had been adrift, casting
about for a decisive direction for his considerable intellectual ambitions.
He had tried Divinity School at Harvard, but a pilgrimage on a shoestring
budget to the Centennial World's Fair in Philadelphia had provided more
inspiration and uplift than the lectures on Unitarian dogma. When his
father died in early 1877, Fenollosa dropped divinity and took up the
study of art. Among his undergraduate teachers, none was more inspir-
ing than Charles Eliot Norton, who looked to art to provide some of the
lost consolations of traditional religion.

Fenollosa had no way of knowing that his haphazard sampling of philosophy, religion, and art, combined with intensive visits to the Japanese

pavilion at the World's Fair, was the best possible preparation for what Edward Morse, a fellow Salem man, had in mind for him. Morse's invitation to teach at Tokyo Imperial University was a lifeline in more ways than one, giving Fenollosa both money and direction. With the two-year offer in hand, the indigent Fenollosa was emboldened to propose marriage to Lizzie Millett, only daughter of a wealthy Salem family. They married in June and two months later moved into their house in Tokyo.

Morse had brought Fenollosa to Japan to teach Western philosophy to the sons of samurai. Fenollosa dutifully taught Emerson and Hegel to Okakura and the rest of his students, but he soon became more engaged by the traditions of Japanese culture than by those of his own. Fenollosa did not go native to the same degree as his friend Lafcadio Hearn, who adopted Japanese dress, a Japanese name, a Japanese wife, and Japanese citizenship. But by the early 1880s Fenollosa was convinced that Asian art was as compelling and continuously evolving as Western art. He became an activist in government circles in Japan, converted to Buddhism, and pleaded for the preservation of Japanese art and artistic methods at a time when, in the craze for Western things, the use of brush and ink was prohibited in the schools.

Okakura, with his gift for languages and his interest in politics—which he studied with Fenollosa—seemed destined for a brilliant career in diplomacy. (His brother, Yoshisaburo, enrolled at Tokyo Imperial University as well, studying English and Japanese philology with Basil Chamberlain and serving briefly as a translator for Lafcadio Hearn.) At the start of his sojourn at Tokyo Imperial University, as though to get all the choices for his life, personal and professional, out of the way at once, a marriage was arranged for the sixteen-year-old Okakura with the fourteen-year-old Motoko Oka. The marriage, predictably for two teenagers, was a disaster from the start, though its very unraveling gave a decisive direction to Okakura's intellectual career. At the university he concentrated on political theory and economics while also taking courses in literature, music, and art. He drafted an ambitious thesis for his degree, with the capacious title "The Theory of the State." During a quarrel—was he paying more attention to the thesis than to her?—Motoko hurled the pages of the all-but-finished thesis into the fire. Two weeks remained until the deadline for handing in completed theses. This time, as though liberated by the ashes in the grate, Okakura hurriedly drafted a thesis on an entirely different subject, "The Theory of Art." Not surprisingly, given such haste, he graduated second to last in his class, but whatever paternal pressures had pushed him toward a diplomatic career were now removed, and Okakura embarked instead on a career in culture and education.

Upon graduation from Tokyo Imperial University, Okakura was appointed to serve as secretary to Luther W. Mason, a Boston musician known in the United States for his progressive techniques for teaching music theory to children. Mason was in charge of bringing Western music to the Japanese public school system; in this capacity he showed off his accomplishments at the New Orleans World's Fair of 1884. In his songbooks for Japanese schoolchildren, he followed a hybrid strategy, fitting Japanese words to Western melodies and using Western musical notation to present traditional koto compositions. Okakura got along well with the kindly Mason and his wife—another maternal presence—even as his own interests were moving away from the aggressive Westernization campaign of the Ministry of Education.

In 1882, after two harmonious years with Mason, Okakura was transferred to the fine arts section of the ministry, where his superior was the Baron Ryuichi Kuki, a suave and gifted bureaucrat from a high-ranking samurai family who was destined to play a decisive role in Okakura's life. Baron Kuki, a connoisseur and collector of note, shared Okakura's interests in the traditions of Old Japan. Kuki also spoke English, though not as fluently as the Washington newspapers claimed when he was appointed Japanese minister to the United States in 1884. Kuki and Okakura found an impassioned ally in Okakura's former teacher Fenollosa, who was appointed to an advisory position in the ministry. As Japan moved gradually from unthinking Westernization toward a more nuanced appreciation of her own cultural traditions, these three men helped define the course of fine arts policy in Japan. They represent a strange alliance of New England values and the traditions of Old Japan.

It was probably at Fenollosa's urging that Okakura published in 1882, when he was nineteen, a passionate defense of calligraphy as a fine art and carried the day with Meiji officials, who had previously excluded calligraphy (since it had no Western counterpart) from government-sponsored art exhibitions. The article was also a personal answer—part penance and part restitution—to that moment ten years earlier when the boy Kakuzo had proved unable to read the characters on Japanese street signs. In conjunction with Kuki and Fenollosa, Okakura helped organize exhibitions and lectures that emphasized continuity with Japanese art traditions. The three men were also involved in government efforts to identify and preserve Japanese treasures housed in Buddhist temples.

During the summer of 1882, Fenollosa and Okakura made the first of an annual series of summer pilgrimages to the temples and shrines of Japan, beginning with an extensive survey of the art collections of Buddhist temples around Kyoto and Nara. Fenollosa's colleague at Tokyo Imperial University, Edward Morse, had a keen interest in these surveys—he was himself collecting ceramics and occasionally accompanied Fenollosa and Okakura on their campaigns into the countryside. During such expeditions Fenollosa, with his imposing stature and carefully trimmed beard, cast himself in the heroic role of the discoverer of ancient cultures, bullying priests into uncovering treasures that had been under lock and key for hundreds of years. His well-publicized discovery of the seventh-century gilded statue of Kannon, the Buddhist deity of compassion, in the temple of Horyuji outside of Nara, quickly became legendary.

The temple of Horyuji rises from the vast plain a few miles from the old capital of Nara. Unlike the many hillside temples of Kyoto that blend into the wooded landscape—Kiyomizudera, Nanzenji, Ginkakuji—there is nothing hidden about Horyuji. It is more like the great monuments of Egypt, proudly exposed, windswept, a beacon in the distance for weary travelers. Enter the front gate and before you are two beautiful buildings, the oldest wooden structures in the world. One is a five-storied pagoda; the other is a broad hall of worship known as the *kondo,* or "golden hall." Built in the seventh century, these buildings—one tall and many-tiered, the other low to the ground—establish between them a mysterious and elegant balance. Even the roofs, black-tiled and, from a distance, seemingly corrugated, make an interesting contrast. The pagoda roofs curve slightly upward, as though for elevation or imminent liftoff. The roofs echo the up-curved pines and cypresses by the main gate. One can see why the Japanese philosopher Tetsuro Watsuji, who wrote a book about his pilgrimage to Nara, detected an affinity between pagodas and pine trees. The *kondo* roof declines more sharply, like a hat for rainy weather, or a protective shell for a tortoise. One building suggests the values of the air, the other those of the earth: the hare and the tortoise, the rocket and the gravity of the globe.

If you take a walk across the gravel courtyard, with the pagoda and *kondo* in line behind you, you come to another, larger expanse called the Eastern Precinct of Horyuji. The most striking building is an octagonal pavilion of a single storey, its roof a shell of eight upturned triangles. This is the Yumedono, or Hall of Dreams. Here, according to legend, Prince Shotoku—founder of Horyuji, son of the emperor, and the man tradition-ally thought to be most responsible for the spread of Buddhism through-out Japan—would meditate on a passage of scripture, and a golden Buddha would appear before him in a dream to explain its meaning.

During the summer months of 1884, something partaking of dream and legend occurred at the Hall of Dreams. It was a time when Buddhism, no longer the national religion, was under siege in Japan, and priests were torn between hoarding their treasures and selling them off for profit. At the gates of Horyuji, Fenollosa and Okakura, government officials wear-ing Western-style suits, presented themselves as saviors of the Japanese artistic heritage. Okakura described what happened when he and Fenol-losa asked to enter the Hall of Dreams.

> The priests said that opening the gates would certainly produce a clap of thunder. . . . And when we began to open the gates they were so afraid that they fled. When we opened the shrine gates, the stench of almost one thousand years assailed our nostrils. Brush-ing aside the cobwebs, we saw a low table of the Higashiyama pe-riod. When we cleared this aside, there, directly before us, was the sacred statue which measured some eight or nine feet in height. The statue was wrapped in many layers of cloth. Surprised by the presence of human beings, snakes and mice suddenly scampered,

frightening us. We approached the statue, and when we removed the cloth wrappings there was underneath a covering of white paper. . . . We saw behind the white paper the serene face of the statue. This was truly one of the greatest pleasures of a lifetime. Fortunately, there was no clap of thunder and the priests were greatly reassured.

The statue was the Guze Kannon, androgynous god of compassion, carved of camphor wood and gilded from head to feet. The standing figure of slightly superhuman size held a jewel in delicate hands. An oversize crown studded with more jewels and scored with swirling motifs of flame rose above the figure's head. A flowing scarf of gold fell to the ground. The face, though, was what held Fenollosa's attention: "The finest feature was the profile view of the head, with its sharp Han nose, its straight clear forehead, and its rather large—almost negroid—lips, on which a quiet mysterious smile played, not unlike Da Vinci's Mona Lisa's." Fenollosa was alluding to Walter Pater's famous account of the Gioconda: "She is older than the rocks among which she sits; like the vampire, she has been dead many times, and learned the secrets of the grave; and has been a diver in deep seas, and keeps their fallen day about her; and trafficked for strange webs with Eastern merchants." The Mona Lisa in the Hall of Dreams is a Mona Lisa of the East, with a mysterious touch of Africa.

Fenollosa and Okakura worked harmoniously together during their travels, but their ultimate aims were different, even to some extent at cross-purposes. Fenollosa worked closely with Japanese experts, but he wished to preserve Japanese art as a resource for Western exploitation. "I must remember," he wrote in his notebook, "that, however much I may sympathize with the past civilizations of the East, I am in this incarnation [note the Buddhist touch] a man of Western race, and bound to do my part toward the development of Western civilization." Even as he and Okakura were lobbying in Japan for National Treasure legislation to prevent the removal of art from Japan, Fenollosa was amassing a magnificent collection of Japanese paintings, which he eventually donated to the Museum of Fine Arts in Boston—precisely the activity the legislation was designed to prevent.

For Okakura, by contrast, Japanese art was a vital national tradition, the roots of which needed cultivating in order to keep the living tree healthy. The West was not a monolithic whole, Okakura insisted in a lecture. "All these countries have different systems; what is right in one country is wrong in the next; religion, customs, morals, there is no common agreement on any of these. Europe is discussed in a general way, and this sounds splendid; the question remains, where in reality does what is called Europe exist?" This stress on national particularity as a way to challenge the wholesale adoption of "European" methods and ideas remained a major part of Okakura's thought. At the same time he rejected, even at this early point in his career, a narrow commitment to preserving and merely duplicating Japanese national traditions in art. "Conformity is the domicile of bad habits," he told his audience, echoing Emerson. "Art is a product of past history combined with present conditions. It develops from this fusion of past and present." Even the adoption of European techniques and media, such as oil paint or naturalistic perspective, was acceptable as long as this was consistent with what Okakura called the organic or "natural development" of Japanese art.

In 1886 Okakura and Fenollosa were appointed to the Imperial Fine Arts Commission to study methods of art education in Europe and the United States with a view toward establishing a national art academy in Japan. (Such study tours, sending Japanese students abroad and importing foreign experts for temporary stays, were typical of the Meiji government's Westernization campaign.) Two years were allotted for the tour, with an ambitious itinerary that included major museums and academies from Boston to Berlin. A photograph from this period shows Okakura in a chic European suit, with a fashionable mustache—the cosmopolitan at home in the modern world.

The summer of 1886, when Okakura and Fenollosa were busily preparing for their fact-finding journey to the West, turned out to be a watershed in Okakura's life. In June two remarkable travelers arrived from the United States—one from the inner government circles of Washington, D.C., and the other from the inner sanctum of the American fine arts establishment. The historian Henry Adams and the painter John La Farge had come to Japan together for an extended visit. Their host was Dr. William Sturgis Bigelow. Bigelow, the wealthy Boston surgeon who had followed Edward Morse to Japan, was a favorite cousin of Henry Adams's wife, Clover. He had taken up residence in Tokyo, converted—in a joint rite with his friends Fenollosa and Okakura—to a sect of Esoteric Buddhism, and become a passionate collector of Japanese art. As his friend Isabella Gardner put it, Bigelow "always carried local color around with him." Bigelow introduced Adams and La Farge to Fenollosa and Okakura, and the five men spent a great deal of time together. Adams and La Farge will have chapters to themselves in the course of this narrative; here, we need to ask what their serendipitous appearance meant to Okakura.

Okakura, who served the two Americans as guide and interpreter, made little impression on Adams at this time. His name is not mentioned in Adams's dozen letters from Japan, and in *The Education of Henry Adams* he is referred to only as La Farge's friend. Okakura's intimate friendship with John La Farge, by contrast, turned out to be crucial for the careers of both men. One of the first Western artists to take an interest in Japanese art, La Farge was particularly susceptible to Okakura's charms. Okakura is everywhere in La Farge's *Artist's Letters from Japan*, including the dedication: "And you too, Okakura San . . . because the memories of your talks are connected with my liking of your country . . . and because for a time you were Japan to me."

With his deep knowledge of the traditions of Asian art and his physical grace, Okakura was La Farge's ideal embodiment of Japan. And it was La Farge who, more than anyone else, taught Okakura how to "be Japanese" for American audiences. La Farge knew precisely where Japan belonged in American culture—he had been mapping it out for twenty-five years—and this was the critical lesson he imparted to Okakura. It was in his many talks with La Farge, during the summer of 1886 and thereafter, that Okakura began to assemble the heady mix of "the wisdom of the East," the charm of Japanese arts and crafts, and a taste for martial valor that so impressed his Western audiences later in his career. If Okakura was—far more than Bigelow or Fenollosa—La Farge's key to the

Orient, La Farge was in turn Okakura's key for opening the West to Japanese culture.

In October 1886, after six months together, all five companions—Fenollosa, Bigelow, La Farge, Adams, and Okakura—boarded a steamer in Yokohama bound for San Francisco. La Farge quickly made Okakura a fixture in his New York studio (he would be the first of a series of attractive Asian men who would fulfill this service for La Farge), and from it Okakura dispensed advice on incorporating Asian themes in American works of art. During that fall of 1886, Okakura was a frequent visitor at the Union Square home of Richard Watson Gilder, editor of the *Century* magazine, and his wife, the painter Helena De Kay, on East Fifteenth Street. The Gilders were the epicenter of genteel New York cultural life; they were always entertaining painters, writers, and musicians. Their converted carriage house was among the first projects of their friend Stanford White; John La Farge (who had taught Helena to paint) contributed stained-glass windows and fire screens. Richard Watson Gilder—the name so perfectly fitted for his role as steward of culture during the Gilded Age—publicized the work of his circle of friends in his popular magazine; it was in the *Century* that La Farge's *Artist's Letters from Japan* first appeared. And when La Farge brought Okakura to meet the Gilders, Okakura charmed everyone he met.

Women were particularly drawn to Okakura, who adopted a lyrical way of talking to match the flowing robes he now wore. The portrait painter Cecelia Beaux, a close friend of Helena Gilder, loved the way Okakura recited classic Japanese poetry and how he "changed his whole personality, voice, and especially facial expression." It was at the Gilders' house that Okakura was introduced to the famous opera singer Clara Louise Kellogg. A quarter of a century earlier, during the Civil War, Kellogg had triumphed in the role of the innocent Marguerite in the New York premiere of Gounod's *Faust*—she was practically identified with the role. During the following decade she was the most popular American diva, valued for her dramatic interpretations of Carmen and other roles, for her graceful figure, and for the purity of her voice. When she met

Okakura she was forty-four, her figure had filled out, and her demanding touring career had drawn to a close. She is the first of a type that recurs in Okakura's life: the mature maternal diva in search of spiritual sustenance to replace her youthful charms.

Here is how Clara Kellogg described her initial encounter with Okakura in her *Memoirs of an American Prima Donna:*

> Okakura was only twenty-six when I first met him at Richard Watson Gilder's studio in New York, but he was already a professor and spoke perfect English and knew all our best literature. When Munkacsy, the Hungarian painter, came over, his colleague, Francis Korbay, the musician, gave him an evening reception, and I took my Japanese friend. It was a charming evening and Okakura was the success of the reception. When he started being introduced he was nothing but a professor. Before he had gone the rounds he had become an Asiatic prince and millionaire. He had the "grand manner" and wore gorgeous clothes on formal occasions.

Okakura maintained the grand manner in a series of love letters to Kellogg that allow us to trace his travels through Europe. "France still lies three nights ahead of us," he wrote on January 4, 1887. "The returning clouds still see the western shore and the ocean rolls back my dreams to you. Your music lives in my soul. I carry away America in your voice; and what better token can your nation offer? But praises to the great sound like flattery, and praises to the beautiful sound like love. To you they must both be tiresome. I shall refrain. You allude to the Eastern Lights. Alas, the Lamp of Love flickers and Night is on the plains of Osaka." In March, from Vienna, he complained that "Europe is an enigma—often a source of sadness to me," and predicted that war was coming: "The policy of maintaining peace by increasing the armies is absurd."

Okakura often wrote to Kellogg of spiritual matters. Rome, he told her, "interests me deeply, as yet the spiritual center of the West," and in Dresden, "the Sistine Madonna was divine beyond my expectation. I saw Raphael in his purity and was delighted." By late July, learning that he had to return to Japan a year earlier than planned, he was ready to serve as Clara Kellogg's spiritual adviser, sprinkling his prose with the imagery of

Esoteric Buddhism: "You say that you have a hope of finding what you long for in Buddhism. Surely your lotus must be opening to the dawn. European philosophy has reached to a point where no advance is possible except through mysticism."

What interrupted Okakura's travels was an abrupt summons to Washington by his former superior in preservationist circles, Ryuichi Kuki. Baron Kuki, serving out his term as Japanese ambassador to the United States, wanted Okakura to accompany his ailing and unhappy wife, Hatsu, back to Japan. Mrs. Kuki wore stylish Western clothes and charmed reporters with her beauty and her spoken English. But she concealed her ties to an earlier, older Japan. For Hatsu in her youth had been a geisha from the Kyoto entertainment district of Gion, trained in the ancient arts of dance, the shamisen, and the tea ceremony. During their monthlong journey to Japan, Okakura and Hatsu embarked on a passionate affair. Roughly nine months after their romantic Pacific crossing, Hatsu gave birth to a son, named Shuzo. There is little doubt that Okakura was his father.

The scandalous attachment with Mrs. Kuki, who lived apart from her husband in a house frequented by Okakura, endured during his rapid rise in the Japanese arts establishment. In 1890, at the age of twenty-eight, Okakura was named director of the new Tokyo Fine Arts School, which he led for eight years. (The American wife of the British ambassador, visiting him at the school in 1892, noticed Okakura's "large brilliant eyes" and "low clear voice," and she noted that "his English is fluent and complete.") He was also appointed curator of art at the Imperial Museum in Tokyo, the forerunner of the National Museum. Eager to cultivate an audience for the Japanese-style painting they favored, called Nihonga, Okakura founded with Fenollosa the leading art magazine, *Kokka*. He helped design the interior of the Japanese pavilion for the 1893 World's Fair in Chicago, for which he also wrote a descriptive brochure in English. Visitors from abroad made a point of meeting him.

Then, around 1896, Okakura's prodigious career ran into trouble. This was partly the result of envy, compounded by his high-handed and flamboyant personal style. He rode a stallion to the art school and designed for himself and his students a theatrical school uniform modeled on the flowing robes of eighth-century Japan. The scandal with Mrs. Kuki strengthened the hand of Okakura's enemies. He began to drink heavily. Mrs. Kuki's son, Shuzo, remembered later that Okakura would generally visit Hatsu in the evening. "I always remember seeing sake bottles on these occasions," he wrote, "and I sometimes saw Okakura with a bright red face." Meanwhile, Okakura's wife, who had put up with him till now and was herself ill and in need of surgery, demanded that he break off the affair. Baron Kuki, determined to put an end to the scandal and punish Okakura, found a way to have Hatsu put in an asylum for the insane.

In 1896 Okakura was forced to resign from the Fine Arts School and from his post at the Imperial Museum. Many of his teachers resigned in protest and joined him in the founding of an alternative art school, the Japan Art Institute. It was "alternative" in other ways as well: there were no formal classes, and the emphasis was on encouraging originality. Several of Japan's leading modern painters in the Nihonga style—including Yokoyama Taikan and Hishida Shunso—emerged from this school and remained fiercely loyal to Okakura. At this time, Taikan painted an extraordinary portrait of Okakura in the guise of the exiled Chinese poet Kutsugen (or Chu Yuan) wandering in the barren hills among windblown narcissus. Of Kutsugen, Okakura later wrote: "By way of self-assertion he wrote great poems of solitude—of the man who stands apart from men—seeking in Nature his only friend, in idealization his only home, and then committed suicide by drowning."

Despite generous contributions from William Sturgis Bigelow, the Japan Art Institute had shaky financial support, and Okakura was an indifferent administrator. Wishing to escape the vipers' nest that Japan was becoming for him, and devastated by the punitive institutionalization of Hatsu, Okakura departed for India in 1901. This was the beginning of a new phase in his career: twelve years of wandering as international celebrity and writer of books for the English-speaking public. Demonstrating his uncanny instinct for cultivating the most influential and interesting people, Okakura lived in Calcutta with the Tagore family and became a close friend of the Bengali poet and partisan Rabindranath Tagore.

The two men were a year apart in age—Okakura was thirty-nine,

Tagore forty—and they had many things in common. Both were profoundly involved with their national traditions and wary of European influences. Both had founded innovative schools on this basis; Tagore's famous school at Santiniketan opened the year of Okakura's arrival. Both subscribed to some of the conventional dualisms of the time: Asia as a spiritual and feminine counterbalance to the male materialism of the West. At the same time, they accepted the notion that Western culture might have certain ideas and techniques worth synthesizing with their own. Isaiah Berlin's summary of Tagore's convictions could easily be applied to Okakura: "Nor is an ancient culture sufficient to keep a modern people going. The new must be grafted onto the old; that is the only alternative to petrification, or the miserable aping of some ill-understood foreign original."

In the Tagore household, Okakura drafted his first book in English, *The Ideals of the East* (1903). He insisted on the original "ideals" of Asian culture in order to counter the widespread view—advanced by Percival Lowell, among others—that the Japanese were a nation of copyists, clever imitators who mimicked the material surface of things. In his pioneering "Essay on Japanese Art" of 1869, John La Farge had cast doubt on whether "the Japanese have an ideal." He conceded that the colossal statue of the Buddha at Kamakura betrayed "a serene ideal of contemplation, a surmise of some one of the things that might have been in Japan." But the great Buddha was an exception, a path not taken. La Farge praised Hokusai's "realism," his clever eye for natural detail in human and animal form, but added that we should not "expect to find in Japanese art that deeper individual personality—the glory of our greatest art . . . which may perhaps be connected . . . with the education of the Western world by Christianity."

Against such dismissive views, Okakura argued that there was indeed an inner or "ideal" dimension to Japanese art, a synthesis achieved over time of Indian mysticism and Chinese moral virtue. There was a political aspect to Okakura's argument as well. If Japan was merely "imitative," her institutions could at best be imitations of their Western counterparts. That Japan had a core of inner ideals onto which she could "graft" alien skills—this remained an article of faith for Okakura and his followers. The periods of Japanese art that Okakura emphasized were those most clearly permeated by "ideals," Buddhist art and architecture above all. And Okakura dismissed the naturalism of Hokusai and other "floating world" artists because it seemed open to the charge of lacking an inner or "ideal" aspect.

Ideals of the East begins with the famous and often quoted line "Asia is one." The opening section and closing pages hold to this pan-Asian idea (the counterpart of Okakura's claim that Europe is fragmented), but the middle of the book is given over to a history of Japanese art. Okakura saw Asian culture as having two major strands: "individual" India, with her mystical tradition emphasizing the individual's search for divinity; and "communal" China, with her Confucian model for a smoothly functioning society. Okakura believed that Japan had achieved the Hegelian synthesis of these dual tendencies. Only in Japan, because of its openness to the culture of China and India and its resistance to foreign military invasion, could one find all the strands of Asian culture. "It is in Japan alone," he wrote, "that the historic wealth of Asiatic culture can be consecutively studied through its treasured specimens." *Ideals of the East* had a profound influence in India and Japan, but Okakura, after a year in India, was on the move again.

During this period, when his prospects in Japan were meager, Okakura remained in touch with his American contacts. After a brief stint in charge of the Asian collections at the Museum of Fine Arts in Boston, Fenollosa had returned to Japan and asked Okakura to help him pursue an intensive study of classic Chinese poetry. Okakura, buffeted by change in his own life, was increasingly drawn to the philosophy of Taoism, with its doctrine of constant transformation. He translated some Taoist poetic texts for Fenollosa. During the spring of 1903, probably at Fenollosa's suggestion, Okakura hosted a delegation of Americans visiting Japan on their way to India: the famous singer Emma Thursby, her sister Ina, and their friend Mrs. Ole Bull, the American wife of the Norwegian violinist. They were enchanted with him; and with Emma Thursby, Okakura developed another of his quasi-romantic ties to maternal women. Meanwhile, William Sturgis Bigelow, aware of Okakura's troubles in Japan, saw a way for him to work for an institution where Asiatic culture could indeed be "consecutively studied." If Japan was closed to Okakura, America, and especially New England, might be "opened" instead.

By the turn of the century, Japan had, for thirty years, been a fantasy world for American aesthetes, and Bostonians in particular regarded it as a sort of exotic suburb of the Hub. Historically connected with Japan by the clipper trade, Boston and Salem had grown accustomed to Japanese porcelain and other decorative objects, and two generations of Bostonians, stretching back to Emerson and Thoreau, had found spiritual sustenance in their image of the East. But Japan had grown up in the meantime. Just as the United States was exerting force in Cuba and the Philippines in the Spanish-American War, Japan was emerging as an imperial power, with special interests in Korea and Manchuria. It had shown in its successful war with China in 1895 that it would not be pushed around in Asia. Then, on February 10, 1904, after failed negotiations over their respective "spheres of influence," Japan declared war on Russia, a war that no one expected the Japanese to win. On that very day, Okakura boarded a ship in Yokohama bound for the United States.

Okakura immediately made effective use of his American contacts. His first destination was New York, where he stayed with Emma Thursby in her Park Avenue apartment. John La Farge, thrilled to have Okakura back in his studio, organized at the Century Club an exhibition of recent work of the two artists, Taikan and Shunso, that Okakura had brought with him. These young artists, trained in traditional Japanese methods but also attuned to Western techniques, were painting luminous landscapes on silk—evanescent waterfalls, mountains, moonlit pilgrimages. These stunning works are only now, fully a century after they were painted, receiving the attention they deserve.

Okakura's theatrical practice of wearing only Japanese clothing in the West, counter to the Meiji practice of adopting Western formal attire, attracted much notice from an admiring press. Okakura once remarked that unless one's English was flawless—as his was—one should wear Western clothes in the West. An anecdote testifying to his dexterity with English is recorded from his New York sojourn in 1904. Okakura and his companions in their traditional Japanese dress were stopped by a wag in the street who asked: "What sort of 'nese are you people? Are you Chinese, or Japanese, or Javanese?" Okakura responded, "We are Japanese gentlemen. But what sort of 'key' are you? Are you a Yankee, or a donkey, or a monkey?"

Then Okakura turned his attention to Boston. La Farge wrote a letter of introduction to the redoubtable Mrs. Isabella Stewart Gardner, now in her sixties, who was known to have the best private collection of European art in the United States. La Farge told Gardner that Okakura was "the most intelligent critic of art, and I might also say of everything, that I know of." On March 27, Okakura first came to Fenway Court, and whenever he came to Boston after that he and Gardner, as her biographer reports, "were much together."

Collectors like Isabella Gardner are a special kind of traveler: They insist on bringing "elsewhere" home with them. When her husband, the railroad financier Jack Gardner, died in late 1898, she found herself with enough money to indulge her dreams of a residential museum in which she would live among her masterpieces. Gardner decided that she liked many things she had seen in Venice—especially paintings by Titian and Giorgione—and these she could afford (after her connoisseur Bernard Berenson had vouched for their authenticity) to buy and ship back to Boston. But what Belle Gardner loved most in Venice was Venice itself. This affection presented an extra challenge for the collector, but Mrs. Gardner was up to it. She made several collecting forays to Italy, shipping home Venetian window frames and archways, columns, cornices, and marble fireplaces. Eight balustrades rescued from the Ca d'Oro on the Grand Canal—it was undergoing a renovation—came straight to Boston. She even located some aging Italian plasterers to reproduce the ornate ceilings of Venice. And then she found a part of Boston, the watery Fens, that was both sufficiently undeveloped and sufficiently swampy—pooling here and there into meandering creeks and ponds—to support her architectural ambition of a Venetian palazzo in the New England city.

The stunning result was Fenway Court, with three stories of balconies—those balustrades from the Ca d'Oro—overlooking an interior courtyard, roofed with glass, of Roman mosaics and fountains. Outdoor staircases and arcades led to high-ceilinged rooms especially designed to house treasures such as Titian's *Rape of Europa* and Rembrandt's *Shipwreck*. To her hall of dreams Mrs. Gardner had no difficulty attracting the sorts of Americans one might encounter among the pigeons of San Marco: Henry James, Henry Adams, the young T. S. Eliot. Fashionable Boston flocked to her official opening, on the evening of January 1, 1903, and wandered among the corridors lit by torches and candlelight (there was no electricity at Fenway Court for another decade). Edward Sylvester Morse came to the opening, wearing his great coat in the courtyard, and so did Edith Wharton, who complained that the food was about as good as one might expect from a French provincial railroad station. (She was not invited again.) William James, echoing the breathless response of most of the guests, called the opening "a Gospel miracle."

Okakura arrived at Isabella Gardner's house a year after its opening,

Okakura with friends in Gloucester, Massachusetts, October 1910.
Isabella Gardner is seated behind Okakura.
Courtesy Isabella Stewart Gardner Museum, Boston.

bearing his glowing letter of introduction from La Farge. Gardner was best known for her collection of European art, but she was knowledgeable about Asia. She had traveled to Japan twenty years earlier during a trip around the world. William Sturgis Bigelow, son of her private doctor, had been her host there, and she had met Fenollosa. She was a close friend of Edward Morse, who had lectured on Japan in her house; she knew something of Japanese customs and folkways. Although she had accumulated through the years some examples of Asian art, mainly through dealers in New York and Boston, and later installed a Buddha Room in her museum, she seems to have made little use of Okakura's expertise. "Mrs. Gardner," as the scholar Anne Nishimura Morse notes, "appears to have been more captivated by Okakura, the Japanese man, than by Japanese art."

Their affection and mutual understanding seem to have been immediate. While Okakura's relationship with Isabella Gardner stoked the rumor mill in Boston high society for many years, the exact nature of their intimacy remains a riddle. She was in love with him, and her mothering instincts appealed to Okakura. Her effusive description of him to Berenson, as "so interesting, so deep, so spiritual, so feminine," hints at complexities. Perhaps her own "masculine" traits—her boldness, her authority, her self-confidence—found a complement in Okakura's sensitivity. He wrote her love poems, like his moonlit tribute, "The Stairway of Jade," that show how much he understood her loneliness.

The One,
Alone and White.
Shadows but wander
In the lights that were,
Lights but linger
In the shadows to be
The Moon
White and alone.

But there was another, more playful, side to Okakura's relationship with Isabella Gardner. To one accustomed to the reverential respect of friends like Henry Adams and Henry James, Okakura's Taoist-inspired informality was a breath of fresh air. Okakura teased her out of her imperious ways, addressing her as "the Presence of Fenway Court" and, during a visit to Japan, sending letters to her cat:

> Ages have passed—are you changed any? Swans sailing across the ocean have brought tidings of your whereabouts and I am glad that fate has dealt kindly with you.
>
> When you left I have felt the loss deeply— My breast has missed your nightly tread, the table was suddenly large without your prowling presence. Even now I write with your picture before me. You have killed all the cats in the world for you are alone,—the only one dear to me.

Again, amid the irreverent playfulness, that hint of loneliness. Okakura enclosed a "small parcel of Japanese Catnip."

Under Okakura's tutelage, Mrs. Gardner introduced Japanese themes among her Venetian furnishings. For a benefit in support of a Boston sanitarium, she transformed her Music Room into a Japanese village, invited guests, and had herself carried about in a "genuine" jinricksha, visiting a little Buddhist temple and a shrine among fake trees. She hired one Professor Uchimura, who had been teaching jujutsu at Harvard, to give a demonstration. The fair took place in May 1905, at a time when American admiration for Japanese military prowess against the Russians was at its peak.

Okakura himself had presided over a more serious occasion the previous January. With much preparatory pomp, he had staged a formal tea ceremony at Fenway Court. Again, the guests arrived by carriage through the darkened Fens, to be greeted by torchlight and candles, and the hushed rituals of the tea ceremony. Isabella Gardner could hardly contain her excitement. She wrote breathlessly to Berenson: "I am still full of the sentiment and flower of the great Tea Ceremony, the 'Cha-no-yu,' which was performed here yesterday at 5 PM (candlelight) by Okakura." So intense were the preparations for this particular tea ceremony that the connoisseur Roger Fry, who had stopped in Boston to examine Gardner's collection, was told that he would have to wait a day until the ceremony was over.

For her birthday in 1911, Okakura wrote Isabella Gardner a special poem, called "The Taoist":

She stood alone on earth—an exile
From heaven. Of all the immortals
She was the flower.
Time receded in reverence at her approach.
Space bowed the way to her triumph. The wind
Brought to her its untrammeled grace, the air
Lent to her voice the balm of its own summer.
Blue lightning swept in her glances, clouds
Draped the flow of her queenly train.

No wonder she loved him. Isabella Gardner told Mary Berenson that Okakura was "the first person . . . who showed her how hateful she was, and from him she learnt her first lesson of seeking to love instead of to be loved."

If Okakura's private life had its own mysterious trajectory, his professional life in Boston is more easily charted. In April 1904, less than a month into his stay, Okakura was appointed adviser on Chinese and Japanese art at the Museum of Fine Arts. Ironically, while his relationship with Mrs. Kuki had caused him to lose his job in Japan, it was his former teacher Fenollosa's affair with an assistant that opened a job for him in Boston. Fenollosa, who had established the Japanese department at the Museum of Fine Arts in 1890, had left his own organizational work incomplete and undocumented. Okakura, armed with a pushy letter of introduction from Bigelow, went to work in his place. "Okakura is busy at the Museum," Mrs. Gardner reported to Berenson, "cataloguing the Japanese things that have been huddled there since Fenollosa's time, and finds forgeries and forgeries!!! And has great contempt for Fenollosa." The souring of the mentor-disciple relationship, which must have had a long fore-ground, shows the emergence of Okakura as his own man. Fenollosa's patronizing ways, and especially his refusal to acknowledge his depen-dence on his brilliant assistant's expertise, rankled over time. Going through the treasures at the museum, Okakura could see proof of how lit-tle Fenollosa could manage without him.

During his first ten months at the museum, Okakura examined more than five thousand paintings, making determinations about authenticity and date, and identifying gaps in the collection that might be filled by further acquisitions. He recognized that the market for Asian art, increasingly dominated by wealthy industrialists like Charles Freer in the United States and Kaichiro Nezu in Japan, had changed, and that the best finds were not in dealers' shops but in temples in Japan and China. Okakura's buying trips to Japan yielded works of extraordinary quality, including the sculptor Kaikei's graceful and naturalistic *Miroku, the Bod-*

Kaikei, Miroku, the Bodhisattva
of the Future, *1189.*

hisattva of the Future (dated 1189), acquired through Okakura's contacts with monks in Nara and Kyoto.

Okakura was soon convinced that China, in political turmoil, offered the best opportunities for acquiring masterpieces of Asian art. Tung Wu, a specialist in Chinese art at the Museum of Fine Arts, makes a strong case for how advanced Okakura's views of Chinese art were for his time. Okakura traveled to China for the museum, collecting ancient ritual jade implements and Taoist sculptures and paintings—including the wry *Three Taoist Transcendants Admire a Toad* (fifteenth century). In such purchases, Okakura went far beyond his contemporaries' penchant for export porcelain, and displayed a witty and idiosyncratic taste. Not all of his identifications withstand current scrutiny, but the number of significant acquisitions made during his tenure is impressive, and his policy of filling gaps in the collection remains in place today.

By 1906 Okakura had spent two decades thinking about the United States, and how best to make a place in it—a sort of cultural beachhead—for Japanese ideas. His first two books in English, *The Ideals of the East* and *The Awakening of Japan* (1904), had followed Fenollosa's ideas about forging a synthesis of East and West. Nationalistic in tone and argument, *The Awakening of Japan* celebrates Japanese prowess on the battlefield. Gone are the fantasies of pan-Asian spirituality as a counterbalance to Western technology, which had permeated *Ideals of the East*. The Hegelian synthesis of spirit and matter that was to be a worldwide affair, uniting Asia and Europe, had now occurred, Okakura argued, within Japan itself, "the result of a brilliant effort to mirror the whole of Asiatic consciousness."

But such arguments remained little more than propaganda, an outsider's harangues without a strategy for infusion and infiltration. What Okakura lacked was something to give focus and force to his thinking, what his friend and admirer T. S. Eliot was to call an objective correlative. Okakura found it in an unexpected subject: tea. It suddenly dawned on him that the synthesis of East and West could be charted in the stunning spread of tea across the world: "Strangely enough humanity has so far met in the tea-cup. It is the only Asiatic ceremonial which commands universal esteem. The white man has scoffed at our religion and our morals, but has accepted the brown beverage without hesitation."

Okakura, in a flash of inspiration, saw that the formal tea party as practiced in New England was a version of the tea ceremony. "The afternoon tea is now an important function in Western society. In the delicate clatter of trays and saucers, in the soft rustle of feminine hospitality, in the common catechism about cream and sugar, we know that the Worship of Tea is established beyond question." As his friend Henry James put it in the first sentence of his *Portrait of a Lady:* "Under certain circumstances there are few hours in life more agreeable than the hour dedicated to the ceremony known as afternoon tea." Part social ritual, part religious rite, the making and partaking of tea united the two cultures of East and West.

In the West, the tea party was primarily a ritual of women. Okakura mentions "the soft rustle of feminine hospitality," while James notes that the men taking tea in his opening scene "were not of the sex which is supposed to furnish the regular votaries of the ceremony I have mentioned." One of Mary Cassatt's most appealing genre scenes, painted at precisely the time James was writing his *Portrait,* depicts two women thoughtfully sharing the tea hour. One woman delicately lifts a teacup to her lips with her gloved hand while the other rests her chin on her raised fingers. Balancing these two figures is a silver tea service—the large sugar bowl and teapot like parody versions of the women themselves. On the mantelpiece sits a large porcelain vase in blue, red, and gold—a hint of Asian splendor. We are in a distinctly women's space of feminine ritual. The Japanese tea ceremony, by contrast, had evolved in the strenuous masculine worlds of Zen monks and samurai. Okakura's challenge in linking the tea rituals of East and West entailed breaking down a division between men and women as well.

The tea ceremony was not exactly unknown when Okakura published his third and most appealing book in English, *The Book of Tea,* in 1906. Many Western visitors to Japan had commented on the ritual of the tea ceremony, with reverence or ridicule. "I dislike sitting on my heels," Henry Adams wrote. "I cannot gracefully touch the ground with my forehead, or suck my breath; or follow the formalities of the *Cha-no-yu,* or five-o'clock tea, which is the only serious labor of Japanese life." But

Okakura correctly sensed that the tea ceremony, performed with sufficient pomp and mysterious ritual, would appeal to Bostonians like Isabella Gardner and her friends.

Such tea ceremonies, to which Okakura invited wealthy, art-
conscious Boston women, were a way to raise awareness of Japanese culture and, indirectly, to raise money for the Museum of Fine Arts. When
Okakura renewed his acquaintance with the painter Cecelia Beaux, he
made a point of serving tea in her studio. She recounted, "The delightful
harmony of the place, its quiet on winter afternoons, was no doubt sympathetic to his aesthetic sensibilities, and he even brought the materials
for formal Japanese tea service one day, and gave me a lesson in the technique of the function."

In The Book of Tea, *Okakura says little about the step-by-step performance*
of the ritual: the boiling of water, the greeting of the guests, the silence,
the stirring of the tea with the bamboo whisk, the inspection of the hand-
crafted tea bowls. He concentrates instead on the meaning of what he
calls the tea cult, including a fine evocation of the tearoom in which the
ceremony is performed. "To European architects brought up on the traditions of stone and brick construction, our Japanese method of building
with wood and bamboo seems scarcely worthy to be ranked as architecture." There is a moral imperative in the austerity of Japanese interiors,
according to Okakura. "To a Japanese, accustomed to simplicity of orna-
mentation and frequent change of decorative method, a Western interior
permanently filled with a vast array of pictures, statuary, and bric-a-brac
gives the impression of mere vulgar display of riches." The simple wood
interiors—which Edward Morse had admired as a counterbalance to New
England clutter—support the two aesthetic principles that Okakura insists upon in the tea cult. The first is the power of suggestion. "The viril-
ity of life and art lay in its possibilities for growth. In the tea-room is left
for each guest in imagination to complete the total effect." The second
principle is what Okakura calls "fear of repetition." "Uniformity of design was considered as fatal to the freshness of imagination. . . . The various objects for the decoration of a room should be so selected that no
colour or design shall be repeated. If you have a living flower, a painting

of flowers is not allowable. If you are using a round kettle, the water pitcher should be angular."

Okakura's aesthetic of the imperfect—Teaism, he wrote in his first paragraph, is "a worship of the Imperfect"—and his sustained attack on "uniformity of design" are aspects of what the Japanese call the *wabi* aesthetic of rustic poverty. *Wabi* is closely associated with the great sixteenth-century reinterpreter of the tea ceremony, Sen no Rikyu. The *wabi* tea master preferred the mended, the flawed, and the rough-hewn. The taste for thatched roofs and unfinished beams was perfectly congruent with the American Arts and Crafts aesthetic, so popular in Boston—what Thorstein Veblen snidely called "the exaltation of the defective." In "The Poems of Our Climate," the poet Wallace Stevens, an enthusiastic reader of Okakura's books, provides a succinct account of the *wabi* aesthetic:

Note that, in this bitterness, delight,
Since the imperfect is so hot in us,
Lies in flawed words and stubborn sounds.

It is easy to read *The Book of Tea* as a mere aesthetic treatise, a Ruskinian plea for refinement in the vulgar and industrialized modern world. But this reading leaves out the nationalist underpinnings. Early on in the book, Okakura links Western incomprehension of the tea ceremony to the recently completed Russo-Japanese War. "The average Westerner . . . will see in the tea ceremony but another instance of the thousand and one oddities which constitute the quaintness and childishness of the East to him. He was wont to regard Japan as barbarous while she indulged in the gentle arts of peace; he calls her civilized since she began to commit wholesale slaughter on Manchurian battlefields."

For Okakura, the Japanese tea ceremony—seemingly so delicate and refined—is actually a rite of national resistance. He traces the origins of the ceremony to twelfth-century China, when Taoist and early Zen traditions raised Song Dynasty art to a level never achieved again in Chinese art. These practices made their way to Japan with the spread of Buddhism. The Mongol invasion of China put an end to the glories of Song culture. Japan, with the help of a *kamikaze*, or "divine wind," that whipped up the waves and destroyed the Mongol fleet, resisted the invaders, thus preserving the aesthetic superiority lost to China. "It is in the Japanese tea ceremony that we see the culmination of tea-ideals," Okakura argues. "Our successful resistance of the Mongol invasion in 1281 had enabled us to carry on the Sung [Song] movement so disastrously cut off in China itself." So, the practice of the tea ceremony in Japan is a sign of Japanese independence and resistance to foreign invasion.

This link of tea and national independence sets off a bell—a Liberty Bell—in Okakura's mind. In a vivid cultural rhyme, he draws a direct connection between the Boston Tea Party and the origins of the tea ceremony in Japan. "Colonial America," he remarks, "resigned herself to oppression until human endurance gave way before the heavy duties laid on Tea. American independence dates from the throwing of tea-chests into Boston harbour." As a performance of independence and resistance to foreign control, then, tea has a special and parallel meaning for the two young imperial powers, Japan and the United States. And, by extension, the "soft rustle of feminine hospitality" at Boston tea parties is intimately linked to the code of the samurai.

The Book of Tea *suggested to Boston audiences that aestheticism and militarism, beauty and war, might be creatively combined.* (Even the flowers in the tea ceremony are impressed into battle: "Some flowers glory in death—certainly the Japanese cherry blossoms do, as they freely surrender themselves to the winds.") Okakura closes his book with an account of the death of Rikyu, the seventeenth-century Buddhist monk who is regarded as the founder of the tea ceremony as we know it. As Okakura tells the story, the death of Rikyu evokes both the martyrdoms of Socrates and Jesus and the death of Lincoln in his sacrifice for national reconciliation. Unjustly accused of plotting against his patron, the great warlord Hideyoshi, Rikyu performs one final tea ceremony with his disciples before ending his life.

On the day destined for his self-immolation, Rikiu invited his chief disciples to a last tea-ceremony. . . . One by one they advance and take their places. In the tokonoma [the alcove in the tearoom] hangs a kakemono [hanging scroll],—a wonderful writing by an ancient monk dealing with the evanescence of all earthly things. The singing kettle, as it boils over the brazier, sounds like some cicada pouring forth his woes to departing summer. Soon the host enters the room. Each in turn is served with tea, and each in turn silently drains his cup, the host last of all. According to established etiquette, the chief guest now asks permission to examine the tea-equipage. Rikiu places the various articles before them with the kakemono. After all have expressed admiration of their beauty, Rikiu presents one of them to each of the assembled company as a souvenir. The bowl alone he keeps. "Never again shall this cup, polluted by the lips of misfortune, be used by man." He speaks, and breaks the vessel into fragments.

The ceremony is over. With a smile on his face Rikyu plunges the shining blade of the dagger into his stomach.

Okakura had gone far, in such passages, from his earlier notions—developed with his friend Tagore—of Asia as woman and spirit and peace while the West is man and material and war. Even in such seemingly aesthetic and feminine a ritual as the serving of tea, Okakura found themes of national resistance, manly self-control, and virile self-sacrifice. This was a message that Bostonians were eager to hear. They were anxious that, in the words of T. S. Eliot, Boston was "refined beyond the point of civilization." The country had become sissified in their view, and the dangerous lower classes and darker races would soon overtake the Anglo-Saxons. The classic expression of this anxiety is William James's essay "The Moral Equivalent of War."

And here was Okakura arguing that one could be an aesthete *and* a soldier, Oscar Wilde and Teddy Roosevelt, that the way of tea and the way of the samurai were one. In the United States, the peace-loving artisan and the strenuous soldier had always been seen in opposition. "Roosevelt's strenuosity remained inextricably tied to militarism," as the cultural historian Jackson Lears notes, "and militarism required a fiercer premodern focus than the peaceful artisan could supply." Okakura found a way to reconcile soldier and craftsman. "In the thoroughness and minutiae of our preparations for war," he wrote, "[one] will recognize the same hands whose untiring patience gave its exquisite finish to our lac-quer." President Charles William Eliot of Harvard, who conferred an honorary degree on Okakura in 1911, praised the "extraordinary artistic qualities of the Japanese as a race, qualities they exhibit in conjunction with . . . an unparalleled energy and devotion in war." Eliot added, "We ought never to have imagined that the sense of beauty harmonized only with softness, fineness, or frailty in the human being."

Such notions of beauty in harmony with toughness appealed to a wide range of readers. Okakura's ideas and writings had a significant afterlife in at least three fields: modern architecture, American poetry, and German philosophy. His chapter on the ornament-free architecture of the tea-room caught the attention of Frank Lloyd Wright, who had seen Okakura's interior of the Japanese pavilion in Chicago in 1893. On several occasions he specified that it was in Okakura's book he first came across the idea of interior space that inspired his own "architecture of within." "I received a little book by Okakura Kakuzo, entitled *The Book of Tea*, sent to me by the ambassador from Japan to the United States," Wright remembered. "Reading it, I came across this sentence: 'The reality of a room was to be found in the space enclosed by the roof and walls, not in the roof and walls themselves.' " For Wright and other American architects in search of a na-tional style, Japan provided a model for stripping architecture down to its essentials—"the elimination of the insignificant," in Wright's phrase. Okakura's description of the streamlined teahouse, with no permanent decor, gave a vivid idea of what this new American architecture might look like. "Japan has now done," Wright remarked, "in her own perfect way, what now lies for study before us."

Okakura's imprint on American poetry has yet to be charted, but it is safe to say that he was a significant influence on at least three major American poets: Wallace Stevens, T. S. Eliot, and Ezra Pound. Each poet was drawn to different aspects of Okakura's writings. Stevens read *The Ideals of the East* and *The Book of Tea* in 1909, when he was beginning to forge his own distinctive poetic language. T. S. Eliot was drawn to Okakura's writings on Buddhism. Ezra Pound became custodian of Okakura's translations from Taoist poems, the results of Okakura's sessions with Fenollosa. The unlikely twists and turns of that story are detailed in the epilogue of this book.

The German philosopher Martin Heidegger, in his rustic little *wabi* world in the Black Forest, also read *The Book of Tea*. Graham Parkes has recently argued that several of Heidegger's fundamental concepts are drawn from the German translations of Okakura's works. Heidegger's ties to Okakura were more intimate still. Shuzo Kuki, Okakura's illegitimate son, made his way to Germany during the 1920s and worked closely with Heidegger. Master and pupil had sustained conversations about the differences between Japanese and German notions of aesthetics.

Frank Lloyd Wright, Martin Heidegger, T. S. Eliot, Ezra Pound—the names, linked as they are with the rise of fascism and Nazism, raise an interesting question. At what point does the vigorous preservation of a nation's traditional arts—what one might call nationalist aesthetics—veer into a claim that the excellence of a nation's arts gives it political legitimacy? A wounded and marginalized people cannot be faulted for seeking national pride in its own ethnic traditions. But Japan's transformation from a little country in need of respect to a dominant world power was so rapid that even its Asian admirers, such as Tagore, had to rethink their ideas about the meaning of Japan. What, then, is the relation between nationalist aesthetics and aesthetic nationalism?

That question was worrying Rabindranath Tagore when he visited Okakura at the Museum of Fine Arts in Boston in February 1913, the year Tagore won the Nobel Prize. Tagore had admired Japan's victory over Russia but was far less enthusiastic about Japan's imperialist forays into Korea and Manchuria. (Was this what "Asia is one" was meant to entail?) After Tagore's departure Okakura felt, as he put it, "a sudden loneliness." This man who had allowed himself to embody Japan for so many Americans—for Bigelow and Fenollosa, for La Farge and Gardner—ended his career isolated and alone, wondering who his true friends were. The tinge of melancholy never far from his prose darkens into gloom in his final letters. "I seem to go back to things that do not belong to me," he had once told Isabella Gardner. It was as though, in shuttling between East and West, he had lost the thread of his identity. His final months, in a remote mountain village west of Tokyo, were spent revising an opera libretto called "The White Fox," about a vixen who takes human form to impersonate the lost love of her benefactor. At the end, forced to renounce her love, the vixen writes a note of farewell to her beloved. "Her hands turn to paws, and she must take the pen in her mouth to complete the writing." She sings a final song:

> *My magic stone to you I leave,*
> *Power and knowledge to bestow.*
> *What need I now of powers and charms,*
> *An empty shell, bereft of love?*
> *To my former haunts I shall return,*
> *A cowering beast, a quarry foul,*
> *Hunted, baited, and devoured by dogs.*
> *Through the moonless night of howling storms,*
> *In fear and hunger I shall prowl alone.*

A SEASON OF NIRVANA

>< >< ><

At Omaha a young reporter got the better of us:
for when in reply to his inquiry as to our purpose in
visiting Japan, La Farge beamed through his
spectacles the answer that we were in search of
Nirvana, the youth looked up like a meteor,
and rejoined: "It's out of season!"

—HENRY ADAMS TO JOHN HAY, JUNE 11, 1886

Henry Adams has entered the mythology of the United States as a man destined by birth and background to serve his country and denied the chance to do so. The grandson and great-grandson of presidents, and the son of a distinguished diplomat who protected the Union's interests in Britain during the Civil War, Henry Adams never got closer to the White House than having friends in high places. It was as a jaundiced observer of government and not as a participant, a watcher rather than a doer, that Adams made his name. He sat out the Civil War in England, serving his father as private secretary. He sat out the period of Reconstruction at Harvard, teaching medieval history. Having shifted his base of operations to Washington, where no one asked for his services, he took up instead the self-appointed post of historian of the young republic. During the early 1880s, when he began to plan a journey to Japan, he was working on a cold-eyed, multivolume history of the administrations of Thomas Jefferson and James Madison.

Whether his failure to find a place in the federal government was

Adams's fault—the result of genetic attenuation across four generations—or the fault of the vulgar society in which he found himself is a question lurking in many pages of his third-person autobiography, *The Education of Henry Adams*. The idea of a family dynasty in decline (or, alternatively, a nation in decline) has encouraged readers to oversimplify Henry Adams, to see him as the quintessential Yankee, a Bostonian born and bred and out of step—by a century or two—with the modern world. In the *Education*, as he enumerates the details of his birth "under the shadow of Boston State House" in 1838, Adams toys with the question of his lack of fit with modern circumstances:

> Had he been born in Jerusalem under the shadow of the Temple, and circumcised in the Synagogue by his uncle the high priest, under the name of Israel Cohen, he would scarcely have been more distinctly branded, and not much more heavily handicapped in the races of the coming century, in running for such stakes as the century was to offer; but, on the other hand, the ordinary traveler, who does not enter the field of racing, finds advantage in being, so to speak, ticketed through life, with the safeguards of an old, established traffic.

There again, in the contrast between the racehorse and the traveler, is the dichotomy between the doer and the watcher. "What could become of such a child of the seventeenth and eighteenth centuries, when he should wake up to find himself required to play the game of the twentieth?"

But for all his talk of being "branded" from birth as an Adams, and his uneasy joking about being as "handicapped in the races of the coming century" as the Jews, Henry Adams left many clues that he was a divided man, a man not so much of parts as of pieces. The best record of this fragmentation is his *Education*, written during 1905 but published only in 1918, a few months after Adams's death. Ideas of doubleness enter the *Education* early. New England weather is double, and so is life. Adams's childhood in Quincy, Massachusetts, and in nearby Boston is an early education in contrasts. "The intense blue of the sea, as he saw it a mile or two away, from the Quincy hills; the cumuli in a June afternoon sky; the strong reds and greens and purples of colored prints and children's picture-books, as the American colors then ran; these were ideals." In contrast, though—the realities against those picture-book ideals—were "the cold grays of November evenings, and the thick, muddy thaws of Boston winter. With such standards," Adams concludes, "the Bostonian could not but develop a double nature. Life was a double thing."

The point is made with sufficient force, but Adams hammers it home in its own two-ply paragraph.

> The bearing of the two seasons on the education of Henry Adams was no fancy; it was the most decisive force he ever knew; it ran through life, and made the division between its perplexing, warring, irreconcilable problems, irreducible opposites, with growing emphasis to the last year of study. From earliest childhood the boy was accustomed to feel that, for him life was double. Winter and summer, town and country, law and liberty, were hostile, and the man who pretended they were not, was in his eyes a schoolmaster:—that is, a man employed to tell lies to little boys.

Division is both the main structural principle and the central subject of *The Education of Henry Adams.* Adams portrays himself as a divided man in a divided country in a divided time. He traces his internal divisions not only to New England weather but to his own split ancestry. It may come as some surprise—so insistent are the associations of the Adams name—that Adams thought of himself as in certain ways an "exotic." His memories of his grandfather John Quincy Adams are charming and often recounted, especially the set piece when the aging president, upon his grandson's stubborn refusal to go to school, takes him by the hand and silently, without reprimand or moral, leads the boy, "paralysed by awe," off to the classroom. "He had shown no temper, no irritation, no personal feeling, and had made no display of force. Above all, he had held his tongue. During their long walk he had said nothing; he had uttered no syllable of revolting cant about the duty of obedience and the wickedness of resistance to law; he had shown no concern in the matter; hardly even a consciousness of the boy's existence." We are meant to admire the tact of the lesson administered by the eighty-year-old president, and to see it as a quintessential New England lesson. Any verbal pointing of the lesson, any irritating planting of "the seeds of a moral education," would, according to Henry Adams, "have fallen on the stoniest soil in Quincy, which is, as everyone knows, the stoniest glacial and tidal drift known in any Puritan land."

A Northerner by upbringing and temperament, Henry Adams had acquired a strain of something else, equally essential to his character, from his Maryland-bred grandmother, John Quincy Adams's wife: "He never dreamed that from her might come some of those doubts and self-questionings, those hesitations, those rebellions against law and discipline, which marked more than one of her descendants; but he might even then have felt some vague instinctive suspicion that he was to inherit from her the seeds of the primal sin, the fall from grace, the curse of Abel, that he was not of pure New England stock, but half exotic." This is jokingly phrased but seriously meant. That he had "inherited a quarter taint of Maryland blood" from the Johnson wing of his family meant that Adams thought of himself as partly a Southerner. Since those "self-questionings" and "hesitations" are what we most associate with Adams's mind and temperament, it is of particular interest that he traces them to his Southern heritage.

His response to the South on his first visit to Washington, D.C.—the city he later chose for his home—is deeply conflicted. Adams is at pains to describe the "sudden change that came over the world on entering a slave state." True to his free-soil convictions, he is appalled at the realities of slavery: "Slavery struck him in the face; it was a nightmare; a horror; a crime; the sum of all wickedness!" But these ready-made responses, schooled in the twelve-year-old boy like so many phrases for classroom or Sunday recitation, constitute his intellectual response to the South: "He had not a thought but repulsion for it; and yet the picture had another side." What follows has almost a *Gone with the Wind* quality, precisely the note we would least expect from an Adams of Quincy and Boston: "The May sunshine and shadow had something to do with it; the thickness of foliage and the heavy smells had more; the sense of atmosphere, almost new, had perhaps as much again; and the brooding indolence of a warm climate and a negro population hung in the atmosphere heavier than the catalpas. The impression was not simple, but the boy liked it; distinctly it remained on his mind as an attraction, almost obscuring Quincy itself."

There is the division sharply drawn: Quincy versus Maryland; thought versus feeling; and, finally, Adams versus Johnson. "The want of barriers, of pavements, of forms; the looseness, the laziness, the indolent southern drawl; the pigs in the streets; the negro babies and their mothers in bandanas; the freedom, openness, swagger, of nature and man, soothed his Johnson blood. Most boys would have felt it in the same way," he concedes, "but with him the feeling caught on to an inheritance." It is an extraordinary admission, compounded by Adams's ensuing reflections about how Boston and Washington were "two worlds [that] could not live together [and] he was not sure that he enjoyed the Boston world more." This geographical split reflects an inner division: "Even at twelve years old he could see his own nature no more clearly than he would at twelve hundred, if by accident he should happen to live so long."

A lingering fondness for the South continued during his years as an undergraduate at Harvard, where Adams felt a "curious sympathy" for three classmates from Virginia, one of whom was Robert E. Lee's son Roony. "Adams liked the Virginians. No one was more obnoxious to them, by name and prejudice; yet their friendship was unbroken and even warm." These North-South alliances are ironic foreshadowings of the Civil War, when Henry Adams, the divided man, would find himself in a divided nation. While his loyalties to Lincoln and the Union are unquestioned, and his older brother Charles Adams, Jr., enters the Federal Army, Henry Adams's main aim in 1860–61, as his father's secretary in Congress, is to keep Virginia in the Union by making "concessions to the border states." Even through the Civil War chapters of the *Education*, when Adams follows his father to Great Britain as the ambassador's private secretary, his highest wrath is reserved not for the Confederacy but for the British leaders who betray the Union cause.

In these chapters on Charles Francis Adams's diplomatic maneuverings, the theme of doubleness recurs. In the chapter called "Diplomacy," Adams seems to want to remind us that the word *diplomacy* is etymologically rooted in doubleness, from the doubled or folded documents of national emissaries. While "diplomacy held diplomats apart in order to save governments," Charles Francis Adams is so English in his manners that he can pass for a local. "In society, few Londoners were so widely at home. None had such double personality and corresponding double weight."

Adams's sympathy for the South survived the carnage of the war, when so many from his Harvard class of 1858 did not. In his satirical novel of Washington life, *Democracy,* published anonymously in 1880, Adams assigned the views closest to his own to a Virginian and Confederate veteran named Carrington. In a famous essay called "A Southern Critique for the Gilded Age," the historian C. Vann Woodward has mulled over Adams's reasons for "deliberately associat[ing] valor, honor, dignity, and the heroic traditions of the past—of whichever side—with Virginia soil and name and place." When Woodward gropes for precisely what it was that turned Adams's sympathies—and those of Herman Melville and Henry James as well—southward, he is almost as vague as Adams himself:

> America's triumph over the South did not mean simply the defeat of an external foe that left the victorious power unchanged and inflicted change and revolution upon the vanquished alone. It also meant the defeat or denial of something within, a tradition perhaps once shared with the fallen rebels, something that shared the downfall of the South. In their search for what was missing in postwar America, these Northern writers turned southward and invoked a tradition only lately renounced.

The search for what was missing in post–Civil War America led Henry Adams farther afield than the American South, however, and I have spent so much time on Adams and the South as prelude to a larger division in Adams's life, and in the structure of the *Education.* Two great forces are at work in the book. One is the Civil War, which definitively destroys the eighteenth-century order so dear to Henry Adams. (The *Education* may well be the best American book to emerge from the Civil War, the best book, that is, about the hole in the heart left in a generation by the war.) The other force in the book is the birth of modern empires, which introduces the twentieth century. It is one of the many paradoxes of the *Education* that, at least for Adams, the nineteenth century lasted for roughly twenty years, and those happen to be the years excluded from the *Education.*

Here, we approach the great gap in the *Education,* one chapter of which, entitled "Failure," ends with Adams's trip to the Far West during the summer of 1871, when he first meets his great friend Clarence King. The next chapter, entitled "Twenty Years After," picks up in January 1892, with Adams's return from a visit to the South Seas with the painter John La Farge. "Education had ended in 1871; life was complete in 1890; the rest mattered so little!" And again, "Life had been cut in halves, and the old half had passed away, education and all, leaving no stock to graft on." All the great books of education, spiritual and intellectual and senti-mental—from Augustine to Rousseau to Benjamin Franklin (all three are mentioned by Adams in his preface)—have a division between the old life and the new. But there is no moment of illumination that separates for Adams the two halves of his life. It might be more accurate to say that there was a period of darkness.

The Education of Henry Adams is a book with a hole in it. Adams's ex-planation is that education ceased during those two decades, during which he tried to apply his education rather than add to it. From scattered remarks in the *Education*, we can learn some of the things Adams did during the twenty excluded years. He taught medieval history for seven years at Harvard, beginning in 1871. And he traveled a great deal, almost incessantly, in fact. He took a trip to the West and a journey to the South Seas. Instead of telling us straightforwardly what exactly has cut his life in two, Henry Adams—in one of those "curious transitions" that Edmund Wilson complained of in the *Education*—places us in front of a statue. He tells us only that on his return to Washington, after those twenty years, he went immediately to Rock Creek Cemetery, to look at a monument there that he had commissioned, six years earlier, from the great American sculptor Augustus Saint-Gaudens.

> His first step, on returning to Washington, took him out to the
> cemetery known as Rock Creek, to see the bronze figure which St.
> Gaudens had made for him in his absence. Naturally every detail
> interested him; every line; every touch of the artist; every change
> of light and shade; every point of relation; every possible doubt of
> St. Gaudens' correctness of taste or feeling; so that, as the spring
> approached, he was apt to stop there often to see what the figure
> had to tell him that was new; but, in all that it had to say, he never
> once thought of questioning what it meant.

"A poem should not mean, but be," wrote Archibald MacLeish, and Adams seems to assume the same attitude with his bronze figure.

> He supposed its meaning to be the one common-place about it,—the oldest idea known to human thought. He knew that if he asked an Asiatic its meaning, not a man, woman or child from Cairo to Kamschatka would have needed more than a glance to reply. From the Egyptian Sphinx to the Kamakura Daibuts; from Prometheus to Christ; from Michael Angelo to Shelley, art had wrought on this eternal figure almost as though it had nothing else to say.

There is that little phrase again—what it had to say. Adams has assembled an intimidating group of monuments and monumental artists to testify to the obvious, the "common-place," message of the bronze figure in the cemetery. But what exactly that message is he refuses to say.

Instead, Adams shifts the perspective, as though he himself is the statue, unmoving and looking back.

> The interest of the figure was not in its meaning, but in the response of the observer. As Adams sat there, numbers of people came, for the figure seemed to have become a tourist fashion, and all wanted to know its meaning. Most took it for a portrait-statue, and the remnant were vacant-minded in the absence of a personal guide. None felt what would have been a nursery-instinct to a Hindu baby or a Japanese jinrickshaw-runner. The only exceptions were the clergy, who taught a lesson even deeper. One after another brought companions there, and apparently fascinated by their own reflection, broke out passionately against the expression they felt in the figure of despair, of atheism, of denial. Like the others, the priest saw only what he brought. Like all great artists, St. Gaudens held up the mirror and no more.

Borrowing from Shelley's imagery in his sonnet "Ozymandias," Adams sees himself as "landed, lost and forgotten, in the center of this vast plain of self-content"—the United States of the 1890s. He implies that he knows the meaning of the bronze figure in Rock Creek Cemetery, even if we do not. And the reason he knows it is that he has paid homage to the Egyptian Sphinx and the great Buddha (or Daibutsu) of Kamakura. He has been pulled by the Japanese jinricksha runner. He has traveled from Cairo to Asia, exploring what he calls "the edges of life—tropical islands, mountain solitudes, archaic law and retrograde types." And all these encounters, extending beyond the limited view of the Americans who stayed home, mark the beginning of the second half of his education.

The architect Henry Hobson Richardson weighed 345 pounds in his stocking feet and designed buildings of commensurable heft. Stone was his favorite material; he arranged it in Romanesque arches and turrets, built to last. The premier American architect of the Gilded Age, Richardson was a literate man who liked to argue, over copious meals and abundant liquor, the relative merits of the Gothic (bad) and the Romanesque (good). The foursquare possibilities of classic European architecture were his instrument, and he left behind enduring masterpieces such as Boston's Trinity Church and the Allegheny County Courthouse in Pittsburgh. Born and raised in New Orleans, educated at Harvard, and perfectly at home in Paris and London, Richardson gave an American ambition and swagger to his intellectual and aesthetic inheritance. Dressed in his bright yellow waistcoat, his opinions erupting like a series of cannon blasts, Richardson had a presence that "filled the mind as it did the eye," wrote Charles Francis Adams.

During the early months of 1884, two prominent friends of Richardson, his Harvard classmate Henry Adams and John Hay, approached him to build a "double house" for them in Washington. The site, Lafayette Square directly opposite the White House, could hardly be more conspicuous. Both Hay and Adams had their reasons for keeping an eye on the presidential residence. As a young man, Hay had served as Abraham Lincoln's private secretary, and he was writing a biography of that president; a gifted public servant, Hay knew he would serve the federal government again in some capacity. Adams, having shifted his base of operations from Boston to Washington, had assumed the unofficial post of historian of the early decades of the United States.

Adams and Hay were part of a tight circle of friends. With the mercurial

Clarence King—golden-haired scientist and aesthete, head of the U.S. Geological Survey, pioneering Pre-Raphaelite, mountaineer in the Sierras, and intrepid traveler in the South Seas—they formed a little club called the Five of Hearts. They met when they could (whenever King drifted into town) for tea, cards, and malicious gossip. Henry Adams's wife, Marian Hooper Adams—Clover to her friends—was the center of the club. Witty, diminutive, with a biting tongue, a "Voltaire in petticoats" according to her admirer Henry James, she served the tea and kept the repartee going. She was a skilled horsewoman and an accomplished amateur photographer; her portraits of her husband's circle—Richardson, Hay, King, and Henry Adams himself—remain the classic images of those important men.

Marian Hooper, 1869.

It was a sort of Washington Bloomsbury, with the brilliant Clover in the Virginia Woolf role, and there were secrets in the Five of Hearts comparable to any in the Bloomsbury circles. Some of the secrets were romantic. John Hay, that pillar of diplomatic skill who almost single-handedly brought the Russo-Japanese War to a close, was a married man. He was also deeply in love with Nannie Lodge, wife of the senator from Massachusetts (and Henry Adams's favorite student at Harvard), Henry Cabot Lodge. Clarence King, who had a penchant for exotic women—"King had no faith in the American woman; he loved types more robust," Adams wrote in his *Education*—had for many years maintained a secret common-law marriage with an African American woman in New York City. And Henry Adams himself was profoundly attracted to a newcomer in Washington circles, the stunningly beautiful Elizabeth Cameron, young wife of Senator Don Cameron of Ohio.

Clover's secret was more private still. Scornful of others and harsh on herself, she had lost her mother early and found herself unable to bear children of her own. Her closest tie was to her father, and his health, during the early 1880s, was fragile. Mindful perhaps of her husband's attentions to the young Mrs. Cameron, Clover felt increasingly isolated. And the occasional bouts of depression that had marked her early married life now extended into something more lasting and menacing.

Clover's condition had first surfaced during the Adamses' honeymoon trip to Egypt, in the fall of 1872. The couple could afford to allow three months for a leisurely journey from England to France and Germany, down to Italy, and on to Egypt, purchasing objects along the way for their new lodgings in Boston. By 1872 the Nile was a popular destination for upscale American tourists. The aging Emerson was on the Nile that summer, and so was the fourteen-year-old Theodore Roosevelt with his parents. The idea was to book passage on one of the boats called a *dahabeah,* which doubled as hotel room. First one made the slow journey to the sublime waterfall known as the First Cataract; then one changed to another boat for the six-hundred-mile journey downstream from Karnak to Memphis.

Henry Adams had a new camera and was eager to photograph the monuments of ancient Egypt. At each stop of the boat, he eagerly headed for the site. But Clover had no such pleasure, and a new note of anxiety enters her correspondence, a tortured sense of being overwhelmed by the temples and monuments. "I must confess," she wrote from Thebes, "I hate the process of seeing things which I am hopelessly ignorant of, and am disgusted at my want of curiosity. I like to watch pyramids, etc., from the boat, but excursions for hours in dust and heat have drawbacks to people so painfully wanting in enthusiasm as I am." A couple of days later she complained that "it is useless to try to tell you how it all looks. I never seem to get impressions that are worth anything, and I feel as if I were blind and deaf and dumb too."

Clover is voicing here a particularly American anxiety, a sense of the "burden of the past." Emerson, never one to carry the weight of the Old World willingly, felt a kindred oppression on his Nile journey; it was, he wrote in his journal, "a perpetual humiliation, satirizing and whipping our ignorance. . . . The Sphinxes scorn dunces; the obelisks, the temple walls, defy us with their histories we cannot spell." Clover learned from another traveler that Emerson had cut short his trip at Thebes and returned by train to Cairo. She found it "quite shocking" that Emerson "was not interested in Egyptian antiquities" but added that "temples do begin to pall. . . . How true it is that the mind sees what it has means of seeing. I get so little, while the others about me are so intelligent and cultivated that everything appeals to them." While Clover was "painfully wanting in enthusiasm," and feeling blind and deaf and dumb, she reported that Henry by contrast was "working like a beaver at photographing."

It was all too much for Clover, who experienced an emotional and psychological breakdown. As her biographer Otto Friedrich puts it, there was "something . . . bothering Clover, something about the awesome antiquity and grandiosity of those gigantic stone figures that stare blindly out from the temples of the upper Nile." There is in Clover's response something similar to those of other New England women oppressed by monumental Europe: Hawthorne's Miriam fainting in St. Peter's, and Henry James's Daisy Miller succumbing in the Colosseum. Clover's depression lifted when she and Henry Adams were back in Italy, though her swipe at the American sculptor William Wetmore Story for spoiling "nice blocks of white marble with his classic Sybils" also suggests her distaste for the monumental.

A dozen years had passed since that honeymoon on the Nile, years in which the Adamses had lived in several houses, first in Cambridge while Henry tried his hand at teaching at Harvard—a failure, in his jaundiced view—and at editing the *North American Review*, and then in Washington, his research for his *History* in the State Department archives interspersed with daily rides with Clover along the Potomac. As H. H. Richardson dawdled over every detail of the new house on Lafayette Square, and Clover and Henry argued over whether there should be any ecclesiastical "carving" on the stone exterior, plans for another journey together began to take shape. Adams had completed the first half of his history, taking the United States through Jefferson's second administration. There was no telling exactly when the house would be ready. The time seemed right for a respite.

The idea of a journey to Japan, as a sort of romantic reprise of the honeymoon on the Nile, had crystallized in Henry's mind by late 1884. Both he and Clover were enthusiastic collectors of Asian art and hoped to decorate the new house with fine Japanese things. Henry Adams had a scholarly interest in Japan as well and pored over articles on the origins of religion and law in the Far East. Soon after they first moved to Washington in 1878, Adams had become a close friend of the Japanese minister Kiyonari Yoshida. Yoshida was one of the first generation of Japanese officials to make themselves at home in America, and he and Adams enjoyed discussing the origins of archaic law. Yoshida gave Adams a sense of aristocratic Japan and taught him the game of Go, which Adams enthusiastically taught to other friends. On December 12, 1880, Clover reported to her father that Yoshida "has given Henry two water colours he brought him from Japan: one about four feet by two, by the best artist there, he says, Run Lin, a winter scene framed with brocade—it covers six feet of our bare wall in the front entry; the other is narrower and not so original, though very nice."

Clover's favorite cousin, Dr. William Sturgis Bigelow, provided an even deeper connection to Japan for the Adamses. Bigelow lived in Japan for seven years, traveling with Edward Morse and building up an extraordinary collection of Japanese art. It was his presence that made a

Japanese journey easy to contemplate for Clover and Henry Adams. On October 26, 1884, Adams informed John Hay that "the new Japanese minister brings me a strong letter from Bill Bigelow." Yoshida's replacement was Baron Ryuichi Kuki, the suave and extremely well informed Japanese aristocrat who had worked closely with Fenollosa and Okakura a couple of years earlier. Kuki's English was not as good as Yoshida's, but Adams was determined to cultivate him, especially after he learned that Kuki knew a great deal about Japanese art. Adams immediately began to arrange a social occasion for John La Farge, Clarence King, and John Hay to meet his friend "Cooky." H. H. Richardson might join the party as well, he told Hay. On November 16, impatient with his friends—"I could wait for you and Lafarge no longer"—Adams reported to Hay that "I had to have the Jap to dinner."

For Henry Adams, Baron Kuki "proved to be decidedly an interesting man." By March of the following year, Adams had sufficiently attuned his ears to Kuki's accent to enjoy regular visits with him, discussing Japanese "water-colors and bric-à-brack" and exchanging gifts. Kuki, he told Clover, "made to me a long speech to the effect that he wanted me to select among his kakimonos [sic] some that I would like. I of course accepted cordially with the remark that I would wait for your approval, as you knew more about the matter than I; and I hoped the minister would allow me to present him with some piece of European work in return."

Japan as Henry and Clover Adams conceived of it—an impression confirmed by the courtly Baron Kuki—was a world of aristocrats and connoisseurs, high ritual and deep wisdom, where exquisite gifts were exchanged rather than bought and sold. This idea was the perfect counterweight to the money-grubbing vulgarities of Gilded Age Washington under President Grant, a corrupt town that was unable to put the proper value on an Adams descended from Adamses. Confucian Japan knew about filial piety and respect for benevolent rulers. There, the scholar and the ruler were one, or so Henry Adams imagined it.

This idea of aristocratic Japan infiltrated the plans for the house on Lafayette Square. It was an idea that even H. H. Richardson with his Roman arches found appealing. As a result, the "double houses" began to diverge dramatically in concept. The Adams house was everything the Hay house was not. For John Hay, Richardson designed a house in the medieval and "Romanesque" style—first used in Trinity Church in Boston and in a hundred public libraries spread across New England—now known as Richardsonian. Hay's house was a four-story fortress with a turret on the corner. Wealthy and eager to show it, Hay spared no expense on gilded ornament and marble detailing.

Clover and Henry Adams wanted precisely the opposite, a plain house where function determined form. Clover in particular demanded a departure from what she called Richardson's "somewhat heavy monumental style." The Adamses expressed their desires largely by negation: they wanted no stained glass, no carving, "no nothing." They wanted "a square brick box" with a "flat roof." Above all, they wanted something utterly distinctive—"unutterably utter," as Adams put it. They wanted a house "original and pleasant to live in and look at"; as it neared completion, Adams wrote to an English friend: "The house would amuse you, for it is a new form of domestic architecture. . . . I foresee it will rouse a riot."

In their rejection of the heavy and "monumental," and their embrace of stripped-down simplicity and function, the Adamses were clearly heading toward an idea of "modern" architecture—in line with the ideas of the next generation of architects, Louis Sullivan and Frank Lloyd Wright. To their surprise, Richardson embraced their leanings. In fact, the double house expressed a certain doubleness in Richardson's own career, for by the 1880s he was beginning to move beyond the Romanesque toward a more "functional" architecture. As the architectural historian Marc Friedlaender notes, Richardson had often spoken of his wish to design grain elevators and riverboats. "This was the side of Richardson that enabled him to find appropriate forms for railroad stations and bridges, sleeping-cars, and warehouses; and that made him the first American architect successfully to accommodate utility to design."

Recent research has shown that as he tried to escape the "Richardsonian," Richardson found in Japanese architecture models for this shift in his work. Specifically, Edward Sylvester Morse, in his Lowell lectures at MIT in 1882 (later summarized and developed in his *Japanese Homes and Their Surroundings*), inspired particular buildings of Richardson's. A copy of the first edition of Morse's book was found in Richardson's private library. Some of Richardson's famous suburban railroad stations, key to his accomplishments during the 1880s, are modeled on Japanese prototypes from Morse's descriptions and photographs. Henry and Clover Adams gave Richardson the chance to apply these ideas to domestic architecture. The two houses, then, are Janus-like, the Hay half retrospective and the Adams half looking toward the future.

Whatever excitement Adams brought to planning the trip to Japan, and bringing Japanese touches to the house on Lafayette Square, was counterpoised by Clover's foreboding. She feared that the longueurs of sightseeing might match her disturbing experience of Egypt. Clover's distaste for the monumental now had two looming sources of anxiety: the temples of Japan, especially the great funerary shrines in Nikko that Henry was determined to visit, and her own endlessly delayed house. There were other clouds on the horizon. Clover's father, Dr. Hooper, was gravely ill, and she made an extended trip to Boston during the spring of 1885 to care for him. His death on April 13 plunged her into a depression that would not lift. While Henry was consumed with his plans for the future, Clover could not shift her mind from the past. A month of horseback riding at the rustic resort hotel in Sweet Springs, West Virginia, was a distraction, nothing more. In the absence of her father, Clover turned to her sister instead. "She was so tender and humble—" Ellen recalled, "and appealing when no human help could do anything—sorry for every reckless word or act, wholly forgotten by all save her. Her constant cry was 'Ellen I'm not real—oh make me real—You all of you—are real!' "

The new house, the impending pilgrimage to Japan—these, Henry Adams kept hoping, would lift Clover from the dark space in which she felt confined. But the prayed-for opening did not come. Instead, husband and wife engaged in obscure quarrels about this and that detail of the house. When Richardson placed an Assyrian lion backed by a cross, the ancient symbol of Saint Mark, between the arches at the entrance of the house, Adams exploded: it was precisely the kind of ecclesiastical carving he most detested in modern houses. He seemed unaware that his wife, shaken by her father's death, was increasingly drawn to exactly this sort of church ornament.

Toward the end of the summer of 1885, Clover seemed momentarily better, and the Adamses traveled to Saratoga Springs for a meeting of the American Historical Association in September. Henry's brother Charles Francis, never very fond of Clover, saw them on the return train and was shocked by her condition. He tried to talk to her. "She sat there pale and careworn, hardly making an effort to answer me, the very picture of physical weakness and mental depression." At this ill-timed juncture, Adams's publisher, Henry Holt, wrote to ask whether he might look for ways to push up the sales of the novel *Esther*, which Adams had published anonymously. Since the novel eerily predicted the sort of mental downslide of a Boston woman, seeking for spiritual solace after her father's death, that Clover was now enacting, Adams begged off. "I never had so many reasons for wishing to be left in peace just now," he wrote.

Sunday, December 6, 1885. Instead of writing her customary Sunday morning letter to her father, Clover sat at her desk in her upstairs study, which doubled as her darkroom, and drafted the opening lines of a letter to her sister Ellen. "If I had one single point of character or goodness I would stand on that and grow back to life," she wrote. "Henry is more patient and loving than words can express. God might envy him—he bears and hopes and despairs hour after hour." The letter broke off, and Clover placed it, unsent, on a corner of the desk. The house was empty. Henry, complaining of an aching tooth, had walked out in search of a dentist. When he returned he found a woman, an acquaintance of his wife, at the closed door. She had rung for Clover and received no response. Adams called up the stairs, then took them two at a time. He found Clover's contorted body, still warm, slumped heavily beside the fireplace. He lifted it to a sofa nearby and sent for a doctor. The smell of bitter almonds filled the closed room. She had drunk a vial of potassium cyanide—he recognized the odor—which she used to develop her photographs.

Life has strange ways of granting us our wishes. Adams had longed for a shift in the predictable pattern of his life: a grand new house, a sec-

ond wedding journey to renew his marriage, embarkation on the second
half of his *History* of the young United States. He had longed for change,
but nothing so radical as what Fate had dealt him. Shreds of myths hung
in the air—the husband seeking the radiance of the future turns back too
soon to share it with his wife, who is pulled ineluctably into the dark
underworld.

The childhood fear of being left behind in the world was now Adams's
daily reality. To Hay, who had offered condolence and companionship, he
wrote: "Nothing you can do will affect the fact that I am left alone in the
world at a time of life when too young to die and too old to take up existence
afresh. . . . I am going to keep straight on." That was his New Year's resolution: *to keep straight on.* Projects begun in partnership with Clover assumed new and unexpected meanings. The double house, built to their
desires, was sufficiently finished for him to move in, as planned, by New
Year's. But it was now more mausoleum than haven. The Japan journey,
that second honeymoon, he was determined to complete as well, though
now it would be as much a journey of mourning as of renewal. He would go
to Japan, he told Hay, "for no other object than to buy kakemonos for my
gaunt walls." The gauntness was spiritual as well as literal.

At this dead end, determined to "keep straight on," Henry Adams, who had
no appetite for a solitary pilgrimage, began to search for a companion for
his Japan journey. By a singular stroke of luck, he hit upon John La Farge.
They did not know each other well, the acerbic historian and the oblique
and fastidious artist; they had only a casual friendship to go on, nurtured
during the short period each had taught, with distaste, at Harvard. It was
during that Harvard year of 1876 that La Farge and Richardson had
worked side by side on Trinity Church in Boston, Richardson on the
building itself, La Farge on the interior decoration, and Adams had often
stopped by to check on the progress. In his novel *Esther,* Adams had
lightly fictionalized the proceedings. *Esther* takes as its central narrative
the design and construction of the church, with characters modeled on La
Farge, Clarence King, Phillips Brooks (the charismatic preacher of Trinity and a cousin of Henry Adams), and—as the woman torn between King
and Brooks, and despondent over the death of her father—Clover Adams.

A culminating scene is set by Niagara Falls. Clarence King read the book, was disappointed with the happy ending, and told Adams that he "ought to have made Esther jump into Niagara."

Unlike Hay and King, who had business and family concerns to keep them stateside, La Farge was desperate to leave the country and, as chance would have it, there was nowhere he would rather go than Japan. Had Adams issued his invitation a couple of years earlier, La Farge might have waved him away. During the early 1880s, flush with his success with Trinity, and with his potentially lucrative discovery of a method for making opalescent stained glass to rival that of the cathedrals of France, La Farge had set about building a New York business for the decoration of houses and churches. But the whole scheme collapsed under the twin

Henry Adams and Marquis, 1883.

strains of La Farge's commercial incompetence and a ruinous lawsuit with Louis Tiffany, who was experimenting with an opalescent recipe of his own. The episode reached its nadir during May 1885, when La Farge was arrested for allegedly stealing valuable drawings and documents from the offices—now in his partner's hands—of the La Farge Decorative

Art Company. The settlement left La Farge, fifty years old and at the top of his creative powers, humiliated and bankrupt.

With a wife and large family stowed away in Newport—he preferred to live alone in bachelor's quarters on Tenth Street in Manhattan—La Farge was desperate for money and took on more commissions than he could possibly complete. The most important of these was a mural for the Church of the Ascension, just around the corner from his studio. When Henry Adams approached him during that spring of 1886, La Farge was stalled on the enormous mural. He had made some preliminary sketches for the traditional subject of Jesus rising to Heaven with his disciples below and angels above. The background was giving him trouble, how-ever: how to make the ascending Christ and attendant angels look believ-able. Neither a historically correct Middle Eastern scene nor a wholly imaginary one seemed right for this modern-day mural. Perhaps, La Farge thought, the fabled sacred mountains of Japan would offer a solu-tion.

On June 3, as he was boarding a train in Boston bound for New York to retrieve La Farge, Adams heard from his brother Charles, head of the Union Pacific Railroad, that the luxurious and private "Director's Car" had arrived in Boston that morning and would return to Omaha the fol-lowing day. Charles wondered if Henry might like to use it. Adams made a brief detour, presumably by previous arrangement, to visit Augustus Saint-Gaudens in his New York studio. The sculptor had worked as La Farge's assistant at Trinity Church, and Clover had admired his work, taking particular pleasure in Saint-Gaudens's memorial for her cousin, Robert Gould Shaw, who had died with his Negro regiment in South Car-olina.

Adams asked Saint-Gaudens to design a bronze figure for the grave he would share with Clover. Adams already had definite ideas about what the monument should not be. It should not depict himself or Clover. It should not carry an inscription of any kind. It should not depict a male or female figure but rather, in some yet-to-be-determined synthesis, both in one. It should not evoke any traditional notion of the divine. Adams mentioned the seated Buddha as a possible template and may also, as Ed-ward Chalfant has suggested, have had in mind William Story's *Cleopa-tra*—a seated, cowled figure contemplating suicide. A boy, one of

Saint-Gaudens's models, happened to be in the studio that day. Adams grabbed an American Indian rug and draped it over the boy's head and shoulders, arranging the arms so that one hand reached up to the boy's chin. Something like that, he told Saint-Gaudens—and he was off.

Then Adams dragged La Farge, "in a disheveled and desperate, but still determined mind," away from his brushes and his paints. From Poughkeepsie, La Farge telegraphed the agent for the Cassell publishing firm that they would have to wait for his illustration of Shelley's "To a Skylark." La Farge paraphrased a line from the poem: "The purple evening melts around my flight." Already Adams was getting a taste of La Farge's mercurial temperament, so different from his own. La Farge, he wrote Hay, "makes a delicate humor glimmer about our path."

On the westward-moving train, Adams, hoping for some surcease from his feelings of guilt about Clover's death, studied the tenets of Buddhism in preparation for the arrival in Japan. He was particularly drawn to ideas about Nirvana, that extinction of individual personality and desire that was, in its Sanskrit meaning, likened to the blowing out of a candle. Meanwhile, La Farge, himself a student of the fleeting nature of existence, sat by the train window and sketched the passing plains and mountains. "La Farge's delight with the landscape was the pleasantest thing in the journey," Adams wrote.

The subtle exchanges that would mark this extraordinary friendship had begun, exchanges that would transform Adams into a more visual and less analytic writer—"Adams, you reason too much!" La Farge repeatedly admonished him—and La Farge into a writer of style and panache. The opera diva Helena Modjeska stopped by for a twelve-o'clock breakfast as they crossed the Humboldt River. In Omaha a young reporter, attracted by the spectacle of the solitary luxury car with its two occupants, shouted a question about their purpose in visiting Japan. La Farge, Adams wrote, "beamed through his spectacles the answer that we were in search of Nirvana." The young reporter, not to be outdone, made a quick rejoinder: "It's out of season!"

Late in life Henry Adams tried to find words for what he owed to John La Farge, the partner in travel who had so unexpectedly changed the tenor and the direction of his life. The trip to Japan that was to have been a second honeymoon had taken on the muted colors of a mourning journey; now it assumed, under La Farge's uninsistent instruction, the character of an education. Traveling with La Farge to Japan meant not only leaving the United States in a geographical sense but leaving it in a cultural sense as well. For Henry Adams, La Farge was himself a foreign land. If the United States stood for reason and smoothly running machinery, Adams decided, "La Farge alone owned a mind complex enough to contrast against the common-places of American uniformity." Americans were forever proclaiming their freedom and individuality, meanwhile settling for whatever was in fashion. La Farge, without trumpeting the fact, was the real, the wholly original thing.

With his intricate background—French by inheritance, American by residence, and Japanese by adoption—La Farge stepped nimbly outside whatever frame was meant to define him. As Adams wrote in his *Education:*

> The American mind,—the Bostonian as well as the southern or western,—likes to walk straight up to its object, and assert or deny something that it takes for a fact; it has a conventional approach, a conventional analysis, and a conventional conclusion, as well as a conventional expression, all the time loudly asserting its unconventionality. The most disconcerting trait of John La Farge was his reversal of the process. His approach was quiet and indirect; he moved round an object, and never separated it from its surroundings; he prided himself on faithfulness to tradition and convention; he was never abrupt and abhorred dispute.

La Farge's combination of conventional behavior with profoundly original thinking never ceased to surprise Adams during the Japan journey. "His manners and attitude towards the universe were the same," he wrote, "whether tossing in the middle of the Pacific Ocean sketching the trade-wind from a whale-boat in the blast of sea-sickness, or drinking the *cha-no-yu* in the formal rites of Japan."

T. S. Eliot once wrote of La Farge's friend and disciple Henry James that he had "a mind so fine that no idea could violate it." Adams conceived of La Farge in the same way, for La Farge did not so much have original ideas as have an original temperament. "One was never quite sure of his whole meaning until too late to respond," Adams noted, "for he had no difficulty in carrying different shades of contradiction in his mind. As he said of his friend Okakura, his thought ran as a stream runs through grass, hidden perhaps but always there; and one felt often uncertain in what direction it flowed, for even a contradiction was to him only a shade of difference, a complementary color, about which no intelligent artist would dispute." A self-portrait painted in 1859, laid out in the flattened forms of Japanese prints, perfectly captures that sinuous quality in La Farge. A winding path in a grassy meadow curves upward through the painting into a stand of trees. Standing at the lower edge of the path, his bent frame following the trajectory of the path's upward curve, La Farge looks almost sacerdotal with his black suit, his hands clasped on a walking stick, and his soft hat tilted into the trees.

If Henry Adams with his Maryland grandmother was "half-exotic" by background, John La Farge was close to the real thing. Born in 1835 in lower Manhattan, La Farge was descended from French émigrés on both sides of his family. His father had come to the New World with Napoleon's troops to put down Toussaint-Louverture's slave rebellion in the French colony of St. Domingue (the present-day Haiti). His mother's father had owned plantations in the West Indies. So La Farge, like that other French American painter Edgar Degas, could look back to an ambiguous family history of martial valor, slaveholding, and aristocratic pretensions. He grew up speaking French, and took some lessons in painting from his maternal grandfather, who specialized in miniatures. When it came time to choose a profession, he yielded to paternal pressure and settled on law, while continuing to paint and draw on the side.

During a year abroad in 1856, La Farge steeped himself in contemporary French art, meeting the Goncourt brothers and Baudelaire, and studying with the well-known romantic painter Thomas Couture. He continued his aesthetic education in New York, spending his free hours in the Pre-Raphaelite circle of the architect Richard Morris Hunt. The sudden death of La Farge's father in 1858 freed him from financial concerns. Richard Hunt encouraged La Farge to study with his painter brother William Morris Hunt, another Couture pupil, who worked and taught in Newport, Rhode Island.

La Farge settled in Newport during the spring of 1859. A picturesque and semirural town, with secluded beaches and unspoiled hills and dunes, Newport was not yet the Gilded Age resort of mansions and display that it was destined to be. Two gifted brothers in their late teens, William and Henry James, were also studying art with William Hunt. La Farge's imprint on Henry James was decisive—James called the painter his "initiator." At a time when James was vacillating between a career as an artist or one as a writer, La Farge nudged him toward writing and encouraged him to read the great French novelists. "Most of all," James later remembered, "he revealed to us Balzac. . . . To reread, even after long years, the introductory pages of *Eugénie Grandet*, breathlessly seized and earnestly absorbed under his instruction, is to see my initiator's youthful face, so irregular but so refined, look out at me between the lines as through blurred prison bars." La Farge's 1862 portrait of Henry James in profile—thoughtful, alert, the hint of a smile on the full lips—is a poignant memento of their friendship, and of the warm fellowship among aspiring artists during those Newport years.

Newport proved decisive for La Farge's growing passion for Japanese art. As a boy he had avidly read early travel accounts of voyages to the East. During his student year in Paris, before the Impressionist vogue for such things, he had become enamored of the "floating world" of Japanese prints. But Newport had its own Japanese valence. Like Salem, Newport had nurtured seafaring men; among these was the great opener of Japan, Matthew Calbraith Perry himself. The Perry family had continued to thrive in Newport. John La Farge met the young Margaret Perry, grandniece of the commodore, soon after his arrival in 1859. The match seemed fated: the artist destined to open Japan culturally, and a Perry descended from the commodore. The young lovers refused to allow religious differences—she was Anglican, he was Catholic—to interfere with their courtship. The Perrys spent the winter months at their plantation in the Bayou Teche region outside New Orleans. When La Farge heard rumors that Margaret had other suitors, he traveled immediately to Louisiana and proposed to her. They were married in 1860. La Farge brought back from Bayou Teche some deeply atmospheric landscapes and a bad case of malaria.

Barely five years had elapsed since Perry's Black Ships sailed into Edo Bay, and trade with Japan was a lively subject of discussion in the Perry circle. With Margaret's brother Thomas and their Newport friend and neighbor John Bancroft (son of the historian Frederic Bancroft), La Farge became involved in a scheme to import Japanese prints and other bric-a-brac to the United States. The Civil War put the Japan trade on hold—weapons and supplies, not exquisite handicrafts, were on the nation's trade agenda. But the porcelain vases and lacquer trays that filled La Farge's shelves and mantelpieces were soon put to unexpected use.

The Civil War hit La Farge hard emotionally. His grandfather had owned slaves in St. Domingue and participated in the slave trade in Africa; La Farge's substantial inheritance came from these sources. Still, he was a passionate Northerner, and only his bad eyes and the lingering effects of malaria kept him from the battlefield. "The war upset all my notions of the future I had sketched out," he wrote. He remained in Newport, "deeply interested in the war, and regretting having no chance to take any part in it." Instead, he and Bancroft pored over their Japanese treasures—"we had at that time no persons interested in such things"— and tried to make sense of the emotional appeal of their bold combinations of color.

La Farge was groping for a visual language to express his profound feelings about the Civil War, and he found it in these Japanese things, so redolent of fragile grace and vulnerability. The bombastic rhetoric of the war—the fiery speeches in Congress, the "Battle Hymn of the Republic" by the Newport visitor Julia Ward Howe—awakened no feeling in La Farge. The death of young men called for some finer, quieter response. What La Farge achieved in Newport during the Civil War years was an alternative American aesthetic, directly in opposition to the monumental and grandiloquent ethos of American art of the period. The age wanted panoramic views; La Farge offered intimate glimpses. The age wanted solidity; La Farge preferred melting and mists. The age wanted Niagara Falls (and got it in Frederick Church's mural-size rendition); La Farge preferred a backyard rivulet. The age warmed to the expansive seascapes of La Farge's friend John Kensett; La Farge placed a seashell on a fragment of velvet instead. The age was assertively masculine; La Farge, by his own admission, had feminine tastes and tendencies.

La Farge's Japan-inspired still lifes from the war years are almost unbearably poignant. Like the rhetoric-shunning miniatures of Emily Dickinson, or the understated saltwater marshes of Martin Johnson Heade, they stake out a private emotional territory sheltered from the grand outpourings of public grief. La Farge's intense paintings during the early 1860s repeatedly used Japanese subjects and materials. He assembled still lifes in which a closed Japanese world was convened in the picture frame. His *Flowers in a Japanese Vase* of 1864 depicts a sturdy cylindrical vase of black-glazed porcelain on a metallic base. The background is a gilded Japanese screen with vaguely discernible pines and mountains and clouds. The vase, brimming over with roses and carnations, is slightly off center; the asymmetry is balanced in turn by the shadow of the vase, and by the painter's calling card, on which lies—it has fallen from the vase—a single bachelor's button. The calling card doubles as the painter's signature, and the bachelor's button gives the whole picture a suggestion of alienation and loneliness. The painting has the force of a confession; it is, like those ink paintings of lone trees that stand in for Chinese scholar-painters of the Yuan period, a self-portrait of a special kind. The contemporary art historian Henry Adams sees premonitions of death in the fallen flower and the vase "shaped like one of the broken-column grave markers of a New England cemetery."

La Farge rapidly progressed from painting Japanese subjects—porcelain bowls and gilded screens and abalone shells—to using Japanese materials in his art. Instead of primed canvas, he experimented with oil paint applied directly to wood panels—many of which were Japanese lacquered trays. The most astonishing of these works is his *Roses on a Tray*, painted around 1861. It is a picture of a Japanese lacquered tray painted *on* a Japanese lacquered tray. Translucent, wind-ruffled curtains are the backdrop for the drama on this little stage, barely a foot by a foot and a half in size. Roses gathered like shipwrecked sailors on a raft float across an iridescent windowsill. Again La Farge had found in Japanese motifs and objects an echo for the emotions of the war. In opening himself to Japan, he opened secrets of Japanese art to an American audience.

The decade after war's end was a difficult one for La Farge, physically, financially, and emotionally. The malaria he had contracted in Louisiana continued to bother him, compounded, in 1866, by a debilitating nerve condition that afflicted his hands and knees, and was traceable, he believed, to lead poisoning from his oil paints. During the late 1860s and into the 1870s he painted little. The first few years of La Farge's family life had floated along on his considerable inherited fortune and the steady growth of his family, seven children born almost annually from 1862 on. But his sales and commissions were limited, while his taste for a luxurious lifestyle was pronounced. The La Farges found themselves verging on bankruptcy. During one particularly difficult period, they were forced to flee Newport under cover of night to avoid creditors, leaving, according to Henry James, "prodigious debts behind them, and one silver spoon in the side-board drawer; the servant's wages unpaid, the house dismantled of its richest ornaments."

The sense of drift and anomie in La Farge's life ended abruptly in 1876, when his career took a decisive new direction. One provocation was the Centennial Exhibition in Philadelphia, at which La Farge haunted the Japanese exhibits, learning all he could from the decorative spirit of the porcelains and prints on show. It was a stroke of singular good fortune that at precisely this moment La Farge was approached by H. H. Richardson to oversee the decoration of Trinity Church, which Richardson was building on Copley Square in the center of Boston. Here was a vast canvas on which La Farge could experiment with some new ideas about "Oriental" decoration, especially involving asymmetrical motifs and patterns. He had come to love the lighting effects of stained glass, and in Trinity he achieved spectacular results with the opalescent glass he had developed.

The Centennial Exhibition and the Trinity commission called for some new direction in La Farge's painting. He found it in the humble challenges of watercolor, long regarded as a medium for amateurs and women. La Farge treated watercolor with ambition and seriousness. In retrospect one can see that the small still lifes of the 1860s aspired to a liquid iridescence. Something about the medium itself—that it was water and produced watery effects—appealed at the deepest level to La Farge's fluid temperament. Water lilies—twenty years before Monet's

Nymphaea—became an obsessive subject for La Farge, fraught with private meanings. Then, in 1879, came the masterpiece of this phase of La Farge's work, the wonderful *Chinese Pi-tong* in the Fogg Museum at Harvard. Painted on a square sheet of paper, it is a tour de force of watercolor effects. Again, the asymmetry of the placement of the vase is key, giving a dynamism to the picture, as though the horseman and dog on the vase are literally driving it across the seemingly liquid surface of the lacquered table.

La Farge's precocious, passionate, and sustained engagement with Japanese art was unmatched by any American of his time. For fifty years John La Farge was the artist most responsible for introducing Japanese ideas and methods into American art. Even before the French Impressionists and their associates began raiding Japanese prints for innovative designs and subject matter, La Farge was collecting them in Paris. The clever naturalistic eye of Hokusai captivated him, and he refined his admiration in a pioneering essay on Japanese art contributed in 1869 to his friend Raphael Pumpelly's account of a tour of the world. For La Farge, it was never a matter of simply adopting this or that Japanese artistic medium or technique—a kind of paper, a calligraphic brush—to produce a particular effect. From his first months as an artist around 1859 until his death in 1910, La Farge continually returned to Japanese sources—in art, religion, folklore, and philosophy—to see what new things he could learn there.

By an extraordinary stroke of luck—though luck goes to those prepared to make use of it—it was during the most intense phase of La Farge's involvement with watercolor that Henry Adams asked his old Harvard friend to accompany him to Japan, all expenses paid. Adams was seeking to fill the gap that Clover's suicide had opened in his life. A kindred gap had opened in La Farge's life. It had taken longer to manifest itself than the sudden rupture of Adams's existence but was no less painful. While the early years of La Farge's marriage were harmonious enough, he and Margaret had found they had sparse emotional resources for dealing with financial and other difficulties. What began as business trips to New York or Boston in search of commissions, especially after the Trinity triumph, steadily hardened into parallel lives, with Margaret staying home in Newport with the family and La Farge living as a bachelor in his old Tenth Street haunts in New York. When Margaret's grandmother died in 1872, leaving her an inheritance, Margaret bought a house of her own in downtown Newport, the title, pointedly, in her name only.

La Farge's children grew up without a father. The more forgiving among them, such as his son John, later a luminary in the American Jesuit order, found a pocket of virtue in their father's selfishness: "With all his faults, there is one thing with which my father cannot be charged, and that is hypocrisy. He never tried to justify his neglect of his home or his family. His conscience remained clear as to principles. He knew his real responsibility, and he was always uneasy on this matter, and would therefore come back home quite unexpectedly and would be all the more concerned when he was away." But there was something else in La Farge's isolation as well, not covered by the claims of commissions or the steady demands for work. There are hints of his emotional unease in his fastidious aversion to shaking hands or, for that matter, to any physical touching. His friend Royal Cortissoz begins his biography of La Farge with this detail as though it is the key to his character: "It was characteristic of John La Farge that he had a distaste for the promiscuous shaking of hands. Something in him shrank with almost feminine sensitiveness from all personal contacts."

La Farge's closest friends wrote in the same insinuating way about his eccentricities. There is Henry James's strange remark about La Farge peering through the prison bars of Balzac's prose—as though La Farge lived a life of confinement. The character based on La Farge in Henry Adams's *Esther* has a shameful secret, which turns out to be the immigrant wife with whom he is afraid to be seen in public. And then there is the confessional nature of certain images in La Farge's own pictures, most poignantly the fallen bachelor's button on the calling card. La Farge preferred the company of men—either cultured companions like Adams or Cortissoz, or exquisite Asian men like Okakura who made little claim on him. Being a good Catholic and striving to be a good father led to guilt, and awkward attempts to reconnect with his children. By the time Adams invited La Farge to travel to Japan, the rift with Margaret was all but final.

In this fraught context, John La Farge's stated reason for going to

Japan, to find a background suitable for his Ascension mural, his painting on the church wall, takes on added emotional coloring. It is, in retrospect, as personal a confession as Adams's search for Japanese decor for his own "gaunt walls." Technical problems were always spiritual and emotional problems as well for La Farge. The two bachelors, Adams and La Farge, "walled in" by circumstance, set out in search of a magical landscape—call it Nirvana, call it Ascension—a plane of existence above the cracks in their own broken lives.

FALLING WATER

>< >< ><

The Master stood by a river and said: "Everything
flows like this, without ceasing, day and night."

—CONFUCIUS, *THE ANALECTS*, 9.17

After a century of civil strife ending with the decisive battle of Sekigahara in
1600, the warlords of the Tokugawa family brought peace and unity to
Japan. It was a harsh peace of authority and subjugation, administered
from the Tokugawa castle town of Edo. A country redoubt when the first
Tokugawa overlord (or shogun) Ieyasu consolidated his power, Edo
steadily grew over 250 years of Tokugawa rule until it became the sprawl-
ing "eastern capital" of Tokyo (as opposed to Kyoto, the western capital,
where the emperor powerlessly lived on). Edo was a city of court admin-
istrators, merchants, armed samurai, and hostages. The 260 or so feudal
lords, or daimyo, of outlying provinces were required to live in alternate
years at the shogunal court. Their wives and heirs were obliged to live
there permanently, to guarantee good behavior and prevent conspiracies
among the daimyo. The festive arrival and departure of a daimyo was a
significant part of the high ritual of Edo life. The daimyo and their en-
tourages of hundreds of retainers would travel with great pomp from station to station on the famous Tokaido Road, which ran along the spine of
the main island of Honshu. These stations—with their inns and teahouses, their courtesans and famous views—became in turn the subjects
for the great woodblock artists of the late eighteenth and early nineteenth
centuries, Hokusai and Hiroshige.

Pomp and ritual were key to Tokugawa power; the shoguns, especially the first and third, Ieyasu and Iemitsu, were revered like the Roman emperors Julius Caesar and Augustus. Great leaders require great tombs. After Ieyasu's death, in 1616, the year Shakespeare died, one of the great Shinto shrines, the Toshogu Shrine in Nikko, was built to house his mausoleum. A thickly wooded refuge in the foothills of the sacred mountain Nantaizan, Nikko lies ninety miles to the north and slightly west of Tokyo. The village of Nikko is accessible by a single road, and the approach is shaded for twenty miles with giant cedarlike cryptomeria trees. By the late nineteenth century, these majestic trees were between 60 and 120 feet tall. Until the Meiji Restoration, only priests and Tokugawa family members, along with their attendant samurai and servants, were allowed to visit sacred Nikko.

Through the centuries Tokugawa artists and architects were hired to use the mountain flanks of Nikko as a giant canvas for their fantasies. Travelers entered the little village from the south, then crossed Nikko's rushing river by an ordinary bridge. The neighboring "Sacred Bridge," made of wood with an overlay of red lacquer and gold, was reserved for the shogun and the emperor. Directly across the bridge, a torii, two vertical beams with a horizontal one balanced across them, opened to a monumental stone staircase that led, thousands of steps and then a broad pathway later, to the burial shrines of Ieyasu and Iemitsu. Tokugawa taste ran to gilded splendor and rococo elaboration. Even the wells and stables of the shrines were decorated with infinite care. On one side of the stables a sculptor depicted with supreme wit the three monkeys that see, speak, and hear no evil. Beyond the main complex of Toshogu Shrine is a door leading to another set of stone steps. Over the door is a famous carving called the *nemuri no neko*, or "sleeping cat." The steps lead up into the pines. Here, in an austere enclosure, is the tomb of Ieyasu. Gilding and whimsy are left behind, and the martial spirit of the Tokugawas in their early generations—the samurai code of honor and austerity—is palpable in the simple bronze grave marker with subdued Buddhist motifs.

With the fall of the Tokugawa reign in 1868 (when Edo was renamed Tokyo), and the restitution of the Meiji emperor, Nikko's significance suffered a change. No longer the sacred burial ground of the ruling family, Nikko retained its luster. And, with the gradual opening of Japan,

Nikko became the one essential destination for foreign travelers. To Nikko came the intrepid British travel writer Isabella Bird in 1878. The following year Ulysses S. Grant, the American Mikado, made a well-publicized visit, gracefully refusing to use the Sacred Bridge reserved for the emperor. Traveling to Japan and not seeing Nikko was like going all the way to Egypt—with which Nikko was always compared—and somehow missing the pyramids. "Who has not seen Nikko," as La Farge quoted the familiar proverb, "cannot say beautiful (*kekko*)."

"Do you happen to know where Nikko is?" Henry Adams wrote to his friend John Hay on July 24, 1886. "If not, I cannot tell you. All I know is that it is in a valley among some green mountains in the insides of Japan; that it is pretty; that the hour is 8 A.M. of a sweet morning; that I am lying, in a Jap *kimono* on the upper verandah of the smallest doll-house your children ever saw; that La Farge is below, in the bath-room, painting our toy-garden, with its waterfall and miniature mountains, and that at nine o'clock we are to step down to the Fenollosas to breakfast."

Adams and La Farge had arrived in Yokohama three weeks earlier, on Friday, July 2, after a rough Pacific crossing, four calm days out of sixteen. Adams, prone to seasickness, wrote that they had been "more miserable by the linear inch than ever two woebegone Pagans, searching Nirvana, were before." As their steamer, *The City of Sidney*, sailed into the bay, they were struck, not for the last time, by how much Japan resembled the woodblock prints. As La Farge wrote:

We were in the great bay when I came up on deck in the early morning. The sea was smooth like the brilliant black paper of the prints; a vast surface of water reflecting the light of the sky as if it were thicker air. Far-off streaks of blue light, like the finest washes of the brush, determined distances. Beyond, in a white haze, the square white sails spotted the white horizon and floated above it.

The slackened beat of the engine made a great noise in the quiet waters. Distant high hills of foggy green marked the new land; nearer us, junks of the shapes you know, in violet transparency of shadow, and five or six war-ships and steamers, red and black, or white, looking barbarous and out of place . . . and spread all around us a fleet of small boats, manned by rowers standing in robes flapping about them, or tucked in above their waists.

There to receive them on the picturesque and bustling quay, or Bund as it was called, after its Shanghai counterpart, was William Sturgis Bigelow, who claimed to have been expecting them for a month. Tall and upright, bearded and handsome in formal Japanese kimono, Bigelow concealed his shyness beneath a military bluff. When Adams had last seen Bigelow, Clover's favorite cousin, in Washington, he was anxious and sunk in depression, in flight from Boston and all it stood for. Now Bigelow— whose own mother had committed suicide, thus linking him to Adams's particular suffering—struck Adams as "an angel of good-humor and unselfishness." He guided them to their rooms at the Yokohama Grand Hotel on the Bund, a stately and foursquare structure with balconies looking out over the bay. They explored the neighborhood by jinricksha, buying cheap souvenirs; again, everything seemed uncannily familiar, already seen, already known. "Wearied by the novelty, every detail of which, however, was known to us before," wrote La Farge, "we walked back in the white, milky sunset, which was like a brilliant twilight."

During the day on the Fourth of July, Bigelow took Adams and La Farge by train to Tokyo, twenty miles north, to visit Fenollosa, a professor at Tokyo Imperial University and recently named Imperial Commissioner of Fine Arts. From the courtly and formal Fenollosa they received their first lessons in early Buddhist art, which Fenollosa—always looking for parallels between Japanese art and European masterpieces—considered on a par with the early Italian art of Giotto and Cimabue. As Fenollosa unrolled scrolls from his private hoard, La Farge, at least, was convinced: "I dislike to use analogies, but before these ancient religious paintings of Buddhist divinities, symbolical of the elements or of protective powers, whose worn surfaces contained marvels of passionate delicacy and care framed in noble lines, I could not help the recall of what I had once felt at the first sight of old Italian art."

Later that day the three friends ventured to a club in the foreign neighborhood called the Bluff, above Yokohama, to watch No plays. "The monotony of impression," La Farge wrote, "was too novel to me to become wearisome." Adams, showing no such tact, found no pleasure in having to "sit on your heels all through five hours at the theatre." Later that night—it was still the Fourth of July—Adams and La Farge could view the American Independence Day fireworks over Yokohama Bay from their rooms in the Grand Hotel.

Such ambitiously scheduled days reflect a sense of urgency: a cholera epidemic had broken out in Yokohama, with mounting deaths reported in the *Japan Weekly Mail.* During their week of residence at Yokohama, Adams and La Farge made daily trips to Tokyo, visiting (under the tutelage of Bigelow and Fenollosa) temples and tombs in Ueno Park—the huge central park of the city—and the shops of dealers. These sightseeing forays betrayed the twin purposes of Adams's Japan journey: to collect impressions and ideas for the monument over Clover's grave, and to collect objects for his own Washington home and for the houses of friends and relatives. He was particularly attentive to the carved mortuary art of the temples in Shiba, underlining in his 1884 edition of John Murray's popular *Hand-book for Travellers in Central and Northern Japan* details such as the "two curiously carved stones dating from 1644, the subject of one being the Entry into Nirvana . . . and of the other the five-and-twenty Boddhisattvas coming with Amitabha (Amida) to welcome the departed soul."

Adams was disappointed in the offerings in Tokyo. "Japan has been cleaned out," he complained to John Hay. "Kakimonos are not to be got. . . . Fine old porcelain is rare and dear. Embroideries are absolutely introuvable. Even books seem scarce." He failed to note the irony that one reason the market was so competitive was that Fenollosa and Bigelow, along with their friend Edward Morse, had already bought thousands of rare objects destined for the Museum of Fine Arts in Boston.

Barely a week into their stay, the mounting cholera epidemic forced a change of plans for Adams and La Farge. Instead of a tour of Kyoto and Nara to the west, where the great temples and cultural centers lay, the cooler mountain climes of Nikko, where Fenollosa and Bigelow had summer houses, promised a healthier destination. The trip overland from Tokyo to Nikko, which Adams and La Farge began on Sunday, July 11, devolved from train to jinricksha, with a stopover in the railroad junction of Utsunomiya. The heat was unbearable, and so were the smells. Open sewers in Tokyo and night soil in the fields shocked Adams's sensibilities. "Tokyo is beastly," he wrote, "nothing but a huge collection of villages, scattered over miles after miles of flat country; without a building fit to live in, or a sewer to relieve the stench of several hundred thousand open privies." The surrounding countryside was just as bad, however, "one vast, submerged rice-field, saturated with the human excrement of many generations of Japanese." Japanese food was inedible, in Adams's opinion, and the green tea was "nauseous." He lived on a diet of boiled rice, black tea brought from home, and cans of mulligatawny soup.

In Utsunomiya, in a noisy Japanese-style inn, Adams and La Farge spent a sleepless night listening to sliding doors slam and bathers shout in the public bath. Both men suffered from food poisoning. By the time the travelers, bouncing around in a horse cart that "understood jouncing," reached the majestic road lined with towering cryptomeria trees leading to Nikko, torrential rains forced them to finish their journey on foot. Exhausted, they collapsed in the little house by the garden—the same house in which Isabella Bird had stayed eight years earlier. "La Farge and I occupy a baby-house, of four rooms," Adams wrote. "We sleep in the two upper rooms, which are open to the air, when we do not draw our paper windows together." Bigelow had made arrangements for use of the house with a priest at one of the temples. It was part of a little cluster of houses up the river from the Japanese village. The Japanese, as Adams wrote, "leave these superb mountain flanks to monkeys, deer and Americans."

Breakfast they took with the Fenollosas, in what Adams called their "more imposing Japanese house" below. The food was American, to Adams's intense relief, but the leisurely meal doubled as a sustained tutorial in Japanese art and religion. Bigelow, Fenollosa, and the newly arrived Kakuzo Okakura provided the expertise. In Okakura, Fenollosa's extraordinarily well informed assistant, La Farge and Adams found someone who could answer their many questions about Asian philosophy and religion.

Then up from Osaka and Tokyo, like another summer storm, came dealers who showered their wares—"stuffs, lacquers, metal-work, books, pictures, crystals and all the curios of Japan"—on this wealthy group of potential buyers. Adams, as he had in Tokyo, bought everything that Bigelow or Fenollosa thought was good, and much that they didn't. Fenollosa prided himself on his knowledge of early Buddhist art and dismissed anything made or painted under the Tokugawa regime. For Old Japan—Japan before Perry—he substituted a Japan still older, before the Tokugawa. He particularly despised the "ukiyoe" art so beloved of Impressionist painters—images of the brothels and theaters of the "floating world"—and scoffed at Adams's taste for such prints and other popular art. He insisted on giving Adams a copy of a recent article he had written for the *Japan Weekly Mail*, in which he attacked Hokusai in terms that reveal his own class anxiety. "In the case of Hokusai and the Ukiyoe," Fenollosa maintained, "we miss all that indefinable something which is implied in the word 'taste,' and we hear only the clever talk of the barber and bartender."

Adams found Fenollosa's rigid and humorless opinions on Japanese culture—his dismissal of Japanese prints and hushed veneration of Buddhist art—hard to take. "Fenollosa is a tyrant who says we shall not like any work done under the Tokugawa Shoguns," he told John Hay. "He is now trying to prevent my having a collection of Hokusai's books. He is a kind of St Dominic, and holds himself responsible for the dissemination of useless knowledge by others. My historical indifference to everything but facts, and my delight at studying what is hopefully debased and degraded, shock his moral sense. I wish you were here to help us trample on him," Adams concluded. "He has joined a Buddhist sect; I was myself a Buddhist when I left America, but he has converted me to Calvinism with leanings towards the Methodists."

It was Nikko with its great mortuary shrines that had originally prompted Adams's journey to Japan; he had hoped to share it with Clover. And with Nikko, its setting and its buildings, he was not disappointed. "In truth the place is worth coming to see," he wrote. "Japan is not the last word of humanity, and Japanese art has a well-developed genius for annoying my prejudices; but Nikko is, after all, one of the sights of the world." It was the overall effect of the place, its singleness of conception, that amazed Adams: "Photographs give no idea of the scale. They show here a gate and there a temple, but they cannot show twenty acres of ground, all ingeniously used to make a single composition. They give no idea of a mountain-flank, with its evergreens a hundred feet high, modelled into a royal, posthumous residence and deified abode. I admit to thinking it a bigger work than I should have thought possible for Japs. It is a sort of Egypt in lacquer and greenth." To another correspondent he wrote that Nikko "is so well worth seeing that in many ways nothing in Europe rivals it. I should class it very high among the sights of the world. . . . Sky, mountains, and trees are exquisite."

On July 21, 1886, one week into his sojourn in Nikko, Adams set the watery scene for friends at home: "Heavy rains have come. The mountains are lost in mist. The temples and tombs of the Shoguns drip with moisture. When the sun comes out, the sudden heat gives one a vapor bath. I wrap myself in my Japanese dress, and lie on my verandah, reading and sleeping, while La Farge sketches our little temple-garden, with its toy waterfall, miniature rocks and dwarf trees."

Listening to the patter of intermittent rain, Adams passed hour after hour on the polished veranda overlooking the garden, writing letters and reading Dante's *Paradiso*. From time to time he drew a lazy analogy between the Nirvana of the Buddhists and Dante's celestial vision. When the sky momentarily cleared, he had a servant drag out Bigelow's heavy camera for a photograph of the garden. To Elizabeth Cameron he wrote: "I enclose a photograph of our garden-waterfall. It splashes a great deal, with very little water."

La Farge, meanwhile, sketched and drafted his "Artist's Letters." Sitting in the bathroom—the room, that is, that enclosed the Japanese bath—below the veranda, he too looked out on the garden with its central waterfall. "We have a little fountain in the middle of the garden, which gives the water for our bath, and sends the noisy stream rolling through the wooden trough of the wash-room. The fountain is made by a bucket placed upon two big stones, set in a basin, along whose edge grow the iris, still in bloom. A hidden pipe fills the bucket, and a long, green bamboo makes a conduit for the water through the wooden side of our house." The

John La Farge.

waterfall, which so annoyed Adams, enthralled La Farge. "I sit in the bath-
room and paint this little picture through the open side, while A——, upstairs in the veranda, is reading in Dante's 'Paradiso,' and can see, when
he looks up, the great temple room of the Buddhist Mangwanji."

La Farge sketched the little waterfall in pencil and painted it in
watercolor—the perfect medium for this floating world. The whole scene
tugged at him; he wrote that he felt, obscurely, that he had always known
this scene: "What I see here that I admire I feel as though I had always
known, had already seen." The image of the waterfall in the garden became his favorite Japanese scene and recurred again and again in his
paintings, murals, and stained glass long after his return to America. For
La Farge, the view of the waterfall in the garden was intimately tied up
with conversations he was having in Nikko—sometimes over breakfast at
the Fenollosas', sometimes in the little garden by the priest's house. Before leaving America, La Farge had studied Edward Morse's book on
Japanese homes and their surroundings. Now, under Okakura's careful
guidance, he was learning the philosophy behind the Japanese house. He

was learning about Lao Tzu's conception of the Tao, or Way. And he was reading Lao Tzu's great contemporary, Confucius. La Farge was particularly drawn to the tenets of Taoism (then all but unknown in America), the doctrine of yielding and constant change. He called a chapter in his *Artist's Letters from Japan*, most of which he drafted in Nikko, "Tao: The Way."

Improvisatory in form and content, the chapter lays out, in a stream-of-consciousness cascade, some of the ideas that La Farge and Adams were exploring in Japan. Chief among them was the conviction that architects and artists in the West had lost the sense of how to build a monument—"the impossibility of finding a designer today capable of making a *monument:* say, for instance, a tomb, or a commemorative, ideal building—a cathedral, or a little memorial." Suddenly, as he meditated on the Taoist notion of yielding rather than force, he had an epiphany about the subtle power of Japanese architecture. "When I began to reflect how this wood and plaster had more of the dignity of art and of its accessible beauty than all that we have at home, if melted together, would result in; that these frail materials conveyed to the mind more of the eternal than our granite, it seemed to me that something was absolutely wrong with us."

There, in the opposition of "frailty" versus "granite," is the great aesthetic realization of La Farge's stay in Nikko. "Nothing in the world / is as soft and yielding as water," wrote Lao Tzu.

> Yet for dissolving the hard and inflexible,
>   nothing can surpass it.
> The soft overcomes the hard;
>   the gentle overcomes the rigid.

"After many years of willful energy, of forced battle that I have not shunned," La Farge mused, "I like to try the freshness of the springs, to see if new impressions come as they once did in childhood." He was learning the lessons of the Tao.

When it didn't rain, Lizzie Millett Fenollosa—a great favorite with both La Farge and Adams—proposed treks on horseback into the surrounding countryside in search of waterfalls larger than the trickle in the garden. Nikko is a valley with steep sides, and during the rainy season numerous waterfalls cascade down toward the river. La Farge was particularly struck by the Buddhist meanings attributed to waterfalls. Under Okakura's tutelage, he learned that waterfalls expressed for Buddhists the flow of life. La Farge was delighted to find that Kannon, the androgynous Buddhist deity of mercy, was often portrayed sitting beside a sheet of falling water. He sketched in one of the temples at Nikko a picture "hanging on the wall, which faces the mountain and the tomb [of Ieyasu], in which Kuwan-on the Compassionate sits in contemplation beside the descending stream of life."

"Of all the images that I see so often," he wrote later in his *Artist's Letters*, "the one that touches me most—partly, perhaps, because of the Eternal Feminine—is that of the incarnation that is called Kuwan-on, when shown absorbed in the meditations of Nirvana. You have seen her in pictures, seated near some waterfall, and I am continually reminded of her by the beautiful scenes about us, of which the waterfall is the note and the charm. Were it not that I hate sightseeing, I should have made pilgrimages, like the good Japanese, to all the celebrated ones which are about."

For Adams, by contrast, waterfalls were the bane of existence in Nikko. "Mrs. Fenollosa drags us to see waterfalls day and night," he complained. "We have a friendly flea at times, and mosquitoes, horse-flies, black flies, and waterfalls. Of the lot I prefer the mosquitoes, but the fleas have points." Only one of the destinations moved him: a deserted little temple, "buried in forests and unworried by tourists," by a skein of cascading rivulets called Somentaki (or Somen-ga-taki). "Now and then, early in the morning, I start off with a boy carrying Sturgis Bigelow's camera," he wrote, "and I photograph a temple or some accident that interests me." Somentaki interested him. Adams photographed it several times, reveling in its picturesque decay. He wrote on the back of one photograph (the basis for a now-lost watercolor of La Farge): "The little shrine and waterfall (taki) at the entrance to the temple. All overgrown with lichens, moss and shrubs." But the allure was the absence: "its value," as Edward Chalfant notes, "began with its desertion." This was the kind of "anti-monument" in the presence—or absence—of which Adams could mourn in peace.

The most ambitious of Lizzie Fenollosa's trips, with Adams and Bigelow in tow, led up from Nikko to the lake of Chuzenji, a sheet of blue water circled with mountain peaks that Adams thought resembled the Sierras. A few minutes away from the lake is the dazzling ribbon of falling, twisting water called Kegon Falls. After a short break by the lake, the party ventured higher still, to the hot springs of Yumoto, which Adams—recalling the last two places he had traveled with Clover—called "the Saratoga, or White Sulphur, of Japan." In Yumoto, something other than waterfalls took him by surprise.

Among Adams's many disappointments with Japan—its nauseating food, its stenches and stinks, its diminutive waterfalls—none is more insistent in his letters than his dismay at Japanese women. His friend Clarence King, himself devoted to the charms of exotic women, had hoped that Adams might find in Japanese women, and especially geisha, some erotic distraction from his loss of Clover. La Farge, convinced that the aristocratic "institution" of geisha was "a reminder of old, complete civilizations like that of Greece," hired two geisha to perform in their house in Nikko and sketched one of them dancing. Adams refused to be enticed—"Wooden, jerky, and mechanical" was how he described them in a letter. "The women all laugh," he told Hay, "but they are obviously wooden dolls, badly made, and can only cackle, clatter in pattens over asphalt pavements in railway stations, and hop or slide in heel-less straw sandals across floors. I have not yet seen a woman with any mechanism better than that of a five-dollar wax doll; but the amount of oil used in fixing and oiling and arranging their hair is worth the money alone."

Entering the gates of the hot springs village of Yumoto, Adams was momentarily transfixed. "I saw at last the true Japan of my dreams," he told Hay, "and broke out into carols of joy. In a wooden hut, open to all the winds, and public as the road, men, women and children, naked as the mother that bore them, were sitting, standing, soaking and drying themselves, as their ancestors had done a thousand years ago." This vision of naked bathers "who paid not the smallest regard to our presence" delighted Adams, with his taste for the "primitive." But he was unsettled by one bather who did seem aware of his presence. "I should except one pretty girl of sixteen, with quite a round figure and white skin. I did notice that for the most part, while drying herself, she stood with her back to us. When this exceptionally pleasing virgin walked away, I took no further interest in the proceedings, though I still regard them as primitive."

A few days later, realizing that he might seem to be backsliding in his views of Japanese women, he added a few lines to his ongoing letter to Hay. "As for returning to my remarks on Yumoto as connected with the sexes, I decline to do it. In spite of [Clarence] King, I affirm that sex does not exist in Japan, except as a scientific classification. I would not affirm that there are no exceptions to my law"—that sixteen-year-old beauty, perhaps?—"but the law itself I affirm as the foundation of archaic society. Sex begins with the Aryan race." Behind the smoke screen of erudition and prejudice, Adams is aware that something unexpected has happened. Amid his pervasively morbid mood—telling Hay that if they should catch cholera, "it will kill us, for it is virulent: but as I don't care, and La Farge seems not nervous, we go ahead"—Adams has experienced a moment of sheer desire, and momentary return to life.

By the last week in August, their sojourn in Japan was two-thirds over, and still Adams and La Farge had seen only one of the four sights considered essential viewing for any visitor. The wonders of Nikko they had winnowed and weighed; Kamakura, Mount Fuji, and Kyoto still remained. Originally, they had planned a leisurely meander through the Kansai—the triangle of the old cities of Nara, Kyoto, and Osaka. But the threat of cholera had kept them overlong in Nikko, and only a month was left for a hurried circuit of the interior. Now, like migratory birds, they followed the promise of cooler weather southward, returning to the comforts of the Yokohama Grand Hotel for another try (heat had previously kept them away) at the early capital of Kamakura, a few miles down the Pacific coast.

"Already seen, already known"—La Farge's mantra applied most fully to the Great Buddha at Kamakura. He had already persuaded Henry Adams, based on photographs, that the thirty-seven-foot bronze statue, cast in 1252, was essential to Adams's quest for the guiding conception for the grave that he would share with Clover. Still, what they saw took their breath away. The cross-legged Buddha, with eyes half shut in meditative repose, was originally housed in a huge temple of stone columns supporting a wooden roof. Roof and columns were carried away by a great tidal wave—like some cresting vision from Hokusai's famous print—in the fifteenth century, leaving the statue in direct contact with the elements. Nothing Adams and La Farge had seen in Nikko matched their awe and admiration as they circled the imposing Buddha.

La Farge pronounced the Great Buddha (or Daibutsu) "the most successful colossal figure in the world," superior to the Sphinx. He was particularly entranced by "the curious gray and violet tone of the bronze" and executed a quick sketch on the spot. Later he used this sketch, as well as Adams's photographs, as the basis for a stunning large watercolor of the Buddha, in which the bronze takes on some of the iridescent shim-

John La Farge, The Great Statue of
Buddha at Kamakura, *circa 1887*.

mer of the clouds, and lushly contrasting green foliage frames the Buddha on two sides. The translucence of watercolor creates an almost mystical effect—seen from below, his head against the sky, the celestial Buddha partakes of the blue and violet heavens.

"Accident" was the keynote, for La Farge, of the whole complex scene. "An accident, the breaking of its prison temple by a great cataclysm of nature, a great wave of the sea coming far inland and destroying the great building, has given to the statue," he observed, "something that it could never have had to the physical eye." That "something" was the way in which the Buddha seemed to sit and meditate on the whole surrounding landscape. "Now, freed from its shrine, the figure sits in contemplation of entire nature, the whole open world that we feel about us, or its symbols—the landscape, the hills, the trees and fields, the sky and its depths, the sunshine playing before the eyes of the seated figure." The "astounding success" of the figure, so steeped in convention, itself seemed to La Farge "partly accidental . . . it seems difficult to grant that there was once a choice in the other mind that caused it, that there were once many paths opened before it." But the most spectacularly "accidental" aspect of the Buddha at Kamakura, in La Farge's view, was the shifting scenery, the "undecidedness of this background of veiled sky and shifting blue, which makes one believe at times that the figure soon must move." In this regard the Buddha resembled Kannon by the waterfall: a figure of profound repose in the midst of "everything around it gently changing."

With his habitual skepticism, Henry Adams first looked askance at the Daibutsu, noting "the mild contempt of his blessed little moustache." At La Farge's request, he took several photographs of the statue from various angles and heights. "I would have given you a present if you could have seen us on our expedition last Friday to what the old books call the *Dye boots*," he wrote to a friend, ". . . as La Farge says it is the most successful colossal figure in the world, he sketched it, and I, seizing the little priest's camera, mounted to the roof of his porch, and, standing on my head at an angle of impossibility, perpetrated a number of libels on Buddha and Buddhism." Again, Adams concealed his emotions behind a veil of wit and invective. His profound respect for the Great Buddha steadily increased; it is not by accident that he mentions it, along with the Sphinx, in the elliptical pages in his *Education* devoted to the Adams memorial designed by Saint-Gaudens.

Kyoto was their quarry now. They took a steamer down to Kobe, the bustling port to the south, then traveled overland by train to the great "Western Capital." As they rattled through the countryside, Adams's conception for the memorial was developing. The Buddha at Kamakura provided decisive clues. Unroofed and unprotected, open to the changing weather, this figure had survived a tidal wave—as Henry Adams had, metaphorically—and remained unmoved. And there was Kannon, merciful witness to the fleeting waterfall of human life. During their final hours in Kamakura, Adams and La Farge had ventured up to the neighborhood of Hase, from which the Pacific Ocean spread out beneath them, and ducked into a dark temple dedicated to Kannon. There they had seen the ghostly glimmer of the statue to La Farge's favorite deity—another clue.

As they neared Kyoto, Adams studied the pages devoted to the city in Murray's guide, carefully underlining each mention of a carved funerary effigy. At this point in their travels, it may be that he was considering an idealized image of Clover for the monument—an idea he had previously rejected. Such statues were a specialty of Saint-Gaudens, as in his superb memorials to Farragut, Sherman, and Robert Gould Shaw. As he consulted the guidebook, Adams was particularly attentive to odd details that reminded him of his own situation. He marked the passage, for example, describing "the sitting effigy of Hideyoshi," in the Zen temple of Kodaiji, "in a shrine having panels of black lacquer with designs in thin gold, taken from his wife's carriage." He noted several effigies carved by their subjects—almost all of them lacquered and gilded and portrayed in a sitting position. This too may have reminded him of his curious plight, as he contemplated the design of his own grave. He noted a Korean-style figure of Kannon, in the temple of Koryuji, outside the city: "The face is supported on two long fingers of the r. hand. Drapery formal. The hair is drawn back from the forehead and tied in a knob at the top. The features are extremely natural, and wear a pensive expression. The hands are beautifully modelled." All these were clues, to be filed away and shared with Saint-Gaudens.

The hotel where foreigners stayed in Kyoto was the rustically Western-style Ya'ami, situated on a steep hill overlooking the city from the east. "I hardly know any inland city except Grenada, so charmingly situated," Adams wrote his secretary, Theodore Dwight. Wide awake at six the morning after their arrival, he wrote excitedly to John Hay: "Kioto at last! . . . we are sitting on our verandah, looking out over the big city, [La Farge] sketching." La Farge's watercolor sketch over light pencil, *View over Kiyoto from Ya Ami*, dated September 17, evokes a liquid, evanescent city:

> The city lies in fog, sometimes cool and gray; sometimes golden and smoky. The tops of pagodas and heavy roofs of temples lift out of this sea, and through it shine innumerable little white spots of the plastered sides of houses. Great avenues, which divide the city in parallel lines, run off into haze; far away always shines the white wall of the city castle; near us, trees and houses and temples drop out occasionally from the great violet shadows cast by the mountain behind us. Before the city wakes and the air clears, the crows fly from near the temples toward us, as the great bell of the temple sounds, and we hear the call of the gongs and the indefinite waves of prayer.

To reach the hotel from the almost dry Kamogawa River that divided the city north to south, they walked through the intimate streets of the Gion, the entertainment district of theaters and teahouses. Hundreds of geisha lived in the Gion and could be seen at dusk hurrying in their multicolored kimonos and clattering wooden sandals to their nighttime assignations. The sound of the plucked shamisen and the laughter of hushed conversations echoed through the narrow streets. Here and there a little stream curled among the ancient, dark-stained wooden buildings of the Gion, with delicately arched wooden bridges. "The gentle little bodies" of "the little geishas trotting about in couples," La Farge noted, "disappeared entirely inside of the folds of the dress and the enormous bows of the sash."

At the point where the straight and level Kyoto cross streets begin to climb into the surrounding hills, the setting shifts abruptly. Now instead of geisha one sees black-robed Buddhist monks making their way amid vast temple complexes surrounded by cypresses and walls. Sacred and profane rub shoulders at the boundary. The road, Shijo or Fourth Avenue, that Adams and La Farge followed in their jinrickshas took them to the ancient park called Maruyama, where gnarled cherry trees hundreds of years old bloom each spring and crowds come to pay their respect to the *sakura*. Just above these sacred trees stood the Ya'ami Hotel.

From their base in the comfortable hotel, Adams and La Farge made hurried tours of temples and shrines, interspersed with more visits to dealers of curios and artifacts. At Kodaiji, the temple built in the eastern hills in honor of the great general Hideyoshi's widow, Adams made a point of seeing the shrine with the stern sitting figure of Hideyoshi, with his robe fanned out like two wings. He lingered in the garden at Kodaiji. "The picturesque effect," according to a passage he marked in his Murray's guide, "is much heightened by the two lofty pine-clad hills which rear their heads over the trees at the back." He also entered a rustic teahouse attributed to Sen no Rikyu. "And we have gone up into the plain little pavilion, sacred to the ceremonies of tea-drinking," wrote La Farge, "where the rough and shrewd adventurer [Hideyoshi] offered to grim, ambitious warriors . . . the simple little cups of glazed clay that collectors prize today."

Bigelow and Fenollosa had insisted that Adams and La Farge visit the earliest Buddhist temples, so they made a hurried pilgrimage south from Kyoto and over the famous bridge at Uji, where, wrote La Farge, "violet butterflies and blue dragon-flies crossed our path in every bar of sunshine." They sipped locally grown tea, the most illustrious green tea in all of Japan, then made the short walk to the Byodoin Temple. There they admired the Phoenix Hall, or Hooden, with its two wings looking out over the water, and listened to the "sweet-toned bell."

Then came Horyuji, where Okakura and Fenollosa had made their great discovery of the Kannon sculpture only four summers earlier in the octagonal Yumedono, or Hall of Dreams. The five-story pagoda caught La Farge's interest; he particularly loved the scenes from the life of the Buddha enacted by little terra-cotta figures in the lowest level. On their tiny stages, as though in a sacred peepshow, they reminded him of Greek

Tanagra figures. From Horyuji to Nara is a short trip, only a few miles, by jinricksha. Nara found the two travelers exhausted, suffering from what La Farge called "an indigestion of information." The sites of the city get barely a mention from either Adams or La Farge.

They took a jostling night journey back to their hotel in Kyoto. Two experiences from their last days there made a lasting impression: an evening at the Shorenin, or Green Lotus Temple, and a final visit to Kiyomizudera, architecturally one of the most dramatic of the Japanese temple complexes. At Shorenin, a temple laid out like a rural villa, with elegant low-lying buildings with verandas for viewing gardens and pools, Adams and La Farge watched a series of temple dances. Adams carefully recorded the sequence in his notebook: "Bird dance; Butterfly dance; Amusements of peace; Four guardsmen sword dance; Amma—two court nobles playing hide and seek. . . . Music all old. Dances older than Nara epoch."

On their last day in Kyoto, Adams and La Farge made a final pilgrimage to Kiyomizudera. The temple is reached by a long uphill route lined with stalls selling trinkets to pilgrims—reminiscent of Assisi or Lourdes. Visitors approach the main building by a circuitous route and walk out along the broad, dark-wood veranda, which is supported by immense piles plunging down to the valley below. The view is stunning. The landscape drops sharply to a deep ravine with trees gorgeous in their fall foliage and waterfalls rippling out of the mountain flanks. As La Farge recounted, he and Adams stepped out onto the wide balcony: "From below rise, with the coolness of the green trees and grass, the sounds of dropping waters. In time we descend the path and the steps, and drink from one of the streams which fall from gigantic gargoyles, out of a great mass of wall."

In its dramatic integration of mountain, waterfall, and temple, the cantilevered design of Kiyomizu reminds one of some of Frank Lloyd Wright's most astonishing creations—especially the house in the Pennsylvania woods known as Fallingwater. It was a fitting final stop before the travelers began their weeklong overland journey back toward Yokohama. At some point during their stay in Kyoto, the travelers had hired an interpreter named Aoki. Aoki accompanied them on their ensuing travels, then followed La Farge back to New York as his private servant, companion, and studio assistant.

———

One more experience, outweighing all others in its uncanny majesty, awaited the travelers. Rattling through the mountain passes and rock-strewn valleys of the Tokaido Road, Adams read snatches of Dante and medieval French, writing brief journal entries in his pocket notebook. Suddenly, without warning, Fuji loomed in the distance. La Farge described the apparition: "For a mile now, perhaps, we ran along between the sea and the abrupt green wall of hills, so steep that we could not see them, and, turning sharply around a corner, beheld Fuji, now filling the entire field of sight, seeming to rise even from below us into the upper sky, and framed at its base by near green mountains; these opened as a gate, and showed the glittering streak of the swollen Fujikawa, the swiftest river in Japan." Except for "one enormous band of cloud halfway up its long slope, and melting into infinite distance towards the ocean," the sacred mountain was fully visible. La Farge realized immediately that he had the answer to the problem he had come to Japan to solve: how to represent the Ascension of Christ "in an atmosphere not inimical, as ours is, to what we call the miraculous." The ascending mountain would be the perfect setting for the ascending savior. With his mural in mind, La Farge made a painstaking study of the whole mountain scene. He noted, "There are turns of the tide which allow you at times to do an amount of work incredible in sober moments."

Adams was just as moved. He told La Farge that "it was worth coming to far Japan for this single day." On one leaf of his pocket notebook he sketched the shape of Mount Fuji as it stood before him, correcting it several times. On the following page, Adams wrote a brief, uncharacteristically scrawled description of the clouds hovering below the cone: "We do not care to scoop away the dazzling cloud that marks and magnifies its summit." Then he wrote two lines, partially translated, from the thirteenth canto of Dante's *Paradiso*, a passage in which Thomas Aquinas is describing the complex weave of the mortal and the divine in human life. The mortal world where we lead our lives is like wax, Dante learns, in which the hand of God imprints his divine intentions. "If the wax were exactly worked, and the heavens were at the height of their power, the light of the whole seal would be apparent," Aquinas explains, "but"—and this is the passage Adams copied—"nature always gives it defectively, working like the artist who in the practice of his art has a hand that trembles." Here is what Adams wrote in his notebook:

Paradiso. Xiii. 76–78.
  Nature is always imperfect
Like the artist
Ch'a l'abito de l'arte ha man che trema.

It is a complicated pun. One can see in his writing that Adams's own hand is trembling, because of the motion of the jinricksha. To attribute to God the Creator a similarly trembling hand is, as the Dante scholar Charles Singleton notes, a daring image, but for Adams it was also a reassuring one. The suffering here below is caused by problems not of divine conception—a terrible thought—but of divine execution. God does his best. Looking out at the clouds obscuring the base of Mount Fuji, Adams found himself treasuring this "imperfection" in the landscape. This scene, both travelers felt, was as close as they would get to Paradise.

Along the Tokaido Adams and La Farge continued their pilgrimage, following rivers and—as they took lunch and tea—appreciating famous views. To the comfortable hotel the Fujiya, in the mountain resort of Miyanoshita near Hakone, the two travelers made their way, encountering the popular artist Theodore Whores, who made a living painting exotic Japanese scenes for his audience back home in San Francisco and New York. In the Fujiya's comfortable rooms with hot springs piped into the baths, they settled for a recuperative couple of nights. In the registry of guests one can still find the carefully rounded signature of "Henry Adams, Washington, D.C.," and the offhand, distracted scrawl of "John La Farge, New York City." The date: September 25, 1886. A week later they were on the *City of Peking*, reunited with Okakura, Bigelow, and the Fenollosas, and bound for San Francisco.

Henry Adams told his friends that he had gone to Japan to buy kakemonos for his gaunt walls. John La Farge had gone on a kindred quest: to find the proper background for his mural for the Church of the Ascension. Each had found what he was looking for—and more. In the gently ascending slope of Mount Fuji, La Farge had discovered a vision of the sacred uncluttered with Western associations. In the "accidental" exposure of the Buddha at Kamakura, freed by the Great Wave to contemplate the changes of weather, and in the serene repose of Kannon by the waterfall, Adams had found a vision of peace that he could live with. While the pilgrims may have come late, Nirvana was not entirely out of season.

A subtle shift had occurred in the process; writer and visual artist had partly exchanged places. La Farge brought home fewer sketches of Japan than he expected and soon came to rely on Adams's photographs as he worked up "scenes of Japan" in his studio on Tenth Street in New York. Instead, La Farge had written copiously and had sufficient material for his vivid book, published by his friend and patron Richard Watson Gilder, *An Artist's Letters from Japan*. Adams had written little on the journey—some jottings in his expense notebook and a handful of letters. Instead, he had taken photographs, made occasional sketches, and studied Buddhist statuary and architecture. These interests were the beginning of a new and important phase in his career: his serious engagement with the arts, as evidenced in his late masterpiece *Mont-Saint-Michel and Chartres*.

The commission John La Farge had won in 1886 for the Ascension mural continued to languish until the following summer, when Okakura—interrupting his European travels—passed through New York on his way to Washington, where the Baron Kuki had summoned him to accompany Mrs. Kuki back to Tokyo. It was under Okakura's sustained and daily tutelage that La Farge made two key decisions about the mural, which together allowed him to bring it to satisfactory completion. While art historians have scanned the figures for echoes of Raphael and other Italian Renaissance prototypes, it is Japan that gives the picture what force it retains. The initial problem, and the one that had interrupted La Farge's work in the first place, was what kind of landscape should surround—and literally ground—Christ's ascent into Heaven. It seemed self-evident to La Farge that a nineteenth-century artist could not simply sketch in the Judean hills. Such naturalism would preclude any genuine feeling of elevation. So La Farge reproduced, on the left side of the mural, his careful sketch of Fuji's exact slope so that Christ hovers above the sacred mountain, one more "view of Mount Fuji" to add to Hokusai's album.

The second challenge was the "hovering" itself. Again, a modern artist could not pretend that Christ simply floated upward. Some believable analogy was needed, a sort of charged wire of visual credibility. La Farge first thought of the high-wire acts of circus performers. Edgar Degas—in this regard and others so similar to La Farge—had constructed his own modern Ascension by painting a black circus performer called Miss La La from a striking angle. La Farge and Okakura talked about the circus as a fund of images. Then Okakura suggested a different analogy: the floating forms of early Buddhist art. In paintings of Buddhist deities and Boddhisattvas, the figures often hover on clouds in the heavens. In La Farge's finished Ascension painting, there is a hint of a waterfall— another Buddhist touch—below Christ's feet.

Henry James, La Farge's close friend and former pupil, visited the

John La Farge, The Ascension of Our Lord, *1886–88.*

Church of the Ascension during his 1905 tour of the United States. He was pleased to find that the two superb Greek Revival churches on lower Fifth Avenue, the Ascension and the First Presbyterian Church, had survived the relentless modernization and commercialization of the avenue. He wrote,

> Let me not, however, forget, amid such contemplations, what may serve here as a much more relevant instance of the operation of values, the price of the as yet undiminished dignity of the two most southward of the Fifth Avenue churches. Half the charm of the prospect, at that extremity, is in their still being there, and being as they are; this charm, this serenity of escape and survival positively works as a blind on the side of the question of their architectural importance.

James entertained no doubts concerning the importance of his old mentor La Farge's mural after having "penetrat[ed] into the Ascension, at chosen noon, and standing for the first time in presence of that noble work of John La Farge, the representation, on the west wall, in the grand manner, of the theological event from which the church takes its title.

> Wonderful enough, in New York, to find one's self, in a charming and considerably dim "old" church, hushed to admiration before a great religious picture: the sensation, for the moment, upset so all the facts. The hot light, outside, might have been that of an Italian *piazzetta*; the cool shade, within, with the important work of art shining through it, seemed part of some other-world pilgrimage— all the more that the important work of art itself, a thing of the highest distinction, spoke, as soon as one had taken it in, with that authority which makes the difference, ever afterwards, between the remembered and the forgotten quest.

For James, the importance of the church lies as much in its survival as in any particular aspect. It stands out in a commercialized city as an embodiment of earlier values. The whole impression of the interior of the church, with the mural and a sequence of stained-glass windows La Farge added later, was to James a sort of portrait of his mentor: "The church, as

it stands, is very nearly as commemorative a monument as a great reputation need wish."

It is all the more interesting, therefore, that the mural in the Church
of the Ascension, one of the most ambitious and highly praised religious
paintings in nineteenth-century American art, is in fact a complex fusion of Eastern and Western ideas of the sacred. Only with the influx of
Japanese ideas, conveyed by Okakura, could La Farge find his way to
"making it new," taking the traditional and timeworn ideas of Italian Renaissance iconography and giving them a reimagined setting and dynamism. In doing so, La Farge and Okakura returned the events of the
Ascension to the East.

The other commission left dangling at the start of the Japan trip was the
monument for the Adams grave. Henry Adams had secured Augustus
Saint-Gaudens's services and had given him an initial concept. The challenge, almost insuperable, was to design a monument to honor (in addition to Adams himself) the memory of someone who despised
monuments. Clover had hated the ancient monuments of Egypt; she had
steered H. H. Richardson away from a "monumental" design of the house
on Lafayette Square; she had chided the sculptor William Wetmore Story
for ruining perfectly good blocks of marble. What is more, Clover had
killed herself—a heroic act for a samurai perhaps, but not generally regarded as such for a well-born nineteenth-century woman from Boston.
What was required was not so much a monument as a countermonument.
And this, miraculously, is what Saint-Gaudens achieved in the Adams
Memorial in Rock Creek Cemetery in Washington, D.C.

In retrospect one can view the journey to Japan as a quest for ideas
for such a paradoxical achievement. The search had led Adams and La
Farge to the Nikko tombs, to the colossal Buddha at Kamakura, to many
temples dedicated to Kannon and other Buddhist deities. After the return from Japan, Adams found himself not yet able to talk about his
wife's death and its meaning for him. (Twenty years later, when he wrote
his autobiographical *Education*, he still could not discuss it.) He dele-
gated La Farge to convey his wishes to Saint-Gaudens. The sculptor was
already poring over photographs of Michelangelo—the figure for sleep

on the Medici tombs was a clear model for the cowled head. Again, Okakura helped bring about a complex cultural synthesis. The calm and sitting position of the Kamakura Buddha had a strong influence—it is quite possible to imagine Saint-Gaudens's figure with legs crossed in the lotus position.

It was Kannon, however, who proved the decisive idea. Indeed, it is not an exaggeration to say that the Adams Memorial is an American Kannon. Kannon, goddess (and sometimes god) of compassion, is among the most popular of Buddhist deities in Japan. One of the many Boddhisattvas, Kannon consented to suffer the fate of humans rather than remain in the realm of Nirvana. As such, she (or he) is a kind of intercessor for suffering humanity, with obvious parallels to Christian ideas and figures (Mary, Jesus) of mercy. La Farge was especially fascinated by the Kannon figure. He reproduced in *An Artist's Letters from Japan* his sketch from Nikko of a painting of Kannon contemplating a waterfall. This became in turn the prototype for two large and ambitious oil paintings of Kannon that La Farge completed after his return to New York. For La Farge, the waterfall was essential to her meaning. It was the endlessly flowing river of life. Kannon and her waterfall were so intertwined that the sight of a waterfall summoned up for him the figure of Kannon. He had written from Nikko: "I am continually reminded of her [Kannon] by the beautiful scenes about us, of which the waterfall is the note and the charm . . . and here [at Urami-no-taki], again, the intense silence, broken by the rush of the waterfall recalled the pictures of the Kwan-on, whose meaning and whose images bring back to me the Buddhistic idea of compassion."

Henry James, a connoisseur of monuments as well as murals, thought the key to the success of Saint-Gaudens's statues was a certain ambiguity, which James first called "equivocal" before revising to the more neutral "double." The statue of Sherman on horseback at the southeast corner of Central Park partook of this doubleness, blending, in James's view, an image of Sherman the Destroyer with Sherman the "messenger of peace." (James confessed that he would have preferred the Destroyer alone, "crested not with peace, but with snakes.") The Adams Memorial is also double, a complex fusion in at least three ways. First, following Adams's explicit request, Saint-Gaudens made an an-

John La Farge, Kannon, *1886, copy of hand
scroll attributed to Maruyama Okyo,
Iyemitsu Temple, Nikko.*

drogynous figure, double in its sexuality. When President Theodore Roosevelt declared in public that the statue was "a strange, shrouded, sitting
woman," Adams was quick to correct him. Like Kannon, the statue was
neither male nor female but a synthesis of both. Second, Saint-Gaudens
created a tension between the stillness of the figure and the apparent
motion of the shroud. In this regard, he fused Kannon and waterfall. Instead of taking on the impossible task of sculpting falling water in the

background, Saint-Gaudens worked the image of a rippling flow right into the bronze figure's cascading robe. Third, he fused East and West, perfectly melding Michelangelo with Buddhist iconography.

The waterfall in the garden at Nikko appeared once more in La Farge's art. Early in 1903 he was approached by the architect Cass Gilbert to design murals for the Minnesota State Capitol in St. Paul. Gilbert wanted La Farge to decorate the Supreme Court room, a cross-shaped space with four semicircular lunettes. Justice would be La Farge's theme, but he shied away from the sort of allegorical treatment—strong female figure holding justice in the balance—so favored by his contemporaries. Instead, he chose four episodes of the workings of justice in human history, none of which had any particular tie to Minnesota. La Farge had a bigger idea in mind: that the United States had inherited and synthesized several cultural traditions. On one panel he showed Moses receiving the Ten Commandments of the Law on Mount Sinai. On another he portrayed Socrates and his friends discussing the ideas of the *Republic.* In a third lunette, Count Raymond of Toulouse adjudicates conflicting claims of civilian and religious authorities.

It is the fourth panel that surprises, for it depicts Confucius and his disciples in their favorite grove. The theme is "The Recording of Precedents." Confucius is not generally regarded as a contributor to the American system of justice. The success of Japan in the early battles of the Russo-Japanese War at the time La Farge was making preliminary sketches may have confirmed the dawning importance of Asia. La Farge made a watercolor study in black and white, using as the setting the garden in Nikko where he and Adams had spent so many pleasant hours two decades earlier. It was in this garden with its thrice-breaking waterfall that Okakura had introduced La Farge to the ideas of Confucius. Five figures in the black-and-white study are roughly brushed in, in a zigzag pattern across the lunette. Their features are a blur, as though awaiting later definition. The waterfall in the background is more carefully rendered.

Then came a stroke of luck. La Farge learned that Okakura was returning to the United States in 1904, at Bigelow's invitation, to take a post at the Museum of Fine Arts in Boston. Okakura came first to New York, accompanied by three Japanese disciples from his school. La Farge, as his friend Cortissoz reports, "loved to talk about Confucius, whom he had found as interesting as a novel when he was studying him with Okakura's help." Now the conversations about Confucius could resume. As La Farge began applying color to the sketched scene, he playfully asked Okakura to inscribe in Chinese characters a saying of Confucius: "First the white, and then the color on top." Something else happened besides the addition of color between study and finished mural. The features of master and pupils, blurred and hypothetical in the study, became Okakura—himself a lawgiver in aesthetic matters— and *his* disciples. The figure in blue, who seems modeled on the young Okakura, now has in front of him a kotolike musical instrument. While Confucius's fondness for music as an analogy for social harmony comes up repeatedly in the *Analects*, the instrument also seems a marker for the artist as lawgiver, as well as a private reminder that Okakura played the koto.

The grove itself is as much a character as the five figures, and the centerpiece is the waterfall, with its three breaks. The scrolls on which the disciples record the precedents echo the flow of the waterfall, and the waterfall is in turn a figure for the passing on of tradition from generation to generation. "Everything flows," as Confucius wrote. La Farge was so taken with the image of Confucius that, when asked for a similar set of decorations for the Baltimore Court House two years later, he painted Confucius again. This time Confucius is playing his koto while two disciples look on. The master looks exactly like Okakura circa 1904. There is no waterfall, but behind the seated Confucius an iridescent curtain falls. Cortissoz again:

He painted another Confucius in one of the panels which he placed in the Court House at Baltimore and for purely decorative reasons he wanted a perpendicular mass in the centre of it. Finally, he thought of putting a white curtain behind Confucius to shield him from the air as he sat, after his wont, beneath a favorite tree. Okakura, coming in, was greatly astonished at La Farge's scholarship and told him that Confucius had various names, one of them being the Man of the Curtain. But the artist had only been solving a technical problem. He recalled the story of Confucius one day making a little music, as he always did, before he began work. A disciple said to him, "that was not like you; it sounded so cruel." The master replied that he had seen a rat in the grass which a cat had killed, and, said he, "The cruelty got into my music." "There," remarked La Farge, "you have your modern music. What you see and feel, what goes on about you, goes into your work."

During the summer of 1887, Henry Adams had his own idea of how to combine Asian and Western motifs. Again, Okakura served as expert. Among the objects Adams had collected in Japan were several kimonos. His aim was to find just the right kimono to show off Elizabeth Cameron's charms, and have La Farge paint her portrait à la Japonaise. Adams gave Lizzie an update from Quincy on August 18: "Quincy is not enlivening. I hope your friend Okakura the Jap will pay me a visit next week. We will ask him to send over some of the more recondite portions of a lady's wardrobe to make the kimonos useful." Okakura is "La Farge's friend" in the *Education* and Lizzie's friend in this passage, but Adams respected his expertise nonetheless, even if it involved undergarments and sashes.

Adams had in mind a group excursion to see the Ames estate in nearby North Easton, where H. H. Richardson had built a magnificent group of buildings, including an enormous living room in the main house with Japanese stenciling—chrysanthemum and lotus crests—and detailing. Adams invited Okakura, Lizzie, and La Farge, who had made some stained glass for the Ames chapel. When Okakura begged off, Adams asked Lizzie to invite Bigelow instead. "Do get Billy Big to send me a message to say when I am to come and matronise you ladies at his house. He is a dangerous fellow, and very Japanese, but he has pretty things if we can only make him give them to us." The pretty things Bigelow had collected included priceless No robes and ceremonial kimonos—possible props for the portrait of Elizabeth Cameron.

All these plans collapsed when La Farge, sensing the depth of Adams's obsession, put him off for several months before writing Adams on November 20, 1887, that he couldn't do it. La Farge explained, unconvincingly, that he had avoided portraits because "I am too sensitive to my sitter's influence. I am not incapable of making a likeness—every painter can do that—but everything affects me to the extent of a paralyzing result." For La Farge, there was an even greater obstacle than portraiture in general. "A face like Mrs. Cameron's has all sorts of difficulties. There is a distinct interior which contradicts the exterior at moments—or rather there are changes which make one wonder whether they are not really most important. All this is stupid as an explanation—but I wish I were a portrait painter who learns to be very cool as he is most interested." The conception of the unpainted portrait of Lizzie could be entrusted to no artist other than La Farge, who had shared the experience of Japan with Henry Adams.

"If only we had found Nirvana—" La Farge wrote in the dedication to Adams of his *Artist's Letters from Japan*, "but he was right who warned us that we were late in this season of the world." Adams had given La Farge directions for how Saint-Gaudens might depict Nirvana, but he hadn't found it for himself, as his feelings for Elizabeth Cameron made clear. Almost from the moment of his return to America, Adams began scheming for a way to return to Asia. China had been his original goal—"I mean to start for China, and stay there," he told John Hay in 1887. "I expect to enter the celestial kingdom by that road, if not sooner by a shorter one." He wanted to circle the world and retrace Marco Polo's journey from China back to Europe. Okakura led him to believe that the paintings and sculpture that had eluded him in picked-over Japan awaited the avid collector in the vastnesses of China. Adams wrote Lizzie on August 31, 1887, that he had received a letter from Okakura "quite breaking my heart by saying he cannot come [hence no "recondite portions of a lady's wardrobe"], and appointing Pekin as our place of meeting."

Adams's growing attachment to Elizabeth Cameron, increasingly embarrassing to her and to their friends, made a trip seem all the more advisable. He dined with his old friend Pumpelly and asked him for information about China. Then he signed up La Farge—eager as always to flee commissions and creditors—to resume their quixotic quest for Nir-vana. Aoki would come as well. When the first brace of volumes of the *History of the United States of America* appeared in October 1889, Adams was ready for departure.

The same split that had marked Adams's response to Japan—exotic hedonism at war with spiritual asceticism—recurred in the South Seas, but there was more time and leisure to pursue and play out both fantasies. Armed with Melville's *Typee* and its idyll of Fayaway the native girl, they proceeded to Hawaii, where the "golden girls" Clarence King had seen twenty years earlier were all grown up and wearing Western clothes, and then to Tahiti. They left Tahiti six days before Paul Gauguin arrived on a kindred quest. Gauguin and La Farge used some of the same photographs of native life as the basis for their own pictures.

The months in the South Seas were a kind of therapeutic holding pat-tern for Adams, the rest and respite he hadn't quite found in the hurried tour of Japan. The real goal, however, was China, and Adams was bitterly disappointed when news arrived that violence against foreigners, which would culminate in the Boxer Rebellion, made travel there impossible. Adams remarked that he did "not know where to go, now that China is shut. . . . India, Central Asia and China are my only hopes, and without China I find Asia unmanageable." *Hope* in this case meant possibilities for collecting. For five years he had assumed that Japan was picked over, and he had wandered from archipelago to archipelago, and from the Pa-cific into the Indian Ocean, scouring island after island for aesthetic beauty, or booty. "For the soul of Siva, how many islands are necessary for me, if all these are not enough?"

The more he traveled, however, the more Japan came to seem, with all its smells and mechanical women, the gold standard for collecting. "I am astonished to find how relatively rich Japan was in every way. From Tahiti to Ceylon I have seen nothing whatever, old or new, in art or na-ture, that has tempted me to get it." "Java is Japan without everything that makes Japan interesting," he wrote. And again, "We see Japan every-where, but it is Japan without the fun, and the dancing was even more conventional than that of the Kioto geishas."

Ceylon, a final stop before swinging up through the Suez Canal to the Mediterranean, had held out a ray of hope that some inkling of the mystery of Asia might be salvaged from the journey. The little teardrop at the tip of India was reputed to be the cradle of Buddhism, and Adams was determined to make the pilgrimage to the sacred city of Anuradhapura. He referred to Buddhism as "our church" and mourned its decline—only in Boston, "where Bill Bigelow and Fenollosa fan faint embers," did the faith flicker. Adams's pilgrimage was scholarly as well; he wanted to brush up on German theories of the "Aryan" origins of certain religious and political practices in the West. He was disappointed to find "not even a stray volume of Max Müller . . . here, except in the little library of the Sacred Tooth."

From the coastal city of Kandy to the sacred ruins of Anuradhapura required a bumpy ride in an ox cart over eighty miles. "We have tracked Buddhism to its lair," Adams wrote John Hay on September 13, "in an oxcart drawn by two little trotting humped oxen, with us stowed close together inside, barely able to peer out over our boots at the moonlight on the jungle." He went on,

> Please imagine a great plain, covered with woods. Dumped on this dry plain are half a dozen huge domes of solid brick, overgrown with grass and shrubs; artificial mounds that have lost their architectural decorations and their plaster covering, but still rise one or two hundred feet above the trees, and have a certain grandeur. Each of these dagobas represents an old temple which had buildings about it, stone bathing-tanks, and stone statues of Buddha, chapels and paved platforms decorated with carved or brick elephant-heads, humped oxen, lions and horses. When Buddha flourished here, two thousand years ago, vast numbers of pilgrims came to worship the relics supposed to be hidden under the dagobas, but still more to pray at the sacred bo-tree, which is the original shoot brought here more than two thousand years ago from the original bo-tree under which Buddha attained Nirwana.

Despite the admiration expressed in phrases like "a certain grandeur," Adams was not particularly impressed, and again Japan was the standard. "To my surprise and disappointment, all the art seems to me pretty poor and cheap. Compared with Egypt or even with Japan, Ceylon is second-rate."

Henry Adams felt not merely a collector's disappointment but a pilgrim's dismay as well. Despite his habitual armor of ironic detachment, Adams was serious about Buddhism, and seriously in search of the release from earthly care—and especially sexual desire—that Buddhism promised. What he particularly missed in Anuradhapura was a specifically religious feeling. It all seemed crassly imagined and cheaply built, like the worst excesses of Gilded Age America that Adams and La Farge were in flight from. The ruins were impressive, "like the Castle of St Angelo run mad . . . but not a square inch of really religious art." This complaint recurs throughout Adams's letters from Anuradhapura. "None of the work is conscientious or religious in feeling. It resembles more the religion of the Roman empire than the Buddhism of Japan.

Nonetheless Adams paid his respects to the sacred tree, and reported the mixed results to Elizabeth Cameron:

> Of course we went at once to the sacred bo-tree, which is now only a sickly shoot or two from the original trunk, and under it I sat for half an hour, hoping to attain Nirwana. La Farge says I am always trying to attain Nirwana, and never get near it. I don't know. Sometimes I think that intellectually I am pretty close to it, if isolation from the world's intellect is Nirwana; but one or two personal interests or affections still bar the last leap to total absorption and silence; even under Buddha's most sacred tree, I thought less of him than of you; which was not the Nirwana that Buddha attained.

By the time Adams and La Farge crept back into their ox cart, "a real cart with two wheels, and two slow, meditative, humped oxen, who are also sacred cattle, and who have the most Buddhistic expression in their humps and horns that ever was reached by God's creatures," Adams was already reconsidering his devotion to Buddha.

The idea Adams was playing over in his mind, and developed as the steamer entered the hotter climes of Arabia, was that he wasn't really able to relinquish altogether those "one or two personal interests or affections" he had mentioned to Lizzie. Perhaps, after all, he was more in the world than out of it, hence more Brahma than Buddha. "For my own part I may say that I returned to Kandy with a poor opinion of Ceylon Buddhism, and a settled determination to devote myself in future to Brahma," he wrote. For an Adams from Boston, this leap to Brahmanism might seem less dramatic than he tried to make it sound. But he amused himself on the voyage toward France by writing a poem of about three hundred lines in blank verse called "Buddha and Brahma."

As a poet, Henry Adams was technically skilled and unoriginal; he rarely put his hand to verse, but when he did, as in the sonnets in *Esther* and the verse translations in *Mont-Saint-Michel*, the results were impressive. As a way of coping with his personal dilemma of embracing life or escaping it, and at the same time placing the choice on a higher, more universal plain, "Buddha and Brahma" is of considerable interest. The poem is built around the contrast between two imposing men, both sitting in silence: the Buddha and the Rajah. As the Buddha sits sunk in silence, one of his disciples asks him three times if the world is eternal. The Buddha's only answer is to lift a lotus flower into the air and lower it. This doesn't suffice for "the last of the disciples," who determines to pose the same question to his father, the Rajah. The Rajah, a warrior and a man of action, first tries to evade the question: "My teaching is not his; mine not his way; You quit your Master when you question me." Pressed by his son, however, the Rajah reveals that he and the Buddha were friends as children, and that both were frustrated by the rules of caste and the priesthood:

> *And in our youths we both, like you, rebelled*
> *Against the priesthood and their laws of caste.*
> *We sought new paths, desperate to find escape*
> *Out of the jungle that the priests had made.*
> *Gautama found a path. You follow it.*
> *I found none, and I stay here, in the jungle,*
> *Content to tolerate what I cannot mend.*

That last line must have had particular personal resonance for Henry Adams. The Buddha

> *. . . failed to cope with life; renounced its cares;*
> *Fled to the forest, and attained the End,*
> *Reaching the End by sacrificing life.*

Adams concludes the poem with the idea—so central to the *Education*—that we are inevitably divided, and hence lead double lives. Buddha

> *. . . breaks a path at once to what he seeks.*
> *By silence and absorption he unites*
> *His soul with the great soul from which it started.*

The rest of us can hope, at best, for Brahma:

> *But we, who cannot fly the world, must seek*
> *To live two separate lives; one, in the world*
> *Which we must ever seem to treat as real;*
> *The other in ourselves, behind a veil*
> *Not to be raised without disturbing both.*

Still, the final word goes to the Rajah, who explains that Buddha and Brahma, while seemingly "worlds apart," are actually one: "The Starting-point must be the End-point too!" The double life of the Brahman is ultimately the higher, more difficult calling, since it encompasses an awareness of the Perfect Life even amid the imperfections of this one.

> *Yet in this world of selfishness and striving*
> *The wise man lives as deeply sunk in silence,*
> *As conscious of the Perfect Life he covets,*
> *As any recluse in his forest shadows,*
> *As any Yogi in his mystic trances.*
> *We need no Noble Way to teach us Freedom*
> *Amid the clamor of a world of slaves.*
> *We need no Lotus to love purity*
> *Where life is else corruption.*

As a reluctant acknowledgment of the claims of life and "personal af-fections," "Buddha and Brahma" is a peculiar sort of love poem. Adams was in no particular hurry to return to Washington to see what he now re-ferred to as his "Buddha grave." The restlessness of the traveler subsided somewhat. Before him still lay Paris and Elizabeth Cameron—life itself. The way of the Brahman, "deeply sunk in silence," was the only ideal he could wholeheartedly embrace.

MESSAGES FROM MARS

>< >< ><

That you glance at Japan as you breakfast,
not in the least surprises me, thronged only
with Music, like the Decks of Birds.

—EMILY DICKINSON

Part 1

Percival Lowell loved heights. Standing on a jagged peak above the clouds, with the humdrum human world forgotten and the stars for aristocratic company, Lowell felt right at home. He was not the first foreigner to climb Ontake, one of the most sacred mountains of Japan, but he knew he was unlikely to meet another *gaijin* on the trail. The guidebook (Murray's of 1891, written by Lowell's close friend Basil Chamberlain) warned that Ontake was "beyond the reach of railways and modern civilization"— music to Lowell's ears—and that the climb was rough. So, in August 1891, he and a companion joined the "rosary of ten thousand pilgrims" who climbed Ontake each summer. They expected to find what Lowell called "probable picturesqueness" along the way: rustic tea huts at leisurely in- tervals, patches of snow and cloud, a view from the top encompassing the peninsula of Noto (the "unexplored corner of Japan" to which Lowell had already devoted a charming travel book), and, on a clear day, Mount Fuji in the distance. "That the mountain held a mystery," Lowell wrote, "was undreamed of."

In a rest hut four-fifths of the way up Ontake, Lowell was sipping bitter green tea and counting his escalating heartbeat. Three pilgrims dressed in white suddenly entered the hut from below. The hut was placed, like a seine in a stream, across the mountain path, but the three pilgrims passed right through, deaf to the hut keeper's entreaties. Intrigued by their single-minded progress, Lowell and his friend decided to follow the pilgrims. What they saw astonished them. "We had not climbed above a score of rods when we overtook our young puritans lost in prayer before a shrine cut into the face of the cliff, in front of which stood two or three benches conspicuously out of place in such a spot. The three young men had already laid aside their hats, mats, and staffs, and disclosed the white fillets that bound their shocks of jet-black hair. We halted on general principles of curiosity, for we had no inkling of what was about to happen." One of the men drew a wand from his sleeve while another, with a spasmodic jerk, tied his fingers in a knot and recited a chant in monotone. The chanter was handed the wand. Suddenly the wand began to twitch, and so convulsively that "it was as if the wand shook the man, not the man it." The man had gone "completely out of himself," wrote Lowell. "Unwittingly we had come to stand witnesses to a trance."

Nothing that Lowell had heard or read about Ontake or about Shinto, the native Japanese religion, which held mountains in reverence, had prepared him for such spiritual practices. It was as though he had stumbled into the mystic rites of Delphi. He watched with fascination.

At the first sign of possession, the exorcist had ceased incanting and sat bowed awaiting the coming presence. When the paroxysmal throes had settled into a steady quiver—much as a top does when it goes off to sleep—he leaned forward, put a hand on either side the possessed's knees, and still bowed, asked in words archaically reverent the name of the god who had thus deigned to descend.

At first there was no reply. Then in a voice strangely unnatural, without being exactly artificial, the entranced spake: "I am Hakkai."

High on Ontake, itself "a volcano sunk in trance," Percival Lowell had discovered in these trances "the hitherto unsuspected esoteric side of Shinto." Why, then, had no one noticed these spiritual possessions before, since they were, after all, "certainly going on all the time"? Lowell concluded that Japan "is still very much of an undiscovered country to us," as unexplored in its spiritual as in its geographical spaces. The average foreigner, as in Poe's case of the purloined letter hidden in plain view, was the least likely to notice things. "What he expects to find does not exist, and what exists he would never dream of looking for."

There are people who are driven to make discoveries, and Percival Lowell was one of these. In addition to the usual requirements—a willingness to travel and take risks, an intellectual boldness and even cockiness, the ability to recognize what others have overlooked—Lowell had other advantages. His eyesight was said to be extraordinary, the keenest, according to the leading ophthalmologist in Boston, that the doctor had ever encountered. Lowell was preternaturally gifted, as well, in mathematics and languages. The great Harvard mathematician Benjamin Peirce hoped that Lowell might someday inherit his chair. His cousin Dr. William Sturgis Bigelow reported that Lowell "learned Japanese faster than I ever saw any man learn a language." Finally, Lowell was a writer of scope and flair, giving his discoveries—and his claims to have discovered things—eloquent and persuasive expression. For ten years Lowell trained his eyes and his intellect on Japan and its people. Then abruptly, and seemingly without transition, he turned his attention to the planet Mars.

Born in Boston in 1855, the son of Augustus Lowell and Katharine Bigelow, Lowell had a Jamesian childhood of education abroad, including two years in a boarding school in Paris, before attending Harvard, from which he graduated in 1876. For six years he was a successful businessman, managing trust funds, running the financial operations of a large cotton mill, and—as his younger brother and biographer, Harvard president A. Lawrence Lowell, puts it—"withal . . . a young man of fashion." Percival Lowell was well connected. His maternal grandfather had been minister to England; his second cousin was the poet James Russell Lowell; his much younger sister, Amy Lowell, became a famous American poet known for her Imagist evocations of Japan. Percy's atmospheric letters to Amy, whom he addressed as "Big Fat Baby," and the objects he sent home set Japan in her mind as a place of beauty and mystery.

Percival Lowell was one of those Bostonian seekers after adventure—along with William Sturgis Bigelow and Isabella Stewart Gardner—who came under the sway of the zoologist Edward Morse's lectures on Japan at the Lowell Institute. "With money enough for his wants," as his biographer puts it, "never extravagant, he felt free in the spring of 1883 to go to Japan to study the language and the people." An enthusiastic photographer, Lowell took along a camera; Morse had made it clear that there would be extraordinary things to see. For the next ten years Lowell spent much of his time in Japan, with sojourns in Boston to check up on his business responsibilities and to write his books.

During his early months in Tokyo, Percival Lowell's precocious talents, linguistic and social, were obvious in foreign circles, especially to his intimate companion and mentor Dr. Bigelow. One suspects Bigelow's hand in the invitation extended to Lowell in 1883 to accompany the first Korean diplomatic mission to the United States. Relations between the countries had been strained, and occasionally bellicose, as when the crew of the American schooner *General Sherman*, on a trading mission to Korea during the late 1860s, was murdered and the ship burned. Negotiations with the so-called hermit kingdom of Korea were comparable to Commodore Perry's with Japan thirty years earlier. As Bigelow explained to Percival's father: "The position practically amounts to his having complete charge and control of the most important legation from a new country that has visited the U.S. since the opening of Japan."

Lowell accompanied the Korean legation to San Francisco and then overland to New York, where they were received by President Chester Arthur. On their return, Lowell accepted an invitation to visit Korea, at a time when the country was virtually unknown to Westerners. A photograph shows him in formal European attire with members of the Korean embassy in robes and ceremonial hats. In his first book, the impressive travel narrative *Chöson* (1885), Lowell included fifty-three photographic images from his Korean sojourn. In *Chöson* he also began to view Asia as a sort of photographic negative of the West: "It is because the Far-East holds up the mirror to our civilization,—a mirror that like all mirrors gives us back left for right,—because by her very oddities, as they strike us at first, we truly learn to criticize, examine, and realize our own way of doing things, that she is so interesting."

Lowell returned to Boston in the fall of 1884 to check on his business and social interests. The following spring, he served as best man at Edith Wharton's wedding. He soon had a new passion as well: the aristocratic game of polo, imported from colonial India to the fields west of Boston. Lowell's base in Boston was the Dedham Polo Club, founded in 1887 by his close friend Samuel Warren, a successful businessman who also served as president of the Museum of Fine Arts. Lowell arranged trains from Boston to Dedham specifically for the polo players and their entourage. Stories were told of Lowell and Warren having a midnight match in the main street of Dedham. New Year's Eve was celebrated with "a steeplechase on all fours, and a neat-ankled maiden leaping rows of candles at midnight."

In 1888 Percival Lowell published his second book, The Soul of the Far East. Almost immediately after his arrival in Yokohama five years earlier, Lowell had observed something about the Japanese language that struck him as a clue to the whole culture around him. He announced to his mother on June 8, 1883, that he had discovered "a key to the Japanese," which he called "impersonalism": "In the Japanese language there is no distinction of persons, no sex, no plural even. I speak of course of their inflected speech. They have pronouns, but these are used solely to prevent ambiguity. The same is true of their genders and plurals. To suppose them, however, destitute of feeling, as some have done, I am convinced would be an error. The impersonalism I speak of is a thing of the mind rather than the heart. I suggest rather than posit." Within a few years Lowell was ready to posit, and this notion of Japanese impersonality became the basis of *The Soul of the Far East.*

Lowell argued that everything in Asia—religion, art, language, and so on—was derived from this impersonal view of life, the diametric opposite, in his view, of European and American individualism. Lowell opens the book with some lighthearted observations about how everything in Japan, to Western eyes, seems, as he puts it, "topsy-turvy": "To speak backwards, write backwards, read backwards, is but the *a b c* of their contrariety. . . . From the standing of a wet umbrella on its handle instead of its head to dry to the striking of a match away in place of toward one, there seems to be no action of our daily lives, however trivial, but finds with them its appropriate reaction—equal but opposite." This is standard travel-book fare, and Morse liked to make the same point—using some of the same examples—in his journals and his lectures. Lowell's major argument, hammered home in chapter after chapter, is that there is an underlying opposition beneath all these amusing contraries, and it is the opposition of Asian impersonality to the Western "sense of self."

The Japanese, according to Lowell, are imitative rather than original. They graft and copy while Europeans invent and create. Like Morse, Lowell was a passionate Darwinian—but it was Herbert Spencer's applications of Darwin to human development that most intrigued him. Lowell maintained that while human evolution was on the fast track in the West, it had come to a premature end in Japan, where "the orderly procedure of natural evolution was disastrously supplemented by man." The Japanese, in Lowell's view, are a "childish" race, a case of arrested development that has moved too quickly, like a stunted tree, to a borrowed perfection. Even their arts, so striking to the eye, are a case of "the survival of the unfittest." Of the beauties of Japanese lacquer Lowell observes: "Our word finish, with its double meaning, expresses both the process and the result." And then, in a strange comparison that we will return to, Lowell writes of Japan: "For we behold here in the case of man the same spectacle that we see cosmically in the case of the moon, the spectacle of a world that has died of old age." Unless Japan adopted the techniques and attitudes of Western progress, the country would vanish, according to Lowell, "off the face of the earth and leave our planet the eventual possession of the dwellers where the day declines."

Lowell made two more trips to Japan. In early 1888 he picked from a map a remote and untraveled region of the country, the Noto peninsula. Noto turned out to be pretty much like other parts of Japan—farmers, villagers, shrines. In a brilliant passage early on in *Noto: An Unexplored Corner of Japan*, concerning his departure from Tokyo, Lowell indulged his love of heights. He had missed the train and decided to pursue his affection for fishing. The fish were the "aerial carp" flying from Japanese rooftops to celebrate the boys' festival, and the rod and reel were Lowell's camera.

The city made a spectacle from above. On all sides superb paper
carp floated to the breeze, tugging at the strings that held them to

the poles quite after the manner of the real fish. One felt as though, by accident, he had stepped into some mammoth globe of goldfish. The whole sky was alive with them. Eighty square miles of finny folk inside the city, and an untold company without. The counterfeit presentments were from five to ten feet long, and painted to mimic life. The breeze entered at the mouth and passed out somewhat less freely at the tail, thus keeping them well bellied and constantly in motion. The way they rose and dove and turned and wriggled was worthy of free will. Indeed, they had every look of spontaneity, and lacked only the thing itself to turn the sky into an ocean, and Tokyo into a sea bottom with a rockery of roof.

This beautiful passage probably inspired his sister Amy's little poem on the same subject. Called "Paper Fishes," it runs as follows:

The paper carp,
At the end of its long bamboo pole,
Takes the wind into its mouth
And emits it at its tail.
So is man,
Forever swallowing the wind.

Lowell wandered into the countryside with Bigelow, floating down the rapids of the Fujikawa—the river below Mount Fuji. And, a recurring pleasure, he photographed pretty Japanese women, the younger the better, despite what he called "my well known antipathy to the sex." He resorted to elaborate measures, as when he tracked down a woman he had first seen strolling in Ueno Park in the center of Tokyo. As he gleefully reported to his Dedham polo-playing friend Frederic J. Stimson:

My boy was sent to ask if I might be granted the privilege of taking her picture. I might but would I wait a moment till she had donned some finer toggery. I then set to work to prospect for a better place than the platform [in Ueno] from which she smote the hearts of men and discovered a nice little back alley among the trees. After an interview with the priest her father she was persuaded so far to condescend. There the deed was done. I discovered subsequently that she was a virgin—to photography.

In 1891 Lowell returned to Japan for a final visit, and this time—roughing it in the mountains to the south of Noto—he made his discovery of the Shinto trances on the sacred mountainside of Ontake.

In the fall of 1893, Percival Lowell left Japan and never returned. Ten years he had spent trying to make sense of Asian culture. And then, with an abruptness as mysterious as it is striking, he shifted his sights to Mars. On his last trip to Japan he had taken along a heavy twelve-inch telescope. He was, he later claimed, deeply impressed by the news that the Italian astronomer Giovanni Schiaparelli—who in 1877 had first discerned the fine lines he called *canali* on Mars—was so troubled by failing eyesight that he could no longer pursue his researches. For some reason, Schiaparelli's neutrally descriptive word *canali* (which means "channels") was early on translated as "canals," with the obvious suggestion of human—or at least intelligent—agency. Lowell was convinced Schiaparelli had discovered evidence that Mars was inhabited. He spent the rest of his life trying to persuade the world of this interesting news.

In 1894 Lowell set up the first, temporary structures of what became his famous Lowell Observatory on the mesa land above Flagstaff, Arizona. He was ready to explore the canals of Mars himself. Like many of his contemporaries, Lowell believed that Mars was further along in its "planetary evolution" than Earth, and that as a consequence water—which had once covered the earth and had receded to the oceans—was in much shorter supply on Mars. Hence, Lowell logically concluded, the pressing need for canals. "Irrigation," he wrote, "and upon as vast a scale as possible, must be the all-engrossing Martian pursuit." He imagined a planet crisscrossed with canals so gigantic that they were visible from the Flagstaff mesa. How could Martians have constructed such enormous things? Lowell reasoned that, since gravity was not as strong on Mars, Martians might be much larger than Earthlings and still move about with ease.

We now know, thanks to better telescopes and to probes sent to Mars, that many of Lowell's assumptions were unfounded. Mars and Earth are the same age, and the Martian landscape is apparently barren—drier than any desert on Earth. If there is life on Mars, it is likely to take the form of microscopic bacteria buried under the polar icecap. There are no canals on Mars, and the fine lines witnessed by Schiaparelli and Lowell seem to have been visible only to them and to their associates—hence Arthur C. Clarke's nasty moniker for Lowell, "the man with the tessellated eyeballs."

Percival Lowell at his telescope.

What was the connection in Lowell's mind between his twin passions of Japan and Mars? The question intrigued his admirers. "It is strange," wrote Lafcadio Hearn in 1902, "that Lowell should have written the very best book in the English language on the old Japanese life and character, and the most startling *astronomical* book of the period,—'Mars,'—more interesting than any romance." Nor was Lowell the only explorer of Old Japan to take an interest in the "old" planet. His good friend Edward Sylvester Morse, of the Peabody Museum in Salem, made extended visits to Lowell's Mars Hill Observatory in Flagstaff. Since Morse, through his lectures in Boston, had first inspired Lowell to travel to Japan, it was fitting that Lowell now inspired Morse's interest in Mars.

In 1906 Morse published his own book about Mars, entitled *Mars and Its Mystery*. The "mystery" of the title was the canals. "What are the canals?" Hearn had wondered back in 1894, as he looked over one of Lowell's letters. "*Are* they canals, or only the lines of a monstrous planetary breaking-up?" Morse thought he had the answer. Like his friend Lowell, he believed the canals were deliberately and intelligently designed. But his evidence, as usual with Morse, was fresh and offbeat. He compared man-made patterns of networks—railroads in Illinois, irrigation canals in Arizona—with "natural" patterns of cracking. Among examples of the latter were cracks in mud and asphalt. And then—a brilliant connection—Morse looked at the accidental crackling in the glaze of Satsuma ware, the most prized of Japanese ceramics. He concluded that the Martian networks had all the hallmarks of deliberate furrows rather than random cracks.

For Percival Lowell, there were other links between Japan and Mars. First, there was the Darwinian connection. In both Japan and Mars, Lowell discovered species endangered by "evolution." Mars, he believed, is "relatively more advanced in his evolutionary career" than Earth. It is tempting to speculate that the network of long, straight irrigation ditches in Japanese rice fields provided a model for his interpretation of the "canals" of Mars.

A deeper connection, however, is expressed most eloquently in the opening pages of Lowell's second book on Mars, *Mars and Its Canals* (1906), where he ascribes his interest in Mars to the thirst for travel. "From time immemorial, travel and discovery have called with strange insistence to him who, wondering on the world, felt adventure in his veins," Lowell begins. He mentions Columbus, and how the same footloose spirit "led the more daring of the Aryans to quit the shade of their beech trees . . . and wander into Central Asia." Maintaining his orotund style, he then draws the obvious link between terrestrial and extraterrestrial travel:

> Something of the selfsame spirit finds a farther field today outside the confines of our traversable earth. Science which has caused the world to shrink and dwindle has been no less busy bringing near what in the past seemed inaccessibly remote. Beyond our earth, man's penetration has found it possible to pierce, and in its widening circle of research has latterly been made aware of another world of strange enticement across the depths of space. Planetary distances, not mundane ones, are here concerned, and the globe to be explored, though akin to, is yet very different from, our own. This other world is the planet Mars.

This idea of new frontiers, connecting remote countries like Japan with remoter planets, is clear enough. Lowell was always eager to discover unknown corners of Japan like Noto, and undiscovered spiritual landscapes like the Shinto trances.

He also draws another, less obvious, connection between his Martian research and his previous travels. The astronomer himself, in Lowell's view, is a sort of high priest and hardy pilgrim, who must travel alone to distant and elevated shrines.

> He must abandon cities and forgo plains. Only in places raised above and aloof from men can he profitably pursue his search, places where nature never meant him to dwell and admonishes him of the fact by sundry hints of a more or less distressing character. To stand a mile and a half nearer the stars is not to stand immune.
>
> Thus it comes about that today besides its temples erected in cities, monasteries in the wilds are being dedicated to astronomy as in the past to faith; monasteries made to commune with its spirit, as temples are to communicate the letter of its law. . . . Primitive, too, they must be as befits the still austere sincerity of a cult, in which the simplest structures are found to be the best.

Lowell called his Flagstaff retreat the Hermitage and evoked the strenuous sublimity of the astronomer's calling. "To sally forth into the untrod wilderness in the cold and dark of a winter's small hours of the morning, with the snow feet deep upon the ground and the frosty stars for mute companionship, is almost to forget one's self a man for the solemn awe of one's surroundings." The solitary pilgrim sipping tea on Ontake and the astronomer high on Mars Hill are one.

There exists a convenient symbol of this odd connection of astronomy and Japan. In the reception room of Miidera, the Buddhist temple high above Lake Biwa in Otsu, where Fenollosa, Bigelow, and Okakura took their spiritual vows, there are two conspicuous gifts from Bigelow: a terrestrial globe on a tripod—and a telescope.

Part II

David Todd fell in love with the girl in the blue raincoat. She was standing in the June rain with her father, like some portrait of youth and age. Slim, brown-eyed, and stylish, she waited with her bearded, slightly disheveled father. Todd, a young astronomer employed by the U.S. Naval Observatory in Washington, had stopped by the Nautical Almanac Office, on that June day in 1877, to borrow a telescope. He knew the father, Eben Loomis, an amiable and eccentric New Englander who had known Thoreau well and Whitman slightly. Loomis had the old New England look about him—starry-eyed and a bit "transcendental," a sage gone to seed. Like Percival Lowell, Loomis had studied with the Harvard mathematician Benjamin Peirce, but Peirce had never suggested any great future for Loomis, who earned a modest living making astronomical calculations for the *Nautical Almanac.* Todd knew Loomis, but he didn't know the girl in blue.

Mabel Loomis spent summers in New England, away from the Washington heat and mosquitoes, with her mother and grandmother in cholera-free Concord. So it wasn't until the following November that David Todd called on her, at one of the many shabby Washington boardinghouses she called home. "Tonight Mr. Todd, a great friend of the Newcombs, called," Mabel confided to her tell-all journal. "He is in the Observatory, and quite charming. Evidently thoroughly at home among *young* ladies, as indeed is every man I know." She noted with satisfaction that Todd was "very good looking, a blond with magnificent teeth, pleasant manners, and immense, though innocent enough, powers of flirting. Well, so also have I." In addition to his magnificent teeth, Todd had a degree from Amherst College (1875) and solid career prospects. It also mattered to Mabel that he was a direct descendant of the famous New England minister Jonathan Edwards—he of the fiery sermon "Sinners in the Hands of an Angry God."

David and Mabel Todd, 1878.

Between his first sighting of the girl in the blue raincoat and his formal call on her, David Todd had made a lucky discovery. That August of 1877, during the same opposition of Mars in which Schiaparelli discovered his "canals," Todd and his boss, Simon Newcomb, were inspecting the Martian atmosphere. Todd took his turn at the telescope. An accidental turn of a screw, which momentarily darkened the vivid red planet, allowed him to identify a previously unknown satellite of Mars. The moon was named Phobos. A year later David Todd married the girl in the rain.

As an astronomer, David Todd lacked Percival Lowell's advantages—good eyes, good math, and money. He failed the mathematics exam for permanent appointment to the Naval Observatory. Todd did have a talent for machinery, however; in 1876, the young Thomas Edison, recognizing his knack for mechanical invention, tried to enlist his aid in his experiments. Todd decided to pursue the less lucrative field of astronomy instead, and his finest work—which eventually attracted patrons like Percival Lowell—was in developing machinery for photographing or otherwise recording astronomical phenomena.

During the first years of their marriage in Washington, the Todds were an attractive young couple and a passionate one. And while David Todd's career as an astronomer was by no means a failure, he is far better known for his participation in his wife's erotic life than for his contributions to astronomy. It is no exaggeration to say that Mabel Todd's love life may be the most fully documented of any nineteenth-century American woman. She herself recorded each erotic detail—sexual encounters and fantasies, menstruation and pregnancy, orgasms and discomforts—with a specificity rare in the Victorian era. Her diaries and journals have been mined in turn by historians of nineteenth-century sexuality. The first volume of Peter Gay's monumental *The Bourgeois Experience: Victoria to Freud* (1984) opens with an analysis of Mabel Todd's complicated affections.

The early married life of the Todds, Gay points out, shows none of the division of domestic repression and furtive transgression that Freud and others have led us to expect of the Victorians. Marriage, writes Gay, "far from dimming the Todds' sexual ardor, or reducing it to pleasant, drowsy monotony, only enhanced it." Gay notes the "steamy domestic atmosphere that Mabel Todd enjoyed and fostered," and the erotic rituals that marked her nights (before her husband's departure, when the sky was clear, to the observatory) and mornings. She wrote in December 1881: "Every night, [David] undressed me on the bright Turkey rug before the fire & then wrapped me up to keep warm while he put hot bricks in the bed. Then he took me in his arms & tucked me safely in bed & kissed me over & over, while he went to his desk & studied an hour or two longer. And after parties, when I came in cold, he did first the same for me— & loved me so!" In the morning, she wrote, David "would get up and brighten the fire, & spread all my clothes around it until they were warm, when he would come for me, & taking me in his arms, set me down on the rug close to the fire, where all my 'toasting hot' garments were awaiting me. Then would come the grapes or figs or apples on which he always re-galed me before breakfast."

In 1881 David Todd was invited to return to his alma mater to teach astronomy and supervise the observatory there, a fine octagonal building located where the first church in Amherst had once stood, on a hill over-looking the town. The move quickly brought the social-climbing Todds into the orbit of the leading family in Amherst, the Dickinsons. The inti-mate relations between the Todds and the Dickinsons brought stunning results for the Todds' marriage, for their careers, and for American liter-ature. Mabel Loomis Todd is best known to literary history as the friend, editor, and energetic publicist of the Amherst poet Emily Dickinson. As the pioneering Dickinson scholar Jay Leyda succinctly put it, "If David Peck Todd had not been appointed director of the Amherst College Ob-servatory in 1881 we might not today know that a poet named Emily Dick-inson ever wrote a poem." It is less well known that Mabel Todd was, in her time, a highly visible traveler to Japan. She was the first Western woman to climb Mount Fuji. While collecting artifacts for Edward Sylvester Morse of the Peabody Museum, she was also the first Western woman to visit Ainu villages in the north of Hokkaido. The Todds recapit-ulate, in unexpected ways, the strange convergence of astronomy and Japan that marked the life of their close friend Percival Lowell.

Mabel Todd was twenty-four when she arrived in Amherst. She quickly discovered that what distinguished society there was to be found in Amherst revolved around the Dickinson family—and specifically around the Italianate villa on Main Street known as the Evergreens, the house of Emily Dickinson's older brother, Austin Dickinson, and his wife, Susan.

Next door was the Homestead, the brick mansion in which the reclusive Emily Dickinson was born, wrote her nearly two thousand poems, and died. Mabel was a frequent guest at the Evergreens, where she played the piano and sang in her lovely soprano. She was deeply impressed with Susan Dickinson. Austin and Susan's twenty-year-old son, Ned, immediately developed a crush on the beautiful and quick-witted Mabel. Flattered by Ned's attentions, Mabel did nothing to discourage him—until she fell in love with his father.

Austin Dickinson, twenty-seven years older than Mabel and a year younger than her father, was the leading lawyer, indeed the leading citizen, in Amherst. Like his father before him, Austin served as the treasurer of Amherst College and had taken a lead in beautifying—with the help of his good friend Frederick Law Olmsted—the college and the town. If David Todd had good teeth and was related to Jonathan Edwards, Austin was, in Mabel's view, "impressive in look & manner, (the finest looking man I ever saw) . . . [and] comes from a staunch old New England family." Mabel Todd's snobbishness is evident in everything she writes about the Dickinsons. After the working-class boardinghouses of Washington, she finally felt welcome in the upper echelons of New England society. And, as Peter Gay notes, "the firmness of her snobbery permitted her to be flexible about her morality."

Indeed, Mabel's social climbing cannot be easily distinguished from her erotic attraction to Austin Dickinson. Until she had experienced a growing intimacy with Austin, as they rambled the countryside around Amherst together, she had (she wrote in her journal) been "perfectly satisfied with roast-beef & lager," but now she was "supping upon the nectar of the gods." After one of those sentimental rambles, on September 11, 1882, Austin confided in his diary the decisive word "Rubicon." When David Todd left town on November 10 to photograph the transit of Venus in California, and Susan Dickinson was attending a wedding in Michigan, Mabel Todd practically moved into the Evergreens. She was Austin Dickinson's not very secret mistress for a dozen years, until his death in 1895.

David Todd not only acquiesced in his wife's affair but reveled in it. He considered Austin Dickinson his closest friend and welcomed the generous gift of a house—the Dell—on the edge of Austin's property. When Mabel was away, Austin and David, as Peter Gay notes, would together "praise the woman they adored." And when she was at home, David did everything he could to facilitate their adultery. The Todds' daughter Millicent remembered how, during her childhood, her father would whistle a tune from the opera *Martha* when he came home from the observatory late at night. "Only later," as Emily Dickinson's biographer Richard Sewall notes, "did she realize that this was a signal to forewarn Austin and Mabel of his coming." The three traveled together—to the Chicago World's Fair in 1893, for example. And Austin had no difficulty imagining, in Susan's hypothetical and wished-for absence, all three under one roof. "I think we three would have no trouble in a house together," he wrote Mabel in 1885, "in living as you and I should wish." In David Todd's behavior there is a clear vicarious pleasure in his wife's erotic attachment to Austin Dickinson.

It later became clear to Millicent Todd, the daughter so often ignored in all these goings-on, that her father had secret affections of his own. Millicent learned from her mother that the Todds "had hardly been married three years when he began to make love to everybody that would accept his advances. He had most of the women guests who came to our house, even beginning on my [i.e., Millicent's] friends when I grew up." Millicent herself had to fend off her father's advances. She described a particularly horrifying scene when, during a visit to her father in the mental asylum where he passed the final years of his life, David Todd grabbed her, kissed her, and thrust his tongue into her mouth "with all the accompaniments." In 1929, clueless to the end, David Todd complained to his friend the singer Emma Thursby, "As a young father all little girls *except her* [Millicent] were very fond of me. *Why* has always been a mystery unsolved to me. Still is." As Gay sums up Todd's multivalent and omnivorous sexuality, he was "incestuous, polygamous, probably homosexual."

Austin Dickinson's two unmarried sisters, next door in the Homestead, also apparently tolerated his affair with Mabel. The sisters had a clear sense of Susan Dickinson's affections, and the painful withdrawal of them. (Austin complained bitterly to Mabel—hardly a disinterested party to be sure—that Susan refused his sexual advances for months at a time.) Emily had herself been half in love with Susan and had written a revealing and—despite its jesting tone—devastating poem about her sister-in-law:

But Susan is a Stranger yet—
The Ones who cite her most
Have never scaled her Haunted House
Nor compromised her Ghost—

To pity those who know her not
Is helped by the regret
That those who know her know her less
The nearer her they get—

For Austin and Mabel, the "haunted house" of the Evergreens was increasingly a place to be avoided. But the Homestead, so long a refuge for Emily Dickinson, became a safe haven for them as well. As Polly Longsworth, author of the definitive book *Austin and Mabel* (1984), has observed: "The Homestead became the safest place for Mabel and Austin to meet, for by 1882 Sue rarely went there. Emily, fully aware of what was occurring in her home, rejoiced in Austin's renewed happiness . . . and enjoyed indirectly the gaiety and spontaneity Mabel brought to the quiet mansion." "Indirectly," because Emily and Mabel—in an apparent concession to propriety—never met face-to-face. Mabel had corresponded with Emily Dickinson, sending her pictures in exchange for poems, and played the piano in the Homestead for the recluse upstairs. But Mabel first saw her lover's sister in May 1886, when Emily Dickinson was lying in her coffin.

A week after Emily Dickinson's death from kidney failure, her sister Lavinia discovered in the house a locked chest that held forty hand-sewn albums of Dickinson's poems in manuscript, as well as many more poems neatly copied on loose sheets. (Only a dozen poems had appeared in print in Dickinson's lifetime, none at her own instigation.) Determined to get these hundreds of poems published, and with no literary expertise herself, Lavinia approached the two potential editors least likely to agree on anything. First she asked her sister-in-law, Susan Dickinson, an obvious choice, since Susan, an amateur poet and occasional journalist, had received more poems from Emily—some 250—than had any other correspondent. When Susan dawdled at the considerable task of choosing among the more than a thousand poems at her disposal, Lavinia asked her to return the albums. In a decision that showed perhaps as much hostility as impatience, she turned to Mabel Loomis Todd, her brother's mistress and Susan's rival. Mabel accepted the challenge with alacrity. But the enormous job of transcribing, editing, and arranging poems for publication would have to await a journey—to Japan.

The Todds had been interested in Japan for some time. The Philadelphia Centennial Exposition of 1876 had created a vogue for Japanese style in furnishings and architecture, and Mabel Loomis Todd was determinedly stylish. When Austin Dickinson offered to build a house for his mistress on his own pastureland south of the two Dickinson houses on Main Street, the Todds settled on a Queen Anne cottage. The mixed style known as Queen Anne, with asymmetrical relations of square and round, and varied window shapes and sizes, leant itself to exotic touches. During the months when the house was being planned, David Todd carefully read through Edward Sylvester Morse's *Japanese Homes and Their Surroundings*. He found inspiration in Morse's discussion of rooflines and window overhangs. When the house was completed, in 1886, Mabel painted blossoming branches in Japanese style across the walls and ceilings of the parlor rooms. With such pronounced tastes for Japanese things, it was natural that, when given the chance to go to Japan, the Todds would seize it.

At precisely the moment Lavinia approached Mabel in 1887 about editing Emily Dickinson's poems, David was planning a trip to Japan. This time he was determined to take his wife with him. So, instead of another passionate interlude in Amherst with Austin, Mabel contented herself with love letters to him. The Todds crossed the Pacific in June, but it felt more like November. Instead of leaving by the usual route, from San Francisco, they took the shorter—and colder—route from Vancouver, arriving in Yokohama "after struggling to keep warm for sixteen days." During their brief stay in Yokohama and Tokyo, Mabel was most struck by a morning spent at a tea-firing factory in Yokohama owned by a Mr. Varnum, the only such establishment where the entire process of preparing the tea for export was accomplished by machinery. As she observed, in the first of three reports to *The Nation* magazine: "The natives bring in the slightly dried tea in boxes or sacks of a hundred or more pounds each—called a picul. Tons of it lie in piles upon the floor—enough for centuries of wakefulness. After this, the various drying processes take place—the sifting, sorting, coloring, and the blowing off of the dust, which is afterwards frequently used to flavor whisky."

In Tokyo, Todd and his associates debated the merits of various locations for the observatory. Mabel hoped for Nikko, "the beautiful summer resort . . . among mountains, groves, and temples . . . but as a daily afternoon thunder-storm is among the probabilities of that region, it was reluctantly abandoned." The choice of Shirakawa, a hundred miles or so north of Tokyo, turned out to be as fickle as Nikko for viewing the eclipse but perfect for Mabel's evocation of Old Japan, and the inroads of modern life. In her articles for *The Nation*, she worked up a contrast between the modern instruments of the Amherst expedition—the telescope, the special photographic plates, and the like—and their picturesque setting. As she wrote to Austin, on July 24, "The eclipse station has been pitched upon the ruins of an old castle . . . which is a marvel of picturesque beauty." The observatory on the battlements of the ancient castle, which was burned to the ground during the revolution of 1868, becomes the dominant symbol for Mabel Todd's reports.

> Nothing now remains but the series of stone embankments, which rise about seventy-five feet above the level of the surrounding rice-fields. Inside is space enough to quarter an army, and the whole is overgrown with grass and ivy and climbing white roses, while a number of the quaint, flat-topped pines with which Japan abounds have rooted themselves in effective niches. The castle was built somewhat more than three hundred years ago, and has had no history worthy of particular note, except that it was one of the last and most difficult strongholds to be taken and subdued in the late rebellion. A more picturesque station could not have been devised, nor one more favorable for the observations to be made.

For Mabel, the ancient castle is a place of transition, whose only significant history was at the moment, 1868, when the Meiji Era ushered in the modernization of Japan. A delegation of samurai—"four feudal knights of the old regime"—arrive in "picturesque loose *kimono*" to pay their respects to the foreign scientists. Mabel draws the obvious irony in the situation: "How changed their life, when they must ask of an American the privilege of visiting their own castle." The aesthetic category of the picturesque, which dominates all her reports from Japan, arises in the disjunction between old and new, ancient and modern.

Mabel Todd's historic ascent of Mount Fuji is similarly grounded in the specific conditions of the Meiji regime. According to the *Dictionary of National Biography*, Todd was "the first woman to climb Fuji-san on foot." In her account for *The Nation*, on October 13, 1887, she explains why: "Until the revolution of 1868, which changed so many old customs and prejudices, foreigners were not allowed to ascend this great peak, as they were looked upon in the light of mere beasts. Neither were women permitted to go higher than the sixth station [of ten]." Again, the interests of modern science were to be served—the "testing," funded by Harvard, of "various mountain peaks for astronomical purposes."

Mabel's description of the ascent is charming if conventional, departing in only a few respects from the accounts by Morse, Hearn, and other travel writers. Like them, she distinguishes the comfortable lower reaches of the mountain from the desolate upper regions according to the Romantic aesthetic categories of the beautiful and the sublime:

> But at length we came out from this woodsy shelter, and beheld the indefinite acres of fire-baked lava ahead and around us. The wild wind here blew free, and we saw what lay before us. . . . All the beauty and dreaminess were dropped in a moment, and no poetry remained, but grandeur alone, except where some little flowers of one kind and another, hardily following the cinders, laid their pink cheeks and their white cheeks caressingly against the black lava.

The clash of old and new is still very much on her mind: "The sweet little single rose, which had long since gone to seed at the old castle where the eclipse station had been located, here turned still a few delicate blossoms to the light." She gives pathetic fallacy a national twist, endowing even

Japanese flowers with native good taste: "Our own familiarly beautiful maidenhair . . . following Japan's universally artistic and decorative tendency, shaped themselves like a low bowl or jar."

Mabel notes the Japanese pilgrims who appear now and again along the strenuous climb to the summit, and the sacred relics and written prayers left at rustic stations along the way. But it is clearly a modern pilgrimage that she wants us to focus on—the modern foreign woman climbing where no woman has climbed before, in the company of those modern priests of the heavens, the astronomers. Overcome with altitude sickness, she records a final view of "our astronomers standing upon the summit, clearly outlined against a sky of deepest blue." As in Percival Lowell's evocation of clear nights at Flagstaff, these newly anointed high priests now rule the desolate heights. "An astronomer is at times a hero," she meditated ruefully, after clouds ruined all attempts to photograph the corona of the sun in August 1887.

After the Todds' return to Amherst, Mabel applied herself to the Emily Dickinson manuscripts. Working in conjunction with Thomas Wentworth Higginson, the Boston man of letters who had served as Dickinson's literary adviser, she produced three popular volumes of Dickinson's poetry from 1890 to 1896, as well as an edition of Dickinson's letters. Mabel Todd, who had published stories and travel sketches in prominent magazines, was an effective publicist for Dickinson's poems, attracting the attention of William Dean Howells and others. But whatever gratitude she had earned from the Dickinsons was shattered when Austin died in 1895, leaving a strip of land to his mistress in his will. Lavinia, daughter and sister of lawyers, was outraged, but she waited until the Todds had returned from a second trip to Japan to pursue legal redress.

Undaunted by the failure to capture the solar corona eight years earlier, the Todds traveled to Japan to photograph the eclipse in August 1896. The occasion offered even more dramatic contrasts of the old and the new. For this time it was determined that the best location would be high in Hokkaido, the northernmost island. This time, the Todds traveled in high style, aboard the 133-foot-long schooner *Coronet,* largest yacht in the New York Yacht Club and winner of a famous race from Long Island to County Cork, Ireland, in March 1886. There was a piano in the main saloon, where Mabel played and sang with the other guests and crew. They docked in Yokohama after a leisurely crossing. Mabel spent a few days exploring Tokyo, with the old Imperial Hotel as her base. On July 2 she made a point of looking for Okakura. As her traveling companion, Harriet James, reported: "We went this afternoon to the Ueno Park School, where we hoped to find the president, Mr. Okakura. Like so many others here, he has gone to the country: and being vacation there was no one at work in the school, and our journey was almost fruitless." While Mabel, staying at the Ya'ami Hotel, looked at temples in Nara and Kyoto, visited Doshisha University (founded by an Amherst College graduate, Joseph Neesima—or Niishima), and admired the cormorant fishing in Gifu, her husband and the rest of the eclipse expedition hurried north to Hokkaido. Mabel followed shortly.

The region around the southern city of Sapporo was already well developed, thanks in large part to the efforts of another Amherst man, William Clark. Mabel knew all about Clark. He was a friend of the Dickinson family, having worked closely with Austin in schemes to decorate Amherst with exotic trees. And during the Civil War an Amherst boy, Frazar Stearns, son of the Amherst College president, had died in Clark's arms, as Emily Dickinson reported in one of her finest letters. A few months later the news reached Amherst that Colonel Clark himself had died in battle. Fortunately it was a false report.

One of the great foreign figures of Meiji Japan, William Clark had come to the country by an interesting and roundabout route. In early 1871 a Japanese delegation had visited President Grant in Washington. They wanted to hire American advisers, since Americans were—as Dallas Finn remarks—"obvious experts at exploring, timbering, mining, farming, and settling a wilderness. Their frontier suggested Hokkaido. The Americans had their Indians, just as the Japanese had their aboriginals, the Ainu." For an expert in agriculture, everyone agreed that William Clark was the man. Clark had founded the first land-grant university in the country, in Amherst, Massachusetts, with a curriculum combining military drill and farming.

Upon his arrival in Sapporo during the summer of 1876, the energetic Clark set about building an American barn, modeled on one in Amherst, and an Imperial Agricultural College, modeled on the college in Amherst. There he trained a generation of Japanese men, drawn mainly from the middle class of Tokyo, under the uplifting motto—still known to all Japanese—"Boys, be ambitious!" (According to some who heard it, he actually said, "Be ambitious in Christ.") The most famous of these ambitious boys was Inazo Nitobe, the great interpreter of Japan to the West, whose face now graces the five-thousand-yen bill. Nitobe married a Quaker woman from Philadelphia, served in various wings of the Japanese government, and wrote a major work on the code of the samurai called *Bushido: The Soul of Japan* (1899). He was drafting *Bushido*, with the help of another Philadelphia woman, Anna Hartshorne, when Mabel Todd visited. It was Nitobe himself—with whom David Todd had corresponded before their departure—who welcomed Mabel to Sapporo. Nitobe "called at once," she reported in her book *Corona and Coronet*, and escorted her to see the sights and the local museum.

For Mabel Todd, as for other visitors, Hokkaido seemed barely Japanese at all. "Can it really be that Japan is seen from the windows of the train bound for Sapporo?" she wondered. The landscape seemed more New England than Old Japan: "The path might have been along some New England hillside. Red and white clover grew luxuriantly, humble heal-all and wild geraniums . . . dear old cinnamon pinks of traditional grandmothers' gardens, and fair purple iris. Young oaks shaded bluebells, homely yarrow sent forth its pungent odor." *Homely* is the key adjective here, with its double meaning. "But Japan—where had that poetic country gone?" William Clark's Agricultural College in Sapporo was even more conspicuously American. "Sapporo seemed the most American city of the Empire," she observed. "The model farm with its buildings, and the whole atmosphere of the place are American, not Japanese, with an effect practical rather than picturesque." It was the picturesque that Mabel was in search of—old, not new Japan. She found it, finally, among the Ainu. She was stunned by her first encounter with a " 'civilized' specimen" in Sapporo, "the most extraordinary figure in my experience. With his wild head of electrified black hair parted in the middle and standing out under a round-crowned and very dingy Derby, huge hoops of brass or German silver in his ears, his face largely hidden by an enormous beard and mustache . . . this anomalous relic of a vanishing nation was infinitely more pathetic than his veriest savage kinsman." She is alluding to that other "vanishing nation," the American Indian, "savage kinsmen" of the Ainu. "Sad it is to see a whole race disappear," she mused, "but this is inevitable in the world's progress."

Mabel Todd had been commissioned by Edward Sylvester Morse to collect Ainu artifacts for the Peabody Museum in Salem, of which he was director. He had hoped that she might acquire "a primitive loom, bows and arrows, elm-fibre garments, musical instruments." Nitobe proved invaluable for this undertaking. As Mabel reported: "Through Professor Nitobe's skill and courtesy I was enabled to purchase a number of rare relics, which induced great elevation of spirits, since Professor Morse had mentioned [that the Ainu] . . . especially dislike parting with their possessions."

Mabel was destined to travel in realms far wilder than this. For apart from Americanized Sapporo, as she noted, "Hokkaido is an unknown region,—one of the few places yet remaining where primitive nature and human nature may still be found, as rude aborigines pursue their unmolested way, and where many hundred miles of trackless forest yet await the first step of outer civilization." David Todd's eclipse station was established in a village called Esashi, on the northern shore of Hokkaido. The town itself was colonized by Japanese and hence not (as Mabel lamented) "picturesque . . . that quality dear to artists." But there were many Ainu villages in the area that she was determined to explore.

Mabel Todd's adventures among the Ainu were a sort of double journey—an ethnographic search for exotic artifacts and customs on the one hand and an inner, self-exploration on the other. She was confident that she was the first Western woman to travel in these remote villages and repeated the claim often, proudly recording "my first walk abroad as the first foreign woman visitor in Esashi." With the help of a Japanese guide she did more collecting for Morse, securing a magnificent Ainu necklace with a round silver pendant and a salmon-skin coat that are among the treasures of the Peabody collection. "To buy anything from an Ainu house," she observed, "requires tact and diplomacy even more than that necessary in purchasing old mahogany or china from some unwilling but hesitating elderly lady on a lonely New England country road." In accord with Morse's special interest in archery, she purchased a bow and poisoned arrows but kept for herself a little wooden eating bowl, "rudely carved" and never washed, "but merely wiped out with the finger after using. . . . I do not use it for bonbons."

Mabel recorded with similar distaste the filthy habits of the Ainu, among whom "bathing is unknown." She was shocked at the "bear festivals," when a bear, raised from cubhood until "too large for a safe playmate in the house," was slaughtered and eaten. Bear festivals, she wrote, "are the opera, theatre, afternoon tea, reception, and dinner-party of the Ainu." She told Anna Hartshorne, Nitobe's friend, that she had even seen a bear cub being suckled by an Ainu woman. The Ainu, Mabel concluded, are "barbarians pure and simple," with "no literature, no written language, and their arts are the simplest." In a sentence reminiscent of Percival Lowell's predictions about the Japanese, she maintained: "The race evidently lacks force, and will be entirely unable to hold its own in the march of nations."

But there is a contrasting current in Mabel Todd's account of the Ainu, centering on the Ainu women and, by extension, on herself. She takes note of the conspicuously inferior position of the Ainu women— how, for example, they are thought to have no souls and always step aside to let a man pass. Not surprisingly, "suicides among them are not uncommon." But an angry woman is given a great deal of respect by Ainu men, "for there seems hardly any end to the vindictive performances with which she will afflict a man who has displeased her, especially if he be her husband." Todd was fascinated by the tattooed "mustaches" on Ainu women, describing them with a mixture of admiration and disgust:

> The process of producing such mouth-decoration is described as exceedingly painful, but the Ainu women have borne it heroically, sustained by their happy certainty of its beautifying result. Horizontal slashes are made with a sharp knife, crossed by slanting cuts very close together and subsequently opened wider. Coloring matter, made from the soot of birch wood scraped from the bottom of an iron kettle, is then rubbed in unflinchingly, and afterward washed with water in which ash bark has been soaked, to produce an indelible stain. For two or three days the lips are so

swollen and sore that moving them, or attempting to eat, is almost impossible. But when once healed, imagine the satisfaction of emerging among one's friends and enemies, decorated for life!

The last sentence, so uncertain in its irony, carries an autobiographical weight. As the woman speaker in Yeats's "Adam's Curse" puts it: "We must labor to be beautiful." Beauty is akin to pain, and to anger. No wonder the Ainu men feared an angry woman.

Even as she recites the dreary tenets of social Darwinism concerning the eclipse of "vanishing" races by "progressive" races, Mabel Todd revels in her "primitive" existence among the Ainu. She deems it "appropriate to travel in a distinctly native way," taking only essentials and packing them in native baskets. She writes her letters "upon long strips of Japanese paper with a camel's-hair brush and native ink" and posts one such letter to America measuring two and a half yards. Her explorations in what she calls "Ainu land" are "quite primitive enough to accord with surroundings." All this is exhilarating, and in line with her wistful observation that "the Ainu are among the few races yet retaining in this over-civilized age an utterly unspoiled simplicity."

Mabel's Ainu explorations were conspicuously fruitful, but the pursuit of the eclipse turned out to be a disappointment—David Todd's second failure to view an eclipse in Japan. So, instead of vivid photographs of the corona of the sun, the Todds packed up their Ainu artifacts and prepared for the return voyage on the *Coronet*. Before they left Esashi, the Todds painted a scroll, in "native ink," as a farewell gift for the town. It was a poem, signed by Mabel and David, and dated August 16, 1896:

This is the land the sunrise washes,
This is the shore of the crimson sea,
How it rises or whither it rushes—
These are the eastern mystery.

The poem is by Emily Dickinson, more or less. Mabel Todd has been much faulted over the years for "fixing" some of Dickinson's poems, by regularizing rhymes, eliminating Dickinson's idiosyncratic punctuation, and so on. But this time she went a step further. For Dickinson had been

describing not the sunrise but the sunset, and not the eastern but the
western mystery:

> *This—is the land—the Sunset washes—*
> *These—are the Banks of the Yellow Sea—*
> *Where it rose—or whither it rushes—*
> *These—are the Western Mystery!*

Part iii

A nasty surprise awaited Mabel Loomis Todd in Amherst. She had departed
in mourning for Austin Dickinson, not knowing that the sliver of land he
had left her in his will would lead to trouble. Shortly after the Todds' return on October 22, 1896, Mabel, suspecting nothing, visited Lavinia
Dickinson and told her of a gift of blue china from Japan that would soon
make its way to the Homestead. A few weeks later she was stunned to
learn that Lavinia was bringing a lawsuit against her. In a protracted trial,
Lavinia sued Mabel for fraud, arguing that Mabel had secured her signature on the deed without informing her exactly what the document concerned. In the trial Lavinia's lawyer effectively contrasted the
stay-at-home, innocent Lavinia with the sophisticated world traveler
Mabel. Mabel's proud demeanor in the courtroom, with such worldly
friends as Mrs. George Washington Cable (wife of Lafcadio Hearn's close
New Orleans friend) sitting beside her in support, merely confirmed the
image.

The suit hung over the Todds for months, with the ever-present possibility that the affair with Austin would become public knowledge. The
trial, which was the talk of Amherst and neighboring Northampton, had
an unexpected observer. Percival Lowell, intrigued by David Todd's inventions in solar photography, had begun corresponding with him in
1895. On November 9 of that year, Lowell wrote Todd to thank him for his
"trans-Neptunian pamphlets," in which Todd had argued that there was a
planet, out of the range of telescopes, beyond Neptune. (Todd's hypothe-
sis, vigorously defended by Lowell, was confirmed when the planet Pluto
was discovered in 1930 at the Lowell Observatory. Pluto, the symbol of

which is a *P* and an *L* joined, was named for Percival Lowell.) "The public takes an interest too: only last winter a man—Prof. Fenollosa, you know him—wanted to know where he could learn about the stranger [i.e., the unknown planet]—I shall send him your first paper." This exchange is another indication of the surprisingly fervent curiosity of Japan hands concerning astronomical research.

In early 1897, during intense months at the observatory in Flagstaff, viewing the night sky and writing by day, Percival Lowell had a serious nervous breakdown and returned to Boston. He first visited the Todds in Amherst on May 8, 1897. "He is very charming," Mabel noted in her diary. In June, Lowell was in Amherst again, asking for a corner room at the Amherst hotel, "better for invalid." In Mabel's diary for September 7, written during a visit in Boston, she noted: "David went to Amherst at three, with Percival Lowell who then started for Flagstaff, and was most *anxious* for David to go too. He has invited him, *hard,* for several weeks."

Lowell spent much of the winter of 1898 in Amherst, visiting the Todds and taking a lively interest in Mabel's lawsuit. His comment on the trial, "Perjury always kills," is recorded in a letter from David Todd to Percival's sister Amy Lowell. "Be that as it may," the Todds' daughter, Millicent, drily remarked, "Lavinia soon took to her bed and died the following year."

Percival Lowell was still not fully recovered when, in early 1900, he and David Todd arranged a joint journey to Tripoli to observe another total eclipse of the sun. Lowell provided the money and Todd the expertise— and manual labor. While Lowell rested on the French Riviera for a few months, Todd set up the apparatus. They stayed in touch by postcard, vying with each other to send the most sexually explicit images they could find. One from Lowell, dated May 5, depicted a naked woman in a lace-decked bathtub. Lowell suggested that Todd, who wasn't feeling well, should "get into this warm tub and slough it off. . . . Apropos of treatment you should take a little more exercise on an empty stomach. Don't ask me whose; any fair Tripolitaine." On the Riviera, as he reported to Todd on one of the postcards, Lowell ran into William James, who was himself recovering from a breakdown, and working at the same time on his Gifford Lectures, which became his famous book *The Varieties of Religious Experience.*

While Lowell was enjoying himself on the Riviera, Mabel Todd was increasingly annoyed by the discrepancy between Lowell's lordly ways and her husband's hard work. She herself passed the time by investigating daily life in Tripoli, taking notes and photographs for a book she planned to write. Mabel had a particular interest in photographing the lives of women. She had taken arresting images of Ainu women with their painfully tattooed upper lips. In Tripoli, she photographed women in harems. At one point she was given permission to photograph an Arab bride and her entourage—without veils—as they prepared for the ceremony. The host of the wedding party arrived at the Todds' hotel that night and claimed his life was in danger. Mabel wrote, "The husbands of all the ladies who were guests at his wedding festivities had each taken an alarm lest his particular wives might have been photographed when I turned the camera on the various balconies and groups." She wondered why they should "take my innocent little camera so seriously." Because, the man explained, "a *man* might develop the negative . . . and so see their faces." To put his fears to rest, Mabel gave him the undeveloped film.

The final days in Tripoli were particularly strained. Lowell had joined the Todds, but he had no intention of sharing the work. On June 13, Mabel wrote in her journal:

> The last week of our stay in Tripoli rushed on, and very gladly would we have stayed for two or three more, but Mr. Lowell was possessed to get away as soon as possible. Indeed, he said before the Eclipse, which occurred Monday, that he saw no reason why we could not pack up and go on the Wednesday boat! An incredible idea—with fifty men we could not have taken down all the telescopes even, to say nothing of packing them. . . . A very wealthy person is usually possessed of the idea that he can do *anything*. And a nervously prostrated person is always unreasonable. The two together make an impossible combination. Mr. Lowell is better, decidedly, than when he was in Amherst, and most of the time he is thoroughly charming—nobody can be more so; but occasionally there are irresponsible bursts that show a diseased mind.

Mabel was so offended by Lowell's hauteur and sloth that she did not mention him a single time in her travel memoir *Tripoli the Mysterious* (1912).

Percival Lowell's electrifying "discovery" of life on Mars, first announced in 1894, had received enormous worldwide attention for a dozen years and resulted in popular fantasies such as H. G. Wells's *War of the Worlds*, as well as numerous Mars-inspired poems, popular songs, and sermons. While Lowell believed no further proof of intelligent life on Mars was needed—he had seen the canals with his own keen eyes—he knew that photographs would clinch the deal. So in the summer of 1907, when Mars would be in favorable opposition—proximity—to Earth, Lowell again enlisted the help of David Todd to direct a well-publicized expedition to the Andes. A telescope was set up near Alianza, Chile, four thousand feet above sea level and, in July, Todd cabled Lowell that photographic plates had captured the canals. "Bravo," Lowell cabled back. "The world, to judge from the English and American papers, is on the *qui vive* about the expedition, as well as about Mars. They send me cables at their own extravagant expense and mention vague but huge (or they won't get 'em) sums for exclusive magazine publication of the photographs."

There were tensions on the Andes expedition, however, and they were centered on the Todds. A young man called Earl Slipher, with expertise in photography, complained that the Todds seemed unhappy with the Alianza location. "I don't see how I can follow Mr. Lowell's directions and also please Prof. Todd," he wrote his brother in late July. "I guess he must ask Mrs. Todd. She seems to wear the trousers." Once the photographs were obtained, there were further squabbles. Lowell wanted to give the *Century* magazine, under Richard Watson Gilder, exclusive use of the photos, but the canals were considered not sufficiently visible in reproduction without retouching, which Gilder refused to do. The whole point of the photographs, as he reminded Lowell, was to be proof of the existence of the canals. The Todds, in the meantime, wished to announce the successful photographing of Mars—which they regarded as their own achievement—in articles in the popular *Cosmopolitan* and *The Nation*. Lowell successfully sought a legal injunction against *Cosmopolitan*, though

Mabel Todd's self-promoting article "Photographing the Canals on Mars" did appear, without photographs, in *The Nation* on September 19, 1907.

After the fiasco over the photographs of Mars, contact between the Todds and Percival Lowell ceased, only to be restored, posthumously, by other events. In June 1907, a few months before the Andes exhibition and still flush with their collaboration, David Todd had arranged for Lowell to receive an honorary degree at Amherst College. A year later, at the age of fifty-three, Lowell married his longtime Boston neighbor, Constance Savage Keith. They honeymooned in London, spending part of their trip in a balloon over Hyde Park, 5,500 feet up, to establish with a camera how markings on Earth appear from a great height. The last years of his life were spent in an increasingly bitter attempt to attract support for his "Martian theory."

At his death, on November 12, 1916, Percival Lowell was buried in his purple Amherst gown, a reminder of the respect once accorded his work. Soon after his death his widow approached the Todds to ask a favor. A posthumous portrait of Lowell had been commissioned, and what more appropriate raiment than the Amherst College gown? But the gown was in the casket, and could hardly be borrowed for the occasion, so Constance wondered whether the Todds might supply one, on loan, for the use of the artist. They were happy to oblige.

There was to be a late connection of the Lowells and the Todds, through Percival's younger—much younger—sister, the poet Amy Lowell. Born in 1874, when Percival was nineteen and attending Harvard, Amy grew up a pampered and overweight tomboy. ("She was never," says the chronicler of the Lowell family, "to be easy and happy with her body.") When Amy was nine, Percival appeared in Boston with the Korean mission, and Amy sat in the lap of his private secretary, a man of seventeen called Miyaoka Tsunejiro, who regaled her with tales of Old Japan. Tsunejiro had been a protégé and student of Edward Morse, and a playmate of Morse's son. Throughout his decade in Japan, Percival had sent his sister a cascade of letters on beautifully decorated paper. "Every mail," she later wrote, "brought letters and a constant stream of picture prints, kakimonos [*sic*] flowed in upon me, and I suppose affected my imagination, for in childhood the imagination is plastic. . . . Japan seems entwined with my earliest memory."

Amy experienced a prolonged bout of "neurasthenia" during the 1890s that coincided almost exactly with Percival's malaise. Whether it had similar causes is unknown, but it apparently had the same cure. Their father's death in 1900 brought a fortune to the siblings, freeing Percival to spare no expense in his pursuit of Mars, and giving Amy a comfortable mansion and time to write. He could leave business for astronomy; she could drop any pretense of seeking a husband and devote herself to a career in literature. In March 1912, Amy met the love of her life, Ada Russell, whom she nicknamed Peter. That same year, in October, Amy published her first book, *A Dome of Many-Coloured Glass*, which included poems inspired by Japanese art.

Amy continued to draw on her brother's letters and sojourns in Japan. The full flowering of her interest in Japan came with the book *Pictures of the Floating World* (1919). So convincing were these poems that Mabel Todd wrote to congratulate her on her vivid translations. But the real purpose of Mabel's letter was to encourage the project Amy Lowell had in mind, a life of Emily Dickinson, with special attention to Dickinson's family and milieu. David Todd, now institutionalized for mental illness, joined in the effort to persuade Amy to take on the challenge.

For five years, from roughly 1920 to 1925, Amy Lowell had labored on her immense book on the brief life of John Keats. Her editors wished to shorten it but, as Carl Sandburg said, "arguing with Amy was like arguing with a big blue wave"—of Hokusai, perhaps. Meanwhile, she was beginning to amass manuscript material on Emily Dickinson. Two things prevented Amy Lowell from writing her life of Dickinson. One was the full biography published in 1924 by Dickinson's niece (and passionate enemy of the Todds), Martha Dickinson. The other was her own precarious health.

The two red volumes of Amy Lowell's life of Keats were published in February 1925. She was set to sail to England on the *Berengaria* on April 26 to celebrate publication of the book. But plans were canceled when she suffered a stroke. She died on May 12. Within a year of her death, her reputation was already on the wane. Edmund Wilson found her verse "hollow and metallic," and compared it to "a great empty cloisonné jar." Van

Wyck Brooks, far more generous and discerning, saw how Amy Lowell, like her astronomer brother, opened up worlds for others to explore.

Was there something Japanese about Emily Dickinson? Mabel Todd thought so, as she painted, with brush and ink, a Dickinson poem for the people of Hokkaido. Amy Lowell seems to have thought so, too, as she turned from her imagery of the "floating world" to the haiku-like nature poetry of the Belle of Amherst. Ernest Fenollosa thought so, when he drafted a talk on Chinese and Japanese poetry in New Orleans, on December 22, 1896, just as the Todds were rounding the Horn on their long way back to Amherst. Fenollosa was trying to identify a property common to all poetical thought. "The harmony of poetic thought and word must be married," he concluded. "Each is a potent magic fluid, completely solvent of the other. Oriental poetry is specially deep in this field. Its highest philosophy was to read soul in nature. . . . There excellence of oriental is very high. Pure emotion. Generally very brief— In this resembles modern tendencies/Emily Dickinson."

The Fenollosas shared their enthusiasm for Dickinson with others in their circle. On April 7, 1898, during their sojourn in Kyoto, Mary wrote in her journal, "We got our Emily Dickinson from Okakura, but not other books." This would make Okakura the first documented Japanese reader of Dickinson. A few years later, in his "Notes for a Lecture on Chinese Poetry" of 1902, Fenollosa again thought of Dickinson in relation to what he called the "condensation and brevity" of the Chinese poetic language: "Like modern English/like our Emily Dickinson/like Emerson/Long poem impure—like long music/impression—."

As Akiko Murakata has noted, Fenollosa "did not live to see the full blossoming of Imagism nor the publication of his lecture at Columbia University in 1901, 'The Chinese Written Character as a Medium for Poetry,' " which Ezra Pound edited and published in *The Little Review* in 1918. This slim volume, in which Fenollosa argued that the Chinese ideogram retained a pictorial and metaphorical force lost to European phonetic languages, had an enormous influence on twentieth-century American poets.

Not that Emily Dickinson herself showed any particular interest in Japan. Though there are scattered references to Asia in her poems and letters, she seems to have mentioned Japan only once. "That you glance at Japan as you breakfast, not in the least surprises me, thronged only with Music, like the Decks of Birds." So she wrote to her childhood friend the novelist Helen Hunt Jackson (who was living in California) in the early spring of 1885. And yet there does seem to be something Japanese in Emily Dickinson's whole stance—something that, by the way, has appealed to generations of Japanese readers and scholars, many of whom make the pilgrimage each year to the big brick house on Main Street in Amherst in which Dickinson was born and died.

With her short, intensely observed poems of natural occurrences, Dickinson resembles those hermit-poets of China and Japan who found in the splash of a frog some clue to the workings of the universe. The change of the seasons—"These are the days when birds come back," "A light exists in Spring," "Further in summer than the birds"—is crucial to Dickinson and crucial to Basho and the classic haiku poets. Emily Dickinson's love for a few conventional stanza shapes also seems somehow Japanese, as does her reticence, her zealously guarded privacy, her love of solitude and silence. Like an epigraph from *The Tale of Genji*, her imperious lines impose a spiritual boundary:

The soul selects her own Society,
Then shuts the door.

THE MOUNTAIN OF SKULLS

>< >< ><

*The first sight of Fuji at dawn is not to
be forgotten in this life or the next.*

—LAFCADIO HEARN

Part I

*When Lafcadio Hearn saw the electric lights go on over the World's Industrial
and Cotton Centennial Exposition,* like a million moons dawning slowly
at once, he knew that it was time to leave New Orleans. The spectacular illumination of the fair, "forty miles of electric wire bursting simultaneously into flame," was the harbinger of a great industrial future for the
New South. But for Hearn—strolling among the moss-draped oaks by the
Mississippi River, seeking relief from bright lights, bad ventilation, and
eager crowds—it was an exit sign. He already knew, during that winter of
1884–85, that a more decisive departure was in the cards.

Hired by a Cincinnati newspaper eight years earlier to cover the
"new" New Orleans, Hearn had come to the Creole City in search, instead, of what remained of the old traditions. With his collapsible pocket
telescope held to his one good eye, he liked to zigzag along the filthy sewers of the French Quarter—in which water moccasins mingled with raw
sewage and dead animals—seeking out voodoo queens and the quaint
cries of street vendors. "I think a man must devote himself to one thing
in order to succeed," he wrote in New Orleans, "so I have pledged me to
the worship of the Odd, the Queer, the Strange, the Exotic, the Mon-

strous." Hearn liked the dilapidated streets of the Quarter, and the crumbling wooden houses with relics of Spanish and French architecture on their "wrinkled faces." He liked the cultivated languor of the Creoles, their threadbare rituals of dueling and masked balls. He liked their aboveground cemeteries and their ancestor worship. He liked their bitter coffee, and shared their bitter longing for an earlier, simpler time.

The pattern of Hearn's life was to arrive in a place just as what he loved there was on the point of disappearing. The year 1877 happened to be the very moment when Reconstruction came to an end, and the South was eagerly developing industry as a way to enter the modern economy. Since 1881 Lafcadio Hearn had been a New Orleans newspaperman, pampered and respected by the editor of the *Times-Democrat*, Page Baker. Baker was one of the voices of the New South. With the lifting of Reconstruction, New Orleans made tentative efforts to improve its fortunes, embracing internal improvements such as railroads and steam-driven streetcars. The big event of the decade, sponsored and promoted by the *Times-Democrat*, was the World's Industrial and Cotton Centennial Exposition, which opened on December 16, 1884. With this fair, New Orleans, known for her languid pace, meant to announce her entrance into the bustling modern world.

Hearn's aversion to the electric lighting was indicative of a greater ambivalence about the whole event. "Never did the might of machinery seem to me so awful," he wrote, "as when I first watched that enormous incandescence; and after having left the buildings and their myriad lights far behind, I found myself still dreaming of that future cycle of centuries wherein the world's labors shall be performed by automatons, and the great duels of nations shall be fought with lightning." Leaving those lights "far behind" was Hearn's principal objective at the fair, and he found a temporary refuge of silence and shadow in the extensive displays contributed by the young nation of Japan. "The attention of the visitor to the Main Building is apt to be especially attracted at the present time by the Japanese exhibit," he began his first dispatch. Of his handful of reports on the fair, four were devoted to the Japanese exhibits. There is a revealing tension in these pieces—Hearn's first concerning Japan—in the thrust of Japan's self-presentation against his version of it.

The main effort of the Japanese exhibits was to demonstrate the extraordinary success of Japanese educational and industrial programs during the early Meiji Era. Hearn's first piece on the exhibits ignores this progressive slant. He dutifully noted the witty deceptions of some recent examples of export art: "Great incense-burners, with double-headed and triple-clawed dragons interlinked about them in monstrous contortion, seem to be wrought in fine bronze; but they are only faience-ware dexterously metal-tinted. Delicate vases of porcelain aspect, covered with grotesque paintings, and surmounted by a cover on which a frog, a tiger, or a gargoyle-shaped creature is sitting, turn out to be made of the finest and hardest statue metal." But Hearn much preferred "the antique art of Nippon" on view, in which he sensed, without being able to name it, the rustic "tea" or *wabi* taste: "The antiquated porcelains have none of that conventional frankness of composition in design nor the flaring color which distinguishes many of the best new pieces; they are sober-tinted; they affect no accepted pattern; their figures are strangely puzzling to the eye at first glance, but when the puzzle is read, what marvellous movement!" He loved the "fans of all values and varieties," porcelain decorated "with stanzas inscribed in those long straggling black characters which Japanese poets compare to a flight of birds winging their way against the light."

Hearn even knew enough about Japanese art to notice what was not on view in New Orleans: rice-paper drawings ("but these are promised at a later day"); swords of the highest quality ("which outrivalled in beauty and temper the blades of Toledo and Damascus"). He closed his piece—as he later would close so many of his Japanese writings—with a flourish about Mount Fuji (or "Fusi," according to the then-prevailing romanization):

> Splendid silks are hanging everywhere; some exquisitely embroidered with attractive compositions, figures, landscapes, and especially views of Fusiyama, the matchless mountain, whose crater edges are shaped like the eight petals of the Sacred Lotos; Fusiyama, of which the great artist Houkousai [Hearn had been reading French art critics] alone drew one hundred different views; Fusiyama, whose snows may only be compared for pearly beauty to "the white teeth of a young girl," and whose summit

magically changes its tints through numberless variations of light. Everywhere it appears, the wonderful mountain—on fans, behind rains of gold, or athwart a furnace light of sunset, or against an immaculate blue, or gold-burnished by some wizard dawn; in bronze, exhaling from its mimic crater a pillar of incense smoke; on porcelain, towering above stretches of vineyard and city speckled plains, or perchance, begirdled by a rich cloud sash of silky shifting tints, like some beauty of Yosiward.

Hearn means Yoshiwara, the pleasure quarter of Tokyo, but one hardly minds the error, so confident is the exotic evocation of a backward-looking world of unerring aesthetic delight, of geisha clad in silk of shifting tints, with Fuji in the distance.

Ichizo Hattori's Japan was quite different. It was a modern Japan of scientific progress, high literacy, proficiency in European music. Hattori (whom Hearn carelessly called Hattoro in his articles) was the commissioner of Japanese exhibits at the New Orleans Fair. He welcomed Hearn to his "cozy private office" and guided him through the elaborate Japanese educational exhibits. A friendly and mild-mannered man, Hattori spoke excellent English. He had, along with a cohort of other Japanese young men, attended Rutgers, graduating in the class of 1875 and delivering (according to the official history of the college) "an oration in Japanese at Commencement." As vice president of the Imperial University in Tokyo, Hattori was a friend and valued associate of Edward Sylvester Morse and other American professors there.

Hattori led Hearn through aisles of scientific publications and apparatus. Amid the profusion of instruments, maps, charts, schoolbooks, kindergarten toys for teaching the law of gravity, school furniture, photographs of university buildings, Hearn paused to admire those objects that demonstrated the Japanese gift for fine workmanship—for example, an anatomical manikin "surpassing the best work of the kind executed in Paris." While Hattori proudly disassembled physically explicit manikins, including some "for obstetric demonstration," in his private office, Hearn admired instead the Japanese tapestries on the office walls, representing birds and flowers in gold and silver. When the tapestry quivered, Hearn noted, "the fighting storks become startling."

Hearn's days were spent at the fair, cultivating and quizzing Hattori and searching for pockets of Old Japan. His nights were spent at his desk, writing about the fair and finishing his finest book, the short novel *Chita*. It is about a great storm that engulfs an island resort in the Gulf of Mexico below New Orleans. Everything on the island—the beautiful old hotel, the elegant Creole dancers, the palms, the pleasure boats—is swept away by a tidal wave. Nobody survives. Nobody except one child, clinging to the dead and floating corpse of her mother. In a way, *Chita* is the story of Hearn's own life.

Lafcadio Hearn spent his life in flight, circling the globe like a migrating bird, from one island to another in a continuous archipelago. He was born in 1850 on the Greek island of Leukas, an outpost of the British Empire. His father, an Anglo-Irish surgeon in the British navy, had an affair with a local woman—illiterate, dark-skinned, beautiful. When she became pregnant Dr. Hearn left her, and their son, with his relatives in Dublin. Abandoned, miserable, and pining for her lost home, she returned to Greece when her oldest son was seven. Patrick Lafcadio (for Leukas, or "Lefkas") never saw her again. Under the apathetic care of a great-aunt, he attended boarding schools in England, where he lost an eye in a playground fight, and in France, where he was a classmate of Maupassant. Having rid themselves of the mother, the Hearns got rid of the child. They gave him a bit of money and shipped him to Cincinnati, supposedly to place him under the tutelage of a distant relative. The relative, unapprised of the plan, wanted to have nothing to do with the dirty and misshapen waif. And so, at the age of nineteen, Lafcadio Hearn (as he now called himself, having left the Patrick behind in Ireland) found himself homeless, jobless, and penniless in the beer-swilling, largely German-speaking city on the banks of the Ohio River.

Hearn was adept at languages and a fluent and observant writer. He took lodgings with a printer and began contributing grisly stories inspired by Edgar Allan Poe. A crime reporter of genius, Hearn learned how to do something special with the murder of a tanyard worker stabbed with a pitchfork and crammed, still alive, into a furnace. Meanwhile, he found a sort of second family among the black drifters and roustabouts along the river. In 1871 Hearn fell in love with a mulatto woman called Alethea Foley, whom he nicknamed Mattie. She was the daughter of a white Irish slaveholder and one of his own slaves. (The parallel to Hearn's divided parentage, abusive Irish father and illiterate "dark" mother, is striking.) Born into slavery herself, Mattie had worked for members of her father's white family in Kentucky—her father presented her as a wedding present to his own white daughter—before moving north after the Civil War. When Hearn met her she was eighteen, making a bit of money as a cook at a boardinghouse, and occasionally as a prostitute, in the dark streets of Cincinnati. In an article, Hearn described Foley's "wonderful wealth of verbal description . . . [and] gift of conversation which would have charmed an Italian improvisatore." She was, by all accounts, strikingly beautiful—"a healthy, well built country girl," Hearn wrote, "whom the most critical must have called good looking." Though she could pass as white, "but for a slight crispness of her hair" (according to a 1906 report), she made no attempt to do so.

Laws against miscegenation prohibited interracial marriage in Ohio, but Hearn—driven by love or guilt—managed to find a black minister who was willing to perform a marriage ceremony, with Mattie pretending this time to be white. Hearn's editor at the *Cincinnati Enquirer* was shocked when he got wind of the marriage in August 1875 and fired Hearn immediately for "cohabiting with a woman of color for four years." A rival newspaper, the *Commercial*, was willing to hire him. But Hearn, disillusioned and angry, and feeling "ostracized, tabooed, outlawed," was ready to escape from "beastly Cincinnati." His loyalty to Mattie was solid, but their marriage seems to have been a difficult one, with Mattie straying into her former life in the streets. She spent some time in Indianapolis in the fall of 1877. When she returned a few months later, she found that Hearn had departed for New Orleans.

Officially, Hearn was traveling as a reporter for the *Commercial*, but he had no intention of returning to Cincinnati. He made his way down the Ohio and then the Mississippi River. From Memphis he wrote an anguished letter about Mattie to his friend Henry Watkin. "I feel all the time as if I saw Mattie looking at me or following me and the thought comes to me of the little present she made me and a little woolly lock of hair she sent me, and her despairing efforts just to speak to me once more, and my only answer being to have her arrested and locked up all night in the police station."

As Hearn's steamboat neared New Orleans, he was drawn to the "sad ruin on the face of the great plantations": "There were splendid houses crumbling to decay and whole towns of tenantless cabins; estates of immense extent were lying almost untilled, or with only a few acres under cultivation; and the vigorous cottonwood trees had shot up in whole forests over fields once made fertile by the labor of ten thousand slaves."

Lafcadio Hearn was sent to New Orleans to cover the election campaign that restored ascendancy to the white population of the city. He took no notice whatsoever of the political shenanigans—the "compromise of 1877"—by which the Republican Rutherford B. Hayes gained the crucial electoral votes of the state of Louisiana in exchange for a promise to lift the policies of Reconstruction. The majority of white New Orleanians had chafed at the systematic—and in their view corrupt—efforts to bring about a government that accorded freed slaves a fair shake in the political process. Four years earlier, in September 1874, hundreds of New Orleanians, under the banner of the "White League," had resorted to violence to seize the state government (then located in New Orleans) and place their own leaders in office. (The military leader of the coup, General Frederick Ogden, was superintendent of the Cotton Exposition.) The coup so alarmed President Grant, who feared a resumption of the Civil War, that he sent federal troops to restore order. With the election of Hayes, these White Leaguers quickly took legally, by elections, the prize that they had tried to seize by force of arms. Hearn's arrival coincided with the beginning of one of the gloomiest periods for black people in the Crescent City.

Hearn's editor in Cincinnati received a series of "letters from New Orleans," but there was nothing in them about politics or Hayes or the New South. The news from New Orleans, as far as Hearn was concerned, was the old stuff that—against all odds—survived there. These "survivals," as Hearn—good evolutionist that he was—called them, filled his dispatches from the city. He noticed immediately that New Orleans was a city divided, but not exclusively along racial lines. The division that interested him most was ethnic: the "Creoles," white and black, on one side and the

"Americans," also white and black, on the other. Before the Civil War, the word *Creole* had denoted anyone born in New Orleans and descended from the French and Spanish who first settled the area. New Orleans was unique among Southern cities in having a large and conspicuous free black population before the Civil War, and many of these free blacks were French-speaking and Catholic—the so-called black Creoles.

As he moved from lodging to lodging in the French Quarter of the city, Hearn busily collected Creole lore and legend. He gathered Creole proverbs and Creole recipes, Creole medicines and Creole spells, Creole catcalls and vendors' cries. He was particularly drawn to ritualistic "survivals" such as voodoo and the traditional dances of Congo Square, where slaves had congregated on Sundays before the war. And he sought out people with some expertise in these matters, such as the writer George Washington Cable and the Creole historian Charles Gayarré. Never mind that Cable, a Negro-rights advocate, and Gayarré, a white supremacist, were sworn enemies of each other.

George Cable was a white New Orleanian by birth and a Confederate veteran. His researches into local history convinced him that whites and blacks were so intertwined in the life of the city, linked by blood and by common interests and traditions, that it was madness to try to separate them. His stories, and his great novel *The Grandissimes*, display this interconnectedness. For Cable, Creoles, white and black, were one family. Gayarré, who had initially dismissed Cable as "no more than a malevolent, ignorant dwarf," became so incensed by Cable's views that he rented a hall to denounce Cable in public, accusing him of proposing as a panacea to Louisiana's ills a bottle labeled "social and conjugal fusion of the blacks and the whites." Rumors circulated that Cable himself had "colored blood."

Cable's writings had inspired Hearn to come to New Orleans in the first place. While living in Cincinnati with Mattie Foley, Hearn had read with passionate interest and recognition Cable's stories of love across the color line. As soon as he arrived in New Orleans, he sought out the Creole cottages that were the settings for Cable's stories. It was only a matter of time before Hearn sought out Cable, and the two of them became a sort of investigative team in search of Creole songs and folkways. With Cable's help Hearn published a Creole cookbook and a book of Creole proverbs to coincide with the opening of the fair, and the two friends collaborated on a guidebook to the Crescent City.

But these were gestures of farewell, futile attempts to fix in time an "Old" New Orleans that Hearn knew was passing away before his eyes. Hearn left New Orleans shortly after the Cotton Exposition closed. He spent two years in Martinique—another island—in search of a more authentic Creole world. Already Japan beckoned as an ultimate goal. Hearn carried with him in Martinique, as a sort of talisman, a Japanese paper fan "with a design upon it of the simplest sort: one jointed green bamboo, with a single spurt of sharp leaves, cutting across a pale blue murky double streak that means the horizon above a sea." While the design might seem "trivial to my Northern friends," Hearn wrote, "to me it causes a pleasure bordering on pain."

Hearn was now involved in a new and consuming quest, which he described succinctly to his friend and *Times-Democrat* colleague Elizabeth Bisland: "I am trying to find the Orient at home." Long before he actually traveled there, Hearn had fashioned his own private Japan. His days at the Japanese exhibits of the New Orleans Fair were preparation. And so was his stray reading in Max Müller's scholarly renditions of ancient Buddhist texts. But the book that really lit a fire in Hearn's mind, confirming Japan as the only goal of his quest, was Percival Lowell's *Soul of the Far East.* "I have a book for you—an astounding book—a godlike book," he told a friend in 1889. "But I want you to promise to read every single word of it. Every word is dynamic. It is the finest book on the East ever written; and though very small contains more than all my library of Oriental books. And an American wrote it!" Though with time Hearn came to question certain tenets of Lowell's book, especially the claim that the Japanese were imitative rather than imaginative, he loved the overriding view that Japan was "topsy-turvy," the opposite in every way to the West. Hearn thought Lowell had discerned "the fluttering of the Human Soul in its chrysalis" and was determined to follow his lead.

Hearn came late to Japan, and he knew it. Edward Morse, in 1877, had seen married women with their teeth blackened, not whitened, for beauty, and indignant samurai reluctant to relinquish their twin swords.

Henry Adams and John La Farge could still see, in 1886, a rural Japan un-changed by Western contact. In proposing a travel book to Harper's, Hearn knew he could promise no discoveries of the kind that Morse or Lowell or Isabella Bird had made along the "unbeaten tracks" of Japan. "In attempting a book upon a country so well trodden as Japan," he wrote in late November 1889, "I could not hope—nor would I consider it pru-dent attempting—to discover totally new things, but only to consider things in a totally new way . . . to create, in the minds of readers, a vivid impression of *living* in Japan—not simply as an observer but as one taking part in the daily existence of the common people, and *thinking with their thoughts.*" On April 4, 1890, book contract in hand and a few months shy of his fortieth birthday, Hearn saw Mount Fuji hovering at dawn above the sea and clouds, like an afterimage of his Japanese fan. He landed in Yokohama for what he thought would be a tour of a month or so. He stayed for the rest of his life.

Part II

Too poor for the Grand Hotel, Hearn found a seaman's rooming house by the Yokohama waterfront run by an American mulatto named Carey. Hearn was an avid reader of Melville, and in Carey's hotel he found a congenial world like the Spouter's Inn in *Moby-Dick:* "an atmosphere of sailors and sealers and mates and masters of small craft . . . a salty medium of water-dogs." Hearn was happy to avoid the poisonous company of luxury travelers and Christian missionaries. From Carey's, he made forays by jinricksha into the back streets and hillside retreats of Yokohama, "cool with the coolness of Japanese spring and wind-waves from the snowy cone of Fuji," finding the city by turns alluring and appalling.

In his manic search for "survivals" of Old Japan, as detailed in "My First Day in the Orient," Hearn kept bumping up against modernity: "a shop of American sewing-machines next to the shop of a maker of Bud-dhist images; the establishment of a photographer beside the establish-ment of a manufacturer of straw sandals." Everything tempted him in the traditional shops, toothpicks of cherrywood, "bound with a paper wrap-per wonderfully lettered in three different colors; even the little sky-blue towel, with designs of flying sparrows upon it, which the jinrikisha man

uses to wipe his face." And everything was cheap. Against the temptations
of the collector, he had this sudden epiphany:

> The largest steamer that crosses the Pacific could not contain what
> you wish to purchase. For, although you may not, perhaps, confess
> the fact to yourself, what you really want to buy is not the contents
> of a ship; you want the shop and the shopkeeper, and streets of
> shops with their draperies and their habitants, the whole city and
> the bay and the mountains begirdling it, and Fujiyama's white
> witchery overhanging it in the speckless sky, all Japan, in very
> truth, with its magical trees and luminous atmosphere, with all its
> cities and towns and temples, and forty millions of the most lov-
> able people in the universe.

Only in the shrouded darkness of Buddhist temples and Shinto
shrines, however, did Hearn find glimmers of the deep Japan he was
after, though here too he could not resist two jokes on himself. One priest
reverently presented him with a bowl of water, in which Hearn dipped his
fingers before realizing he was being offered a drink. And deep within
another temple, in "the dimness of an inner sanctuary, haunted by faint
odors of incense," Hearn approached what he hoped might be the mystery of mysteries only to find "a mirror, a round, pale disk of polished
metal, and my own face therein, and behind this mockery of me a phantom of the far sea." For his first day in Japan, this seems about right.
Hearn had brought his Orient along with him, and found himself wondering "whether I shall ever be able to discover that which I seek—outside
of myself! That is, outside of my own imagination."

Hearn arrived in Japan knowing two names. One was that of Hattori,
his friendly guide at the Japanese exhibits in New Orleans. The other was
that of Basil Chamberlain, professor of Japanese literature at the Tokyo
Imperial University, with whom he had corresponded about Japanese
folklore. Chamberlain, an Englishman, had translated classic Japanese
texts, revised Murray's guide to Japan, and written *Things Japanese*, a
lively and authoritative compendium, arranged in alphabetical order, of
commentary on Japanese culture from "Abacus" to "Zoology" (the latter
begins, "Japan is distinguished by the possession of some types else-

where extinct—for example, the giant salamander—and also as being the most northerly country inhabited by the monkey"). His Japanese was flawless and his scholarship wide-ranging. Two more influential friends could hardly be imagined: Hattori in 1890 was vice minister of education, and Chamberlain was a powerful voice in the university system. When Hearn conveyed his desire to remain in Japan, they found an opening for a teacher of English at a boys' high school in Matsue, a deeply traditional castle town on the Sea of Japan, on the other side of the main island of Honshu.

The astonishing thing about Hearn's fourteen years in Japan is that he managed, by luck and guile, to experience the different phases of Japan's modernization by his choice of geographical locale, thus fitting himself as an effective spokesman for the evolution of the country. Three towns—Matsue, Kumamoto, and Tokyo—were home to Lafcadio Hearn, and each gave him a vivid sense of one crucial stage in Japan's progress.

In immemorial Matsue, waking to the rhythmic thump of a huge mortar and pestle pounding rice (a young man climbed up the wooden shaft to weigh it down, then jumped off to release it), Hearn lived for an idyllic year a samurai's life in Old Japan. Here in this placid town were "survivals" in spades, unchanged since the centuries before contact with the West. Hearn taught his reverent pupils by day and at night cataloged the festivals and folkways of Matsue. When the winter cold and his own domestic ineptitude left him bedridden, a Japanese friend proposed a solution: an arranged marriage with a quiet, twenty-two-year-old samurai's daughter named Setsuo Koizumi. Her name may have seemed an uncanny sign to Hearn; Setsuo means "the true," just as Alethea, Mattie Foley's given name, means "truth." The match was advantageous on both sides: Setsuo took care of Hearn, and Hearn, with his generous salary, took care of her impoverished extended family. With servants, grandparents who remembered a feudal past, and a traditional samurai's house called Kitabori, located between the old hilltop castle of Matsue and a forest filled with the cooing of doves, Hearn could imagine Japan before Perry.

A different world awaited in Kumamoto, Hearn's next posting. This was the proud and decimated garrison town in Kyushu that Edward Morse had visited soon after the civil war of 1877, when General Saigo's siege had led—like Sherman's march on Atlanta—to the burning of the city. Hearn was not prepared for this awkward, transitional city of modern railroad stations and Western-style brick school buildings in the new university where he was to teach. His students were older and less respectful, their ambitions pragmatic. Hearn complained to Chamberlain that Kumamoto had "no poetry—no courtesy—no myths—no traditions—no superstitions."

Lafcadio Hearn.

And yet, three hard years in Kumamoto inspired Hearn's best writing on Japan. The very lack of external "survivals" in this scorched town turned his attention inward. He began to look for what he called Kokoro, or "Heart Things." He hired translators, including Okakura's younger brother Yoshisaburo, to provide him with literal versions of Japanese poems and folktales. Meanwhile, he questioned friends and chance acquaintances for anecdotes that revealed the deep psychological traits of Japan.

His stark sketch "At a Railway Station" recounts the moment when a captured thief and murderer is brought back to Kumamoto to face charges and encounters the wife and child of the police officer he had killed while making his escape: "I went with a great throng of people to witness the arrival at the station. I expected to hear and see anger; I even feared possibilities of violence. The murdered officer had been much liked; his relatives would certainly be among the spectators; and a Kumamoto crowd is not very gentle. I also thought to find many police on duty. My anticipations were wrong." Instead, the arresting officer guided the criminal to the son of the murdered man. "Little one," he said, "this is the man who killed your father four years ago." The child began to sob, and the murderer threw himself at the child's feet, begging for pardon. That "the appeal to remorse had been made through the criminal's sense of fatherhood," this, for Hearn, was the "heart thing" revealed by the anecdote, an indication of "that potential love of children which is so large a part of the soul of every Japanese."

If Matsue was an unpicked pocket of Old Japan, and Kumamoto an uneasy truce of old resentments and modern structures with lingering "heart things" hidden in the interstices, Tokyo—where Hearn settled in 1895—represented the radioactive core of Westernization and the "New Japan." Hearn's appointment to the prestigious chair of English literature at Tokyo Imperial University was surprising for at least three reasons. First, he had no training or degree in British literature and much preferred French authors. Second, as the modernizing university par excellence, Tokyo Imperial University was a bad fit for Hearn, all of whose instincts were conservative. And third, the timing was exceedingly odd. In 1895 Japan, as Hearn himself noted approvingly, was sending its foreign teachers home. In the flush of victory in its war with China, and resentment over the terms imposed by European powers (who were afraid of a powerful Japan and wanted China for themselves), Japan was in a proud and xenophobic mode. When the offer from Tokyo Imperial University came, at a time when Hearn had fled Kumamoto and was doing freelance work for his old New Orleans newspaper, he was momentarily puzzled.

The idea to hire Hearn for the chair had come from his old patrons, Hattori and Chamberlain. Toyama, poet and head of the university (he

had hired Morse and Fenollosa so many years earlier), was also enthusiastic. Hearn realized that these men were no longer in need of foreign experts to train the Japanese in the ways of the West. Japan had caught up.
Hearn was hired not as an expert but as a propagandist. His book *Glimpses
of Unfamiliar Japan*, published in Boston in 1894, was a huge success. Its
idyllic chapters on Hearn's first day in the Orient and on daily life in
Matsue had revived interest in Japan at a time when American fascination with the country was in danger of waning. (The adjective *unfamiliar*,
at a time when many things about Japan were all too familiar in the West,
was carefully chosen.) Hearn was the most prestigious Western writer to
fall in love with Japan. He could be trusted, his Japanese patrons felt, to
continue to write in praise of the country. Chamberlain wrote that "the
kind of man the Japanese like to retain is one who keeps their name
prominently before the great world." And Hearn himself recognized the
implied pact of his Tokyo post. In 1896, soon after he had started to teach
in Tokyo, Hearn wrote to a friend: "I fear—I suspect that this position has
been given unto me for a combination of reasons, among which the dominant is that I may write at ease many books about Japan."

The novelist Natsume Soseki succeeded Hearn in the chair of English
at Tokyo Imperial University. There is an interesting scene in Soseki's
novel *Sanshiro* in which two students at Tokyo Imperial University talk
about Hearn's years there. The implication is that Hearn did indeed see
his main responsibility at the university as the writing of books.

> They entered the Red Gate together and strolled around the pond.
> The student told Sanshiro how Professor Lafcadio Hearn . . . had
> always disliked the faculty room. After his lectures he would walk
> round and round the pond. He spoke as if Hearn himself had told
> him this. Sanshiro asked why Hearn never mixed with the other
> teachers.
>
>   "It stands to reason, doesn't it? You've heard their lectures.
> Who could he have talked to?"

In any case, Lafcadio Hearn knew the value, beyond propaganda, of
his successive sojourns in Matsue, Kumamoto, and Tokyo. In his important story "A Conservative," he summed up what he had learned of

Japan's—and his own—inner progress. "A Conservative" is a composite portrait of the creative elite of the generation of Meiji—such men as Okakura, Hattori, Soseki, and the rest. It is also a veiled self-portrait of Hearn, and was recognized as such by admirers of the story such as Hugo von Hofmannsthal. In sketching the biography of the son of a samurai, Hearn traces the sequence of "heart things" along Japan's path. The boy grows up in the feudal world of the samurai, in a city "where no foreigner had ever been." There he learns the martial arts—"archery and riding, wrestling and fencing"—coming to manhood "in that innocent provincial life of Old Japan," where "a young samurai might grow up exceptionally pure-minded and simple-hearted."

The arrival of Perry's Black Ships represents the end of innocence. As Japan is humiliated by foreign visitors and foreign treaties backed by foreign weapons, the nation rushes to catch up. The young samurai learns English from a British teacher and comes under the influence of an aged missionary who resembles James Hepburn. The missionary introduces him to the New Testament and puts his extensive library at the young man's disposal. The young samurai, surprised to find "among the doctrines of the 'Evil Sect' ethical precepts like those of Confucius," converts to Christianity and travels to Europe "to see for himself the influence of religion upon morals in the Occident." What he finds appalls him: "That world had no faith. It was a world of mockery and masquerade and pleasure-seeking selfishness, ruled not by religion, but by the police." A sadder, wiser man, he resolves to return to Japan: "Foreign civilization had taught him to understand, as he could never otherwise have understood, the worth and beauty of his own." The story concludes with his return and draws on Hearn's own memory of arriving in Yokohama in the April dawn:

It was through the transparent darkness of a cloudless April morning, a little before sunrise, that he saw again the mountains of his native land—far lofty sharpening sierras, towering violet-black out of the circle of an inky sea. Behind the steamer which was bearing him back from exile the horizon was slowly filling with rosy flame. There were some foreigners already on deck, eager to obtain the first and fairest view of Fuji from the Pacific; for the first sight of Fuji at dawn is not to be forgotten in this life or the next. They watched the long procession of the ranges, and looked over the jagged looming into the deep night, where the stars were faintly burning still—and they could not see Fuji. "Ah!" laughed an officer they questioned, "you are looking too low! higher up— much higher!" Then they looked up, up, up into the heart of the sky, and saw the mighty summit pinkening like a wondrous phantom lotus-bud in the flush of the coming day: a spectacle that smote them dumb.

The returning samurai repeats like a mantra the words of the ship's officer, "making vague rhythm with an immense, irresistible emotion swelling in his heart," as the meaning of his journey dawns on him. "Then everything dimmed: he saw neither Fuji above, nor the nearing hills below, changing their vapory blue to green; nor the crowding of the ships in the bay; nor anything of the modern Japan; he saw the Old."

Part III

The story, as Mary Fenollosa told it in her soft Alabama accent, and wearing her kimono for her distinguished guest ("thinking it would be a subtle compliment"), was simple and straightforward. A young monk dies, and his task of expiation in purgatory is to climb a mountain. But for Lafcadio Hearn, as he turned it over in his mind for weeks afterward, the story took on new meanings and a new shape, until it crystallized as one of the best pieces in his volume In Ghostly Japan.

A Boddhisattva—one of the myriad helpers in the Buddhist pantheon— was guiding a pilgrim up a steep mountain. Sunset turned to twilight; the landscape became ever more desolate, "neither token of water, nor trace of plant, nor shadow of flying bird." As the two climbers mount higher and higher, the pilgrim looks down. "For there was not any ground,—neither beneath him nor about him nor above him,—but a heaping only, monstrous and measureless, of skull and fragments of skulls and dust of bone." The pilgrim is horrified. But the Boddhisattva, cheerful and energetic, keeps up the pace: "Hasten, hasten, my son!" he cries. "The day is brief, and the summit is very far away." The pilgrim balks: "I fear!—unutterably I fear! . . . there is nothing but skulls of men!" "A mountain of skulls it is," concedes the Boddhisattva. "But know, my son, that all of them *are your own*! Each has at some time been the nest of your dreams and delusions and desires. Not even one of them is the skull of any other being. All,—all without exception,—have been yours, in the billions of your former lives."

Maybe it was Mary Fenollosa's Southern accent, so familiar to his ears, or maybe it was something in the story itself, but Lafcadio Hearn was overwhelmed with emotion. "Had I only eleven more stories of such quality, what a book could be made out of them!" he sighed. Hearn had some difficulty giving final shape to the tale, as if it possessed some special, private meaning. "As for the Mountain of Skulls—yes: I have written it,—about seven or eight times over," he told Mary's husband, Ernest Fenollosa, "but it still refuses to give the impression I feel, and can't define,—the impression that floated into my brain with the soft-flowing voice of the teller." For Mary Fenollosa, the story was about death. "The Buddhist story which I had for him," as she noted in her memoir of Hearn, "and which made his fine face glow with swift appreciation, was of a young monk who, immediately after the change called death, found himself in the Buddhist purgatory with his task of expiation, the climbing to the summit of a towering mountain of human skulls." The germ of the tale, for Mary Fenollosa, was a Buddhist version of the myth of Sisyphus: an endless climb with no clear meaning or reward.

But Hearn, who was always on the lookout for material from friends and acquaintances, made two small but significant changes. First, he did not specify that the story was set in the time "immediately after the change called death." Second, he made the skulls into remnants of the pilgrim's own former lives: "Each has at some time been the nest of your dreams and delusions and desires." The idea fit in neatly with one of Lafcadio Hearn's deepest convictions. He believed that we inherit memories from our ancestors—what he called "the immense evolutional fact of psychical inheritance."

When Hearn first met the Fenollosas, on April 1, 1898, the idea of former lives was very much in the air. Hearn and Fenollosa had encountered each other briefly in 1890, when Hearn had just arrived in Japan and Fenollosa was leaving, to take his new job at the Museum of Fine Arts in Boston. Hearn was looking for work in Japan; Fenollosa, whose contract was not renewed by a Japanese government done with its foreign experts, had to look elsewhere. At the museum, Fenollosa had fallen in love with his young and beautiful assistant, Mary McNeil. He divorced his first wife; a scandal ensued; and he left Boston under a cloud of resentment and indignation. Now he was back in Japan, looking for a job. The trajectories of the two men had crossed. Hearn was now ensconced in the Imperial University, Fenollosa's former bailiwick, while Fenollosa checked the local high schools—where Hearn had once been forced to teach English. The Fenollosas were accompanied by Mary's close friend, a New Orleans writer called Anne Dyer. Anne, as fascinated with Hearn as Mary was, noted that he "carries his own environment with him." They had talked, predictably, of Buddhism and of Herbert Spencer, and the striking analogies between reincarnation and evolution. The Fenollosas had converted to Buddhism, which had a deep appeal for Hearn as well. The story of the Mountain of Skulls—with its hints of evolution—fit the Buddha-Darwin affinity so dear to both Hearn and Fenollosa.

But there was something else to the impression left by the story, and it concerned the specific former lives of these Americans gathered in Tokyo. They had all passed through the American South, and specifically through New Orleans. Hearn, as everyone knew, had first made a name for himself as a journalist in New Orleans. It was on the strength of his work there that he had been invited to travel to Japan. Hearn wondered, in turn, if he had read some of Mary's stories in the New Orleans newspapers. She recalled, "Said he had seen some of my writings under the name Mary M. Scott (alas!) and hoped that Mary Fenollosa was the same person." She was.

Mary McNeil had grown up in rural Alabama among poor folk who remembered a life as plantation gentry before the Civil War. She married at seventeen, but her husband died of pneumonia searching for oil in Texas. An old beau, Ledyard Scott, heard she was a widow and proposed that she join him in Kobe, Japan, where he was the United States consul. She arrived in Japan in July 1890, three months after Hearn. The marriage foundered almost immediately, but not before Mary had acquired a feel for Japanese language and culture. The couple returned to Alabama, were divorced and, soon afterward, Ledyard Scott was struck by lightning while sailing on Mobile Bay. Mary M. Scott began writing for newspapers in New Orleans, where she forged lasting friendships with established New Orleans writers such as Grace King.

When Ernest Fenollosa gave a lecture in New Orleans on Japanese art, Mary Scott made a point of meeting him. Fenollosa needed an assistant at the Museum of Fine Arts, and this woman, a skilled writer who knew her way around Japanese materials, and beautiful as well, seemed to him just right for the job. When their affair and subsequent marriage turned them into outcasts in Boston, they made their way back to Japan—first to Kyoto and then Tokyo. Here is Grace King's description of the Fenollosas as she knew them during their periodic visits to New Orleans:

> Fenollosa was a Spaniard in appearance, and a very handsome one. Tall, graceful, and polished in manner, his face was most attractive, with regular features, olive complexion, and the dignified yet cordial courtesy of the true Spaniard. . . .
>
> His wife was from the South, belonging to a distinguished family of Mobile, and Fenollosa's heart, like hers, was filled with sympathetic admiration of the South, notably of Alabama and Louisiana. She was a typical Mobilian, dark-haired, dark-eyed, vivacious.

As Hearn, that first afternoon with the Fenollosas, mulled over the story of the mountain of skulls, playing with the idea that it was about the persistence of memory, the conversation turned to specific memories and what prompted them to reenter consciousness. Mary Fenollosa reported in her journal:

> As [Hearn] stayed on, he became more confidential, charming and close. He told us of the book in progress, a book of "Why's" which he calls "Retrospectives"—a series of essays trying to explain by science and karma the subtle memories that attack us. He told us of conversations with Dr. von Koeber and a French priest at the University that once in speaking of the mysterious power of

perfume he had quoted Schopenhauer as saying that "perfume is
the blood of memory."

Dr. von Koeber was a professor of philosophy at Tokyo Imperial University who introduced German philosophy to the Japanese. He was one
of Hearn's only close friends on the faculty. As for the Fenollosas, they
arranged a few more meetings, but Hearn had gotten, with "The Mountain of Skulls," what he needed from them. Like Henry Adams, Hearn
seems to have tired of Fenollosa's pomposity and dogmatism. Soon he
sent Fenollosa a note announcing the end of their friendship: "My dear
Professor—I have been meditating, and after the meditation I came to
the conclusion not to visit your charming new home again—not at least
before 1900. I suppose that I am a beast and an ape; but nevertheless I
hope to make you understand."

The reverence accorded Lafcadio Hearn in Japan—he is more deeply loved
and respected than any other Western writer—remains a mystery for
American readers. Why would this trafficker in exoticism and quaintness, who had already invented a charming "Old Japan" long before arriving in Yokohama, be held up as the greatest interpreter of Japan to the
West? How did Hearn eclipse the likes of his friend Basil Chamberlain,
who knew so much more about the land and the language? It is true that
Hearn viewed Japan through an idealized haze of ghostly "survivals" from
antiquity. But this is not the major reason for his veneration among the
Japanese. What Hearn, almost alone among Western commentators, gave
eloquent voice to was Japanese anger—and specifically anger against
Western visitors and residents in Japan.

When Hearn arrived in Yokohama in 1890, what was immediately
conspicuous to him was the casual arrogance of foreigners in Japan, rich
ones in particular. He noted how the English-language newspapers directed toward the Japanese "the language of ridicule or contempt." He
saw how the Japanese, eager to learn the ways of modern trade, put up
with obnoxious Western merchants and tolerated practices that "plainly
expressed the foreign conviction that all Japanese were tricksters."
Japanese merchants traded with Westerners or worked for them, Hearn

noticed, "while secretly detesting them." The time would come—indeed, Hearn arrived at the very moment of Japan's dawning sense of self-sufficiency—when Japan would have its own merchant marine, its own banking agencies abroad, its own foreign credit, "and be able to rid herself of these haughty strangers." In the narrow streets of Yokohama one heard the "endless tinkling of piano practice"—the sound of foreign skills being acquired. Japan, Hearn concluded, "was only paying to learn; and her patience was of that kind which endures so long as to be mistaken for oblivion of injuries." Hearn viewed with satisfaction signs that Japan, in its educational policies, was stepping back from the wholesale adoption of Western practices, such as making English the official language, or one of the languages, of the country, or "the idea of changing ancestral modes of feeling and thinking."

When war broke out between Japan and Russia in 1904, Hearn was quick to see the conflict as Japanese revenge for ill treatment at the hands of Westerners. "This contest, between the mightiest of Western powers and a people that began to study Western science only within the recollection of many persons still in vigorous life, is, on one side at least, a struggle for national existence." In one of his last—and best—essays, written a month before his death, Hearn examined the effects of the war on the home front. He reported on the craze for photographs of soldiers, placed in the reverential alcove, or *tokonoma*—"photography has added something new to the poetry of the domestic faith." But what truly fascinated Hearn during the months of Japanese naval victories was the ingenuity of the Japanese in celebrating their prowess in clothes, personal ornaments, and children's toys. He saw hairpins topped with tiny battleships, scarves decorated with the full text, in beautiful calligraphy, of the Imperial Declaration of War, dresses for baby girls showing submarine mines exploding. After the first attack on the Russian fleet at Port Arthur, Hearn noticed a towel depicting "a procession of fish in front of a surgeon's office—waiting their turns to be relieved of sundry bayonets, swords, revolvers, and rifles, which have stuck in their throats."

Some readers, on the whole sympathetic to Hearn's writings, noted with distaste his antipathy toward Westerners in Japan. "In righting the Japanese," his good friend Chamberlain remarked, "he seems to us continually to wrong his own race." But Chamberlain, for years a professor of literature at the Imperial University, was precisely the kind of "haughty stranger" Hearn thought the Japanese could do without. These teachers, among whom Hearn himself had worked, had performed a service, but Hearn was convinced that, as with foreign trade, their legacy was mixed: "Perhaps Japan will remember her foreign teachers more kindly in the twentieth century [than in the nineteenth]. But she will never feel toward the Occident, as she felt toward China before the Meiji era, the reverential respect due by ancient custom to a beloved instructor; for the wisdom of China was voluntarily sought, while that of the West was thrust upon her by violence."

Chamberlain seems to have been oblivious, or at least impervious, to Japanese criticism. When Hearn asked him if he could recommend a translator, someone who could turn some traditional Japanese songs and verses into literal English, Chamberlain recommended his favorite student in philology, Okakura's younger brother Yoshisaburo. Yoshisaburo dutifully translated some texts, and Hearn had a tantrum about his attempts to translate Japanese idioms into English idioms. So Chamberlain, with haughty modesty, offered to try his own hand.

Now it might be assumed that Okakura was grateful for his training by the great Chamberlain. But recently his true view has come to light. The Japanese scholar Akiko Murakata discovered in Fenollosa's papers at Harvard University the draft for Fenollosa's favorable review of Hearn's *Glimpses of Unfamiliar Japan* and *Out of the East*. In the review, published in *The Atlantic Monthly* in June 1895, Fenollosa wished to compare Hearn's sympathetic books, written after four or five years in Japan, with Chamberlain's "misleading" *Things Japanese*, the result of "twenty-five years of study." In a passage excised by the *Atlantic* editors, Fenollosa called *Things Japanese* "the exact antipodes of Mr. Hearn's writings, and of which his favorite pupil said that, were it reprinted in Japanese, his [Chamberlain's] life could not be guaranteed twelve hours. It is cynical, unfeeling, blind to all the higher meaning of Oriental life and light, sour and self-conscious, like much of English comment on alien standards." Now this "favorite pupil" can only be Yoshisaburo Okakura. As a footnote in the history of Japanese cultural exchange, the comment confirms Hearn's suspicions regarding the true feelings of Japanese "students" of the West, of whom the Okakura brothers were two of the most prominent.

———

Lafcadio Hearn's lifelong love of ghosts and revenants had a strange and fitting coda. One thing he had treasured about the black wife he left behind in Cincinnati was her seeming access to the spirit world. (Mattie Foley's given name of Alethea, or "truth," derives from the Greek for "unconcealment.") Hearn was convinced that she was a "ghost-seer," whose large dark eyes could apprehend a deeper truth, "as though she were ever watching the motions of Somebody who cast no shadow, and was invisible to others." But it was Hearn's own ghost that haunted Mattie. She claimed that she had received a document verifying his death in Louisiana, sent from Baton Rouge in 1880. Whether the forgery was Hearn's or her own, Mattie remarried later that year—this time to a black man. Twenty-five years later, in 1904, came the news, the real news, that Lafcadio Hearn was dead—and a famous man as well.

During the summer of 1906, two years after Hearn's death, Mattie Foley made a claim on Hearn's estate, based on their marriage in 1874, in probate court. Hearn's publishers made a simple but devastating case against her. Since racially mixed marriages were prohibited by Ohio law from 1861 to 1877, the marriage of Hearn and Mattie was invalid—based as it was on the fraudulent claim that Foley was white. She lost the case, but Hearn's long-kept secret was out of concealment. From the Cincinnati papers he had written for, it spread to the national press, where the reception of Elizabeth Bisland's two-volume biography of 1906 (which made no mention of Foley) brought renewed attention to the many lives of Lafcadio Hearn—the skulls of his private mountain.

The scandal over Hearn's alleged bigamy was especially painful to the Japanese, for he had died a Japanese citizen, a Japanese hero, with a Japanese wife and child. It was felt that someone of stature should come to his defense. Kakuzo Okakura happened to be in Tokyo that fall of 1906, preparing for a collecting campaign in China on behalf of the Museum of Fine Arts in Boston. "I hear with regret that some shadows are being cast over the memory of Lafcadio Hearn," he wrote in a letter published in *The New York Times* in October. Okakura placed Hearn above all other foreign writers on Japan, for he "has reached nearest the heart of our people." In Okakura's view, Hearn was both "a spokesman of Eastern ideals" and a "brilliant contributor to literature." As such, he should be defended from the "ignominious charges . . . brought against him when he has hardly left us." Even if the charges proved true ("and we believe that they are not"), Okakura reminded his readers that "the man whose memory we love did but share the weaknesses of your Byron, your Burns, and the host of other fallible geniuses who have enriched our lives and made them nobler. The pathology of genius is a painful study." He concluded with an Eastern proverb: "He who slanders another is one who has no other way of praising himself."

THE JUDO ROOM

>< >< ><

Man at his birth is supple and weak; at his death,
firm and strong. So it is with all things. . . .
Firmness and strength are the concomitants of death;
softness and weakness, the concomitants of life.
Hence he who relies on his own strength
shall not conquer.

—LAO TZU, *TAO TE CHING*

Part 1

*The president was learning jujutsu in the White House. He had a separate
room—the Judo Room—set aside for his lessons.* He startled the members
of his cabinet by announcing, on the morning of April 26, 1904, that his
"Japanese wrestler" (a master of judo) had throat muscles "so powerfully
developed by training that it is impossible for any ordinary man to stran-
gle him." This was peculiar news for a cabinet meeting, and Secretary of
State John Hay copied it down in his diary. Hay added the interesting detail (so typically Japanese) that if the president managed on occasion to
get the upper hand, the teacher said, "Good! Lovely!"

Of course, the cabinet members were accustomed to President
Theodore Roosevelt's preoccupation with fitness regimens and martial
arts—signs of obsessive compensation, according to his biographers, for
being born with weak eyes and a puny physique. Roosevelt's life, as the

historian Richard Hofstadter remarked, "was cluttered with the paraphernalia of physical culture—boxing gloves, dumbbells, horizontal bars,
and the like." What was new was the Oriental turn that Roosevelt's exer-
tions had taken, ever since Dr. William Sturgis Bigelow, three years earlier, had demonstrated to the president the grips of jujutsu. On that
occasion, Dr. Bigelow had asked the secretary of war to lie down on the
floor. Bigelow then showed how to keep him there.

Bigelow was a passionate preservationist of all the arts of Old Japan.
Like the other traditional aristocratic arts—the tea ceremony, haiku,
archery, and the rest—the samurai art of jujutsu (sometimes Anglicized
as jiu-jitsu) had fallen into disuse under the Westernization program of
the 1870s following the Meiji Restoration. Various schools of jujutsu, derived from Chinese martial arts traditions, had survived for three centuries. At the core of all of them was the Taoist idea of "conquering by
yielding." *Ju*, meaning "yielding" or "softness," was the word Lao Tzu
used in warning against mere strength, the "concomitant of death," while
praising softness as the path of life.

The key figure in the preservation of jujutsu was Jigoro Kano. The
American journalist Julian Street, who knew Kano well, explained that he
was hardly a professional athlete but rather "a gentleman of samurai
family." Kano enrolled in the Faculty of Letters at Tokyo Imperial University in 1877, the same year as Okakura, and was for a long time the
headmaster of the Peers' School in Tokyo, the prestigious preparatory
school for the future leaders of Japan. Street's account of Kano's endeav-
ors to preserve the fighting arts of the samurai bears a striking resemblance to the efforts of Fenollosa and Okakura to preserve Japanese
aesthetic traditions.

> As after the [Meiji] Restoration the craze for all things American
> and European spread through Japan, the old arts of jiu-jutsu,
> which for more than three centuries had been practiced by samu-
> rai, fell into disuse. Before that time there had been many differ-
> ent schools of jiu-jutsu, teaching a variety of systems, but as the
> old masters of the art became superannuated no followers were
> arising to take their places.

In 1878, when Mr. Kano took up the study of jiu-jutsu, he saw that, through lack of interest, many of the fine points of the art were likely to be lost.

Working with several aging jujutsu masters, Kano systematized the fine points of each into what he called judo—the "way of softness"—and gave an early demonstration of his prowess for Ulysses S. Grant when Grant visited Tokyo in 1879.

As recent historians have pointed out, Kano's modernization of an ancient set of practices was as much a new creation, in tune with modern times, as an act of preservation. Kano's own education at Tokyo Imperial University was thoroughly imbued with Western values, especially the late-nineteenth-century ideal of physical culture; judo, like so many other products of the Meiji Era, was a synthesis of East and West. As Kano himself wrote, "Following the scientific method, I selected the best elements of older schools of *jujutsu* and constructed a new system which is most suited to today's society." It was no accident that judo was the first of the martial arts to become an Olympic sport, and Kano was chosen in 1909 as the first Japanese representative on the International Olympic Committee.

And it was one of Kano's pupils, as Julian Street points out, who taught judo to President Roosevelt. Street noted parallels between the childhoods of Kano and Roosevelt. Kano's "first interest in jiu-jutsu arose through the fact that he had been a weak child and wished to make himself a strong man. I was reminded of Theodore Roosevelt's sickly childhood when Mr. Kano told me that; and it is interesting to recall that it was President Roosevelt who first caused jiu-jutsu to be widely talked of in the United States, and that he studied it, while in the White House, under one of Mr. Kano's pupils." So Kano's achievements in the martial arts were known to not one but two American presidents, Grant and Roosevelt.

William Sturgis Bigelow, a staunch partisan of Japan and the Japanese, realized that judo might be a way to enlist the president's sympathies for the country. Roosevelt had built his career around militarism and manliness; his mantra was that all the "great masterful races have been fighting races." When he was only twenty-eight, Roosevelt had complained in a *Century* article that "the general tendency among people of culture and high education has been to neglect, and even to look down upon the rougher and manlier virtues, so that an advanced state of intellectual development is too often associated with a certain effeminacy of character." No one knew better than Bigelow, who was busy building up the Japanese collections at the Museum of Fine Arts in Boston, that Japan was widely regarded as a country of peace-loving artisans and aesthetes. Roosevelt preferred the company of cowboys and frontiersmen, and in 1895 replied to Harvard president Eliot's criticism of him as a jingoist with the retort that Eliot was fostering at Harvard "a flabby, timid type of character which eats away the great fighting qualities of our race." A man like Roosevelt could hardly be brought to admire Japan by looking at prints of Hiroshige or Hokusai. So Bigelow would court the president's favor instead by representing Japan as the land of the *bushi*, or samurai, a sort of Rough Rider of the East.

It was Bigelow's boyhood friend, the longtime senator of Massachusetts Henry Cabot Lodge, who brought Bigelow and Roosevelt together. During the spring of 1887, just after his precocious but unsuccessful run for mayor of New York City, Roosevelt was honeymooning in Paris with his second wife, Edith. Bigelow, who was on his way back from Japan, where he had lived for seven years, happened to be there as well. "In Paris we dined at the Jays, and there, to our great delight, met Bigelow," Roosevelt reported to Lodge, "and the following evening . . . dined with him at a restaurant. He was most charming; but, Cabot, *why* did you not tell me he was an Esoteric Buddhist? I would then have been spared some frantic floundering when the subject of religion happened to be broached." The previous year Bigelow had been confirmed—with his friends Ernest Fenollosa and Kakuzo Okakura—in the tenets of Tendai Buddhism. Dr. Bigelow quickly learned that Esoteric Buddhism was not the way to Roosevelt's heart. During the 1890s, he watched his young friend's rise with admiration and patiently looked for ways to engage Roosevelt's sympathies with Japan.

Roosevelt's connections in Washington were impeccable, but his career was not always smooth. Lodge, from his powerful position in the

Senate, tried in vain to get Roosevelt named assistant secretary of state. He did manage to land a job for Roosevelt in the Civil Service Commission. By the summer of 1889, Roosevelt was happily ensconced in Washington, a frequent guest of the Lodges, and of Lodge's favorite professor from his Harvard days, Henry Adams. Roosevelt, like Hay and Adams, was a scholar with an interest in politics—his best-selling book, *The Winning of the West*, had just appeared. Adams, Hay, and their British friend Cecil Spring Rice enjoyed Roosevelt's gusto and bluff, and generally shared his imperialist convictions, but they refused, as Hofstadter remarks, "to take him altogether seriously as a person." "You must always remember," Spring Rice later wrote, "that the President is about six."

During the 1890s Dr. Bigelow kept a close eye on Roosevelt, afraid that the promising young man would squander his talents. As with his other protégés—Percival Lowell, Ernest Fenollosa, and Lodge's son Bay—Bigelow sought whenever possible to advance Roosevelt's interests. When Roosevelt seemed overburdened with his responsibilities as police commissioner in New York City, the job he took after his stint with the Civil Service Commission, Bigelow urged Lodge to find an appropriate position back in Washington. "Theodore Roosevelt dined with me the other night," he wrote Lodge, in late November 1895. "He had grown several years older in the last month. He looks worn & tired, for him, and has lost much of his natural snap & buoyancy." He was, according to Dr. Bigelow, on the verge of a "breakdown," and the only thing to do was "to get him *shifted* somehow, to an *easier place* that he can hold on till the next Presidential year, when he ought to have anything he wants." Lodge pulled strings, Roosevelt was named assistant secretary of the navy, and Bigelow pronounced Lodge's behind-the-scenes maneuvers "nothing short of *masterly.*"

Having secured a comfortable place for Roosevelt in Washington, Bigelow was dismayed by his protégé's plans to raise a regiment for the Cuban war. Bigelow opposed both the war and Roosevelt's participation in it. As Akiko Murakata explains in her detailed account of the Bigelow-Roosevelt relationship, Bigelow "was afraid that the war would give the European powers a chance to combine against the United States as the tripartite intervention of Germany, France, and Russia had forced Japan to give up the spoils of the Sino-Japanese War of 1894." But Roosevelt, who had trumpeted the virtues of the soldier all his life, was not about to miss his chance on the battlefield. The much-celebrated campaign of the Rough Riders, during which Roosevelt had reportedly killed a Spaniard with his bare hands, had propelled him to the governorship of New York and the vice presidency, but Bigelow was still concerned that Roosevelt needed rest. Bigelow's men-only island retreat on Tuckernuck, near Nantucket, would be just the thing. "Dear Mr. Vice-President—" he wrote

William Sturgis Bigelow.

on March 18, 1901, "I note you are billed to appear in this town at the Annual Benefit of the Market-man's Benevolent Association, or some such thing, & merely wish to remind you that if repose is what you want there is a 'umble but 'appy 'ome yawning for you here, where the women cease from troubling and the wicked are at rest." Six months later, in September 1901, President William McKinley was assassinated. At age forty-three Bigelow's protégé, ready and rested, became the twenty-sixth president of the United States. And the Japanese had a friend in high places.

Having found an effective way to introduce the strenuous virtues of Old Japan into the White House, Bigelow—himself a skilled practitioner of jujutsu, which he practiced with his friend Okakura—pressed his advantage. The president, he insisted, should hire Professor J. J. O'Brien, the first American teacher of this martial art that "all the police and army officers learn" in Japan. Roosevelt obliged, reporting that he was having "a great time with O'Brien." Soon the Japanese naval attaché in Washington, Commander Takeshita, was offering further tips to Roosevelt and his sons. The artist Cecelia Beaux, dining one night at the White House, reported that "the President talked of Jiu-Jitzu at some length" in relation to a passage in the medieval epic the *Chanson de Roland.* When Bigelow returned from a visit to Japan in 1903, he brought six judo jackets, a book about judo, and a supply of Japanese green tea for the president and his family. And to ensure that Roosevelt understood the larger worldview of the samurai, Bigelow sent him a copy of Inazo Nitobe's *Bushido: The Soul of Japan.* This was the same Nitobe, married to a Quaker woman of Philadelphia, who had guided Mabel Loomis Todd around Sapporo in 1896, helping her to buy Ainu artifacts.

President Roosevelt was suspicious of *bushido* (literally, "the way of the bushi," or samurai), however. Too many ideas, not enough force. It is difficult to imagine Roosevelt relishing Nitobe's easy equation of *bushido* with medieval chivalry. (Nitobe's opening sentence—"Chivalry is a flower no less indigenous to the soil of Japan than its emblem, the cherry blossom"—struck precisely the wrong, effeminate, note, as did the Quaker Nitobe's claim that jujutsu "differs from wrestling in that it does not depend upon muscular strength.") Roosevelt assured Bigelow that both he and his son, Theodore Jr., had read the book. This was honor enough, apparently, for Nitobe to add the following words to his preface to the tenth edition of *Bushido* in 1905: "Exceedingly flattering is the news (which reaches me from a trustworthy source) that President Roosevelt has done me the honor of reading the treatise and of distributing copies among his friends." Nitobe's "trustworthy source" could only have been Bigelow.

Roosevelt read *Bushido*, but he did not like it. "Now," he wrote Bigelow, "do you know enough to say whether that is really studied in Japan, and represents home Japanese philosophy, and not Japanese philosophy for export? The last is alleged by the enemies of Japan." The president's question shows an unexpected sophistication concerning Japanese exports, and the important distinction between arts and crafts made especially for foreign trade and those for domestic use. Bigelow was quick to defend Nitobe's book:

> "Bushido" is the real thing. There is no trace of manufacture for export about it. The Japanese value the book highly. For instance:— when I landed two years ago an old friend—a Samurai who had fought through the Satsuma rebellion on the losing side, been imprisoned, and now holds a high government place in Tokyo under his former enemies—a man whom I have always called the typical Samurai—brought me the book as the best thing extant in English. Nothing could be farther from the truth than the suggestion that it is a gallery-play.

Bigelow at that moment was particularly sensitive to the question, and to any suggestions by the "enemies of Japan." Russia and Japan were jockeying belligerently for influence in Korea, China, and Manchuria. As Roosevelt wrote Bigelow on February 8, 1904, "Poor Japan has more important things to attend to than Jiu Jitsu at present!" Two days later Japan and Russia were officially at war.

Almost everyone in Roosevelt's circle, including Russia sympathizers such as Henry Adams and Henry Cabot Lodge, admired the pluck of the Japanese during the war. Many observers compared the early Japanese victories against the aging Russian regime with the precocious American thrashing of Spain a few years earlier. "Teikoku Banzai!" (Hurrah for the Empire), Bigelow wrote Roosevelt as the Japanese progressed. "The papers say that Europe is trying to get you to stop the fight.—I hope you will see them damned first. [Generals] Kuroki and Nogi will stop it fast enough after they get together. All they need now is to be let alone." "Banzai!" Roosevelt responded in kind on January 7, 1905. "How the fur will fly when Nogi joins Oyama!"

The Japanese prowess on the battlefield forced Americans to re-assess their notions of the Japanese, and editorialists wrestled with what *The Nation,* in its April 28, 1904 issue, two months into the war, called the "paradox" of Japanese education. How did this nation of artisans—devoted to "minute and exquisite workmanship"—so quickly master the basics of modern war? The writer for *The Nation* concluded that it was this very lack of "superstitious respect for machinery" that served the Japanese so well: "The cherry-stone carvers have been preparing to hold the lever and the trigger." The Western hand, by contrast, is "numbed and almost superseded, as an instrument of precision, by the machine." The writer concluded that feudal Japan, with its samurai virtues of phys-ical and spiritual discipline, had been a better preparation for war than industrial expertise. "The successes of Japan today in scientific warfare are due to that immemorial discipline of hand, heart, and head which has made the Japanese mind."

There were shades of difference, however, in how Roosevelt's friends interpreted these successes. The question was whether the key to the conflict was Japanese prowess or Russian weakness. "The Japanese fought it admirably and for all it was worth," Lodge conceded to Roosevelt on June 3, 1905, as the war was drawing to a close, "but the Russians sim-ply collapsed apparently." He compared the ineptitude of the Russians with that of the Spanish in 1898: "So that it does not test very thoroughly what the Japs would have done against a first class enemy or even one that would have put up a fairly good fight. The Russians seem to have become panicstricken and not fought at all. They did not so far as I can judge show as much pluck or fight as the Spaniards against us. . . . What fighting the Russians did seems to have been very bad,—as bad as the Spaniards."

Henry Adams, applying the concepts of modern physics to history, felt much the same way. He admired Japanese diplomacy, which he had followed carefully since the days of Yoshida and Kuki—men he knew well. But he agreed with Lodge that Russia was not much of a test for the Japanese military. He wrote in his *Education:* "Nor could the force of

Japan be mistaken for a moment as a force of inertia, although its aggressive was taken as methodically,—as mathematically,—as a demonstration of Euclid, and Adams thought that as against any but Russians it would have lost its opening." Russian "inertia" rather than Japanese "force" seemed to Adams the key to the outcome of the Russo-Japanese War. And the complete breakdown of Russia, an important European nation, seemed to him a bigger problem for world stability than a strong Japan. In Adams's view, "the workings of Russian inertia" constituted the riddle that America—thinking for the first time "as a world-power"— needed to solve, since Europe averted her eyes from the Russian collapse. "Never had so modern and so vital a riddle been put before western society, but society shut its eyes. Manchuria knew every step into war; Japan had completed every preparation; Alexeieff had collected his army and fleet at Port Arthur, mounting his siege guns and laying in enormous stores, ready for the expected attack; from Yokohama to Irkoutsk, the whole east was under war conditions; but Europe knew nothing." In Adams's imperialist view, the United States could play a role in a drama that Europe ignored. This was an opening for Roosevelt, and for Adams's friend John Hay.

The first phase of the Russo-Japanese War, during the early months of 1904, happened to coincide with preparations for the World's Fair in St. Louis. The war and the fair opened, so to speak, during the same season. Many spectators, alerted to the early military successes of the Japanese, saw a relation between the two. When the director of the Louvre was unable to deliver his promised address at the fair, during the spring of 1904, Kakuzo Okakura was invited to speak in his stead and seized the occasion to trumpet the special strengths of Japanese culture at this moment of its "awakening." Mabel Loomis Todd, sent by *The Nation*, needed no special enticements to visit the Japanese exhibits—including a huge replica of the great gate at Nikko. "Japan is particularly well represented," she noted. "Besides its own charming houses and gardens in the neighborhood of 'Jerusalem' and 'Morocco,' and its 'Pike' temple and teahouse and attendant jinrikishas, nearly every building shows extensive and complete exhibits from this most versatile of nations."

Secretary of State John Hay, ailing and overworked, was dragged away from his daily diplomatic efforts of trying to balance the competing claims of Russia and Japan—as the United States remained officially neutral. President Roosevelt wanted him to speak at the fair. "May 12. Bade the President good-bye," Hay wrote in his diary. "He said, with jeering good nature, he hoped I would enjoy my well-earned rest." Henry Adams, an inveterate "pilgrim of World's Fairs," as he called himself, went along at Mrs. Hay's invitation. Adams, who had been deeply impressed by the fairs at Chicago in 1893 and Paris in 1900, took a perverse pleasure in the vulgar, artificial splendors—white palaces lit by thousands of electric candles—of St. Louis. "One enjoyed it with iniquitous rapture, not because of exhibits but rather because of their want. Here was a paradox like the stellar universe that fitted one's mental faults. Had there been no exhibits at all, and no visitors, one would have enjoyed it only the more." A month later Adams was in France, admiring the more lasting cathedrals of Bayeux and Coutances—"where the people of Normandy had built, towards the year 1250, an Exposition which architects still admired and tourists visited."

That summer of 1904 offered three distractions for an ironic observer like Adams: the fair, Roosevelt's campaign for reelection, and the intensification of fighting along the eastern frontier of the Russian Empire. By late August, Japanese forces were concentrated on two targets. The first was the Russian fortress at Port Arthur, on the tip of the Liaotung Peninsula; whoever controlled Port Arthur was in an advantageous position to rule Korea and Manchuria—the prizes Japan coveted. The second target was the inland plain around Liao-yang, where the Russian army had dug in for the coming winter. On August 20, General Maresuke Nogi decided to storm Port Arthur with wave after wave of Japanese troops. It was a suicidal strategy, unimaginative and predictable. Fifteen thousand dead and wounded resulted for the Japanese in the August assault alone, and two others followed before Nogi, the former samurai—too proud to change his strategy—was relieved of his command. Fighting was even fiercer during nine horrific days at Liao-yang. "Three hundred thousand soldiers tried to kill one another on roads and fields and hills," writes Edmund Morris. "The Russians . . . fell back mile by mile, battered by Japanese frontal pressure and harassed by surprise attacks on their rear communications.

They summoned ten thousand reserves to stay their retreat, in vain." Roosevelt wrote John Hay, "The Russians think only with half a mind. I think
the Japanese will whip them handsomely."

A month later Port Arthur still resisted, but the Russian army was in
flight south of Mukden—an ancient city in the central plains of
Manchuria. Roosevelt saw signs of weakness on both sides—"Look how
long they've been predicting its surrender!" he wrote of Port Arthur—and
an opportunity for American peacemaking. Japan and Russia seemed to
him like two tired wrestlers ignorant of jujutsu: "I would like to see the
war ending with Russia and Japan locked in a clinch, counterweighing
one another, and both kept weak by the effort." Such a balance of power
would protect American interests in the Pacific, including Hawaii, from
Japanese predation. On November 8, 1904, Roosevelt was reelected by a
wide margin and promised not to seek a third term. He celebrated by attending, at Henry Adams's urging, the final days of the St. Louis World's
Fair, arriving on November 26. He raced through the exhibits. "His
hurry," according to his biographer, "was less a matter of urgency than
camouflage: unbeknownst to reporters, he was nursing several boxing
and riding injuries, including a burst blood vessel that had spread a
bruise 'big as two dinner plates' across the inside of his thigh." On January 2, 1905, news reached Washington that Port Arthur had surren-
dered; on March 10, six days after Roosevelt's inauguration, Mukden fell
to the Japanese as well. It was time for Roosevelt and his secretary of state
to engineer a peace treaty.

These were John Hay's last days, and everyone knew it. The extraordinary
career that had begun when the young man from Ohio came to Washington to serve as Abraham Lincoln's private secretary would end with Hay's
masterly solutions to the war in the Pacific. For Henry Adams, the Russo-
Japanese War "had no personal value . . . except that it gave Hay his last
great triumph. . . . St. Gaudens came on to model his head," Adams
wrote, "and Sargent painted his portrait, two steps essential to immortality which he bore with a certain degree of resignation." As a final monument to his closest friend, Adams, who had "set his heart on seeing Hay

close his career by making peace in the east," ended his *Education* with an account of the "diplomatic perfection" of Hay's work: "In his eight years of office he had solved nearly every old problem of American statesmanship, and had left little or nothing to annoy his successor. He had brought the great Atlantic powers into a working system, and even Russia seemed about to be dragged into a combine of intelligent equilibrium based on an intelligent allotment of activities. For the first time in fifteen hundred years a true Roman *pax* was in sight, and would, if it succeeded, owe its virtues to him."

Only peace between Russia and Japan had eluded Hay. And even that seemed in sight during the summer of 1905, especially after the decisive battle of Tsushima on May 27, when the Japanese navy destroyed the Russian fleet and killed four thousand men. The final entry in Hay's diary is dated June 19, 1905: "Spent the evening at the White House. The President gave me an interesting account of the Peace Negotiations—which he undertook at the suggestion of Japan. He was struck with the vacillation and weakness of purpose shown by Russia; and was not well pleased that Japan refused to go to The Hague."

John Hay died of a stroke on the morning of July 1, 1905. Adams, as he tells us in the last paragraph of his *Education*, was strolling under the trees in Paris when he heard the news. "It was time to go," he reflected, having lost both Hay and Clarence King. "The three friends had begun life together; and the last of the three had no motive—no attraction—to carry it on after the others had gone." This master of the deepest ironies ended his book with an irony as profound, in historical hindsight, as it was unintended:

> Education had ended for all three, and only beyond some remoter horizon could its values be fixed or renewed. Perhaps some day— say 1938, their centenary,—they might be allowed to return together for a holiday, to see the mistakes of their own lives made clear in the light of the mistakes of their successors; and perhaps then, for the first time since man began his education among the carnivores, they would find a world that sensitive and timid natures could regard without a shudder.

In August, a month after Hay's death, the president convened the Russian and Japanese delegations over a table in a hotel in Portsmouth, New Hampshire. Concessions were made on both sides, a treaty was signed, and Roosevelt was awarded the Nobel Peace Prize for his efforts—it was the first time the prize was awarded.

Part II

The strongest voices in President Roosevelt's inner circle concerning the present and future status of Japan were Dr. William Sturgis Bigelow and Henry Cabot Lodge. As childhood playmates growing up on Beacon Hill in Boston, Bigelow and Lodge had gleefully toppled over a marble nymph in the Lodges' garden. Their friendship had always had an air of puerile high jinks about it. As Harvard undergraduates on holiday in New York City, they made a clandestine visit to see what Lodge described as "a disgusting exhibition called 'Kahn's Medical Museum' " ("which I wonder," he sniffed in his memoirs, "should have been permitted to open its doors for the delectation of boys"). As grown men they liked to lounge around in pajamas and swim naked at Bigelow's island retreat of Tuckernuck. Both Boston Brahmins of the old school, with admiration for old money and older rituals, the two men were united by ties of friendship and family. Bigelow's favorite cousin, Clover Hooper, had married Henry Adams, who was in turn Lodge's favorite Harvard professor. Two of Lodge's sons, George Cabot Lodge (known to everyone as Bay) and John Ellery Lodge, were under Bigelow's tutelage. Bay, a gifted poet, was particularly close to Bigelow, who initiated him into Esoteric Buddhism. His early death in 1909, at age thirty-six, was devastating for Bigelow and for the Lodges; Henry Adams wrote his short biography. Bay's younger brother, John, worked under Okakura at the Museum of Fine Arts.

Bigelow and Lodge differed sharply in their views, however, and in how they lived their lives. Bigelow escaped the confines of Boston to find a second home in Japan. It was he who attended the Philadelphia Centennial Exposition of 1876, reporting back to Lodge that "this exposition does not amount to much—Outside the Jap. dept. I have not seen a thing so far . . . that I ever want to see again." Bigelow claimed he didn't marry because of his fears, confirmed in his cousin Clover Adams's suicide, that mental imbalance ran in the Sturgis family. While pretending to court the likes of Edith Wharton and Isabella Gardner, Bigelow preferred the company of men. Bashful, big, and a little overweight, he concealed his homosexuality behind "manly" pastimes such as judo and falconry. He had a taste for behind-the-scenes intrigue, essentially running the Japanese collections at the Museum of Fine Arts, for example, while he shied from the public eye.

Lodge, by contrast, was never happier than when he was pontificating in the well of the Senate. He never went to Japan, and one cannot imagine him—like Bigelow—wandering around the less traveled regions and eating raw fish. Profoundly xenophobic, Lodge could stand a brief sojourn in some safely civilized spot like London or Paris; he could never understand why America should open its doors to anyone other than Anglo-Saxons. At times he seemed to think that Boston had gone wrong in admitting anyone other than Cabots and Lodges. Lodge was a family man, a public man, the very embodiment—in his own view—of old New England. In his autobiography, *Early Memories*, he lamented the old days, when "it was the height of vulgarity to refer to money or to what anything cost," and "it was not good manners to discuss physical ailments in general society."

Lodge, in short, was the upright Puritan from Boston, Bigelow the exotic exile of Tuckernuck. But in other ways the two were strikingly similar. There is an air of repression, of self-concealment, in both men. Bigelow strove to appear strenuous in public; he was the man who brought judo (and helped bring Roosevelt) to the White House. But contemporaries noticed the strain, and expressed it in veiled language, as when a friend of Bigelow's said that he "emanated a peaceful radiance mingled with a faint fragrance of toilet water."

Lodge put himself forward as the pillar of virile Boston rectitude and came off as a prima donna—"the Oscar Wilde of American statesmanship," as a fellow senator called him. He made things worse by defending himself against the charge in the most priggish manner possible: "I suppose the allusion [to Wilde] was really meant to convey the idea that the statesmanship of Massachusetts and of New England is 'effeminate.'

That is a very easy accusation to make. It is the view which naturally is taken of a high civilization by a lower one. It is the view which would naturally be taken of the civilization of the public school by the civilization of the shotgun." Lodge's shaky marriage—his wife, Nannie, pursued a long-standing affair with John Hay, ending only with Hay's death—confirmed the public view that the shotgun was winning out over the school. While Bigelow and Lodge resented any imputation of effeminacy, they seemed in the know about homosexual circles. There was, for example, the matter of Matthew Prichard, curator of classical art at the Museum of Fine Arts. Prichard, an Englishman, was a close friend of Mrs. Gardner and of Okakura; like them, he was a passionate advocate of authentic works of art and wished to have plaster casts (a fixture of nineteenth-century art galleries) removed from the museum. Bigelow disagreed and sought to have Prichard removed from the staff. He somehow knew of Prichard's former connection with Oscar Wilde's circle. Bigelow thought Henry James might have still more information, and he asked Lodge to approach James about it. Prichard eventually fled the museum and took up residence in Paris.

During and after the Russo-Japanese War, the two friends, Bigelow and Lodge, engaged in a private tug-of-war for President Roosevelt's allegiance with regard to Japan and the Japanese. They disagreed sharply on three issues in particular: the status of the warring nations, the terms of the peace agreement, and the aftermath of the war, especially with respect to Japanese immigration to the United States.

It was common for Americans to think of Russia as a European power while consigning Japan to the status of a barbarous island nation of the benighted Orient. Bigelow believed the exact opposite. As the two vast armies slaughtered each other on the plains outside Mukden during the fall of 1904, he reminded Roosevelt that Japan, unlike Russia, was a nation that combined the fighting instinct with a deep respect for cultural traditions. Bigelow was deeply concerned about the fate of Mukden, the ancient capital of the Manchus, where there was a great library—"a sort of second Alexandrian library business," he told Roosevelt. "There are things of the greatest value, and others beyond valuation—for instance the only copies of the earliest Chinese translations of Indian MSS. of which the originals are lost, even in India." Contrasting the barbarism of

the Russians with the cultural sophistication of the Japanese, Bigelow requested a favor of the president:

> When the war broke out the Japanese scholars sent a petition to
> the Minister of War asking him to save the palace and library [at
> Mukden] if possible. —If the Japanese get it it will be safe.
>
> But the Russians in Pekin quartered their troops in the tem-
> ples, and tore up the books of the temple-libraries to sleep on. The
> Chinese paper is soft, and they piled it on the floors thickly
> enough to be comfortable.
>
> They may be doing the same in Mukden now. And if they evac-
> uate the city, they will burn it, and then everything will go.

He wanted to know if Roosevelt would be willing to cable the British, the
German, and the French chiefs of state "to put some combined pressure
on Russia—in the form of a united request—that will prevent the disas-
ter." Roosevelt dutifully passed the request to John Hay. After the
Japanese took Mukden, much of the treasure was safely conveyed to
Tokyo, only to be destroyed in the earthquake of 1923.

While Lodge supported the terms of the Portsmouth peace treaty of August
1905, Bigelow was deeply distressed. Japan had formally approached
Roosevelt, as a neutral party, to help negotiate the treaty, demanding
neither indemnity nor the disputed island of Sakhalin. Instead, Japan
settled for international recognition of her control over Korea, as well as
Russia's lease of the Liaotung Peninsula and the South Manchurian
Railway.

Bigelow was shocked that after their brilliant victory the Japanese
had won so little. Many Japanese shared this view and rioted in Tokyo
against the government and against foreigners. Roosevelt complained to
Lodge, "If Sturgis Bigelow, who ought to know better, does not see things
straight about the Russian-Japanese peace, no wonder the Japanese mob
goes crooked." Lodge quickly reassured Roosevelt that Bigelow "thinks
you the greatest of modern Statesmen. Don't think his admiration of you
has ever waned. Not at all. But he thought that the Japs yielded too much

Theodore Roosevelt, with representatives from Japan and Russia,
negotiating peace treaty at Portsmouth, New Hampshire, 1905.

and was terribly disappointed." Bigelow wrote Roosevelt an angry letter
from Tuckernuck:

> Apparently Japan is worse off in some ways than before the Con-
> ference met. —Cabot says the Japanese have now got, without the
> indemnity, all they said they wanted before the war. —I answer that
> no nation goes to war for an indemnity any more than a man goes
> to law for costs. —The costs go with the verdict. The indemnity
> goes with the victory. . . . Cabot says he knows for certain that it is
> all right, which I am only too glad to believe. But from outside what

the Japanese have done appears as unintelligible as if the Germans in '70 had suddenly made peace [with the French] and gone home just before [their victory at] Sedan.—I can't make head or tail of it.

Roosevelt, for his part, thought it was a good thing that the Japanese did not get all they wanted. Three times in his letters he referred to the danger of the Japanese "having their heads turned." Soon after the Russian defeat, on June 5, 1905, he predicted to Lodge that Japan "will have her head turned to some extent" by her victory. On September 6, 1905, Roosevelt claimed that the rioting in Tokyo was "unpleasant evidence that the Japanese mob—I hope not the Japanese people—had had its head completely turned." A third mention of "having their heads turned" occurs in Roosevelt's letter to Lodge two days later, when he notes that the riots were "directed . . . partly against foreigners and Christians." The rioting "shows that the people have not advanced as far as their Government and that it is a good thing for mankind that the war should have ended as it did, without the Japanese getting an enormous indemnity and with them still facing Russia in East Asia. I shall do everything I can to help Japan and have a most friendly feeling for her; but it would be a bad thing for her and for all mankind if the hopes of her ultra admirers like Sturgis Bigelow had been gratified; for evidently the Japanese people have been in great danger of having their heads turned."

The simplistic psychology displayed here—reward the Japanese but do not spoil them—is typical of Roosevelt's foreign policy, even toward countries he admired. That policy is summed up in his June 5 letter to Lodge: "But if as Brooks Adams says, we show ourselves 'opulent, aggressive and unarmed,' the Japanese may some time work us an injury. In any event we can hold our own in the future, whether against Japan or Germany, whether on the Atlantic or the Pacific, only if we occupy the position of the just man armed."

The postwar issue that divided Lodge and Bigelow concerned Japanese immigration to the United States. In a letter of May 15, 1905, to Lodge—before the final battles of the Russo-Japanese War—Roosevelt expressed his dismay over agitation in California to exclude Japanese immigrants "exactly as the Chinese are excluded"—in other words, since the Chinese Exclusion Acts following the Boxer Rebellion. This seemed to Roosevelt not only offensive but bad policy in the long run. "The California State Legislature and various other bodies have acted in the worst possible taste and in the most offensive manner to Japan. . . . How people can act in this way with the Russo-Japanese war going on before their eyes I cannot understand." Roosevelt saw a contradiction between antagonizing Japan by excluding her citizens while at the same time refusing to develop the American navy to defend against Japanese hostility. In a letter of June 5, he added:

> These Pacific Coast people wish grossly to insult the Japanese and to keep out the Japanese immigrants on the ground that they are an immoral, degraded and worthless race; and at the same time that they desire to do this for the Japanese . . . they expect to be given advantages in Oriental markets; and with besotted folly are indifferent to building up the navy while provoking this formidable new power—a power jealous, sensitive and warlike, and which if irritated could at once take both the Philippines and Hawaii from us if she obtained the upper hand on the seas. Most certainly the Japanese soldiers and sailors have shown themselves to be terrible foes. There can be none more dangerous in all the world.

In the same letter, Roosevelt drew an interesting connection between Japanese discontent abroad and domestic events in California: "I have no doubt that [with regard to the terms of peace] some Japanese, and perhaps a great many of them, will behave badly to foreigners. They can not behave worse than the State of California, through its Legislature, is now behaving toward the Japanese." Lodge's solution to labor troubles in California was simple: "to have an arrangement with Japan by which she excludes our labor and we exclude hers. We must treat her as an equal of course and these idiots [rioting teamsters in Chicago who voted for a resolution against Japanese labor] by raving do all they can to make any arrangement impossible. . . . I am utterly against both Chinese and Japanese labor but we should at least behave like gentlemen and see that by decency alone can we hope to carry our point."

Through the fall of 1905, the issue of Japanese in California boiled over, as white laborers demanded curbs on Japanese workers. Bigelow recommended naturalization for Japanese. To his surprise, Roosevelt agreed. *The New York Times* ran the headline "President Demands Citizenship for Japanese. Says he will use all the present power, civil and military, to meet the present emergency in California." The agitation on both sides concluded with the agreement of February 1907 known as the Gentlemen's Agreement, by which Japan curbed Japanese immigration in exchange for access to American markets.

Part III

It remained for Lafcadio Hearn to make the case that the whole foreign policy of Japan was based on jujutsu. Hunched and half-blind, Hearn was hardly an athlete, though he did pride himself on his prowess as a swimmer. Perhaps because, like Roosevelt, he had been bullied in his youth (and had lost the use of one eye in a schoolyard fight), Hearn was drawn to the idea at the base of judo: that a weaker opponent could use an aggressor's strength against him. One day Hearn wandered into the huge judo room at the Imperial University in Tokyo. "Should you happen to enter the Zuihokwan while jiujutsu is being practiced," he reported, "you would see a crowd of students watching ten or twelve lithe young comrades, barefooted and barelimbed, throwing each other about on the matting."

Hearn drew special attention to the fact that, unlike practitioners of Western wrestling or boxing, "the master of jiujutsu never relies upon his own strength. . . . Then what does he use? Simply the strength of his antagonist. The force of the enemy is the only means by which that enemy is overcome." He was particularly impressed by a discussion he had with the master Jigoro Kano himself, who presided over the *dojo* at Tokyo Imperial University. Hearn had admired a particularly strong pupil and was amazed when Kano remarked that the pupil was difficult to teach. Why? "Because he relies upon his enormous muscular strength, and uses it." The pupil had not grasped the cardinal principle of jujutsu: "to conquer by yielding."

In a brilliant intellectual leap, Hearn argued that Japan's whole attitude toward the West was based on jujutsu, a yielding rather than a caving in. To the claim—voiced most persuasively by Percival Lowell—that Japan was merely imitative, Hearn countered: "Those who imagine the Japanese to be merely imitative also imagine them to be savages. As a fact, they are not imitative at all: they are assimilative and adoptive only, and that to the degree of genius." Hearn discerned this genius in all phases of Japan's progress:

> It is still uncertain whether Japan will ultimately win all her ends by jiujutsu, although never in history did any race display such courage and such genius in facing colossal odds. Within the memory of men not yet old, Japan has developed her military power to a par with that of more than one country of Europe; industrially she is fast becoming a competitor of Europe in the markets of the East; educationally she has placed herself also in the front rank of progress, having established a system of schools less costly but scarcely less efficient than those of any Western country. And she has done this in spite of being steadily robbed each year by unjust treaties, in spite of enormous losses by floods and earthquakes, in spite of political troubles at home, in spite of the efforts of foreign proselytizers to sap the national spirit, and in spite of the extraordinary poverty of her people.

He argued that the Westernization decried by so many of Japan's friends had in fact not occurred. Despite her adoption of telephones and public schools and military systems and railroads—all on Western models—Japan remained fundamentally unchanged.

> Now in all this she has adopted nothing for a merely imitative reason. On the contrary, she has approved and taken only what can help her to increase her strength. She has made herself able to dispense with nearly all foreign technical instruction; and she has kept firmly in her own hands, by the shrewdest legislation, all of her own resources. But she has *not* adopted Western dress, Western habits of life, Western architecture, or Western religion; since the introduction of any of these, especially the last, would have diminished instead of augmenting her force.

Hearn claimed that Japan "remains just as Oriental today as she was a thousand years ago." He concluded, "She has been able to remain herself, and to profit to the utmost possible limit by the strength of the enemy. She has been, and still is, defending herself by the most admirable system of intellectual self-defense ever heard of,—by a marvelous national jiujutsu."

Hearn drafted his "Jiujutsu" essay in 1893, revised it in 1894, and went over the proofs as Japan was humiliating China in the war of 1895. "What none could have predicted in 1893 the whole world recognizes in 1895 with astonishment and with admiration," he wrote in an appended note. *"Japan has won in her jiujutsu."* In a passage remarkably close to— and likely a source for—Okakura's famous remark about Japan winning admiration not in the arts but on the battlefields of Manchuria, Hearn observed: "What neither her arts nor her virtues could ever have gained for her, she has obtained by the very first display of her new scientific powers of aggression and destruction." With a bit too much optimism, perhaps, he proclaimed that Japan "has passed forever out of Western tutelage . . . the day of Occidental influence upon her—whether direct or indirect—is definitely over."

In the body of the essay, Hearn had ventured an interesting prediction regarding the fate of Japan. "Will she stumble?" he wondered. "It is very hard to predict. But a future misfortune could scarcely be the result of any weakening of the national spirit. It would be far more likely to occur as a result of political mistakes,—of rash self-confidence." In other words, Japan might stumble if she relied on her strength, instead of on jujutsu.

Part IV

Did the Japanese rely on jujutsu to win the Russo-Japanese War? Or did they put too much confidence in their newly won strength? It is difficult to say. President Roosevelt's analysis of the war sometimes suggests a wily Japan versus an unwieldy Russia. He noted admiringly, for example, that "the entire Japanese force was always used to smash some fraction of the Russian force." A clever tactic, no doubt, though "divide and conquer" is hardly a mainstay of judo. The Russians, in their overwhelming strength, had indeed shown an unyielding rigidity. Had the war been allowed to continue, Roosevelt believed, "Russia, in spite of her gigantic strength, was, in my judgment, apt to lose even more than she had already lost." That too has the sound of jujutsu, though Jigoro Kano might have made one correction: Russia would lose *because* of (not in spite of) her gigantic strength.

Nonetheless, the Japanese had not exactly followed the "way of softness" either. The mindless slaughter on the plains of Mukden showed as little strategy on both sides as the bloodbaths of Antietam or Fredericksburg. General Nogi's disastrous siege of Port Arthur had followed the most old-fashioned model: frontal assault, strength against strength, in a battle of attrition. In this regard the general had pursued, instead of the yielding of jujutsu, another samurai tradition, that of ritual suicide for one's lord and leader. That tradition is memorably evoked in a letter to Jigoro Kano himself from Commander Yuasa of the Japanese navy, a former pupil at Kano's judo academy. Commander Yuasa was about to sink the steamer *Sagami Maru* as part of the blockade of the harbor at Port Arthur.

> We shall do all that human power can, and leave the rest to Heaven. Thus we can calmly ride to certain death. I am happy to say that among the members of this forlorn hope are three of your former pupils: Commander Hirose, Lieutenant Commander Honda, and myself. . . .
>
> Though I greatly regret that while living I could not do justice to the kindness you have shown me, still please accept as an expression of my gratitude the fact that I lay down my life for the sake of our country, as you have so kindly taught us, in time of peace, to be ready to do.

Only Honda, who was wounded by a Russian shell, survived the mission. In the assault on Port Arthur, thirty thousand Japanese soldiers died. That General Nogi lost both his sons in battle helped his reputation, though it left him a deeply unhappy man, never reconciled to his own bitter survival.

Japan had secretly approached President Roosevelt to bring about an end to the war by negotiation. Why had she not pressed her apparent advantage after the victories at Port Arthur and Mukden? Because, as Roosevelt later wrote, "the Japanese had to have peace. Their money was exhausted. So was their credit. The villages from one end of the country to the other had been so drained of men that the greatest difficulty was experienced in harvesting the rice crop. When I intervened, Japan was on the verge of collapse. She was bled white."

The evidence suggests that in 1905 Japan came perilously close, in her confident swagger, to precisely the fate Lafcadio Hearn feared when he wondered if Japan might "stumble." Hearn did not doubt Japan's strength against Russia, but he worried that victory would hasten the disappearance of those last vestiges of Old Japan that he loved above all else. As it happened, Hearn witnessed neither Japan's brokered victory in 1905 nor her near suicide forty years later, when her "rash self-confidence" led to disaster. He died in September 1904. The previous week he had instructed his wife not to announce his death. If anyone asked, he told her, she should reply, "Oh, he died some time ago!"

EPILOGUE
CIRCA 1913: THE ESCAPE FROM TIME

> < > < > <

If ever the search for a tranquil belief should end,
The future might stop emerging out of the past,
Out of what is full of us; yet the search
And the future emerging out of us seem to be one.

—WALLACE STEVENS

Will Europe become <u>what it is in reality</u>—
that is, a little promontory on the continent
of Asia?

—PAUL VALÉRY

An epilogue is a gamble, especially when, as in this book, several biographical narratives are braided together, and there cannot be a clear and simultaneous ending for all of them. A cultural historian is not a novelist after all; no narrative sleight of hand can bring his cast of characters to marry or die in unison. I hope nonetheless that my selection of 1913 or thereabouts will not seem wholly arbitrary. Mine will not be the first book to imply that the world after 1914 was in significant ways a different and more dangerous place. The United States and Japan, the two nations given pride of place in this book, have long accorded those awkward and concurrent transitional eras that ended around 1913—the Gilded Age and the Meiji Era—a special status in their national narratives. Toward the beginning of this period, impressed by American military might, a

*Westernizing Japanese emperor welcomed the United States to Japan's xenopho-
bic shores. Toward the end of the period, impressed by Japanese military might,
a Japanophile American president welcomed Japan to the company of world
powers. The simultaneous exit from the public stage of the emperor and the president "circa 1913" renders that date a compelling moment to round off one's
story. A certain chance accumulation (as in the novelist's deliberate art) of
deaths and abrupt shifts in careers and capacities—an accumulation that has
surprised this historian while easing his task—has reinforced the sense of an
ending. To follow (as I have here) the "great wave" of Japanese influence a few
years into the cultural moment we used to call modernism, located principally
in Paris, merely suggests that the wave may not yet have crested.*

On July 30, 1912, the news spread through Japan that the emperor was dead.
The Meiji Era, during which Japan had transformed herself from an isolated feudal backwater to a modern industrial and military power, was
over. When he heard the news, General Maresuke Nogi retired to his austere house in the Aoyama section of Tokyo and prepared for his own
death. Built like an army barracks with rough-hewn logs on the outside,
and with a mix of traditional Japanese and Western rooms within, the
house embodied Nogi's own complex relations with the modern world. A
redbrick stable by the road, modeled on Prussian cavalry stables he had
admired during his youthful journey to the West, provided more luxurious accommodations for Nogi's horses than his own stern furnishings.

In the popular imagination, General Nogi was "the last samurai." His
career had spanned the military history of the Meiji Era. In the Satsuma
Rebellion of 1877, he had lost the banner of his regiment in battle—a humiliating episode that he felt he had never sufficiently atoned for. His
old-fashioned siege of Port Arthur in 1905, during the Russo-Japanese
War, had resulted in thousands of Japanese deaths, including those of his
two sons—and eventual victory. Nogi's postwar reputation resembled that
of General Grant—both were hard men willing to sacrifice any number of
soldiers to achieve their goals.

On a September evening a few weeks later, as a succession of cannon
blasts announced the funeral rites of the emperor at the nearby Imperial
Palace, General Nogi informed his wife that the time had come. His lord

was dead; according to his own interpretation of *bushido*, the ancient code of the samurai, Nogi must die as well. With brush and black ink, he wrote a poem of farewell, and prepared the weapons. Then he plunged a dagger into his wife's chest and quickly slit his own stomach. Word of General Nogi's death was almost as electrifying as the news of the emperor's passing. No one expected such behavior in modern Japan. It was as though the ritual of *seppuku*, so redolent of Old Japan, was the final act of the Meiji Era. Committed by the very general who had contributed most to moving Japan into the ranks of the modern powers, the ritual suicide marked the end of an era. Nogi's house became a shrine. In the backyard, where the bloody clothes of Nogi and his wife were buried, General Douglas MacArthur many years later planted a magnolia tree in Nogi's memory.

Frank Lloyd Wright had planned to travel to Japan that fall with his companion, Mamah Borthwick; the trip was delayed until January 1913 by the emperor Meiji's death. Wright, whose career was languishing in the United States, had two schemes in mind to make some much-needed money. He was involved in a shady arrangement to provide thousands of Japanese prints for the American market. And he wanted to secure the commission for the new Imperial Hotel in Tokyo. The Imperial, Wright explained to a friend, "is to cost seven million dollars—the finest hotel in the world. Of course I may not get it—then again I may—it would mean forty or fifty thousand dollars and a couple of years employment if I did—so wish me luck." The manager of the Imperial, Aisaku Hayashi, had considered several other architects for the job, including Japanese, by the time he received a letter from the Chicago connoisseur and collector Frederick Gookin recommending Wright.

Wright was singularly lucky that the decision was Hayashi's to make. Hayashi had worked as an art dealer for years, connected to the Yamanaka firm in New York. Ernest Fenollosa had been a close friend: Hayashi had sponsored a lecture series by Fenollosa in New York in 1907 and had brought his ashes back to Japan for burial near Lake Biwa. In hiring Hayashi, the directors of the Imperial Hotel, as Julia Meech notes, "believed that an artistic turn of mind was the most important qualification in a hotel manager"; the hotel facilities, they felt, "must stir an aesthetic response." Gookin assured Hayashi that Wright could be counted on to provide precisely such a response.

The story of Wright's Imperial Hotel has become, with his eager connivance, a legend. On a visit to Nikko in 1905, when he stayed in the Kanaya Hotel, Wright had become enamored of the volcanic tufa stone from nearby Utsunomiya. (A fireplace and bar made of the stone, clearly designed by Wright, can still be seen at the Kanaya.) The design of the Imperial owes as much to Mayan temple architecture as to Japanese, though it immediately became the inspiration for many other Japanese hotels. Eventually built from 1920 to 1922, the Imperial was completed just in time to undergo the ultimate test of its structural soundness. The Great Kanto Earthquake struck the very day of its official opening, in September 1923; Wright received a telegram from the hotel owner, the Baron Okura, informing him that after the quake struck only the Imperial was still standing amid the rubble.

In late March 1913, during their stay in Japan, Wright and Borthwick received an invitation from Baron Ryuichi Kuki to join him in "an old fashioned tea ceremony" at his country house outside Kyoto. "I assure you that the tiffin will not quite satisfy you," Kuki added, "because it is an old fashioned Japanese one." He was right to worry. Wright had greatly admired *The Book of Tea*, by Kuki's rival Okakura, going so far as to say that he had first encountered his key concept of "architecture from within" in its pages. But Wright despised the physical torments of the tea ceremony, despite the philosophical "tea-ideals" that Okakura ascribed to it: "On tortured knees . . . I have painfully participated in this 'idealized' making of a cup of tea following a Japanese formal dinner, trying to get at some of these secrets if secrets they are. I confess that I have been eventually bored to extinction by the repetition of it all and soon I would avoid the ordeal when I could see an invitation coming."

Kuki also wished to show Wright his collection of Japanese art. Apparently the visit in Kyoto went well enough for Kuki to invite Wright, in late April, to come to his Tokyo lodgings to see the remainder of his collection. Wright, as Meech notes, "was attracted to aristocratic and cultivated men like Kuki." Still, he seems to have realized that events had broken the spirit of the man he called "poor old Baron Kuki." As a young

man the baron had brought his beautiful bride to Washington and befriended Henry Adams; he had risen quickly in the Ministry of Education, which he had headed for a time. Then came the scandal, when his
associate Okakura ran off with his wife. The man Frank Lloyd Wright encountered in 1913 was a "lonely aged diplomat still celebrated for his cui-
sine and his 'collections.' "

In early 1913 Theodore Roosevelt was recovering from a gunshot wound. While
campaigning in Milwaukee the previous October for a third term as president, under the banner of his progressive "Bull Moose" Party, Roosevelt
was approached by a man wielding a pistol. He was shot in the chest, but
groped his way to the podium, telling his appalled audience that "it takes
more than that to kill a bull moose." On the day after Christmas he reported, "I am just about to go on to stay with Sturgis."

In 1913 the California legislature again sought to limit the rights of
Japanese immigrants, passing the Alien Land Law, which prohibited
Japanese Americans from acquiring, possessing, or inheriting land.
Again Bigelow and Henry Cabot Lodge took opposite sides on the issue,
with Roosevelt in the middle. "It is just like the situation six years ago,"
Roosevelt wrote Bigelow, "only [President] Wilson is not taking hold of it
the right way, and meanwhile [former President] Taft has done what he
could to tangle things up." Bigelow, remembering Roosevelt's sympathy
toward the Japanese in the labor battles of 1905, responded that he
wished Roosevelt were still in charge. But Lodge, in a letter to Bigelow of
May 15, argued that the United States had blundered into one "race problem" and was on the verge of another: "We can exclude anybody we
choose to exclude. . . . I think exclusion should go much further, and you
well know my views about [limiting] European immigration, but in the
case of Asian immigration there is the further objection that it involves
race problems. We have one race problem in this country, which has been
with us for a good many years and has been a pretty expensive one. I do
not want another."

Bigelow responded by invoking Japan's own disastrous policy of exclusion, which the United States had found intolerable: "We established
the precedent, by Perry's expedition and what followed, that such reluc-

tance to receive visitors may be overcome by force of arms even if the process involve a complete overturn of the government of the country concerned." As for Lodge's remarks about "race problems," Bigelow argued, in a Darwinian flourish, that the Japanese were more a racial solution than a problem: "The real fact about it is that the Japanese, from the point of evolution and survival of the fittest, are the superior race."

In 1913 David Todd made a flamboyant and well-publicized attempt to establish radio contact with Martians. "Assuming that there is life on Mars," he told *The New York Times,* echoing the views of his old friend and patron Percival Lowell, "the evolution of intelligence through the cycle of a million years must be advanced beyond the best efforts of our puny intellects. . . . Possibly they carry on ordinary conversations at all distances on their planet, where to them miles are as inches. If so they have been trying for years to get into conversation with us and perhaps they wonder what manner of stupid things we are not to respond." Todd and Leo Stevens, chief instructor of ballooning for the U.S. Army, ascended in a hot-air balloon in western Massachusetts to the height of 22,000 feet. After twenty-six hours in the air, the balloon was blown northward into Quebec. Todd flashed some messages to Mars with a mirror and listened intently to a wireless receiver—but he reported no response.

That same year of 1913, at the age of fifty-six, Mabel Loomis Todd suffered a severe stroke, which paralyzed the right side of her body. She never recovered full use of her right hand and foot. Her husband's progressively bizarre behavior necessitated his early retirement from the Amherst College faculty in 1917, and his institutionalization in 1922. After her stroke Mabel retreated to the house in Coconut Grove purchased for her by another of her admirers, Arthur Curtiss James, owner of the yacht *Coronet,* who had taken the Todds to Japan in 1896. To the Florida house she gave the Japanese name Matsuba, or "Place of Pines." Among the close friends Mabel made in Florida were the Thursby sisters, Emma and Ina. (Kakuzo Okakura had traveled with the Thursbys in India, hosted them in Tokyo, and stayed with them, in 1904, in New York.) And Mabel Todd continued to try to persuade Amy Lowell to write a definitive biography of Emily Dickinson.

———

In 1913, Amy Lowell and her companion Ada Russell, whom she had met the previous year, toured Europe in their mulberry-hued Pierce-Arrow, with polished brass radiator and two mulberry-clad chauffeurs. Her personal style was extravagant. "Her bed had eighteen pillows," wrote Van Wyck Brooks, "and she had ten thousand black cigars and seven megatherian sheep dogs that mauled and all but murdered her visitors." During her European honeymoon, Amy made common cause with Ezra Pound, at the famous Imagist dinner of July 17, 1914. Pound and Lowell were entrepreneurs of modern poetry as well as poets. Brooks called Lowell "the shrewdest of salesmen . . . like the old China traders" from whom she was descended. There was a clear rivalry between Pound and Lowell. Both aspired to be the leader of the Imagist group of poets, a loose-knit confederation bent on eliminating stodgy phrasing and conventional imagery from poetry in English. Both were using Asian sources to provide new imagery and a pared-down style for American poetry. Neither poet ever traveled to Asia, but both could claim—as of 1913—impressive mentors, and hence authority, for their Asian work. Amy Lowell had her brother Percival. Ezra Pound had Ernest Fenollosa.

On the evening of September 29, 1913, Ezra Pound had dinner with Mary McNeil Fenollosa, widow of Ernest Fenollosa. They met at the London home of the Bengali nationalist poet Sarojini Naidu. Mary Fenollosa was looking for someone who could make sense of her late husband's copious papers and notes on Japanese and Chinese literature. She disliked academic experts—her publication of Fenollosa's two-volume *Epochs of Chinese and Japanese Art* in 1911 had reinforced her aversion—and her reading in some of Pound's poetry had convinced her that he was the man for the job. It is no exaggeration to say that their meeting changed the course of American literature.

Before the fall of 1913, when he turned twenty-eight, Pound had searched in various literary traditions for a renewed poetic language. He had ransacked Provençal lyrics of the late Middle Ages, and French Symbolist poetry of the late nineteenth century. Instinctively pursuing a language of dynamic verbs and crystalline images, he had begun exploring, during the spring of 1913, Japanese prints in the British Museum along with whatever Asian literature he could find in books by French and English scholars. In an early experiment Pound caught in the compass of nineteen syllables the seasonal atmosphere and abrupt cognitive shift of haiku:

IN A STATION OF THE METRO

The apparition of these faces in the crowd;
Petals on a wet, black bough.

During their first meeting, Pound listened intently as Mary Fenollosa outlined her husband's earlier career as a scholar of Chinese and Japanese art, and his more recent years, before his death in 1908, as principal adviser for Charles Freer's rapidly growing collection—or, as Pound put, "selector of a lot of Freer's stuff." It was only at the second meeting, at the Café Royal a week later, that Mary disclosed another phase of her late husband's scholarship: his sustained work on classical Chinese literature, under the tutelage of several Japanese experts. She described the notebooks in which Fenollosa had recorded his tutorials with Professors Mori and Ariaga, as well as with his close associate and former student Kakuzo Okakura. Mary wondered if Pound might consider going through these documents, serving in effect as Ernest Fenollosa's literary executor. That William Heinemann, who had published Fenollosa's *Epochs of Chinese and Japanese Art*, was also present suggests that Mary believed the notebooks were close to being publishable. In mid-December 1913, Pound received the boxes of material, mailed from the Fenollosa estate of Kobinata—named after their Tokyo villa—in Mobile, Alabama.

The "Fenollosa manuscripts," as Pound came to refer to the notebooks, contained draft translations of early Chinese poetry, writings attributed to Confucius, and Japanese No plays—materials that Pound would draw on for the rest of his long life. This unexpected "windfall," as he called it, allowed Pound to travel far beyond the aestheticized *Japonisme* of Amy Lowell and others. Under the guidance of his tutors, Fenollosa had gone deeply into the spiritual inspiration behind many of the poems, especially the Taoist and Chan (Zen) strains. What Pound introduced into American poetry, via the Fenollosa-derived poems of his epoch-making *Cathay* (1916), were precisely those qualities—concision, suggestivity, detachment, vivid imagery—that he found in Fenollosa's draft translations and notes.

One of the notebooks Mary Fenollosa sent was labeled "Chinese Poetry: Okakura," with the notation "begun with Kakuzo—March 12 1900." The notebook is a memento from the fraught period when both men had been fired from their positions because of romantic scandals. At loose ends professionally, the two determined to collaborate on a survey of Chinese culture. In late 1899 Mary had referred in her diary to "the decision to have Ernest and Okakura start the big book." And on February 4, 1900: "Ernest had a full day. In forenoon a long talk with Okakura about the book." Mary never fully trusted Okakura, however; she considered him unreliable, eccentric, and a snob. "He was never loyal," she had written during the summer of 1899. "He went off constantly with such men as La Farge and Gilder." In March 1900 she noted in her diary that Fenollosa "has begun study [of Chinese poetry] with Okakura. This last will be most valuable, all if O. only sticks." During this excruciating moment in his life, just before his departure for India, the question of whether Okakura would "stick" was a genuine one.

The Chinese poems that Okakura discussed with Fenollosa were Taoist in inspiration. If the spirit of Taoism entered American architecture through Frank Lloyd Wright, via Okakura's *Book of Tea*, it is no less true to say that Taoism entered American literature through Ezra Pound, with Okakura again serving as the intermediary. Concision was the quality Pound most admired in Chinese poetry. After his second meeting with Mary Fenollosa, he wrote to his wife: "There is *no* long poem in Chinese. They hold if a man can't say what he wants to in twelve lines, he'd better leave it unsaid." This idea of the brevity of Chinese poetry—not always borne out in actual poems—continued to influence Pound. Two of the Taoist poems he reworked from the Okakura notebook are exactly fourteen lines in length and have some of the feel of a classical English sonnet—the Taoist sonnet, one might say, a new and unlikely genre.

To limit the anonymous "Ballad of Mulberry Road" to fourteen lines, Pound simply ignored the forty or so additional lines of the poem as translated by Okakura (and not the scholar Mori, as Pound mistakenly labeled it). The fourteen-line fragment follows closely the contours of a Shakespearean sonnet, with shifts of theme and perspective, or turns, after the fourth, eighth, and twelfth lines, and a closing epigrammatic couplet. The poem, about a beautiful young woman who rejects a married suitor, begins with Pound's explicit attempt to convey the illusion of the Chinese written character in English verse:

> *The sun rises in south east corner of things*
> *To look on the tall house of the Shin*
> *For they have a daughter named Rafu, (pretty girl)*
> *She made the name for herself: "Gauze Veil"*

("The sun rises in the South East corner," Fenollosa had written from Okakura's dictation.) Pound gives an inadvertent Japanese orientation to this Chinese poem: "She makes the shoulder-straps of her basket from the boughs of Katsura." "Katsura," a Japanese tree, comes directly from Okakura. The Taoist spirit of the poem is harder to decipher, especially in the fragment that Pound uses. The underlying sense, however, seems to be the closeness of nature and a human exemplar. The girl calls herself Gauze Veil because "she feeds mulberries to silkworms."

"Sennin Poem by Kakuhaku" is more explicitly Taoist in spirit. Here again the shifts of perspective resemble the Shakespearean sonnet, with turns after the fourth and eighth lines and a closing couplet. The opening four lines are a vivid evocation of nature:

> *The red and green kingfishers flash between the orchids and clover,*
> *One bird casts its gleam on another.*
> *Green vines hang from the high forest,*
> *They weave a whole roof to the mountain.*

Then comes the first turn in the poem, as a solitary hermit appears in the landscape and the view of the kingfishers is revealed to be his:

> *The lone man sits with shut speech,*
> *He purrs and pats the clear strings.*

This is Pound's version, but it follows closely what Fenollosa, under Okakura's tutelage, wrote in his notebook. The first line in the Okakura notebook, for example, is "Red and green kingfishers play among the orchids and clovers."

The poem bears a striking resemblance in theme and spirit to Gerard Manley Hopkins's famous sonnet "As kingfishers catch fire, dragonflies draw flame." There is the superficial link of the kingfishers that flash into flame, and the deeper synaesthetic evocation of the plucked strings of a musical instrument juxtaposed with the colorful birds. The first group of lines is Pound's, the second by Hopkins:

The lone man sits with shut speech,
He purrs and pats the clear strings.
He throws his heart up through the sky

Stones rung: like each tucked string tells, each hung bell's
Bow swung finds tongue to fling out broad its name.

It is tempting to say that Hopkins's poem goes even further in a Taoist direction than Pound via Okakura. What could sound more like a translation from the ancient Chinese than Hopkins's "the just man justices" from the same sonnet?

After reading T. S. Eliot's *Waste Land,* Pound wrote the following couplet:

These are the poems of Eliot
By the Uranian muse begot.

The lines offer a secret doorway into a little known moment in Eliot's life, a moment that includes Okakura, Henri Matisse, and the "Uranian" Matthew Prichard. If, as Virginia Woolf claimed after seeing the show of "Post-Impressionist" art organized by her friend Roger Fry, "in or about December, 1910, human character changed," this charged moment in Paris allows us to see such change from the inside.

Thomas Stearns Eliot at twenty-two had fled his native St. Louis to attend Harvard, where he had majored in philosophy and written his first verses. Upon graduation in 1910, he decided to spend what he called a "romantic year" in Paris, perfecting his French and attending the lectures of the philosopher Henri Bergson. By December, Eliot was living in a pension near the Sorbonne, practicing French conversation with the writer Alain-Fournier, and becoming very close friends with a fellow boarder, a medical student named Jean Verdenal. During the first months of 1911, he joined the cultlike audience at Bergson's Friday lectures at the Collège de France. Conspicuous among the crowd was a tall, blond Englishman of aristocratic bearing named Matthew Prichard.

As a young man, Prichard had been a member of Oscar Wilde's circle; after Wilde's arrest and imprisonment on sodomy charges, Prichard had pursued his interests in art history, especially the statuary of ancient Greece. While wandering famished on the Pincio in Rome, he had found a patron in Edward (or Ned) Warren, a connoisseur from a wealthy Beacon Hill family. Warren had established what he called a Uranian community—Uranian was a code word for homosexual—in a huge manor house in the town of Lewes, in Sussex. The Uranians lived a life of aesthetic ease. Drawing on Prichard's expertise, Warren purchased Greek and Roman antiquities for the Museum of Fine Arts in Boston, an institution run by his brother, the businessman and lawyer Samuel Warren. Yet a third brother, the hunchbacked recluse Henry Clarke Warren, was a Harvard professor and the leading American authority on the ancient texts of Buddhism. (T. S. Eliot credited Warren's translation of Buddha's "Fire Sermon," on extinguishing the inner fires of desire, as the source for his own "Fire Sermon" section of *The Waste Land.*)

Through the Warren brothers, Prichard was hired as a curator at the Museum of Fine Arts, where he developed close friendships with his colleague Okakura and with Isabella Stewart Gardner, who served on the board. Prichard had come with little training or expertise, but he developed strong and progressive ideas about how a museum should be run. In 1904 he ran afoul of a conservative faction of the board when he suggested that the plaster casts be removed from exhibition in favor of authentic works of art. The battle that ensued, which pitted him against William Sturgis Bigelow, led to Prichard's resignation and return to Europe. Of the fray Prichard wrote to Mrs. Gardner: "I wish I could regard it, like an Okakura, with grim humor and indifference." And as news of continuing difficulties at the Museum of Fine Arts reached him, especially concerning the reluctance of the museum board to support major collecting in Central Asia, Prichard wrote of "things which I confess occasionally have surpassed my imaginings and seem to answer Okakura's famous question, Am I in fox-land?, in the affirmative."

In the galleries and lecture halls of London and Paris, Prichard—driven by his own hatred of the "academic" conservatism he had left behind in Boston—pursued his own emerging interest in new tendencies in modern art. "To worship the antique is to ferret in a charnel house," he wrote Mrs. Gardner. He looked increasingly to Asian art as an instigation: "I am tired, tired to death of western imaginativelessness which leads to all this arithmetic materialism, the counterpoise comes from the east." Prichard wanted art to escape the confines of traditional Western conceptions of space and time, which he associated with Kant. In the decorative "rhythms" of Islamic art he thought he had a glimpse of what he was after. And Bergson, whom Prichard called "the emperor of thought," had developed a philosophy of flux and feeling, process and "intuition," that seemed the perfect expression of this opening.

Prichard had also discovered in Paris a modern painter who was on the same track: Henri Matisse. In abandoning the tricks of verisimilitude, including perspective, Matisse had, with Prichard's avid encouragement, broken out of the prison of Western rationality and the "scientific" worldview. Prichard and Matisse traveled together to see the great Islamic exhibition in Munich in November 1910. By 1913, in a letter to Mrs. Gardner, Prichard could confidently announce that the "Byzantine and Islamic methods" of Matisse were "intuitive," hence superior to the "Greek-Renaissance-Academic position." Matisse was not yet well known, and it was Prichard's custom to introduce his friends to the artist and his work. Okakura passed through Paris in January 1911, attended Bergson's lectures, and went to the Louvre to study the latest archaeological finds unearthed in Central Asia by the Frenchman Paul Pelliot and the Englishman Aurel Stein—"That is the kind of thing Okakura would have had the Boston people do," Prichard remarked to Mrs. Gardner. Prichard took Okakura—"in a samurai's robe, black silk with flowers of silver," according to another guest—to meet Matisse in his studio.

Okakura, who was unmoved by earlier encounters with Cubist and other modernist works, was entranced with Matisse's Orientalist inventions. The deliberate elimination of perspective and modeling of light and dark, or chiaroscuro, in paintings such as *Harmony in Red* (1908) and *The Red Studio* (1911) seemed not at all outlandish to someone familiar with Japanese prints and paintings. To signify the escape from traditional conceptions of space and time in *The Red Studio*, Matisse depicted objects floating "rhythmically" in space, including a clock without hands. "Clock-time is the quantified, anonymous time of the scientist," the art historian Mark Antliff writes in his comprehensive study of Matisse and Bergson. "Real duration can only be grasped through intuition, it is part of a creative process. To signal the suspension of the former experience of time in favor of the latter, Matisse removed the hands from the clock and let it stand as testimony to a concept of time he consciously rejected."

According to Camille Schuwer, a friend of both Prichard and Matisse, Okakura and Matisse discussed Bergson's idea of "la durée" in relation to Matisse's great painting *La Danse* of 1910. The following summer, during a sojourn in Morocco, Matisse wrote of Okakura's visit: "It is a great comfort for an artist to believe that what's best in him can reach kindred spirits at such a great distance." Schuwer translated Okakura's libretto "The White Fox" into French, with the expectation that Matisse would provide illustrations—a project that was, alas, never completed.

"Okakura . . . took TSE to meet Matisse," according to Eliot's widow, Valerie Eliot. The introduction would have occurred in January 1911, but it would probably be more accurate to say that Prichard introduced both Eliot and Okakura to Matisse. By that time an intense circle of friends had gravitated around Prichard. On March 12, he wrote to Matisse: "If it won't bother you, I am planning to visit you next Tuesday afternoon. I will bring along my friend M. Eliot and the young Frenchman, M. Verdinal [Verdenal] to whom I introduced you last Sunday."

During World War I, Prichard was interned by the Germans as a suspected British spy. Jean Verdenal served as a medical officer in the French army during the fall of 1914 and was killed the following year. News of Verdenal's drowning in the Dardanelles campaign (he actually died at Gallipoli in May 1915) led Eliot to dedicate his first volume of poems, *Prufrock and Other Observations* (1917), to Verdenal, "mort aux Dardanelles." Verdenal's death inspired some of Eliot's most intense poetry, including the "Death by Water" section of *The Waste Land*, drafted in 1918. It was a particular favorite of Ezra Pound, as he shaped Eliot's manuscript into the poem as we know it:

> *Phlebas the Phoenician, a fortnight dead,*
> *Forgot the cry of gulls, and the deep sea swell*
> *And the profit and loss.*
> > *A current under the sea*
> *Picked his bones in whispers. As he rose and fell*
> *He passed the stages of his age and youth*
> *Entering the whirlpool.*

Among the artists in Matthew Prichard's circle was the American potter and jewelry designer Florence Koehler. After he left Paris, Okakura wrote a note to Koehler from his ship, dated February 14, thanking her for a decorative pin. At the bottom of the note he added a characteristic injunction: "Remember that trials are always best."

In February 1913, Rabindranath Tagore visited Okakura at the Museum of Fine Arts. It was Tagore's first trip to the United States, and he had undertaken it primarily for medical reasons. The American Midwest was then a center of homeopathy; Tagore hoped to find a nonsurgical cure for his hemorrhoids. The two men talked of China, then at the center of Okakura's thinking. Okakura urged Tagore to travel to China and promised to be his guide to "the real China." Tagore later wrote of the conversation:

> It at once strengthened my interest for the ancient land, my faith in her future, because I could trust [Okakura] when he expressed his admiration for those people [the Chinese] . . . who were, according to him, waiting for another opportunity to have the fulness of illumination, shedding fresh glory upon the history of Asia. When I first met him I neither knew Japan nor had I any experience of China. I came to know both of these countries from the

personal relationship with this great man whom I had the good fortune to meet and accept as one of my intimate friends.

Tagore made his way back to India via London, where he underwent successful surgery. It was through his London admirers, Ezra Pound and William Butler Yeats in particular, that Tagore's writings had become known throughout Europe. Pound wrote in the December 1912 issue of *Poetry* that Tagore's poetry "brings to us the pledge of a calm which we need overmuch in an age of steel and mechanics." Back at his school of Santiniketan in Bengal, in November, Tagore learned that he had won the Nobel Prize in literature for 1913.

Portrait of Okakura by Denchu Hiragushi, 1963.

On September 4, 1913, Isabella Stewart Gardner received a four-word telegram from Okakura's brother Yoshisaburo. It read: "Kakuzo died Tuesday Nephritis." A week later, on September 11, Yoshisaburo sent a letter to Mrs. Gardner in carefully worded English (Yoshisaburo, Basil Chamberlain's favorite student, was a professor of English) describing Okakura's final days. Okakura had been feeling poorly: "Even fishing which had been his only recreation for these many years began to lose its charm for him." Okakura had sought refuge in "the cool Akakura in the north with its grand mountain scenery and thermal springs," but there too his condition worsened. His eyesight dimmed and his heartbeat was "sudden and violet"— Yoshisaburo meant "violent." Okakura mentioned Mrs. Gardner's name "in full consciousness," Yoshisaburo reported, "and wanted me to send you his heartfelt gratitude for your long friendship." Then, "at 3 minutes past 7 a.m. of the 2nd" of September, "my brother breathed his last in the world very peacefully and 'with good will and good wishes for everybody,' as he repeatedly expressed on his deathbed." Okakura was fifty years old.

Mrs. Gardner arranged a Shinto ceremony in honor of Okakura's passing. She also had built in the subterranean recesses of her mansion, down from the great stone staircase memorialized by Okakura in a poem, a special "Buddha Room" to house the three gilt Buddhas she had purchased from Yamanaka's in New York. Here was the perfect setting for displaying Okakura's implements for the tea ceremony by candlelight: his bamboo whisk and tea scoop, his earthenware bowl and iron kettle.

Shuzo Kuki, Okakura's illegitimate son with Hatsu, the former Kyoto geisha, had begun his graduate work in philosophy in 1912, the year before his father's death, at Tokyo Imperial University. There he studied with Lafcadio Hearn's old friend Raphael von Koeber, who introduced German philosophy to Japan. In 1921 Kuki was sent by the Department of Education for further study in Europe. What Kuki accomplished during his eight years in Europe almost defies belief. First, he studied Kant in Heidelberg with a young professor called Eugen Herrigel, the author, some decades later, of the classic treatise *Zen and the Art of Archery.* Kuki lived in

Paris for the next three years, reading Bergson, whom he befriended, and steeping himself in the aesthetic culture of the French Symbolist poets. While in Paris, Kuki wrote prose poems of distinction and originality, fusing the refined elegance of eighteenth-century Japan with the perspective of the cultivated urban wanderer, or *flâneur*, of Baudelaire. The ghost of his mother hovers over works of this period such as "The Geisha," in which Kuki (following the lead of the *Flowers of Evil*) tries to reclaim the "harmonious union of voluptuousness and nobility" of the courtesan. The same ambition animates the major philosophical work that Kuki began drafting in Paris, *Iki no Kozo*, or "The Structure of 'Iki.' "

Iki according to Kuki is a key concept in Japanese art, especially of the "floating world" of the eighteenth-century pleasure quarters. Iki, the closest English equivalent of which is probably "chic" or "cool," arises from refined elegance with an almost concealed promise of the erotic. A geisha dressed in a kimono of subdued browns or greens, with a tiny dash of red on her *obi* or sash—that is iki. An art of subtle hints and suggestion, restoring aesthetic dignity to sensual pleasure, this was Kuki's imaginary world. Okakura, in his effort to restore the realm of inner "ideals" to Japanese art, had shunned the art of the eighteenth century and its perceived "naturalism." Kuki restored it to serious attention by insisting that iki was itself an ideal—an inner concept manifesting itself in particular contrasts and details. Kuki suggested a fanciful etymology for *iki*, relating it to the Japanese word *ikiru*, "to live." Kuki implied that iki was a way of life, a distinctive way of being in the world.

In 1927, with drafts of his book on iki and a second book on rhyme in Japanese poetry in hand, Kuki returned to Germany. At Freiburg, in the home of the philosopher Edmund Husserl, Kuki met Martin Heidegger. Heidegger was a year younger than Kuki but already a force in German philosophy; his *Sein und Zeit*, translated as *Being and Time*, was published that very year. Its impact was immediate, especially its reigning idea that time is not something people exist apart from and in relation to but rather the very ground of human existence. (We are beings *in* time.) In November, Kuki moved to Marburg specifically to study with Heidegger. Each of these young men had a big idea to share. They had extended conversations about iki and the meaning of time, and about other aesthetic concepts enmeshed in the German and Japanese languages and national

cultures. Heidegger realized that his own emerging thinking had analogies to Asian ways of thought; his conviction that man was always *unter-
wegs,* "under way," was in harmony with the Chinese idea of the Tao, or
"Way." Heidegger was already familiar with Okakura's work—a Japanese
scholar pointed out that the first appearance in German of the phrase *in-
der-Welt-sein* (a key concept in *Being and Time* referring to our un-
escapable "embeddedness" in the everyday world) was in a translation of
The Book of Tea. And Kuki was himself studying Okakura's works in the
original English at this time.

Many years later, as a kind of testimonial to Kuki, Heidegger reproduced these conversations from memory in his important essay "A Dialogue on Language," in which he converses with "a Japanese" about Kuki
and his ideas. "You know Count Shuzo Kuki. He studied with you for a
number of years," begins the Japanese visitor. "Count Kuki has a lasting
place in my memory," Heidegger remarks, adding, "I am happy to have
photographs of Kuki's grave and of the grove in which it lies." "Yes, I
know the temple garden in Kyoto," says the Japanese visitor. "Many of
my friends often join me to visit the tomb there. The garden was established toward the end of the twelfth century by the priest Honen, on the
eastern hill of what was then the Imperial city of Kyoto, as a place for reflection and deep meditation." Of iki, Heidegger confesses: "I never had
more than a distant inkling of what that word says." After many pages of
reflection, he comes upon this attempt at a definition: "the pure delight
of the beckoning stillness." The heart of iki, it would appear, lies in an-
ticipation.

Kuki's *Lehrjahre* in Europe had one more chapter. Kuki returned to
his beloved Paris for the summer of 1928 and looked for a tutor with
whom to read French writers such as Paul Valéry and the philosopher
Alain, author of short sketches called *Propos.* Kuki's private tutor was
Jean-Paul Sartre, who was just finishing his own studies at the Ecole
Normale Supérieure. So it was Kuki who introduced Heidegger's ideas
to Sartre, thus initiating that confluence of German phenomenology
and French "absurdity" that became Existentialism. When Sartre traveled to Germany in 1933, he carried a letter of introduction to Heidegger from Kuki.

Herrigel, Husserl, Heidegger, Sartre—the extraordinary sequence of encounters reminds one of Okakura's talent for aligning his fate with remarkable men. Late that summer, just before his return to Japan in December, Kuki had the opportunity to distill the meaning of his eight years in Paris and Germany. Since 1910 a select group of French thinkers and artists had gathered each summer, along with invited international counterparts, in the medieval abbey of Pontigny, in the region of Burgundy, to converse on a chosen theme. In August 1928 the theme was "Man and Time. Repetition in Time. Immortality or Eternity." Kuki contributed two talks. On August 11 he spoke on "the notion of time and repetition in Oriental time," and on August 17 on "the expression of the infinite in Japanese art." In Kuki's audience under the trees of Pontigny were luminaries such as André Gide, Lytton Strachey, the Russian philosopher Nicholas Berdyayev, and the German literary scholar Ernst Robert Curtius. The two lectures—which were the first presentation of some of Heidegger's ideas in France—were published that fall in Paris under the title *Propos sur le temps, Considerations on Time.*

Like Okakura, Kuki was tall and thin and cut a dashing figure, the very picture of the "extremely well-to-do samurai," according to a German friend. With his sharp, "almost European" nose and delicate hands, he was always impeccably dressed—imbued with iki in his clothes and bearing. As he spoke in flawless French to his distinguished audience, Kuki seemed both the embodiment of Old Japan and a sophisticated intermediary to the West, precisely the role adopted by the man he called his spiritual father, Okakura. And his aim, as Okakura's had been, was to disclose the "ideals" behind the superficial charm of Japanese art. Kuki wished to take issue, above all, with the popular European view that—as one French critic expressed it—Japanese art "never turns inward, even disdains this."

The theme "Man and Time" gave Kuki an opening. In his two talks, Kuki—echoing Heidegger and the *Tao Te Ching* by turn—deftly invoked the burden of time and death on humankind, and sketched two contrasting Japanese responses, two ways in which a person might "liberate himself from time." There is no time without human will, or desire, according to Kuki. A rock does not experience time. So, the man who wishes to escape from time is left with two choices, and two choices only. One way is the annihilation of the will, that extinction of desire that Buddhists call Nir-

Kuki at Pontigny, 1928, with (from left to right)
Dominique Parodi, Emile Namer, Alexandre Koyré,
Raymond Aron, and Vladimir Jankélévitch.

vana. "*Nirvana* is the negation of the will," Kuki remarked. "And since time is of the will one can in this way liberate oneself from time." Kuki suggested an analogy between Bergson's concept of the *durée* and that of Buddhism. "The Bergsonian idea of the *durée*, expressing itself in the image of 'flowing water,' is precisely the fundamental idea of Buddhism: the ceaseless flight of things, a watery flux." For Bergson, only through an act of "intuition" could a person get a true sense of our rootedness in time. Such intuition reminded Kuki of Zen and the leap of intuition known as Nirvana. "Bergsonism and Zen are both served by analogous, albeit independent, methods of intuition."

Against Buddhism, Kuki invoked an opposing moral ideal, that of *bushido,* the way of the samurai. If Nirvana is the successful annihilation of the will, he argued, *"Bushido* is the affirmation of the will, the negation of the negation, in a sense the abolition of *nirvana."* Twenty years before the emergence of Existentialism in France, here was Kuki at Pontigny maintaining that the samurai was the perfect Existentialist. "The infinite good will, which can never be entirely fulfilled, and which is destined always to be deceived, must ever and always renew its efforts. . . . And it does not matter if it is an unsatisfied will, an unrealizable ideal—the life of misfortune and sadness . . . in sum, that 'time lost' perpetually repeating itself." The Buddhist Nirvana "consists in denying time by means of the intellect in order to live, or rather to die, in nontemporal 'deliverance,' in 'eternal repose,' " whereas *bushido* "consists in an unconcern with time, in order to live, truly live, in the indefinite repetition of the arduous search for the true, the good, and the beautiful."

Then, at the close of Kuki's essay on time, something extraordinary. Two decades before the French philosopher Albert Camus based a book upon it, Kuki devoted an entire paragraph to the myth of Sisyphus as the very embodiment of the moral ideal of *bushido.*

> That the Greeks saw damnation in the myth of Sisyphus has always appeared superficial to me. Sisyphus rolls a rock almost to the summit of a hill, only to see it tumble back down again. And he is, thus, set to perpetually beginning anew. Is there misfortune, is there punition in this fact? . . . I do not think so. Everything depends on the subjective attitude of Sisyphus. His good will, a will firm and sure in ever beginning anew, in ever rolling the rock, finds in this very repetition an entire system of morals and, consequently, all its happiness. . . . He is a man impassioned by moral sentiment. He is not in hell, he is in heaven.

Everything that Camus found in the myth of Sisyphus is here, even the idea of the absurdity of the task and its nobility. "The struggle itself toward the heights is enough to fill a man's heart," Camus, born in 1913, concluded. "One must imagine Sisyphus happy." But Kuki had already imagined Sisyphus happy. There can be only two explanations for the congruency here. Either Camus knew Kuki's French text, likely enough since Sartre would have known it well and Raymond Aron, another philosopher from their circle, was in Kuki's audience at Pontigny. Or Kuki showed remarkable prescience in seizing on this of all myths to show the allure of choosing to act despite the certainty of defeat: the essence of Existentialism—and *bushido*.

Kuki preceded Camus in another way as well, by relating *bushido* to suicide. If the guiding question in Camus's *Myth of Sisyphus* is the moral vindication of suicide ("There is but one truly serious philosophical problem," Camus wrote, "and that is suicide"), Kuki found the greatest modern act of *bushido* in the suicide of General Nogi.

> On the day of the Meiji emperor's funeral he committed "sep-
> puku," formerly a means of death reserved for samurai and con-
> sisting in the opening up of the stomach with a sword. Most
> Europeans will not understand this event. They will say it is the
> barbaric habit of sacrificing oneself for the emperor. . . . Some-
> thing ignorant and naïve will be seen there. Yet, in my opinion,
> just this negative appreciation is confession of ignorance and
> naïveté.

Kuki concluded: "And if European civilization condemns this moral idea, we for our part will condemn this civilization, so long as it remains blind to the nobility and heroism of the human soul."

Kuki began his second talk at Pontigny, "The Expression of the Infinite in Japanese Art," with an invocation of his father: "Okakura said very justly that 'the history of Japanese art becomes the history of Asiatic ideals.' " Again, the escape from strictures of time and space was at issue, and Kuki wrote of the "arbitrary composition" of Japanese painting, with its re-fusal of perspective and its deliberate departure from "natural forms." Like Okakura, he stressed the importance of "suggestion" and pockets of "emptiness" in Japanese art: "The spectator is, thus, placed in a situation in which he must exercise the spontaneity of his spirit, in order that he may himself reproduce the natural forms of things." He also spoke briefly of Japanese music—"I will assume that you know almost nothing about it," he told his audience. Instead of trying to describe it, Kuki mentioned several European melodies, by Debussy and Ravel, "which come closest to approximating our music." Kuki quoted a friend and editor of Debussy, who reported that the composer had in his workroom "a Hokusai print, depicting a gigantic wave breaking. Debussy had a particular dilection for this work; he was inspired by it while he composed *La Mer*; he asked us to have it reproduced on the cover of the printed copy of this work." What one hears in *La Mer*, according to Kuki, is "the effort to be liberated from stereotypic time"—"and this is justly the characteristic of Japanese music, as well as of Japanese art in general."

The brilliant closing section of Kuki's talk is devoted to haiku. He knew what his audience expected on the topic: a miniaturized aesthetic domain of moon viewing and delicate evocations of waterfalls and insects. Kuki's choice of haiku for discussion was arrestingly astringent. From Basho:

There's the nightingale,
Its droppings on rice cakes
On the veranda.

And again:

A swaying willow
Gently touched
My abscess!

Basho's poetic world, according to Kuki, was a world of loss and pain— redeemed by art. In his choice of haiku, Kuki displayed what the poet Wallace Stevens might have called "a mind of winter."

And the dried salmon,
And the gaunt monk Kuya,
Both in cold winter.

At the end of the talk, Kuki returned to the overriding question of the escape from time, quoting a final lyric from Basho:

> *O, tachibana blossoms!*
> *When? It was in the fields.*
> *Listen, the cuckoo!*

After venturing a paraphrase ("Basho inhales the fragrance of the tachibana blossoms. He remembers that long ago he had inhaled the same fragrance from the same blossoms while hearing a cuckoo in the fields"), Kuki asks to be allowed "to present a commentary" on Basho's three lines.

> But let a sound already heard or an odor caught in bygone years be sensed anew, simultaneously in the present and the past, real without being of the present moment, ideal but not abstract, and immediately the permanent essence of things, usually concealed, is set free and our true self, which had long seemed dead but was not dead in other ways, awakes, takes on fresh life as it receives the celestial nourishment brought to it. A single minute released from the chronological order of time has recreated in us the human being similarly released, in order that he may sense that minute.

Marcel Proust was one of the first authors Kuki studied with Sartre; Kuki's "commentary" on Basho comes from a culminating passage late in the final volume, *Time Regained*, of Proust's *Remembrance of Things Past*. What Kuki discovers in Basho via Proust is a third way to escape time, neither the annihilation of desire called Nirvana nor the apotheosis of desire called *bushido*. This third way is the way of memory. Such memory is necessarily "involuntary," according to Proust, if the past moment is truly to be recovered, and the "permanent essence of things" drawn out of concealment and set free.

A final tea ceremony. The first volume of Proust's Remembrance of Things Past, entitled in English *Swann's Way*, was published in 1913. In a famous scene, Proust discovers in a cup of tea his first inkling of the vast world of the past opened up by involuntary memory. Into the tea provided by his mother, he dips

> one of those squat, plump little cakes called "petites madeleines," which look as though they had been moulded in the fluted valve of a scallop shell. And soon, mechanically, dispirited after a dreary day with the prospect of a depressing morrow, I raised to my lips a spoonful of the tea in which I had soaked a morsel of the cake. No sooner had the warm liquid mixed with the crumbs touched my palate than a shudder ran though me and I stopped, intent upon the extraordinary thing that was happening to me. An exquisite pleasure had invaded my senses, something isolated, detached, with no suggestion of its origin. And at once the vicissitudes of life had become indifferent to me, its disasters innocuous, its brevity illusory.

Proust (as we may call for convenience the unnamed narrator) takes another sip, and another, searching for the source of this unexpected happiness.

> And suddenly the memory revealed itself. The taste was that of the little piece of madeleine which on Sunday mornings at Combray (because on those mornings I did not go out before mass), when I went to say good morning to her in her bedroom, my aunt Leonie used to give me, dipping it first in her own cup of tea. . . . The sight of the little madeleine had recalled nothing to my mind before I tasted it. . . . The shapes of things, including that of the little scallop-shell of pastry, so richly sensual under its severe, religious folds, were either obliterated or had been so long dormant as to have lost the power of expansion which would have allowed them to resume their place in my consciousness.

Proust is describing an alternative Sunday mass, a pilgrimage into the past, for which the sacred vessels are a pastry in the shape of a scallop shell—the age-old badge of the pilgrim with its "severe, religious folds"—

and a cup of tea. In that sacramental infusion, the past comes to life, opening and unfurling. Proust anchors this ceremony with an evocation of Japan: "And as in the game wherein the Japanese amuse themselves by filling a porcelain bowl with water and steeping in it little pieces of paper which until then are without character or form, but, the moment they come wet, stretch and twist and take on color and distinctive shape, become flowers or houses or people, solid and recognizable," so it is with the writer's own lost past—"the whole of Combray and its surroundings, taking shape and solidity, sprang into being, town and gardens alike, from my cup of tea."

Henry Adams spent the summer of 1913 in Paris looking for twelfth-century songs. "They are fascinating," he wrote Elizabeth Cameron in May, "and, like the stained-glass windows, their contemporaries, all our own, for no one else will ever want to hear them." A stroke in April of the previous year had left Adams partially paralyzed for several months. Mrs. Cameron was even deeper in the past, floating down the Nile to the ruins at Abu Simbel. Adams had brought with him to Paris his own photographs of Abu Simbel from his honeymoon journey of 1872–73. As he transcribed the ancient songs with his paid companion, the aptly named young musician-secretary Aileen Tone, Adams was inclined to retrospect.

That same year, Adams authorized publication by the American Institute of Architects of his own pilgrimage into the past, *Mont-Saint-Michel and Chartres*. The book was edited by Ralph Adams Cram, architect of the Cathedral of St. John in New York and a critic of Japanese architecture. *Mont-Saint-Michel and Chartres* is in one sense a profound analysis of the twelfth-century art of the cathedrals, in which the "marriage" of masculine Romanesque art (as exemplified by parts of Mont-Saint-Michel) lay in perfect equipose with feminine Gothic (Chartres). But the book was also an indirect tribute to John La Farge, and to those habits of mind and sensibility that Adams had first experienced on the mountain flanks of Nikko. It was La Farge's work in stained glass, Adams wrote in his *Education*, that had "led him back to the twelfth century and to Chartres where La Farge not only felt at home, but felt a sort of ownership. . . . In conversation, La Farge's mind was opaline," Adams wrote, "with infinite shades and refractions of light, and with color toned down to the finest gradations." Adams had needed a guide to the twelfth century, and "only La Farge could help him."

Adams memorial, by Augustus Saint-Gaudens,
Rock Creek Cemetery, Washington, D.C.

John La Farge had died, insane and raving in a Providence asylum, in November 1910. "Of course we miss La Farge horribly," Adams wrote soon after. "Nobody is left! Nobody will ever be worth speaking to again!" For just a moment, La Farge seemed to come alive in Henry James's memoir *Notes of a Son and Brother*, which appeared in 1914. But there was something suffocating and self-satisfied about the book. Adams wrote to Mrs. Cameron on March 8, complaining that James's memoir had "reduced me to dreary pulp." He went on, "Henry James thinks it all real . . . actually still lives in that dreamy, stuffy Newport and Cambridge, with papa James and Charles Norton—and me!" Adams asked himself if he really belonged to this already petrified nineteenth century. "Why did we live?" he wondered. "Was that all?"

Henry Adams died in his sleep on the morning of March 27, 1918, at the age of eighty. At a party at his house on Lafayette Square in Washington the night before, guests had sung old French songs after dinner. Adams was buried next to Clover at the foot of Saint-Gaudens's statue of the merciful Kannon in Rock Creek Cemetery.

ACKNOWLEDGMENTS

>< >< ><

My parents first took me to Japan when I was sixteen, and I wish to thank them for a year of pottery, judo, intensive language study, and the freedom to travel and to read at whim. The editors of *The New York Review of Books*, Robert Silvers and Barbara Epstein, made it possible for me to return to Japan to write about Okakura as collector and connoisseur. Nancy Novogrod, editor of *Travel & Leisure*, gave me the dream assignment of retracing, in the company of my wife, Mickey, the Japanese itinerary of Henry Adams and John La Farge. My brother Stephen Benfey, longtime resident of Tokyo and Kyoto, is so intertwined with the genesis of this book that it could not possibly have gotten written without our continuing conversations. Melanie Jackson and Ann Godoff were steady in their support and enthusiasm for each stage of this book. I am deeply grateful for a fellowship from the American Council of Learned Societies and a faculty research fellowship from Mount Holyoke College. Among so many friends, helpers, and supporters I wish to thank, in particular, Sven Birkerts, Meredith Blum, Nick Bromell, Carol Clark, Ellen Conant, Sharon Domier, Jillian Dunham, Joseph Ellis, Robert Herbert, Ruth Jones, Jerome Liebling, Polly Longsworth, David Michaelis, Akiko Murakata, Anne Nishimura Morse, Francis Murphy, James O'Gorman, Karen Remmler, Frederic Sharf, Barton St. Armand, Masako Takeda, Hiroko Uno, James Young, and Harriet and Paul Weissman. Samuel Morse, Doris Bargen, Stephen Benfey, and, at Random House, Susan

M. S. Brown, Maralee Youngs, and Sybil Pincus combed the book for errors of fact and emphasis; needless to say, what errors remain are my own.

I relied heavily on the Massachusetts Historical Society, the Yale University Library, the Houghton Library at Harvard, the Yokohama Archives of History, the Mount Holyoke College Library, as well as the collections of the Museum of Fine Arts, Boston, the Metropolitan Museum of Art, New York, and the Peabody-Essex Museum, Salem. While my debt to previous scholars should be clear from my endnotes, I wish to mention in particular the indispensable work of Hershel Parker on Melville; F. G. Notehelfer and Victoria Weston on Okakura; Henry Adams and James Yarnall on La Farge; Akiko Murakata on Fenollosa, Hearn, Bigelow, and Roosevelt; Ellen Conant on Fenollosa; Polly Longsworth and Peter Gay on Mabel Todd; Leslie Pincus and Stephen Light on Kuki.

NOTES

In these notes, I have tried to strike a balance between the needs of scholars and the impatience of the general reader with pedantry and scholarly display. As in the text, Japanese names are generally cited according to the Western system, family names last.

INTRODUCTION: THE MAP

xi   "The same waves wash": Herman Melville, *Moby-Dick*, ch. 111. All quotations from *Moby-Dick* are drawn from the Library of America edition of Melville's *Redburn, White-Jacket, Moby-Dick* (New York, 1983), with texts established by Harrison Hayford, Hershel Parker, and G. Thomas Tanselle.

xii   "In these days": Phillips Brooks, *Letters of Travel* (New York: Dutton, 1893), 238.

xiii   "The coarse, materialistic civilization": Richard Hofstadter, *The American Political Tradition* (New York: Vintage, 1948), 206.

xiv   "There was a time": Natsume Soseki, *And Then* (New York: Perigee, 1982), 69.

xvi   "For Old Japan was like an oyster": Basil Chamberlain, *Things Japanese*, 3d ed. (London: Murray, 1898), 320.

xvi   "To us, their less tried successors": Joseph Conrad, *Lord Jim* (1899; New York: Signet Classic, 1961), 170.

THE FLOATING WORLD

3   "If that double-bolted land": Melville, *Moby-Dick*, ch. 24.

4   "'Tis in the chilly night": See Donald R. Bernard, *The Life and Times*

of John Manjiro (New York: McGraw-Hill, 1992), 55; and Emily V. Warinner, *Voyager to Destiny* (Indianapolis: Bobbs-Merrill, 1956), 69. For the narrative of Manjiro's life, I rely on both these books, supplemented by the account in Katherine Plummer's *The Shogun's Reluctant Ambassadors: Japanese Sea Drifters in the North Pacific* (Portland: Oregon Historical Society Press, 1991).

4   One Sunday morning: Bernard, *Life and Times*, 55–56; and Warinner, *Voyager*, 68–69.

7   Grogshops, brothels, and gambling dens: For a description of Honolulu at mid–nineteenth century, see Hershel Parker, *Herman Melville: A Biography*, vol. 1 (Baltimore: Johns Hopkins University Press, 1996), 244–48.

8   Perched on the roof: See Gerrit P. Judd IV, *Dr. Judd: Hawaii's Friend* (Honolulu: University of Hawaii Press, 1960), 77. On Judd, see also Parker, *Herman Melville*, 238–40.

8   The men cried "Dai Nippon": See Warinner, *Voyager*, 48, 77; and Bernard, *Life and Times*, 32.

9   Spires jutting into the sky: See Bernard, *Life and Times*, 36.

10 Even the *John Howland:* Bernard, *Life and Times*, 39.

12 Heroes of the Revolutionary War: Parker, *Herman Melville*, 2–3, 742. My account of Melville's life is drawn primarily from Parker's biography and from Laurie Robertson-Lorant, *Melville: A Biography* (New York: Clarkson Potter, 1996), supplemented by Jay Leyda, *The Melville Log*, 2 vols. (New York: Harcourt, Brace, 1951).

12 "the East India Company's Souchong": Herman Melville, *Mardi*, in *Herman Melville: Typee, Omoo, Mardi* (New York: Library of America, 1982), 958. Volume edited by G. Thomas Tanselle.

12 Herman "so completely happy": Parker, *Herman Melville*, 184; and Robertson-Lorant, *Melville*, 92.

13 the "demoniac din" of birds: The short sketches of Melville's "The Encantadas" first appeared in his *Piazza Tales* (1856).

13 "the sky above": Melville, *Typee*, ch. 1. Quotations from *Typee* and *Omoo* are drawn from the Library of America editions (1982) of these works.

14 Manjiro had left Honolulu: See Warinner, *Voyager*, 78.

14 Melville was indignant: Melville, *Typee*, ch. 26.

15 Melville, employed at the time: See Charles Anderson, *Melville in the South Seas* (New York: Columbia University Press, 1949), 332. In 1873 the Reverend Samuel C. Damon, who provided refuge for both Melville and Manjiro, identified Melville's employer as Isaac Montgomery (Anderson, 332).

15 "High in the favor": Melville, *Typee*, appendix. The description of the "Polynesian saturnalia" comes from the same text.

16 "A visit from Herman Melville": Leyda, *Melville Log*, vol. 1, 250.

16 During his sojourn in Honolulu: On Melville and the Reverend Mr. Damon, see Parker, *Herman Melville*, 249, 254.

17 Fearing that Dr. Judd: See Robertson-Lorant, *Melville*, 116.

17 "a person wandering from one island": Melville, *Omoo*, preface.

19 While hunting whales: Plummer, *Shogun's Reluctant Ambassadors*, 49; and Warinner, *Voyager*, 68.

20 Damon raised money: Bernard, *Life and Times*, 112.

20 "like noiseless nautilus shells": Melville, *Moby-Dick*, quoted in Samuel Eliot Morison, *The Maritime History of Massachusetts, 1783–1860* (1961; reprint, Boston: Northeastern University Press, 1979), 318.

21 "I have a sort of sea-feeling": Leyda, *Melville Log*, vol. 1, 401.

22 From the outset: See Russell Reising and Peter J. Kvidera, "Fast Fish and Raw Fish: *Moby-Dick*, Japan, and Melville's Thematics of Geography," *The New England Quarterly* (June 1997), 285–305.

22 Melville's descriptions evoke: See Reising and Kvidera, "Fast Fish and Raw Fish," 287–88. The authors also note "Japanese allusions" in Melville's description of Fedallah (296).

25 In 1845 the whaling ship *Manhattan*: See Plummer, *Shogun's Reluctant Ambassadors*, 210–17; and Sister M. Blish, "Melville and the Sea Drifters of Japan," *Melville Society Extracts* 76 (February 1989), 15.

25 Perhaps the most tantalizing: Blish makes the connection between Melville and Manjiro's *Franklin* in "Melville and the Sea Drifters," 15. See also Plummer, *Shogun's Reluctant Ambassadors*, 192–93.

27 "I never forget your benevolence": Plummer, *Shogun's Reluctant Ambassadors*, 152.

27 How, he wondered, did they move: Warinner, *Voyager*, 120.

28 "The climate of New England": Warinner, *Voyager*, 127.

28 "placed over holes in the ground": See James Fallows, "After Centuries of Japanese Isolation, A Fateful Meeting of East and West" *Smithsonian* (July 1994), 24.

28 "They have an iron box": Warinner, *Voyager*, 125–26. The telegraph is described on page 126.

29 The American president: Warinner, *Voyager*, 127.

29 "American ships entering ports": Warinner, *Voyager*, 129.

30 The lost child Manjiro: Plummer, *Shogun's Reluctant Ambassadors*, 140.

31 The daimyo of the Tosa clan: Plummer, *Shogun's Reluctant Ambassadors*, 155.

31 "The fan painting that hung": Kenzaburo Oe, *The Silent Cry*, translated by John Bester (Tokyo: Kodansha, 1981), 63. See also pages 116 and 204.

31 Japan's more progressive thinkers: This account draws on Fallows, "After Centuries."

32 "When you came here today": Plummer, *Shogun's Reluctant Ambassadors*, 156.

32 "I wonder . . . if that American": Plummer, *Shogun's Reluctant Ambassadors*, 156.

32 A ceremonial exchange of gifts: See Fallows, "After Centuries," 27.

33 "Commodore Perry called": Leyda, *Melville Log*, vol. 1, 494.

34 His sixteen-year-old bride: On Manjiro's marriage, see Derick Dreher et al., *Nakahama Manjiro's Hyosen Kiryaku: A Companion Book* (Philadelphia: Rosenbach Museum, 1999), 23. See also Warinner, *Voyager*, 172.

34 "From my twenty-fifth year": Leyda, *Melville Log*, vol. 1, 413.

35–37 "Took a long walk": Leyda, *Melville Log*, vol. 2, 529. For the quotations immediately following, see pages 529, 531, 626, 627, 628, 629.

38 "Manjiro is certainly": Bernard, *Life and Times*, 193.

38 "the first fully authorized voyage": Marius B. Jansen, *The Making of Modern Japan* (Cambridge: Harvard University Press, 2000), 319.

37 "decidedly the most magnificent display": Quoted in Clay Lancaster, *The Japanese Influence in America* (New York: Walton H. Rawls, 1963), 19. Lancaster also quotes Whitman's poem.

39 "when that is done": Bernard, *Life and Times*, 201.

39 "I have had charge": Bernard, *Life and Times*, 201.

39 Upon his return to Japan: Warinner, *Voyager*, 197; see also F. G. Notehelfer, editor, *Japan Through American Eyes: The Journal of Francis Hall, 1859–1866* (Boulder, Colo.: Westview, 2001), 189.

39 Francis Hall, a bookseller from Elmira: See Notehelfer, *Japan Through American Eyes*, 121, 157; and Warinner, *Voyager*, 187.

41 "If it is not John Mung": Bernard, *Life and Times*, 210–11.

41 Manjiro's final decades: Bernard, *Life and Times*, 213.

41 "Long shall we cherish": Warinner, *Voyager*, 229–30.

41 "Mangero is quite an old-looking": Isabella Bird quoted in Warinner, *Voyager*, 226–27.

42 The central plot: See Warinner, *Voyager*, 230–33.

42 "Probably, if the truth were known": Obituary quoted in Leyda, *Melville Log*, vol. 2, 836. Hearn is quoted on page 800 and La Farge on page 831. The Adams quotation comes from J. C. Levenson,

Ernest Samuels, et al., editors, *The Letters of Henry Adams*, vol. 3 (Cambridge: Harvard University Press, 1982), 277.

43 "how Melville passed": La Farge quoted in Leyda, *Melville Log*, vol. 2, 833.

A COLLECTOR OF SEASHELLS

45 "Nothing we know": Paul Valéry, "Man and the Sea Shell," in James R. Lawler, editor, *Paul Valéry: An Anthology* (Princeton: Princeton University Press, 1977), 132.

45 A typhoon was blowing: See Edward S. Morse, *Japan Day by Day* (Boston: Houghton Mifflin, 1917), vol. 1 (hereafter *JDBD*), 168–72. See also Van Wyck Brooks, *Fenollosa and His Circle* (New York: Dutton, 1962), 12–13.

51–54 "I got acquainted": Dorothy G. Wayman, *Edward Sylvester Morse: A Biography* (Cambridge: Harvard University Press, 1942), 7. For quotations immediately following see pages 7, 13, 79, 224, 222.

54 "What a wonderful change": Wayman, *Morse*, 222–23.

55 "Salem ceased to be an important seaport": Morison, *Maritime History*, 223. See also pages 223 and 214.

56 "No one who is not a collector": Morse, *Japan Day by Day*, vol. 2 (Boston: Houghton, Mifflin, 1917), (hereafter *JDBD2*), 138.

57 "The Japanese exhibit": Edward S. Morse, *Japanese Homes and Their Surroundings* (1886; reprint, New York: Dover, 1961), xxix.

57 At the fair, presumably by prior arrangement: See Peter Fetchko and Junichi Kobayashi, editors, *Worlds Revealed: The Dawn of Japanese and American Exchange* (Tokyo: Edo-Tokyo Museum, and Salem, Mass.: Peabody-Essex Museum, 1999), 150.

57 "Begin to write always": Hawthorne quoted in Morse, *JDBD*, viii.

58–60 The workers' clogs: Morse, *JDBD*, 3. For quotations that follow see pages 12, 292, 154, 1, 288, 289.

61 "Conceive my astonishment": Wayman, *Morse*, 241.

61 "I scanned the walls closely": Morse, *JDBD*, 166.

62 "Find some hobby": Wayman, *Morse*, 258.

63 "Fenollosa never took up chanoyu": Christine M. E. Guth, *Art, Tea, and Industry: Masuda Takashi and the Mitsui Circle* (Princeton: Princeton University Press, 1993), 113.

64 "In one balcony rail": Morse, *JDBD*, 22.

66 "Sturgis Bigelow appeared at midnight": Ward Thoron, editor, *The Letters of Mrs. Henry Adams* (Boston: Little, Brown, 1936), 261.

66–67 "After an absence from Japan": Morse, *JDBD2*, 208. For quotations immediately following, see pages 214 and 216.

67 "We shall see a little": Morse, *JDBD2*, 239.

67–68 "We were greatly entertained": Morse, *JDBD2*, 217. For quotations immediately following, see pages 223, 320, 324.

68 "Fenollosa, being disgusted": Morse, *JDBD2*, 265. For quotations immediately following, see page 266.

68 The Japanese house, he argued: Morse, *Japanese Homes*, 10.

69 "so many features are absent": Morse, *Japanese Homes*, 7. For quotations immediately following, see pages 10 and 12–13.

69 "abject enslavement": Lowell quoted in Morse, *Japanese Homes*, 117.

69 "After studying the Japanese home": Morse, *Japanese Homes*, 309.

70 "Here in these shells": Frank Lloyd Wright quoted in Hugh and Marguerite Stix and R. Tucker Abbott, *The Shell: 500 Million Years of Inspired Design* (New York: Abrams, 1972), 14.

71 "The only thing I don't like": Bigelow quoted in Morse, *JDBD*, ix.

72 "preserving the methods of handling": Edward Sylvester Morse, "Ancient and Modern Methods of Arrow-Release," *Bulletin of the Essex Institute*, vol. 17 (1885), 145.

72 ". . . the record of an itinerary": Morse, *Japanese Homes*, xxx.

THE BOSTON TEA PARTY

75 "Under certain circumstances": The opening sentence of *The Portrait of a Lady* (1881).

75 Hakagawa for Okakura: I am indebted to Professor James Loucks, in personal correspondence, for this identification.

76 "as a stream runs": Dedication to Okakura in John La Farge, *An Artist's Letters from Japan* (New York: Century, 1897), ix.

77 "The Bluff is very pretty": Isabella Bird, *Unbeaten Tracks in Japan*, vol. 1 (New York: Putnam, 1881), 47.

77 Okakura's father, Kan'emon: Details of Okakura's early life, personal conflicts, and administrative career are drawn from F. G. Notehelfer, "On Idealism and Realism in the Thought of Okakura Tenshin," *Journal of Japanese Studies* (Summer 1990), 309–55. I have also relied on Yasuko Horioka, *The Life of Kakuzo* (Tokyo: Hokuseido, 1963).

78 As Isabella Bird reported: Bird, *Unbeaten Tracks*, 46.

78 On the train, the father made: On Okakura's education, I rely on Notehelfer's account in "Idealism and Realism."

79 Salem born and bred: On Fenollosa, see Lawrence W. Chisolm, *Fenollosa: The Far East and American Culture* (New Haven: Yale University Press, 1963); and Brooks, *Fenollosa and His Circle*.

81 Mason was in charge: Luther Mason describes his efforts in U.S.

Bureau of Education, *Educational Exhibits and Conventions at the World's Industrial and Cotton Centennial Exposition, New Orleans, 1884–'85* (Washington: Government Printing Office, 1886), 40–41. On Mason, see also Jansen, *Making of Modern Japan*, 475–76.

81 It was probably: On Okakura and calligraphy, see Notehelfer, "On Idealism and Realism," 323–25.

83 "The priests said": Okakura quoted in Bunsaku Kurata, *Horyu-ji: Temple of the Exalted Law* (New York: Japan Society, 1981), 30. See also Ernest Fenollosa, *Epochs of Chinese and Japanese Art*, vol. 2 (London: Heinemann, 1912), 51, where Fenollosa describes the statue.

84 "I must remember": Fenollosa quoted in Kevin Nute, *Frank Lloyd Wright and Japan* (London: Chapman & Hall, 1993), 75.

85 "All these countries": Okakura quoted in Masaaki Kosaka, *Japanese Thought in the Meiji Era*, translated by David Abosch (Tokyo: Pan-Pacific, 1958), 220, 221.

86 Bigelow "always carried local color": Gardner quoted in Louise Hall Tharp, *Mrs. Jack: A Biography of Isabella Stewart Gardner* (Boston: Little, Brown, 1965), 87.

87 "changed his whole personality": Cecelia Beaux, *Background with Figures* (New York: Houghton Mifflin, 1930), 234.

87 A quarter of a century: On Kellogg, see Peter G. Davis, *The American Opera Singer* (New York: Anchor, 1999), 53–68.

88 "Okakura was only twenty-six": Clara Louise Kellogg, *Memoirs of an American Prima Donna* (New York: Putnam, 1913), 219. Okakura's letters to Kellogg are quoted on pages 221–25.

89 Okakura's "large brilliant eyes": Mary Crawford Fraser, *A Diplomat's Wife in Japan*, edited by Hugh Cortazzi (New York: Weatherhill, 1982), 326.

90 "I always remember seeing sake bottles": Shuzo Kuki quoted in Notehelfer, "Idealism and Realism," 343 n. 106.

90 "By way of self-assertion": Kakuzo Okakura, *The Ideals of the East* (1903; reprint, Rutland, Vt.: Tuttle, 1970), 60.

91 "Nor is an ancient culture": Isaiah Berlin on Tagore in *The Sense of Reality: Studies in Ideas and Their History* (New York: Farrar, Straus, 1997), 260.

91 "the Japanese have an ideal": John La Farge, "An Essay on Japanese Art," in Raphael Pumpelly, *Across America and Asia* (New York: Leypoldt, 1870), 201.

92 "It is in Japan alone": Okakura, *Ideals*, 6.

92 and with Emma Thursby: See Richard McCandless Gipson, *The Life of Emma Thursby* (New York: New York Historical Society, 1940), 379.

93 evanescent waterfalls, mountains: For examples of Taikan and

Shunso's work, see the exhibition catalog *Okakura Tenshin and the Museum of Fine Arts, Boston* (Nagoya: Nagoya/Boston Museum of Fine Arts, and Boston: Museum of Fine Arts, Boston, 1999), 29–36.

94 "What sort of 'nese": Quoted in Elise Grilli, "Okakura Kakuzo: A Biographical Sketch," appended to *The Book of Tea* (1906; reprint, Rutland, Vt.: Tuttle, 1956), 128.

94 as her biographer reports: Morris Carter, *Isabella Stewart Gardner and Fenway Court* (Boston: Houghton Mifflin, 1925), 223. See also Victoria Weston, *East Meets West: Isabella Stewart Gardner and Okakura Kakuzo* (Boston: Isabella Stewart Gardner Museum, 1992).

94 She made several collecting forays: On the design and construction of Gardner's museum, and on her life as collector, I rely on Douglass Shand-Tucci, *The Art of Scandal: The Life and Times of Isabella Stewart Gardner* (New York: HarperCollins, 1997).

95 "a Gospel miracle": William James quoted in Shand-Tucci, *Art of Scandal*, 213.

96 "Mrs. Gardner . . . appears to have been": Anne Nishimura Morse, "Promoting Authenticity: Okakura Kakuzo and the Japanese Collection of the Museum of Fine Arts, Boston," in *Okakura Tenshin and the MFA, Boston*, 147.

96 "so interesting, so deep": Rollin Van N. Hadley, editor, *The Letters of Bernard Berenson and Isabella Stewart Gardner, 1887–1924* (Boston: Northeastern University Press, 1987), 351.

96 "The Stairway of Jade": Shand-Tucci quotes the poem in *Art of Scandal*, 262–63.

97 "Ages have passed": Kakuzo Okakura, *Collected English Writings*, vol. 3 (Tokyo: Heibonsha, 1984), 139.

97 She hired one Professor Uchimura: Tharp, *Mrs. Jack*, 254.

97 "I am still full": Hadley, *Letters of Bernard Berenson and Gardner*, 360.

97 the connoisseur Roger Fry: Denys Sutton, editor, *The Letters of Roger Fry*, vol. 1 (New York: Random House, 1972), 235. Dr. William Sturgis Bigelow wrote of the same occasion that Mrs. Gardner had succeeded "in bringing not only the bones but the soul of Cha-no-yu to the Fenway." See Akiko Murakata, *Selected Letters of Dr. William Sturgis Bigelow* (Ann Arbor, Mich.: University Microfilms, 1971), 266.

97–98 "The Taoist": The poem is quoted in Shand-Tucci, *Art of Scandal*, 256–57.

98 "the first person . . . who showed her": Gardner to Mary Berenson, in Barbara Strachey and Jayne Samuels, editors, *Mary Berenson: A Self-Portrait from Her Letters and Diaries* (New York: Norton, 1983), p. 194.

98   "Okakura is busy at the Museum": Hadley, *Letters of Bernard Berenson and Gardner*, 335.

99   During his first ten months: For Okakura's achievements as a collector, I rely on Morse, "Promoting Authenticity," 145–50. Tung Wu's article, "Keeping Company with Antiquity: Okakura Kakuzo and China," is in the same volume, 137. The exhibition and catalog are reviewed in Christopher Benfey, "Tea with Okakura," *New York Review of Books* (May 25, 2990), 43–47, an early version of this chapter.

100   "the result of a brilliant effort": Kakuzo Okakura, *The Awakening of Japan* (New York: Century, 1904), 65.

100   "Strangely enough humanity": Okakura, *Book of Tea*, 11.

101   "The afternoon tea is now": Okakura, *Book of Tea*, 11.

101   One of Mary Cassatt's: The painting, *Cup of Tea* (1880), is in the Museum of Fine Arts, Boston.

101   "I dislike sitting on my heels": Levenson, Samuels, et al., *Letters of Henry Adams*, vol. 3, 28.

102   "The delightful harmony of the place": Beaux, *Background with Figures*, 233.

102–105   "To European architects": Okakura, *Book of Tea*, 53. For the quotations immediately following, see pages 69, 70, 6, 33, 13, 107, 114.

105   "refined beyond the point": The remark, from an early essay on Henry James, is quoted in Lyndall Gordon, *T. S. Eliot: An Imperfect Life* (New York: Norton, 1998), 26–27.

105   "Roosevelt's strenuosity remained": T. J. Jackson Lears, *No Place of Grace: Antimodernism and the Transformation of American Culture* (New York: Pantheon, 1981), 96.

105   "In the thoroughness and minutiae": Okakura, *Awakening of Japan*, 194.

106   "extraordinary artistic qualities": Charles William Eliot quoted in Chisolm, *Fenollosa*, 163.

106   "architecture of within": See Meryle Secrest, *Frank Lloyd Wright* (New York: Knopf, 1992), 270.

106   "I received a little book by Okakura": Wright quoted in Nute, *Wright and Japan*, 122.

106   at least three major American poets: For Stevens's interest in Okakura, see Holly Stevens, editor, *Letters of Wallace Stevens* (New York: Knopf, 1966), 137. See also Joan Richardson, *Wallace Stevens: The Early Years* (New York: Morrow, 1986), 555 n. 40, for evidence that Stevens was familiar with *The Book of Tea*. I am grateful to Francis Murphy for alerting me to Stevens's interest in Okakura.

107   Graham Parkes has recently argued: See Parkes, "Rising Sun over

Black Forest: Heidegger's Japanese Connections," appended to Reinhard May, *Heidegger's Hidden Sources: East Asian Influences on His Work*, translated by Graham Parkes (London and New York: Routledge, 1996), 95, 114 n. 75.

107 "a sudden loneliness": See Stephen N. Hay, *Asian Ideas of East and West: Tagore and His Critics in Japan, China, and India* (Cambridge: Harvard University Press, 1970), 49.

107 "I seem to go back to things": Okakura, *Collected English Writings*, vol. 3, 71.

108 "Her hands turn to paws": Okakura's "The White Fox" is included in Okakura, *Collected English Writings*, vol. 1., 329–65. The quoted words come from the "Argument," page 331, and the song on pages 363–64.

A SEASON OF NIRVANA

109 "At Omaha a young reporter": Levenson, Samuels, et al., *Letters of Henry Adams*, vol. 3, 12. Adams's letters from Japan, twelve in all, can be found on pages 14–42 of this volume. Except for extended passages, I have chosen not to identify every quoted phrase in these notes.

110 "Had he been born": Adams, *The Education of Henry Adams*, in Ernest Samuels and Jayne N. Samuels, editors, *Novels, Mont-Saint-Michel, The Education* (New York: Library of America, 1983), 723.

110–13 "The intense blue of the sea": Adams, *Education*, 728. Quoted passages immediately following appear on pages 728, 732, 737, 759, 760, 773, 816, 832.

114 In a famous essay: C. Vann Woodward, "A Southern Critique for the Gilded Age," in *The Burden of Southern History*, rev. ed. (Baton Rouge: Louisiana State University Press, 1968), 123, 138. Woodward also discusses the congenial Confederate veterans in James's *The Bostonians* and Melville's *Clarel*.

115 "curious transitions": Edmund Wilson, *The Shores of Light* (New York: Vintage, 1961), 109.

115 "His first step": Adams, *Education*, 1020.

117 "the edges of life": Adams, *Education*, 1040.

117 The architect Henry Hobson Richardson: For details of Richardson's life and career, I have relied on James F. O'Gorman, *Living Architecture: A Biography of H. H. Richardson* (New York: Simon & Schuster, 1997).

117 "filled the mind": Charles Francis Adams quoted in Marc Friedlaender, "Henry Hobson Richardson, Henry Adams, and John Hay," in

Journal of the Society of Architectural Historians (October 1970), 238. I
am grateful to Professor James O'Gorman for this citation.

119　there were secrets in the Five of Hearts: See Patricia O'Toole, *The Five of Hearts: An Intimate Portrait of Henry Adams and His Friends* (New York: Ballantine, 1990).

119–20　Clover's condition had first surfaced: This account of Adams's honeymoon follows closely the version in Otto Friedrich, *Clover* (New York: Simon & Schuster, 1979). For the quotations from Clover's letters, see pages 164, 162, 166, 163. Friedrich quotes Emerson on page 165.

120　"something . . . bothering Clover": Friedrich, *Clover*, 165.

121　Yoshida "has given Henry": Thoron, *Letters of Mrs. Henry Adams*, 242.

121　"the new Japanese minister": Levenson, Samuels, et al., *Letters of Henry Adams*, vol. 2, 554. On Kuki, see also pages 555, 556, 585.

123　"somewhat heavy monumental style": See Friedlaender, "Henry Hobson Richardson," 237. Adams's remarks are quoted on the same page.

123　"This was the side of Richardson": Friedlaender, "Henry Hobson Richardson," 238.

123–124　A copy of the first edition: See Margaret Henderson Floyd, "Inspiration and Synthesis in Richardson's Paine House," in Maureen Meister, editor, *H. H. Richardson: The Architect, His Peers, and Their Era* (Cambridge: MIT Press, 1999), 48, 50–51.

124　"She was so tender and humble": Ellen Hooper quoted in Lincoln Kirstein, *Memorial to a Marriage* (New York: Metropolitan Museum of Art, 1989), 71.

125　"She sat there pale and careworn": Charles Francis Adams quoted in Ernest Samuels, *Henry Adams* (Cambridge: Harvard University Press, 1989), 199. For Adams's response to Holt, see also page 199.

125　"If I had one single point": Clover Adams quoted in Samuels, *Henry Adams*, 200.

126　"Nothing you can do": Henry Adams quoted in Kirstein, *Memorial*, 73.

126　"for no other object": Levenson, Samuels, et al., *Letters of Henry Adams*, vol. 3, 3.

127　"ought to have made Esther jump": Clarence King quoted in Edward Chalfant, *Better in Darkness: A Biography of Henry Adams, His Second Life, 1862–1891* (North Haven: Archon, 1994), 514.

127　The episode reached its nadir: See James L. Yarnall, *John La Farge: Watercolors and Drawings* (Yonkers: Hudson River Museum of Westchester, 1990), 15.

128 William Story's *Cleopatra:* Chalfant, *Better in Darkness,* 515.

129 La Farge, "in a disheveled . . . mind": Levenson, Samuels, et al., *Letters of Henry Adams,* vol. 3, 12. For the other quotations on the departure, see page 12.

130 "The American mind": Adams, *Education,* 1058.

130 T. S. Eliot once wrote: "Henry James," in Frank Kermode, editor, *Selected Prose of T. S. Eliot* (New York: Harcourt and Farrar, Straus, 1975), 151.

131 A self-portrait: The painting is in the Metropolitan Museum of Art.

132 La Farge's imprint on Henry James: See the contemporary art historian Henry Adams's account of La Farge's influence on James in "The Mind of John La Farge," in Henry Adams et al., *John La Farge* (Pittsburgh: Carnegie Museum of Art, 1987), 16–17. For James on Balzac, see page 17. La Farge's portrait of Henry James (The Century Association) is reproduced on page 15.

132 During his student year in Paris: See Adams, "Mind of John La Farge," 21. On La Farge's interest in Japanese art before the Impressionist vogue, see Henry Adams, "John La Farge's Discovery of Japanese Art: A New Perspective on the Origins of Japonisme," *Art Bulletin* (September 1985).

133 "The war upset all my notions": Royal Cortissoz, *John La Farge: A Memoir and a Study* (Boston: Houghton Mifflin, 1911), 121.

134 His *Flowers in a Japanese Vase:* The painting is in the Museum of Fine Arts, Boston.

134 "shaped like one of the broken-column": Adams, "Mind of John La Farge," 21. My discussion of La Farge's still lifes owes a great deal to Adams's analysis of them.

134 *Roses on a Tray:* The painting is in the Carnegie Museum of Art, Pittsburgh.

135 "prodigious debts behind them": Henry James quoted in Yarnall, *John La Farge,* 24.

136 A kindred gap had opened: For details of La Farge's marriage, I rely on Yarnall, *John La Farge,* 24–26, 30.

137 "With all his faults": John La Farge, S.J., *The Manner Is Ordinary* (New York: Harcourt, Brace, 1954), xx.

137 "It was characteristic": Cortissoz, *John La Farge,* 1.

FALLING WATER

139 "The Master stood by a river": Simon Leys, translator, *The Analects of Confucius* (New York: Norton, 1997), 41.

141 "Who has not seen Nikko": La Farge, *Artist's Letters,* 26.

141 "Do you happen to know": Levenson, Samuels, et al., *Letters of Henry Adams*, vol. 3, 22. Adams wrote twelve letters from Japan, all included on pages 14–42 of this volume. I have not given individual citations for each quotation.

141 "We were in the great bay": La Farge, *Artist's Letters*, 1.

142 "an angel of good-humor": Levenson, Samuels, et al., *Letters of Henry Adams*, vol. 3, 28.

142 "Wearied by the novelty": La Farge, *Artist's Letters*, 8. For details of La Farge's sojourn in Japan, I have relied on James L. Yarnall, *Recreation and Idleness: The Pacific Travels of John La Farge* (New York: Vance Jordan Fine Art, 1998).

142 "I dislike to use analogies": La Farge, *Artist's Letters*, 14. See Yarnall, *Recreation and Idleness*, 15.

143 "The monotony of impression": La Farge, *Artist's Letters*, 21.

143 his 1884 edition of John Murray's: Adams's marked copy of Murray's *Hand-book* is in the Massachusetts Historical Society in Boston. Ernest Mason Satow and A.G.S. Hawes, *A Hand-book for Travellers in Central and Northern Japan*, 2nd ed. (London: Murray, 1884).

145 "In the case of Hokusai": Adams's copy of Fenollosa's article is in the Massachusetts Historical Society, 33.

146 "We have a little fountain": La Farge, *Artist's Letters*, 125.

147 "What I see here that I admire": La Farge, *Artist's Letters*, 101. The quoted passages immediately following are on pages 106, 100.

148 "Nothing in the world": Stephen Mitchell, translator, *Tao Te Ching* (New York: HarperPerennial, 1992), 78.

148 "After many years": La Farge, *Artist's Letters*, 117. The quoted passages immediately following are on pages 95 and 175.

149 "The little shrine and waterfall": See Yarnall, *Recreation and Idleness*, 35.

149 "its value . . . began with its desertion": Chalfant, *Better in Darkness*, 518.

150 "a reminder of old, complete civilizations": La Farge, *Artist's Letters*, 190.

152 large watercolor of the Buddha: The picture is in the Metropolitan Museum of Art, New York.

151–53 "An accident, the breaking": La Farge, *Artist's Letters*, 226. La Farge's other remark on the "accidental" success of the figure appears on page 227.

154 Kyoto was their quarry now: I am indebted to Yarnall, *Recreation and Idleness*, for details of Adams and La Farge's itinerary.

154 "the sitting effigy of Hideyoshi": See Adams's copy, in the Mas-

sachusetts Historical Society, of Satow and Hawes, *A Hand-book for Travellers*, 371, 359.

155 "The city lies in fog": La Farge, *Artist's Letters*, 231. Yarnall reproduces the watercolor (Museum of Fine Arts, Boston), 46.

155 "The gentle little bodies": La Farge, *Artist's Letters*, 246, 249.

156 "The picturesque effect": *Murray's Handbook*, 371. See also La Farge, *Artist's Letters*, 234.

156 "violet butterflies": La Farge, *Artist's Letters*, 235.

157 "an indigestion of information": La Farge, *Artist's Letters*, 232.

157 "Bird dance; Butterfly dance": Adams's notebook, at the Massachusetts Historical Society, is quoted in Yarnall, *Recreation and Idleness*, 48.

157 "From below rise": La Farge, *Artist's Letters*, 252.

157 Aoki accompanied them: See Yarnall, *Recreation and Idleness*, 49.

158 "For a mile now, perhaps": La Farge, *Artist's Letters*, 265–66. See also Yarnall, *Recreation and Idleness*, 53.

158 "it was worth coming": Quoted in Chalfant, *Better in Darkness*, 520.

158 "We do not care to scoop": Adams, travel notebook, Massachusetts Historical Society.

158 "If the wax were exactly worked": I give Charles Singleton's translation, *The Divine Comedy, Paradiso* (Princeton: Princeton University Press, 1975), 145.

162–63 "Let me not, however, forget": Henry James, *Collected Travel Writings: Great Britain and America* (New York: Library of America, 1993), 432–33.

163 a countermonument: I borrow this idea from James E. Young's *The Texture of Memory: Holocaust Memorials and Meaning* (New Haven: Yale University Press, 1993), 48.

164 "I am continually reminded": La Farge, *Artist's Letters*, 180.

164 a certain ambiguity: James, *Collected Travel Writings*, 498.

165 "a strange, shrouded, sitting woman": See Chalfant, *Better in Darkness*, 850.

167 "loved to talk about Confucius": Cortissoz, *John La Farge*, 181.

167 "First the white": Cortissoz, *John La Farge*, 181. See also Okakura, *Ideals*, 53: "Thus Confucius says 'all painting is in the sequence of white.' "

167 "He painted another Confucius": Cortissoz, *John La Farge*, 182. The painting is reproduced in Adams et al., *John La Farge*, 162.

168 "Quincy is not enlivening": Levenson, Samuels, et al., *Letters of Henry Adams*, vol. 3, 73.

168 "Do get Billy Big": Levenson, Samuels, et al., *Letters of Henry Adams*, vol. 3, 78.

169 "I am too sensitive": La Farge, correspondence, Yale University Library Archives.

169 "A face like Mrs. Cameron's": Arline Boucher Tehan, *Henry Adams in Love* (New York: Universe, 1983), 102.

169 "I mean to start for China": See Chalfant, *Better in Darkness*, 521.

169 "quite breaking my heart": *Letters of Henry Adams*, vol. 3, 75.

170 Gauguin and La Farge used: For example, Gauguin's *Mysterious Water (Papa Moe)* (1897, private collection) and La Farge's *After the Bath: A Memory of the South Seas* (Weatherspoon Art Gallery, University of North Carolina at Greensboro). The basis for both is a photograph by Charles Spitz. Yarnall in *Recreation and Idleness*, 184, n. 434, establishes the relationship between the two works and dates the La Farge around 1895.

170–73 he did "not know where to go": Levenson, Samuels, et al., *Letters of Henry Adams*, vol. 3, 532–33. The quoted passages that follow are on pages 539, 533, 536, 542, 531–32, 544, 532, 544, 551.

MESSAGES FROM MARS

177 The title of this chapter is drawn from a 1908 lecture by Mabel Loomis Todd called "A Message from Mars."

177 "That you glance at Japan": Thomas H. Johnson, editor, *The Letters of Emily Dickinson*, vol. 3 (Cambridge: Harvard University Press, 1958), 867.

177 "beyond the reach of railways": Basil Hall Chamberlain and W. B. Mason, *A Handbook for Travellers in Japan*, 3d ed. (London: Murray, 1891), 239.

177 "That the mountain held a mystery": Percival Lowell, *Occult Japan: or, The Way of the Gods: An Esoteric Study of Japanese Personality and Possession* (Boston: Houghton Mifflin, 1895), 2.

178–79 "We had not climbed": Lowell, *Occult Japan*, 4. The quotations immediately following are on pages 6, 5–6, 14. Samuel Morse informs me that the rites Lowell witnessed were actually a hybrid of Shinto and Buddhist practices.

179 His eyesight was said to be extraordinary: A. Lawrence Lowell, *Biography of Percival Lowell* (New York: Macmillan, 1935), 61.

179 Lowell "learned Japanese faster": A. Lawrence Lowell, *Biography*, 6, 12.

179 "withal . . . a young man of fashion": A. Lawrence Lowell, *Biography*, 8.

179 Percy's atmospheric letters: See Lancaster, *Japanese Influence*, 261.

180 "With money enough": A. Lawrence Lowell, *Biography*, 8.

180 Relations between the countries: See Christine Wallace Laidlaw, editor, *Charles Appleton Longfellow: Twenty Months in Japan, 1871–1873* (Cambridge, Mass.: Friends of the Longfellow House, 1998), 37 n. 14.

180 "The position practically amounts": Bigelow quoted in A. Lawrence Lowell, *Biography*, 12.

180 "It is because the Far-East": Lowell, *Chöson: The Land of the Morning Calm* (Boston: Ticknor, 1886), 107.

181 Stories were told of Lowell and Warren: See Martin Green, *The Mount Vernon Street Warrens* (New York: Scribner's, 1989), 106.

181 "In the Japanese language": Lowell quoted in A. Lawrence Lowell, *Biography*, 10.

181 "To speak backwards": Percival Lowell, *The Soul of the Far East* (New York: Macmillan, 1911), 1–2.

182 "the orderly procedure of natural evolution": Lowell, *Soul of the Far East*, 11. The quotations immediately following are on pages 8, 10, 8–9.

182 "off the face of the earth": A. Lawrence Lowell, *Biography*, 37.

182 "The city made a spectacle": Percival Lowell, *Noto: An Unexplored Corner of Japan* (Boston: Houghton Mifflin, 1891), 15–16.

183 "my well known antipathy": See Ferris Greenslet, *The Lowells and Their Seven Worlds* (Boston: Houghton Mifflin, 1946), 352. Lowell's letter to Stimson is quoted on the same page.

184 "Irrigation . . . and upon as vast a scale": Lowell quoted in A. Lawrence Lowell, *Biography*, 84.

185 "It is strange": Elizabeth Bisland, editor, *Japanese Letters of Lafcadio Hearn* (Boston: Houghton Mifflin, 1910), 479.

186 Since Morse, through his lectures: The point is made by Masao Watanabe, *The Japanese and Western Science*, translated by Otto Theodor Benfey (Philadelphia: University of Pennsylvania Press, 1990), 62.

186 "What are the canals?": Hearn, *Japanese Letters*, 377.

186 Mars, he believed: See A. Lawrence Lowell, *Biography*, 83.

186–88 "From time immemorial": Percival Lowell, *Mars and Its Canals* (New York: Macmillan, 1906), 3. The quotations immediately following are on pages 4, 7, 8.

188 "Tonight Mr. Todd": Mabel Todd quoted in Polly Longsworth, *Austin and Mabel* (New York: Holt, 1984), 37. Details of David Todd's career are drawn from Longsworth's account. Mabel Todd's journals are in the Yale University Library Archives.

190 He failed the mathematics exam: Longsworth, *Austin and Mabel*, 46. For Todd and Edison, see page 42.

190 "far from dimming the Todds' sexual": Quoted in Peter Gay, *The Bourgeois Experience: Victoria to Freud* (New York: Oxford University Press, 1984), 81. The quotation that immediately follows is on page 82.

191 "If David Peck Todd": Leyda quoted in Richard Sewall, *The Life of Emily Dickinson* (New York: Farrar, Straus, 1980), 170.

192 "impressive in look & manner": Gay, *Bourgeois Experience*, 101. The quotations immediately following are on pages 97 and 94.

193 "Only later . . . did she realize": Sewall, *Life of Emily Dickinson*, 180. Austin's remark on a possible ménage à trois appears in Gay, *Bourgeois Experience*, 95.

193 "had hardly been married": Gay, *Bourgeois Experience*, 95. The quotations that follow are on page 96.

194 "The Homestead became the safest place": Longsworth, *Austin and Mabel*, 64.

195 During the months when the house: David Todd's journal, with multiple mentions of Morse's book on Japanese homes, is in the Yale University Library Archives.

195 "after struggling to keep warm": See Mabel Todd in *The Nation* (September 1, 1887).

196 "The eclipse station": Longsworth, *Austin and Mabel*, 281.

196 "Nothing now remains": Mabel Todd in *The Nation*.

199 "We went this afternoon": Harriet P. James, *Cruise of the Yacht "Coronet" to the Hawaiian Islands and Japan* (New York: Wm. C. Martin, 1897), 61.

199 "obvious experts at exploring": Dallas Finn, *Meiji Revisited: The Sites of Victorian Japan* (New York: Weatherhill, 1995), 51, 56.

200–201 Nitobe "called at once": Mabel Todd, *Corona and Coronet* (New York: Houghton Mifflin, 1898), 258. Quotations that follow are on pages 256, 255, 257, 260, 259, 273, 284, 283.

201 a magnificent Ainu necklace: On Mabel Todd as collector, see Christine M. E. Guth, "The Formation of the Japanese Collections in the Peabody Essex Museum," *Orientations* (May 2001), 70–71. Photographs of the necklace and coat are in Money Hickman and Peter Fetchko, *Japan Day by Day* (Salem: Peabody Museum, 1977), 166, 172.

201 "To buy anything from an Ainu house": Mabel Todd, *Corona and Coronet*, 312. See also pages 312–13, 296, 311.

202 she had even seen a bear cub: See Anna Hartshorne, *Japan and Her People*, vol. 2 (Philadelphia: International Press, 1902), 17.

202–203 "barbarians pure and simple": Mabel Todd, *Corona and Coronet*, 295. Quotations that follow are on pages 317, 302, 303, 262, 295, 294.

203   "This is the land": I wish to thank Professor Hiroko Uno for this citation.

204   a gift of blue china: See Longsworth, *Austin and Mabel*, 409.

205   "The public takes an interest": Lowell's letter is in the Yale University Library Archives, David Todd Papers.

205   "better for invalid": Lowell telegram to Todd, June 23, 1897, Yale University Library Archives, David Todd Papers.

205   "Perjury always kills": The letter, in the David Todd Papers at Yale, is quoted in Millicent Todd Bingham, *Ancestors' Brocades: The Literary Debut of Emily Dickinson* (New York: Harper, 1945), 376. Bingham writes that "Percival Lowell, the astronomer, was living in Amherst during the winter of 1898." Her wry remark on Lavinia's death also appears on page 376.

205   "get into this warm tub": Lowell's postcards to Todd are in the David Todd Papers, Yale University Library Archives.

206   "The husbands of all the ladies": Mabel Todd, *Tripoli the Mysterious* (Boston: Small, Maynard, 1912), 101. The exchange that follows is on pages 101–102.

206   "The last week of our stay": Mabel Todd's journal, Yale University Library Archives.

207   numerous Mars-inspired poems: See William Graves Hoyt, *Lowell and Mars* (Tucson: University of Arizona Press, 1976), xiv.

207   "Bravo," Lowell cabled back: See Hoyt, *Lowell and Mars*, 190.

207   "I don't see how I can follow": Hoyt, *Lowell and Mars*, 190.

208   "She was never": Greenslet, *The Lowells*, 375.

208   "Every mail . . . brought letters": Amy Lowell quoted in Greenslet, *The Lowells*, 376.

209   "arguing with Amy": Sandburg quoted in Greenslet, *The Lowells*, 390.

209   "hollow and metallic . . . a great empty cloisonné jar": Wilson, *Shores of Light*, 240, 243.

209–10   Van Wyck Brooks, far more generous: See Brooks, *New England: Indian Summer* (New York: Dutton, 1940), 533–38.

210   "The harmony of poetic thought": Quoted in an unpublished manuscript on "Emily Dickinson and Japan" (1986) by Akiko Murakata.

210   "We got our Emily Dickinson": Mary Fenollosa journal, Museum of Mobile, Mobile, Alabama. I owe this citation to Akiko Murakata. Conversations with Ellen Conant were of great help in my work on Mary Fenollosa.

210   "condensation and brevity": Ernest Fenollosa, "Notes for a Lecture on Chinese Poetry" (1902), quoted in Murakata, "Dickinson and

Japan." The Fenollosa draft is in the Ernest Fenollosa Papers, Houghton Library, Harvard University.

210 Fenollosa "did not live": Murakata, "Dickinson and Japan." See also Ernest Fenollosa, *The Chinese Written Character as a Medium for Poetry*, edited by Ezra Pound (1936; San Francisco: City Lights, 1968).

THE MOUNTAIN OF SKULLS

213 "The first sight of Fuji at dawn": Lafcadio Hearn, "A Conservative," in Lafcadio Hearn, *Writings from Japan*, edited by Francis King (New York: Viking Penguin, 1984), 308.

213–16 "forty miles of electric wire": Hearn's writings on the Cotton Exposition are collected in Lafcadio Hearn, *Occidental Gleanings* (New York: Dodd, Mead, 1925), 209–40.

213 "I think a man must devote himself": Elizabeth Bisland, *The Life and Letters of Lafcadio Hearn*, vol. 1 (Boston: Houghton Mifflin, 1906), 328.

216 "an oration in Japanese": William H. S. Demarest, *A History of Rutgers College* (New Brunswick, N.J.: Rutgers College, 1924), 441.

218–19 Foley's "wonderful wealth of verbal description": See Mary Keys, "Lafcadio Hearn and Alethea (Mattie) Foley," in *Lafcadio Hearn Journal* (Spring 1993), 7–8, for a full account of this relationship, including Hearn's remarks quoted here.

219 The coup so alarmed President Grant: On this era in Louisiana history, see Christopher Benfey, *Degas in New Orleans* (New York: Knopf, 1997), ch. 10.

220 "no more than a malevolent": Gayarré quoted in Joseph G. Tregle, Jr., "Creoles and Americans," in Arnold R. Hirsch and Joseph Logsdon, editors, *Creole New Orleans* (Baton Rouge: Louisiana State University Press), 179.

220 Cable's writings had inspired Hearn: See Lafcadio Hearn, "The Scenes of Cable's Romances," in *Century* (November 1883), 40–47. Cable also gave Hearn the germ of the novel *Chita*.

221 a Japanese paper fan: See Lafcadio Hearn, *Two Years in the French West Indies* (1890; reprint, New York: Interlink, 2001), 324.

221 "I am trying to find the Orient": Bisland, *Life and Letters*, 390.

221 "I have a book for you": Bisland, *Life and Letters*, 460.

222 "In attempting a book": Hearn quoted in Elizabeth Stevenson, *Lafcadio Hearn* (New York: Macmillan, 1961), 197.

222 "an atmosphere of sailors": Quoted in Stevenson, *Lafcadio Hearn*, 203.

222 "cool with the coolness": Lafcadio Hearn, "My First Day in the Orient," in Hearn, *Writings from Japan*, 20.

223 "a mirror, a round, pale disk": Hearn, "My First Day," 35. This passage provides the title and main idea for Robert Rosenstone's *The Mirror in the Shrine: American Encounters with Meiji Japan* (Cambridge: Harvard University Press, 1988).

225 "no poetry—no courtesy": Hearn quoted in Pat Barr, *The Deer Cry Pavilion* (New York: Viking Penguin, 1988), 226.

226 "I went with a great throng": Lafcadio Hearn, "At a Railway Station," in Hearn, *Writings from Japan*, 144.

227 Hearn was hired . . . as a propagandist: See Yuzo Ota, *Basil Hall Chamberlain: Portrait of a Japanologist* (Richmond, Surrey: Curzon Press, 1998), 162–63.

227 "the kind of man": Chamberlain quoted in Ota, *Basil Hall Chamberlain*, 162. Hearn's remark about the position is also on page 162.

227 "They entered the Red Gate": Natsume Soseki, *Sanshiro*, translated by Jay Rubin (New York: Perigee, 1982), 33.

227 "A Conservative": "A Conservative" is included in Hearn, *Writings from Japan*, 291–309.

229 "thinking it would be a subtle compliment": Mary Fenollosa quoted in Akiko Murakata, " 'Yugiri O Kyaku San (The Guest Who Leaves with the Twilight)': The Fenollosas and Lafcadio Hearn," *Review of English Literature* (Kyoto University English Department, March 1991), 58.

229–30 "neither token of water": Lafcadio Hearn, "Fragment," in Lafcadio Hearn, *In Ghostly Japan* (1899; reprint, Rutland, Vt.: Tuttle, 1971), 3. The other passages quoted appear on pages 5–7.

230 "Had I only eleven more stories": Bisland, *Life and Letters*, vol. 2, 383.

230 "The Buddhist story which I had": Mary Fenollosa quoted in Murakata, "Yugiri O Kyaku San," 66.

230 "the immense evolutional fact": Lafcadio Hearn, *Exotics and Retrospectives* (Boston: Little, Brown, 1898), 193.

231 he "carries his own environment": Anne Dyer quoted in Murakata, "Yugiri O Kyaku San," 58.

231 "Said he had seen some": Mary Fenollosa quoted in Murakata, "Yugiri O Kyaku San," 60.

231 Mary McNeil had grown up: On Mary Fenollosa's early life and career, see Chisolm, *Fenollosa*, 120–21.

232 "Fenollosa was a Spaniard": Grace King, *Memories of a Southern Woman of Letters* (New York: Macmillan, 1932), 210.

232 "As [Hearn] stayed on": Mary Fenollosa quoted in Murakata, "Yugiri O Kyaku San," 59.

233   "My dear Professor": Hearn quoted in Francis King, "Introduction" to Hearn, *Writings from Japan*, 13.

233–34   "the language of ridicule": Lafcadio Hearn, "A Glimpse of Tendencies," in Hearn, *Writings from Japan*, 262. The quoted passages immediately following are on pages 259 and 271.

234   "This contest, between the mightiest": Lafcadio Hearn, "A Letter from Japan," in Hearn, *Writings from Japan*, 151. The quoted passages that follow are on pages 153 and 157.

234   "In righting the Japanese": Chamberlain, *Things Japanese*, 60.

235   "Perhaps Japan will remember": Hearn, "Glimpse of Tendencies," 272.

235   In a passage excised by the *Atlantic:* See Murakata, "Yugiri O Kyaku San," app. 1, 75–76.

236   "as though she were ever watching": See Keys, "Lafcadio Hearn and Alethea (Mattie) Foley," 7. Keys's account of Foley's claim on Hearn's estate is on page 8.

236   "I hear with regret": Okakura to *The New York Times* in Okakura, *Collected English Writings*, vol. 3, 79. In the same volume, the editors claim that Hearn's *In Ghostly Japan* "contains an essay about Okakura" (389). The essay would seem to be "Suggestion," a conversation about androgyny and reincarnation. In the introduction to vol. 1 of Okakura's *Collected English Writings*, both Hearn and Henry James are listed among his acquaintances (xiii).

THE JUDO ROOM

239   "Man at his birth is supple": The passage, from the seventy-sixth section of the *Tao Te Ching*, serves as epigraph to Lafcadio Hearn's essay "Jiujutsu," in Lafcadio Hearn, *Out of the East: Reveries and Studies in New Japan* (Boston: Houghton Mifflin, 1895), 183.

239   the Judo Room: See Akiko Murakata, "Theodore Roosevelt and William Sturgis Bigelow: The Story of a Friendship," *Harvard Library Bulletin* (January 1975), 95.

239   throat muscles "so powerfully developed": *Letters of John Hay* (1908; reprint, New York: Gordion, 1969), 354.

240   "was cluttered with the paraphernalia": Hofstadter, *American Political Tradition*, 210.

240   Dr. Bigelow had asked the secretary: See Murakata, *Selected Letters of Bigelow*, 193.

240   "As after the [Meiji] Restoration": Julian Street, *Mysterious Japan* (New York: Doubleday, 1921), 193.

241   "Following the scientific method": Kano quoted in Allen Guttmann

and Lee Thompson, *Japanese Sports: A History* (Honolulu: University of Hawaii Press, 2001), 100. My account of Kano's career relies on this study.

241   Kano's "first interest in jiu-jutsu": Street, *Mysterious Japan*, 193–94.

241–42   "great masterful races": Roosevelt quoted in Hofstadter, *American Political Tradition*, 213. Hofstadter quotes Roosevelt's *Century* article on page 208 and his response to President Eliot on page 213.

242   "In Paris we dined at the Jays": Henry Cabot Lodge, ed., *Selections from the Correspondence of Theodore Roosevelt and Henry Cabot Lodge*, vol. 2 (New York: Scribner's, 1925), 52.

243   "to take him altogether seriously": Hofstadter, *American Political Tradition*, 229. Rice is quoted on page 236.

243   "Theodore Roosevelt dined with me": Murakata, *Selected Letters of Bigelow*, 92–93.

243–44   "to get him *shifted* somehow": See Murakata, "Roosevelt and Bigelow," 92–93. For details of the Roosevelt-Bigelow relationship, I have relied on Murakata's account. Murakata quotes Bigelow's reservations on the Cuban war on page 93 and his invitation to Tuckernuck on page 94.

245   "all the police and army officers": Murakata, "Roosevelt and Bigelow," 93.

245   "the President talked of Jiu-Jitzu": Beaux, *Background with Figures*, 232.

246   "Now . . . do you know enough": On Roosevelt and *bushido*, see Murakata, "Roosevelt and Bigelow," 95.

246   "Bushido" is the real thing: Murakata, *Selected Letters of Bigelow*, 267.

246   "Poor Japan has more important things": Murakata, "Roosevelt and Bigelow, 95.

246–47   "Teikoku Banzai!": Murakata, "Roosevelt and Bigelow," 96. Roosevelt's response is on the same page.

247   "The Japanese fought it admirably": Lodge, *Selections from the Correspondence of Roosevelt and Lodge*, vol. 3, 128.

247–48   "Nor could the force": Adams, *Education*, 1144. The second passage quoted is on page 1142.

248   "Japan is particularly well represented": Mabel Loomis Todd, *The Nation* (June 30, 1904).

249   "May 12. Bade the President good-bye": *Letters of John Hay*, 354.

249   "One enjoyed it": Adams, *Education*, 1146. The following quotation is on page 1147.

249–50   "Three hundred thousand soldiers": Edmund Morris, *Theodore Rex*

(New York: Random House, 2001), 352. The Roosevelt quotations immediately following are on pages 352 and 356.

250 "His hurry": Morris, *Theodore Rex*, 367.

250 "had no personal value": Adams, *Education*, 1144–45. The quotations that follow are on pages 1179 and 1180.

251 "Spent the evening at the White House": *Letters of John Hay*, 406–407.

252 "a disgusting exhibition": Henry Cabot Lodge, *Early Memories* (New York: Scribner's, 1913), 109.

252 "this exposition does not amount": Murakata, *Selected Letters of Bigelow*, 53.

253 "it was the height of vulgarity": Lodge, *Early Memories*, 217.

253 "emanated a peaceful radiance": Quoted in R. W. B. Lewis, *Edith Wharton: A Biography* (New York: Harper, 1975), 281.

253 "the Oscar Wilde of American statesmanship": See John Arthur Garraty, *Henry Cabot Lodge: A Biography* (New York: Knopf, 1953), 121. Lodge's defense is on the same page.

254 Lodge's shaky marriage: See O'Toole, *Five of Hearts*, 217–20.

254 the matter of Matthew Prichard: Murakata, *Selected Letters of Bigelow*, 274.

254 the fate of Mukden: For Bigelow's correspondence with Roosevelt on Mukden, see Murakata, "Roosevelt and Bigelow," 96.

255–57 "If Sturgis Bigelow, who ought to know better": Quoted in Murakata, "Roosevelt and Bigelow," 97. Murakata quotes also the letter from Bigelow on page 98. See also Lodge, *Selections from the Correspondence of Roosevelt and Lodge*, vol. 2, 190, 192, 193.

257 "But if as Brooks Adams says": Lodge, *Selections from the Correspondence of Roosevelt and Lodge*, vol. 2, 135.

258 "exactly as the Chinese": Lodge, *Selections from the Correspondence of Roosevelt and Lodge*, vol. 2, 122. The passages from the letter of June 5, 1905, are on pages 134 and 135.

258 "to have an arrangement": Lodge, *Selections from the Correspondence of Roosevelt and Lodge*, vol. 2, 127.

259 "President Demands Citizenship": Quoted in Murakata, "Roosevelt and Bigelow," 100.

259–61 "Should you happen to enter": Hearn, "Jiujutsu," in Hearn, *Out of the East*, 185. All the Hearn quotations that follow are from pages 183–242.

261 "the entire Japanese force": Albert Bushnell Hart and Herbert Ronald Ferleger, editors, *Theodore Roosevelt Cyclopedia* (New York: Roosevelt Memorial Association, 1941), 548. The quote immediately following is on page 549.

262 "We shall do all that human power": Quoted in Street, *Mysterious Japan*, 194–95.

263 "the Japanese had to have peace": Hart and Ferleger, *Theodore Roosevelt Cyclopedia*, 549.

EPILOGUE: CIRCA 1913: THE ESCAPE FROM TIME

265 "If ever the search": Wallace Stevens, from "Like Decorations in a Nigger Cemetery," in *The Collected Poems of Wallace Stevens* (New York: Vintage Books, 1990), 151. The Valéry passage is from "The Crisis of the Mind," in Lawler, *Paul Valéry: An Anthology*, 102.

266 General Nogi was "the last samurai": Jansen, *Making of Modern Japan*, 494.

267 The Imperial . . . "is to cost": Wright quoted in Julia Meech, *Frank Lloyd Wright and the Art of Japan* (New York: Japan Society, 2001), 84. My account of Wright's 1913 visit to Japan relies on Meech's book.

267 "believed that an artistic turn": Meech, *Frank Lloyd Wright*, 84.

268–69 "an old fashioned tea ceremony": Quoted in Meech, *Frank Lloyd Wright*, 130. Meech quotes Wright's reaction to the tea ceremony on page 131 and his assessment of Kuki on page 131.

269 "I am just about to go": Lodge, *Selections from the Correspondence of Roosevelt and Lodge*, vol. 2, 427.

269 "It is just like the situation": Quoted in Murakata, "Roosevelt and Bigelow," 104. For Lodge on exclusion, see page 105.

269 "We established the precedent": Murakata, "Roosevelt and Bigelow," 105.

270 "Assuming that there is life": See "David Todd and the Martians," quoted in Daniel Lombardo, *Tales of Amherst* (Amherst, Mass.: Jones Library, 1986), 73–75.

271 "Her bed had eighteen pillows": Brooks, *New England*, 533. Quotation immediately following is on page 532.

271 They met at the London home: See interview with Ezra Pound in George Plimpton, editor, *Writers at Work: The Paris Review Interviews*, 2d ser. (New York: Viking, 1963), 49.

272 "selector of a lot of Freer's stuff": Pound quoted in Zhaoming Qian, *Orientalism and Modernism: The Legacy of China in Pound and Williams* (Durham, N.C.: Duke University Press, 1995), 24.

272 especially the Taoist and Chan (Zen) strains: See Qian, *Orientalism and Modernism*, 99–100.

273 One of the notebooks: The Okakura notebook is in the Pound collection at the Beinecke Library at Yale University.

273 "the decision to have Ernest": Mary Fenollosa journal, Mobile (Ala.) Historical Society, 117. See also pages 194, 147, 238.

273 "There is *no* long poem": Pound quoted in Qian, *Orientalism and Modernism*, 25.

273–74 as translated by Okakura: In Pound's *Cathay*, the translation is mistakenly attributed to Mori.

275 "These are the poems of Eliot": Quoted in Robert Craft, "The Perils of Mrs. Eliot," *New York Review of Books* (May 23, 2002), 32.

276 "romantic year" in Paris: See Peter Ackroyd, *T. S. Eliot: A Life* (New York: Simon & Schuster, 1984), 40.

276 While wandering famished: See Murakata, *Selected Letters of Bigelow*, 274: Edward Warren "is said to have come across Prichard in Rome sitting on a bench in the Pincio half starved."

276 Yet a third brother: On the Warren brothers, see Green, *Mount Vernon Street Warrens*.

276–77 "I wish I could regard it": Prichard to Gardner, November 3, 1904, Isabella Stewart Gardner Museum.

277 "things which I confess": Prichard to Gardner, May 1, 1910, Gardner Museum.

277 "To worship the antique": Prichard to Gardner, November 24, 1906, Gardner Museum. "I am tired, tired to death" comes from a letter of July 12, 1911.

277 Prichard wanted art to escape: See Mark Antliff, "The Rhythms of Duration: Bergson and the Art of Matisse," in John Mullarkey, *The New Bergson* (Manchester: Manchester University Press, 1999), 184–208.

277 "Byzantine and Islamic methods": Quoted in Antliff, "Rhythms of Duration," 187.

277 "That is the kind of thing": Prichard to Gardner, July 12, 1911, Gardner Museum.

277 "in a samurai's robe": The description comes from Camille Schuwer's preface to his translation into French of Okakura's "The White Fox" libretto, Georges Duthuit Archives, Paris. Rémi Labrusse provided this citation, along with other information about the circle around Matisse, in personal correspondence. Labrusse's doctoral thesis, "Esthétique décorative et expérience critique: Matisse, Byzance et la notion d'Orient" (Paris: Sorbonne, 1996), explores this circle. See also Rémi Labrusse, *Matisse: La condition de l'image* (Paris: Gallimard, 1999).

278 "Clock-time is the quantified": Antliff, "Rhythms of Duration," 192.

278 "It is a great comfort": Matisse quoted in Rémi Labrusse, "Matisse

et les arts Japonais," sent to the author. Schuwer on Okakura and Matisse is quoted in the same article.

278 "Okakura . . . took TSE": Valerie Eliot, editor, *The Letters of T. S. Eliot* (San Diego: Harcourt Brace, 1988), 93 n. 2. Valerie Eliot dates the meeting in 1910.

278 "If it won't bother you": The letter, quoted by Rémi Labrusse in personal correspondence, is in the Archives Matisse in Paris. The translation is my own.

279 "Remember that trials": Okakura to Florence Koehler, February 14, 1911, Schlesinger Library, Harvard. I wish to thank Rémi Labrusse for suggesting that I track down Koehler's papers and this previously unknown Okakura letter.

279 Tagore hoped to find: See Hay, *Asian Ideas of East and West*, 48. Hay quotes Tagore on Okakura and China on the same page.

280 "brings to us the pledge": Pound quoted in Noel Stock, *The Life of Ezra Pound* (New York: Avon, 1974), 175.

281 "Kakuzo died Tuesday": Yoshisaburo Okakura to Gardner, Gardner Museum. The letter of September 11 is also at the Gardner Museum.

281 Mrs. Gardner arranged a Shinto ceremony: See Shand-Tucci, *Art of Scandal*, 257. See also Weston, *East Meets West*, 33–34.

281 Shuzo Kuki, Okakura's illegitimate son: While Kuki's paternity is still debated, he takes pleasure in noting, in his "Memories of Mr. Okakura Kakuzo," his physical resemblance to Okakura. I wish to thank Sharon Domier for her translation of this text, which also mentions that Okakura attended Bergson's lectures in Paris.

281 What Kuki accomplished: See Leslie Pincus, *Authenticating Culture in Imperial Japan: Kuki Shuzo and the Rise of National Aesthetics* (Berkeley: University of California Press, 1996), 56–60; and Stephen Light, *Shuzo Kuki and Jean-Paul Sartre: Influence and Counter-Influence in the Early History of Existential Phenomenology* (Carbondale: Southern Illinois University Press, 1987), 4–7.

282 *Iki* according to Kuki: I have relied on John Clark's translation of Shuzo Kuki, *The Structure of "Iki"* (London: Published in typescript "for the East Asia Library, Columbia University," 1979, 1980). Clark's translation has been published as *Reflections on Japanese Taste: The Structure of Iki* (Sydney: Power Publications, 1997).

283 Heidegger was already familiar: On Heidegger and Okakura, see Parkes, "Rising Sun over Black Forest," 96 and 114 n. 75.

283 "You know Count Shuzo Kuki": Heidegger, "A Dialogue on Language," in Martin Heidegger *On the Way to Language*, translated by Peter D. Hertz (New York: Harper, 1971), 1.

283 "the pure delight": Heidegger, "Dialogue," 45.

283 When Sartre traveled to Germany: See Pincus, *Authenticating Culture*, 58.

284 Kuki contributed two talks: On Kuki at Pontigny, see Light, *Shuzo Kuki and Sartre*, 6–7.

284–86 "never turns inward": André Suarès, quoted by Kuki, "Considerations on Time," in Light, *Shuzo Kuki and Sartre*, 63. Stephen Light provides his own translations of the two talks Kuki gave at Pontigny. "The Notion of Time and Repetition in Oriental Time" is on pages 43–50, and "The Expression of the Infinite in Japanese Art" is on pages 51–63. All quotations, including those from Basho, are from Light's translations. Kuki's discussion of Nirvana and *bushido* is on pages 49–50, that of Sisyphus on page 50.

286 "The struggle itself": Albert Camus, *The Myth of Sisyphus and Other Essays*, translated by Justin O'Brien (New York: Vintage, 1955), 91.

287 Raymond Aron . . . was in Kuki's audience: See Claire Paulhan, editor, *De Pontigny à Cerisy: Un siècle de rencontres intellectuelles* (Paris: IMEC, 2002), 17.

287 "On the day of the Meiji emperor's funeral": Kuki, "The Japanese Soul," in Light, *Shuzo Kuki and Sartre*, 80.

287–88 "Okakura said very justly": Kuki, "Expression of the Infinite," in Light, *Shuzo Kuki and Sartre*, 51. On Japanese painting, see page 53, on Japanese music, 60.

288–89 The brilliant closing section: See Kuki, "Expression of the Infinite," 55–60.

290–91 "one of those squat, plump little cakes": Marcel Proust, *Remembrance of Things Past*, vol. 1, translated by C. K. Scott Moncrieff and Terence Kilmartin (New York: Random House, 1981), 48. For the quoted passages that follow, see pages 50 and 51.

291 "They are fascinating": Quoted in Edward Chalfant, *Improvement of the World: A Biography of Henry Adams: His Last Life, 1891–1918* (North Haven, Conn.: Archon Books, 2001), 453.

291 Cram . . . a critic of Japanese architecture: Cram had been a guest of the Fenollosas in Japan and had fallen in love with Anne Dyer, Mary Fenollosa's friend. See Douglass Shand-Tucci, *Boston Bohemia* (Amherst: University of Massachusetts Press, 1995), 261.

291 "led him back to the twelfth century": Adams, *Education*, 1059.

292 "Of course we miss La Farge": Levenson, Samuels, et al., *Letters of Henry Adams*, vol. 6, 482.

292–93 "Henry James thinks it all real": Quoted in Chalfant, *Improvement of the World*, 467.

293 "some of the old French songs": Levenson, Samuels, et al., *Letters of Henry Adams*, vol. 6, 792.

INDEX

Note: Page numbers in italics refer to illustrations.

CREDITS

Grateful acknowledgment is made to the following
for permission to use illustrative material:

Page 5, courtesy of Rosenbach Museum and Library, 2010 DeLancey Place, Philadelphia, PA 19103; p. 10, courtesy of Millicent Library, Fairhaven, Mass.; p. 18, courtesy of Berkshire Athenaeum, Pittsfield, Mass.; p. 49, frontispiece to *Edward Sylvester Morse: A Biography*, by Dorothy G. Wayman (Cambridge, Mass.: Harvard University Press, 1942); p. 95, © Isabella Stewart Gardner Museum, Boston; p. 99, Chinese and Japanese Special Fund, © 2002 Museum of Fine Arts, Boston; pp. 118, 127, 147, and 244, courtesy of the Massachusetts Historical Society, Boston; p. 152, frontispiece from *An Artist's Letters from Japan*, by John La Farge (New York: The Century Co., 1897); p. 161, courtesy of The Church of the Ascension in the City of New York; p. 165, from *La Farge, An Artist's Letters from Japan* (p. 96); p. 185, © Lowell Observatory, used by permission; p. 189, courtesy of Yale University Library; p. 225, courtesy of Lafcadio Hearn Collection, Clifton Waller Barrett Library, University of Virginia Library; p. 256, courtesy of Theodore Roosevelt Collection, Harvard College Library; p. 280, gift of Denchu Hiragashi, © 2002 Museum of Fine Arts, Boston; p. 285, © Fonds iconographique de Pontigny/Cerisy; p. 292, Courtesy of National Sculpture Society, New York.

About the Author

CHRISTOPHER BENFEY teaches literature at
Mount Holyoke College, where he is codirector of the
Weissman Center for Leadership. He writes for many
magazines, including *The New Republic*, *The New York
Times Book Review*, and *Travel & Leisure*, and for two
years he was the regular art reviewer for *Slate*. Benfey is
the author of *Emily Dickinson and the Problem of Others*,
The Double Life of Stephen Crane, and *Degas in
New Orleans*. He lives in Amherst, Massachusetts,
with his wife and two sons.

About the Type

The text of this book was set in Filosofia. It was
designed in 1996 by Zuzana Licko, who created it for
digital typesetting as an interpretation of the
sixteenth-century typeface Bodoni. Filosofia, an
example of Licko's unusual font designs, has classical
proportions with a strong vertical feeling, softened by
rounded droplike serifs. She has designed many
typefaces and is the cofounder of *Emigre* magazine,
where many of them first appeared. Born in
Bratislava, Czechoslovakia, Licko came to the
United States in 1968. She studied graphic
communications at the University of California at
Berkeley, graduating in 1984.